Feminist Geography Unbound is a call to action—to expand imaginations and to read and travel more widely and carefully through terrains that have been cast as niche, including Indigenous and decolonial feminisms, Black geographies, and trans geographies. The original essays in this collection center three themes to unbind and enable different feminist futures: discomfort as a site where differences generate both productive and immobilizing frictions, gendered and racialized bodies as sites of political struggle, and the embodied work of building the future.

Drawing on diverse theoretical backgrounds and a range of field sites, contributors consider how race, gender, citizenship, and class often determine who feels comfort and who is tasked with producing it. They work through bodies as terrains of struggle that make claims to space and enact political change, and they ask how these politics prefigure the futures that we fear or desire. The book also champions feminist geography as practice, through interviews with feminist scholars and interludes in which feminist collectives speak to their experience inhabiting and transforming academic spaces. *Feminist Geography Unbound* is grounded in a feminist geography that has long forced the discipline to grapple with the production of difference, the unequal politics of knowledge production, and gender's constitutive role in shaping social life.

———

Banu Gökarıksel is professor, Michael Hawkins and Christopher Neubert are PhD candidates, and Sara Smith is associate professor in the department of geography at the University of North Carolina at Chapel Hill.

GENDER, FEMINISM, AND GEOGRAPHY

Jennifer L. Fluri, Series Editor
Amy Trauger, Series Editor

FEMINIST GEOGRAPHY UNBOUND

DISCOMFORT, BODIES, AND PREFIGURED FUTURES

Edited by
**Banu Gökarıksel, Michael Hawkins,
Christopher Neubert, and Sara Smith**

WEST VIRGINIA UNIVERSITY PRESS / MORGANTOWN

ISBN 978-1-949199-87-1 (cloth) / 978-1-949199-88-8 (paperback) / 978-1-949199-89-5 (ebook)

Library of Congress Cataloging-in-Publication Data

Names: Gökarıksel, Banu, editor.

Title: Feminist geography unbound : discomfort, bodies, and prefigured futures / edited by Banu Gökarıksel, Michael Hawkins, Christopher Neubert, and Sara Smith.

Description: First edition. | Morgantown : West Virginia University Press, 2021. | Series: Gender, feminism, and geography | Includes bibliographical references and index.

Identifiers: LCCN 2020045744 | ISBN 9781949199871 (cloth) | ISBN 9781949199888 (paperback) | ISBN 9781949199895 (ebook)

Subjects: LCSH: Feminist geography. | Human geography. | Feminism. | Feminist theory.

Classification: LCC HQ1233 .F476 2021 | DDC 305.42—dc23

LC record available at https://lccn.loc.gov/2020045744

Book and cover design: Than Saffel

Cover image: Saba Taj

CONTENTS

ACKNOWLEDGMENTS

This book is in your hands only because Jennifer Fluri and Amy Trauger invited us to make it happen. We are profoundly grateful to them for encouraging and supporting this project. It is exciting to be part of their Gender, Feminism, and Geography series at West Virginia University Press. At the press, Derek Krissoff has been helpful, supportive, and patient throughout this project. We are also grateful to Sara Georgi for her work coordinating the editing and publishing of the book, to Rachel Fudge for her careful copyedits, Lynne Ferguson for the index, and the West Virginia University Press staff members who made this work possible, and our department managers, Nell Phillips, Barbara Taylor, and Dan Warfield. We also thank the two anonymous reviewers for their generous and insightful comments. We are delighted to feature the visual artist Saba Taj's artwork on the cover of this book. Thanks to Saba Taj for contributing to this project and to the Institute of Arts and Humanities at the University of North Carolina at Chapel Hill for making this cover possible. Taj's provocative artwork pushes for transformation towards "miraculous possibilities" beyond bodily and cultural boundaries, sexual boundaries, and the human/nonhuman divide.

We have been so lucky to work with this set of contributors, who took up our invitation after we were inspired by their conference presentations at the 2017 Feminist Geography Conference at the University of North Carolina at Chapel Hill. They worked enthusiastically and patiently with our sometimes-too-many rounds of revisions. We have been fortunate to learn and grow alongside them throughout this project.

We are grateful to the conference organizers in Chapel Hill. So many people worked together and contributed to the organization of the conference, including the other members of the conference organizing committee (in alphabetical order): Amy Braun, Sherah Faulkner, Pallavi Gupta, Nina Martin, Adeyemi Olatunde, Elizabeth Olson, Michelle Padley, Sertanya Reddy, Gabriela Valdivia, Pavithra Vasudevan, and Willie Wright. Each of these organizers not only helped with the months of planning and last-minute (sometimes frantic) details that led to a successful conference, but as our friends, colleagues, mentors, and students they have also sharpened and provided the ideas that shaped the conference and, in turn, this book. Francisco Laso took photographs and videos, and Spencer Green and others provided much-needed logistical support at the conference. The energy during those two days in Chapel Hill was infectious, and we are thankful for everyone who participated. In particular, the keynote panel, including LaToya Eaves, Lorraine Dowler, Kumarini Silva, and Kia Caldwell, set the tone of the conference and has provided us with inspiration for this volume. Before this conference was dreamed up, feminist geography in our department was made possible by Altha Cravey, and we are profoundly thankful for the space she opened up for us. We are also grateful to our dangerous playground writing group, who provided feedback on the introduction: Maya Berry, Andrew Curley, Danielle Purifoy, Jecca Namakkal, and Annette Rodríguez.

The conference was also shaped by absences. Donald Trump's travel ban targeting several Muslim-majority nations made traveling to this conference impossible for some scholars from outside the United States. Two of the organizers of our session on Muslim geographies—Azita Ranjbar and Negar Behzadi—were forced to withdraw their abstracts when their visas were denied. Lauren Hull and Shannon Groll, two activists and students from Baton Rouge, withdrew their paper on academic solidarity after the Department of Justice refused to charge officers in the shooting death of Alton Sterling. They wrote to us, "our community is in upheaval. We continue to be actively engaged in events that unfold and in supporting the Baton Rouge Community and thus cannot attend." Petra Doan—and likely others as well—declined to attend the conference due to North Carolina's anti-trans legislation, HB2.

This conference was built on the foundations of the previous conference organized at the University of Nebraska Omaha by Karen Falconer Al-Hindi and Pamela Moss. In initiating the first Feminist Geography Conference, they inspired us through their creative approach to running the conference, and then subsequently by providing funding, organizational information, and attending the conference. This conference would never have happened without them, and subsequent to our conference, a third Feminist Geography conference was held in Montreal. We are strengthened by the community that these conferences have fostered. The conference also received support from the Department of Geography, Department of Women's and Gender Studies, the Department of Communication, College of Arts and Sciences, Institute for the Arts and Humanities, and the Social and Economic Justice Minor.

INTRODUCTION

Banu Gökarıksel, Michael Hawkins, Christopher Neubert,
and Sara Smith

This book seeks to unbind the stitching that obscures feminism's fractures and pretense, to encourage feminist geographers to engage more widely, expansively, and intentionally with sites of struggle and erasure in the discipline of geography and within feminist circles. Gendered bodies are a terrain of struggle, through which difference, colonization, and liberation are enacted, refused, and complicated. Understanding how our embodied relations to one another and to the past and present are constrained by and reiterate oppressive power structures is necessary for refiguring the future. For us, claiming the title of feminist proclaims a willingness to accept or provoke discomfort in order to question and destabilize the status quo while simultaneously acknowledging that the arrangement of this discomfort is uneven and falls along lines of privilege and power. We find ourselves in a moment when feminism is sold to us as a balm, with T-shirts and baby clothes that proclaim "the future is female." What might feminism look like if we refuse to aspire to the solace of "lean in" and "feel good" feminisms of pink pussy hats and US flag hijabs that deny the violence of nationalism, capitalism, and imperialism? To adapt Ahmed's (2010) formulation, what do we consent to when we consent to this kind of happiness? This feminist happiness is proffered in the form of glossy, marketized, and neoliberal solutions: the woman who has it all, the #girlboss.

To question comfort is not to reject pleasure, joy, and generosity, but to consider its costs and distribution. How can feminism take seriously the legacies and current embodiments of structural inequalities and respond to the rise of the global right in contemporary times? How might feminists remain attentive to the possibility that we are complicit in racialized and imperial domination? How should feminist geographers' attention to the body as a political site enable productive work toward a different future? Taking up the work of feminism requires that scholars either become uncomfortable, by questioning received truths, disciplinary boundaries, or their own situated position within structures of knowledge production, or that they acknowledge their own already-existing discomfort, the ways that they cannot yet bring their full selves into disciplinary spaces without translation or "becoming a problem" (Du Bois [1903] 1989; Bayoumi 2009). Thus, this book considers the wearying institutions that make us uncomfortable, and centers the potential in discomfort and the cost of surviving spaces that ask too much (Berry et al. 2017; Muhs et al. 2012; Puwar 2004).

In these pages, scholars grapple with unpleasant and illuminating moments in job interviews and in the field where offhand remarks or questions that linger as puzzles for all that they contain. For Carrie Chennault, white volunteer gardeners in Iowa disparage the Latinx communities they are working to feed, and, as researcher, she mulls over the moment for years. In her analysis of the racialized effects of toxicity in an aluminum company town in North Carolina, Pavithra Vasudevan theorizes the ethics of her proximity to Black suffering as a Brown scholar. Anusha Hariharan reflects on the difficulties of creating legacies and maintaining feminist networks of care and kinship across generations of activists in her research with the Dalit women's movement in India. Kumi Silva considers the pink pussy hat as a sign of exclusion and calls into question "comfort feminism" for its failure to include women of color and to address imperialism.

Contributors and interviewees recall being pushed to their breaking points, working in collectives to create spaces for those marginalized in the academy, and fragile and fleeting moments of uneven solidarity. Petra Doan describes how an intense moment—sobbing in a Quaker meeting upon being told that trans women are not welcome at a women's event—leads to empathy, a break, a reckoning, and a reconfiguration of relations that redefines the boundaries of "woman" for the group. Sofia Zaragocin carries theory with her across borders and finds her embodied and intuitive understandings move across rocky terrain, as when her use of Sara Ahmed is understood as *"muy gringo"* back in Ecuador. Melanie Yazzie and Andrew Curley write on how, for the Diné Bikeyah (Navajo Nation), settler colonialism and capitalism are the vehicles of gender binaries and gender-based oppression that enact and reconfigure public/private divides, evacuate and pervert women's sources of strength; they also describe how Indigenous feminists work for sovereignty and survival. Tia-Simone Gardner builds a tiny house in the racialized and gentrifying context of Minneapolis, and reflects on this home as a Black vernacular architecture of liberation.

We require a feminism that can hold and account for all these stories without flattening or erasing them, or rendering commensurate the incommensurable. Rather, we need an *abundant* feminism that enables the centering of contextually rooted struggles: Indigenous sovereignty, the capacity to live in your own body in the way that feels right, to thrive as a Black woman in a home that you have made yourself. We hope the contributors to this book and the feminist scholars who inspire their work challenge us to do the labor of reading and learning across sites of struggles in order to better engage and "walk alongside" (Nagar 2019) those coming from differently located feminist traditions. This book presents points of departure for charting feminist geographies that flourish in the cracks, fractures, and uncomfortable moments of our lives.

THE ORIGINS OF *FEMINIST GEOGRAPHY UNBOUND*

This book is the result of conversations that began during the May 2017 Feminist Geography Conference in Chapel Hill, North Carolina, when more than 130 scholars and activists gathered for two days of workshops, presentations, and community-making. This group of geographers and other scholars in gender studies, urban planning, religious studies, anthropology, and media studies formed new connections and strengthened ties among feminists working together for years and those at their first conference. We gathered just four months after the Women's March on Washington (and global counterparts) and during a tumultuous spring in the United States that saw the materialization of xenophobic, sexist, and racist rhetoric through specific, targeted legislation and executive action. While we took care to foster an inclusive, productive conference, this was also a moment of absence and exclusion. A number of scholars could not travel to North Carolina because of Trump's "Muslim ban," economic precarity, or the hostile environment our state's HB2 bathroom bill created for transgender and genderqueer scholars (see Doan and Silva interviews in this volume). We discussed the effects these exclusions and absences had on who could attend the conference, who could connect remotely, and who could not participate at all. These policies and discourses deepened existing differences among feminist scholars (in terms of nationality, queerness, economic resources, location) and created new lines of division. We aimed to recognize these intensifying or emergent fractures by orienting ourselves toward modes of connecting across difference and building solidarity.

In selecting "The Insides and Outsides of Feminism" as our conference theme, we sought papers and presentations that explored the poles of inclusion and exclusion and asked: What counts as feminist geography? The conference program invited participants to collectively query, build, and question feminism's capacities to cross, break down, and reinforce borders as ideas travel across the discipline, and encouraged exploration of the relationship among theory, politics, and activism. Discomfort hummed in the background of paper sessions, question and answer periods, workshops, and informal conversations. In the conference's opening plenary, LaToya Eaves described questions that keep her from getting "too comfortable behind her computer screen" in her position as a researcher, rather than engaging with those beyond the campus. Through the case of a death at a fraternity hazing, Lorraine Dowler interrogated university structures that protect institutions against those more vulnerable, and Kia Caldwell called for transnational solidarities that take on the difficult work of understanding feminist struggles across borders (Caldwell 2018).

As Silva stated at the panel and expands on in her interview, "for those of us who grew up in the tropics, and therefore were never taught to knit (why would we, when the temperatures hover around eighty-eight all year round?), those of us whose vaginas aren't various hues of pink, or those who don't have vaginas but identify as women were left out of that conversation even though we were and continue to be among the most vulnerable since the 2016 elections." Here Silva's problematizing of the knitted pink pussy hat popularized during the Women's March on Washington signals the need for intersectional feminism (Crenshaw 1989, 1991; see also Puar 2012) as a necessary framework to go beyond lip service to diversity and the intentional curation of "other" bodies for the purposes of feel-good white liberal feminism (see also Moss and Maddrell 2017). Crenshaw's (1989, 1991) concept of intersectionality teaches us that oppressive state and societal structures of patriarchy and racism are interrelated but not equivalent, and that the experience of a Black woman navigating both these systems is different from either a white woman or a Black man (for related analyses, see Collins 1990; hooks 1981; Lorde 1984).

In the intimate work of building solidarity, questions of positionality cannot be papered over through superficial engagement with difference that leads to comfort feminism rooted in assumptions of shared experiences (see Silva, ch. 4 this volume). Comfort feminism often functions as an illusion of sisterhood that overlooks how white women have and continue to be complicit in or collude with imperial violence, from European colonialization to the US wars in Afghanistan and Iraq (e.g., Abu-Lughod 2002; Farris 2017; Fluri 2011; Legg 2010; McClintock 1995). As we argue elsewhere (Gökarıksel and Smith 2017), putting a Muslim woman in a US flag hijab in the name of feminism does little to address anti-Muslim racism and ongoing US imperialist wars in Muslim-majority countries.

By questioning the political work discomfort can do for feminism, we do not intend to abandon the project of feminist collaboration and community-building. We suggest that efforts to build solidarity and community can be successful only if they directly grapple with difference, no matter how uncomfortable. We find Nagar's (2014) framework of "radical vulnerability" helpful as it provides a means to work against empire with others across our differently situated positions. This notion calls for acknowledging dissimilar positionings and our already-intimate entanglements, rather than disguising them with easy stories of sisterhood. Shared vulnerability can become a starting place for solidarity and collective action (Butler 2014), but it also requires the queering of kinship structures, so that we come to understand our relationships to one another differently (Eng 2010; Haraway 2016; Muñoz 2009; Oswin 2012). Brought to proximity and entangled across difference, vulnerability must be shared, and power differences must be acknowledged. Otherwise, intimacy and intimate spaces can become the site of monstrosity (Sharpe 2009; see also Pain 2015).

In this book, we center insights drawn from scholarship and activism that have been "ethnographically detained," or in other words, have been taken as particular (Weheliye 2014 in reference to Spillers 1987; Wynter 2003). We ask how race, gender, and the histories of slavery, colonialism, and settler colonialism that have produced these categories are fundamentally constitutive of our social worlds, even as these theorizations are often cast aside as niche fields applicable only to specific histories or geographic location (i.e., writing for and about Black women) in favor of an unmarked universal "human" that can supposedly transcend context (Da Silva 2013; Lowe 2015; McKittrick 2014; Perry 2018; Spillers 1987; Weheliye 2014; Wynter 2003). When we begin from a place of ethnographic detainment that centers an unmarked universal subject—for instance, by championing women's rights without attention to the category of woman itself—we miss the ways that the discourse of rights itself is premised on liberal humanism formed through empire, in which the fullness of humanity was itself defined through the right to own property and subjugate others (see Gardner, ch. 6 this volume; Lowe 2015; Perry 2018; Tadiar 2015). We miss the ways that patriarchal norms and gender binaries traveled through the violence of settler colonialism and capitalism (Arvin, Tuck, and Morrill 2013; Denetdale 2006, 2008; Yazzie 2018; Yazzie and Curley, ch. 7 this volume). We also miss how hewing to the category of woman reiterates a patriarchal gender binary that harms people who are gender nonconforming, and reinforces patriarchal structures that harm us all as it simultaneously normalizes and universalizes a binary rooted in a particular European and settler colonial context (Cofield and Doan this volume; Doan 2010; Hunt and Holmes 2015). This flattening obscures the ways that, for instance, Indigenous women's struggles toward sovereignty and decolonization may be incommensurate with or exceed concepts like equity or parity, because the logic of heteronormative patriarchy has been bound to Native elimination (Arvin, Tuck, and Morrill 2013; Simpson 2014; Yazzie and Curley, ch. 7 this volume).

LEGACIES AND FUTURES OF FEMINIST GEOGRAPHY

Feminist geography has long aimed to unbind geography, asking challenging questions about who geographers are, what counts as geographic theory and practice, which spaces geographers study, and whose spaces inform theory. Pointing to the masculinism of geography and the exclusion of women and women's geographies, earlier works expanded the boundaries of geography and transformed concepts, methods, practices, and institutions (Monk and Hanson 1982; Moss et al. 2002; Rose 1993). Moving from the margins to the center (hooks 1984) and drawing attention to "absented presences" that have always been central (McKittrick 2006, xxv), feminist geographers have questioned the whiteness (Kobayashi and Peake 2000; Mahtani 2014; Pulido 2002) and Eurocentricism of the discipline and its embeddedness in imperialism (Domosh 2013; Tolia-Kelly 2016). Self-reflexivity and positionality have been key concerns of this feminist geographic scholarship (England 1994; Faria and Mollett 2016; Kohl and McCutcheon 2015; Laliberté and Schurr 2016). We aim to continue the feminist project of opening boundaries for new modes of thinking about and doing geography that are nondeterministic and nonessentialist, embrace uncertainty and nonlinearity, undermine dominant power structures, and contribute to a re-presentation of geography (McKittrick 2006, xxiv–xxvi).

How can we, as feminist geographers, engage theoretically with difference, privilege, and hierarchy more carefully and more radically, as we also keep the problem of ethnographic detainment in mind? In a moment when geographers continue to engage with the unending labor of decolonization (e.g., Esson et al. 2017; Jazeel 2017; Naylor et al. 2018; Noxolo 2017), we consider what this means for feminist geographers, who for decades have worked to understand questions of knowledge production, positionality, and power structures (Moss and Maddrell 2017; Oberhauser et al. 2017; Graff, Kapur, and Walters 2019). The authors in this volume address this question by considering discomforting encounters, gendered bodies as a terrain of political struggle, and the embodied work of building the future, in which we all participate.

Building on these frameworks, contributors in this volume ask how the social production of difference and the pervasive geographies of inequality constitute spaces and experiences in our world. Their research projects explore how the repetition of cultural practices, notions of racialized difference, and gendered social relations become naturalized onto bodies in ways that legitimize prevailing power relations and unequally delimit possibilities. At the same time, they locate potential for transforming our worlds and building new futures by engaging discomfort, bodies, and temporality. The chapters in this book are organized into three main sections: first, discomfort across encounters; second, gendered bodies as a terrain of political struggle; and third, building futures through the ways we engage the past and the present.

PART I: DISCOMFORT ACROSS ENCOUNTERS

Discomfort haunts feminist scholarship. It is in discussions of field research and in university hallways and conference rooms, but is rarely analyzed in scholarship. In one passing instance, Geraldine Pratt (2004, 70) points to the significance of thinking about discomfort when reflecting on why Canadian women felt anxious when she asked questions about their Filipina nannies' educational attainments: "These questions are uncomfortable, because they call into attention not only to north/south relations of inequality, but to the intensely fraught terrain of motherhood and the morality of the working mother." It is moments like these that Part I brings to focus when doing fieldwork research (Vasudevan, ch. 1), engaging in food justice alliances (Chennault, ch. 2), or simply looking for a public bathroom as a gender-non-conforming or transgender person (Cofield and Doan, ch. 3).

The spaces and encounters of everyday life and work are structured to make those in power feel comfortable and the marginalized uncomfortable, all the while hiding the violence of this uneven distribution of discomfort. White patriarchy seeks domestication: to extract pleasure and solace from people and from the earth, while obscuring the violence of this extraction (Hage 2017). Many comforts proliferate at the expense of others. The infrastructure of academic life is provided by precarious and inexpensive laborers, who are vulnerable to dangerous chemicals, sexual harassment, and daily exploitation. This includes not only laptops, computers, and mobile phones produced far away by people unknown to us but also the toilets in our academic buildings cleaned by people during night shift and rendered invisible to those who occupy faculty positions (Dimpfl 2017; Dimpfl and Smith 2018). Adjuncts and graduate students increasingly carry higher teaching loads with no job security and for below-poverty stipends (Mountz 2015; Peake and Mullings 2016; Slaughter and Rhoades 2000). Most faculty and administrative academic labor also relies on the work of precarious housekeepers, nannies, and daycare workers, often drawing from marginalized migrants and people of color. This unevenness is rendered invisible or insignificant by capitalist, imperialist, and patriarchal processes. As academics inhabiting these institutions, the pretense of distance from suffering cannot enact the innocence that we may desire. Confederate statues on university campuses, the signage of sex-segregated bathrooms, or insistent questions about where you are *really* from are reminders that certain bodies are out of place on university campuses (Puwar 2004).

Part I begins with Vasudevan's exploration of the complex and uncomfortable intimacies of being a Brown scholar in Black studies. Tracing a series of awkward and heartbreaking fieldwork encounters as a "South Asian, middle-class, highly educated" immigrant, working on anti-Black violence in Badin, North Carolina, Vasudevan asks how careful engagement with the complexity of research and our subject positions can function as a tool for social change. For Vasudevan, working to undo foundational anti-Blackness requires the affirmation of racial capitalism's dependence on the devaluation of Black lives, the narration of stories of Black suffering, and generative work that fosters solidarities opposed to racial capitalism. She calls us to sustained engagement and action through reflections on a conversation in which she is asked to explain her proximity to suffering, and observes that we are *all* proximate to, and implicated in, suffering. The chapter ends with a challenging question: Is it possible to encounter Black suffering without fixing power in whiteness and pathology in Blackness and without exploiting Black people?

Chennault's chapter similarly explores moments of discomfort that arise in fieldwork encounters with Master Gardeners participating in an agricultural extension program to grow food in collaboration with community food recipient agencies in Iowa. In a momentous encounter with other white gardeners providing fresh food to the local community, Chennault finds herself remaining silent when a conversation reveals the white privilege and anti-immigrant sentiment of her fellow gardeners. Asking how to perform an antiracist feminism in the face of failed or impossible alliances, Chennault turns her gaze inward, then outward to question her own position and feminist praxis on one hand, and the racial foundations and structural causes of food insecurity on the other. She notes relationships between US agriculture and geopolitics, between the deterritorialization of Latinx migrants and insistent narratives of judgment that link food insecurity to moral failing. Chennault reimagines how agricultural extension programs might restructure their organizations to embrace solidarity, and challenges feminist geographers to engage in lifelong practices of radical vulnerability, collaboration, and risk-taking.

For people who are transgender or gender nonconforming, questions of discomfort follow through daily life, even in the mundane task of finding a bathroom. Simultaneously, through associating the rights of transgender people with bathrooms and sexuality, politicians and right-wing activists "facilitat[e] the classification of [gender-nonconforming people] as disgusting threats" (Cofield and Doan, ch. 3 this volume). Cofield and Doan draw on Ahmed's (2004) work on the cultural politics of emotion to understand how disgust and fear are mobilized against transgender people. While evidence suggests that it is *transgender* people who face danger in public bathrooms, right-wing rhetoric reorganizes risk to position them as predators. This evokes the need for a masculine state to protect women and girls. Thus, the bathroom is generated as a political and dangerously intimate space, and fear is *generated* for political ends by anti-trans legislation. Perversely, heightened awareness for transgender people has led not necessarily to more safety or security but rather heightened policing. Likewise, the intimacy of legislation that seeks to tie protections and police behavior according to the sex assigned at birth is an insidious and policing form of intimacy, and one that escapes the confines of the bathroom and other private spaces to uphold patriarchal binaries of gender for all, not only for people who are transgender or gender nonconforming. These themes are also picked up in Barefoot's (ch. 8 this volume) analysis of how trans-exclusionary women-only spaces exceed their demarcation and reinforce patriarchal gender binaries more widely.

There is nothing inherently *productive or transformative* about discomfort or intimacy. Affectively ambivalent, discomfort can mobilize a desire for easy comforts within existing webs of power, but it can also urge a questioning of those power structures. Vasudevan's and Chennault's chapters suggest that questions of proximity and discomfort can be productively engaged through attention to methodology. What does it mean to be intimate in the field? What are the ethical obligations of feminists? How is it related to the author's positionality? Autoethnography and queering ethnography are places of potential for grappling with intimacies. The contributors to this section demonstrate that we can think about discomfort and intimacy spatially, through disentangling proximity and culpability, through understanding how the regulation of gender in one site exceeds that site, and through seeing geopolitical morality work through rural contexts that reference global tropes.

PART II: GENDERED BODIES AS A TERRAIN OF POLITICAL STRUGGLE

In Part II, we bring in new ways of engaging with one of feminism's major contributions to geographic scholarship: gendered bodies as terrains of struggle. This section features stories of ordinary people deploying their gendered and gender-troubling bodies to take up the work of decolonization, grappling with the category of woman, and seeking to build new worlds by building tiny houses. Feminist geographers have long attended to bodies as sites of conflict and contestation (Das 1995; Gökarıksel 2012; Hyndman and Giles 2004; Longhurst 2000; Pain and Staeheli 2014). The chapters in this section push us further by placing these ideas in relation to Indigenous strategies to claim sovereignty and survival (Valdivia et al., ch. 5 this volume, and Yazzie and Curley, ch. 7 this volume), Black feminist work for "humanly workable" geographies (Gardner, ch. 6 this volume, citing McKittrick 2006), and trans theorizations of patriarchy (Barefoot, ch. 8 this volume). This section centers the praxis of gendered bodies to claim space and to thrive.

Feminist analyses of the body show how intimate spheres structure our worlds and are crucial spaces for the production of social difference (Brickell 2014; Mountz and Hyndman 2006; Pain and Staeheli 2014; Pratt and Rosner 2012; Spillers 1987). Bodies are also key sites for bridging differences, forming alliances, and working together to transform our societies. This work has been taken up by feminist political geographers who have demonstrated that nations are defined in and through bodies (e.g., Dowler and Sharp 2001; Hyndman and Giles 2004; Mayer 2004; Nast 1998; Torres 2018). We claim and bound space through the body, and geopolitics and politics are enmeshed in embodied life (Dixon 2014; Pain and Staeheli 2014; Smith 2012). Yet many of us can do more to engage with the life of these ideas beyond the discipline, much of which remains "anemic" (Domosh 2015; Kobayashi and Peake 2000; Oswin 2018; Pulido 2002).

The contributors to this section work in conversation with theorizations that hold great promise to decenter white Eurocentric understandings of the body and its relationship to space. Engagement with decolonial theory and decolonial feminism (e.g., Naylor et al. 2018; Zaragocin 2019) asks us to consider the ways that gender itself unspools from the same forms of imperial European whiteness that wrote race onto bodies. That is, empire and colonization necessitated the reconstitution of gender relations and the positioning of Indigenous people as those who must be subjugated and remade into gendered human subjects rather than being human on their own terms (Lugones 2010). Decolonial struggle thus requires grappling with the historical constitution of gender and with the role of language in writing our gender scripts (Butler 1990; Lugones 2010). Interrelated but distinct in scholarly lineage, Black feminists take on the ways space has been configured to be antihuman, particularly for Black women, and, thus, the reconfiguration of space becomes a question of ontological survival and the future (Gardner, ch. 6 this volume; hooks 1995; McKittrick 2006). This section, then, uncovers a feminist spatial praxis. When structures of race and gender are written into the built environment (Cofield and Doan, ch. 3 this volume; Gardner, ch. 6 this volume), how do we dismantle these structures or live apart from them? Can we dismantle territorial structures and the imposition of state violence that challenges our sovereignty?

Focusing on Alicia Weya Cawiya and Manuela Omari Ima Omene, two Waorani women leaders (chapter coauthors) and their embodied Indigenous feminist mobilization, Valdivia et al. examine how women deploy multiple and spatially variant strategies to protect Indigenous culture and to contribute to the survival of their communities in the face of ongoing resource extraction. Their discussion reveals the complex positionings of these feminists: as authentic Indigenous women and as cosmopolitan global citizens, as subjects rooted in the Amazon and as world travelers at ease in airports, as traditional weavers and craftswomen and as savvy entrepreneurs with their fingers on the pulse of the latest fashion trends and tastes of American and European customers. They perform forms of authentic Indigeneity through their dress, bodily adornments, and handmade crafts that are easily legible to non-Indigenous audiences. At the same time, they embody Waorani ontology through these performances, bring the spirit of the jaguar into the spaces they occupy, and establish connections with the people they encounter. They both confirm and challenge conceptions of Indigeneity and reshape the "social skin" that connects us.

A concern with embodiment also runs through Gardner's chapter that centers on the question of how to thrive in a city not built for you. Arguing for a consideration of vernacular architecture in relation to the anti-Black structures of US cities, specifically the Twin Cities in Minnesota, Gardner brings Black feminist thought to bear on the connectivity, invasiveness, racialized devaluation, and exploitation built into US cities that act as the "Master's house." She traces a genealogy in the Black geographies of the shotgun house that is distinct from the Tiny House movement that celebrates this architectural form as a new niche market for the white middle class. She reflects on her own experience and interviews with women of color to show their collective attempts to create affordable spaces to live and work in a "loophole of retreat" (citing Jacobs [1861] 2000). Gardner asks how vernacular self-built tiny houses show the creative ways Black women and women of color transform space, evade surveillance, and produce what Katherine McKittrick (2006) calls more humanly workable geographies in opposition to state-led processes of racialized displacement and settler colonialism.

In their chapter, Yazzie and Curley highlight Native and Marxist forms of feminism as a way to understand how settler colonialism and patriarchy are entangled in the relationship between the Navajo Nation and the US government. Using the case of Navajo coal workers and a powerful Navajo woman leader—Annie Wauneka—they argue that settler colonialism reshapes gender relations in order to entrench capitalist modes of production within the Navajo Nation. Native feminist scholarly and activist engagement takes on these twinned mechanisms of violence as a way to understand endemic violence against Native women. Their intervention urges feminist geographers to better understand approaches to feminism that intersect with and support Indigenous claims to sovereignty (Daigle 2016; De Leeuw and Hunt 2018; Dennison 2012; Smiles 2018). This requires intention, for decolonization is *not* a metaphor (Tuck and Yang 2012) but should be aimed at the repatriation of life, land, and sovereignty to Native peoples.

Through analysis of two trans-exclusionary feminist organizations in the United States, Barefoot asks who and what defines what a woman is and is not. By exploring the ways that Women's Liberation Front (WOLF) and Deep Green Resistance's Women's Caucus (DGR) define the category of woman as "survivor of girlhood" and gender "victim," she demonstrates that these definitions render trans women illegible and illegitimate by positioning them as men due to their childhood socialization. Barefoot argues that these organizations' influence extends beyond their limited sphere through the way they interact in public space, gain media coverage, and attempt to influence policy. As Barefoot observes, this is fraught, as "women-only spaces . . . face the challenge of creating a space for women while acknowledging that there are no 'real' women" (ch. 8). Barefoot's contribution draws attention to the forms of feminist politics that unspool from how gender itself is defined. This can be read in relation to the territorialization of gender into particular spaces (e.g., bathrooms), as well as in the territorialization of gender onto the bodies of others—as in the trans-exclusionary radical feminists' impulse to impose maleness onto trans women's bodies and sense of self.

The chapters in Part II center Indigenous, Black, and trans women. Turning to Indigenous and decolonial feminisms and trans geographies, these chapters destabilize the normalization of gender roles, racial inequalities, and sexual exclusions. The histories they tell show the production of gendered and raced bodies in relation to the forces of extractive capitalism, the territorial logic of settler colonial states, racist urban design and architecture, and trans-exclusionary notions of gender in seemingly radical feminist and environmental organizations. However, their analysis also points to how these forces that appear to be universal are never completely totalizing but contain traces of previous modes of living otherwise and the potential for other forms of being. In exploring how subjects sustain life within these structures, we see how bodies claim, create, and transform space. The cracks and fissures in these systems— whether tiny houses that escape surveillance and control and refuse private land ownership or through a transnational weaving of social skins that forge connections across multiple worlds—remind us of the submerged potential and previous forms of cooperating that are always present.

PART III: TEMPORALITY AND FEMINIST FUTURES

In Part III, we ask how the production of knowledge across time and space is a struggle over the future. Feminism is necessarily tied to praxis, and as feminist geographers we question what kind of knowledge we are making for the future and how our embodied experiences inform and transmit that knowledge. If knowledge makes the world and feminism seeks to make a new world, we would do well to engage questions of temporality. How do the historical and contemporary conditions, processes, and displacements that unevenly devalue lives across racialized, gendered, and geographic lines inform how we envision, plan for, and build our futures? Contributors in this section discuss innovative urban planners crafting new worlds through their presence and perspective as feminists in a masculinist and homogenous discipline; the transmission and translation of feminist knowledge across borders, languages, and disciplinary boundaries as the *transloca* carries disruptive knowledge within her; and the ways that feminist activists struggle to transmit their vibrant organizing skills and knowledge across generations as they age and require care. The willingness (or failure) of younger generations to learn from past activists in India, the subversive tactics used by feminists to change urban-planning scholarship, and the work of translating across languages and intellectual histories in these chapters contain the capacities to provoke new geographical imaginations.

Geographers have paid attention to how social movements work to prefigure the future in the present through enacting the social relations and political configurations they desire (Cheng 2014; Dyson and Jeffrey 2018; Lam-Knott 2017). Here, however, we suggest feminist geography could do more to engage with understandings of temporality. Afrofuturism, Indigenous futurity, and questions of design have inspired scholars, musicians, activists, and writers to produce renderings of the future where power relations are transformed (e.g., Davis and Todd 2017; English and Kim 2013; Gumbs 2018; Whyte 2016; Yaszek 2006). They ask: When is the future? Who do we imagine being included in it? What work do we do with the past? If knowledge was part of the production of anti-Blackness and settler colonial logics of elimination, how can feminist scholarship build humanly workable geographies for the present and future?

Prefiguring, but distinct from, contemporary Afrofuturism, thinkers like W.E.B. Du Bois and Ralph Ellison questioned "whether or not there will be any future whatsoever for people of color" (Yaszek 2006, 43). In a Du Bois ([1920] 1999) short story, a comet that strikes the earth and kills the hero's child is "not really a disaster," but an "extremely fortunate event," as only an apocalypse could destroy racism (Yaszek 2006, 52). Afrofuturist artists enable us to "aesthetically reconstitute the (un)limits of humanity and construct alternative conceptions of ecological ethics within our present world and beyond it" (Frazier 2016, 40). This future visioning echoes the concerns of Sara Ahmed (2010) and Lauren Berlant (2011), who suggest we might need to break or destroy the world and our cruelly optimistic longings for happiness in order to abandon the patriarchal structures that have provided only "cruelty love" (Silva 2018).

Sharpe's "wake work" (2009; see also Vasudevan and Smith, forthcoming) is likewise a political project for us to understand a present and future irrevocably shaped by foundational and ontological violence. Emerging from entangled but distinct contexts, writers on Indigenous futurity ask us to question the universal timelines that figure the future as potentially apocalyptic, instead of understanding the ways that we are already part of a postapocalyptic and deeply haunted world (Davis and Todd 2017; Tuck and Ree 2013; Whyte 2016, 2018). Their concerns with historical narratives and temporality signal key questions that we can attend to as feminist geographers. Where do we place ourselves in relation to temporalities of violence? If we intend to break the world to build a new one, what kind of intergenerational relationships do we wish to forge with those who came before us? How can we move with ideas and ontologies across contexts that have been differently shaped by these violent timelines? How might we prefigure the future we desire?

Part III opens with Hariharan's chapter on the Dalit feminist movement's project of building a digital archive of aging activists' stories. Hariharan analyzes the political and affective dimensions of collective memory and the caring work this archive seeks to accomplish. Her work arrives as the Dalit feminist movement is facing a crisis: the political and economic landscape has shifted to make organizing much more difficult, youth are no longer interested in joining the movement, and lifelong activists are aging. While the movement was sustained through kinshiplike solidarity and intergenerational caring, the networks are currently breaking down, powerfully embodied by the story of one feminist activist who faces old age alone. The digital archive project responds to the anxieties feminists feel in the midst of this crisis. Building the archive is a practice of caring for the movement; the archive aims to define a legacy for a new generation of activists, to foster care, and to leave an inheritance.

Gauger turns to oral histories and institutional archives to tell us how women entered the field of urban planning in the 1970s and early 1980s. The scholars Gauger profiles understood feminism as a theoretical intervention and commitment to gender equality and social justice in a masculine discipline that valued notions of objectivity and distance. Gauger examines the specific tactics women used to share resources and make space in order to transform their discipline and the institutions in which they worked. She argues that these women not only altered scholarship and disciplinary canons and traditions but also enabled a different future. Her careful tracing of the barriers and strategies used to reshape their institutional contexts offers insight into disciplinary knowledge production and the ways change happens (or does not) due to the exclusion of certain people and embodied knowledges from disciplinary practices and spaces.

Writing as a scholar who has returned to Ecuador after growing up and studying as an immigrant in the US and UK, Zaragocin not only navigates national borders but also moves through communities structured by shared meanings and languages. Through her teaching and scholarship she asks how she can carry feminist commitments across these spaces. Zaragocin draws on the transloca (Alvarez 2014), the figure who embodies theoretical ideas and experience as she moves across epistemological worlds, giving her a productive view into where theory does and does not match up. The transloca also experiences the incommensurability of translating ideas and language as she works to bring together decolonial epistemologies that evoke another world with feminist politics that remain grounded in the "Western" academy that it tries to dismantle. Thus, this chapter considers the role of translation across linguistic and epistemological boundaries and across ways of being in the world and political orientations.

Part III explores temporality in relation to feminist praxis, focusing on strategic feminist practices that enable the future through interventions into the present. This might mean actively reworking academic institutions to engender feminist urban planning, or building an archive to forge collective memories and foster intergenerational feminist networks of care. It might also mean using embodied knowledges for translating and transforming geographic theory across transnational boundaries. Part III shows us that the inequalities and displacements that shape today will remain fundamentally constitutive of our future as it considers how we might intervene now to change those futures.

CONCLUSION

What happens when we unbind feminist geography, when we pull at its borders and boundaries, and seek to understand what they hold and what they hide? As feminist geographers, how can we engage more deeply and more carefully with questions central to feminist geography: How do we produce knowledge? What and who is knowledge for? What is the relationship between embodied experience and the spaces that we inhabit? Prefiguring in the present the kind of world that we dream of inhabiting requires understanding uneven distributions of comfort and unease. It means asking how we might better understand the limitations of our existing languages, and theorizing the possibilities and horizons emerging from work by scholars based in decolonizing thought and praxis and who center trans, Indigenous, and Black bodies in their interventions.

This volume argues that our lives are intimately entangled across differences produced in a world that is riven with violence and injustice, but also rebuilt each day through creative acts of care, love, and solidarity. Here, we seek a way forward that interrogates our proximity to and complicity in forms of gendered and racialized inequalities that forge the ongoing ruination of the imperial present (Stoler 2013). We ask, how do we forge a collective future that is abundant (Collard, Dempsey, and Sundberg 2015), that accounts for the epistemological, ontological, and visceral violence that require action from us, without allowing such frameworks to foreclose or overdetermine future horizons? What forms of feminist praxis are adequate to this task? Our contributors provide us with starting places. These emerge through invocations of the transloca, who carries embodied knowledge across borders of space and translation (Zaragocin), and through questions posed about the possibility of working in solidarity with those who are suffering from anti-Black violence (Vasudevan), or those whose ontologies may be different from ours (Chennault). They begin from the work of those who continue Indigenous struggles for sovereignty (Yazzie and Curley, Valdivia et al.). Feminist futures are built by those activists who try to connect generations through collective memory, legacy, and care (Hariharan) and through understandings of vernacular architecture as a form of praxis to dismantle the racialized and patriarchal family relations that structure US cities (Gardner). Transforming disciplinary knowledges and institutional spaces (Gauger) provides another point of departure for feminist work, as does continuing to struggle against the gender policing of bodies (Barefoot) and the imposition of heteronormativity (Cofield and Doan). We witness this praxis in the rich, messy, and provocative life of feminism as told by Petra Doan, Kumi Silva, and LaToya Eaves in their interviews, and as it unfolds in the meetings and creative ventures of feminist collectives.

This book reframes discomfort not as something to be dismissed or suppressed but as a rupture that exposes the norms, structures, and hierarchies of value that constitute our social world (Dowler, Afterword this volume). Turning to discomfort might help us question complicity and complacency and enhance self-reflexivity in feminist research and mobilization. The widely discussed and impossible-to-ignore global turn to the right necessitates leaving behind our comfort if that means perpetuating existing structures of power. The instances of racialized violence, imperial overreach, and patriarchal retrenchment that we witness today are certainly *not* new; they are amplified echoes and reverberations of past violence that has been passed down to us through legal systems that exclude, language that renders people's experience invisible, and ancestries and histories cut short or sustained only through creative fugitivity (Gumbs 2016; Harney and Moten 2013).

We assembled *Feminist Geography Unbound* as courageous activists on our own campus deepened their calls for justice, and insisted on the fundamental humanity of those who are the targets of white supremacy, heteronormative patriarchy, and xenophobic violence. We saw those who are vulnerable portrayed as threats, and those who are powerful act with impunity, and these processes have rendered any distinction between global geopolitics and embodied daily life untenable: our bodies and those we care for are the terrain of ideological battles around migration, reproductive health, and state violence.

We have been privileged to share space with students and community members who toppled the confederate statue that was a signal monument to white supremacy on our campus, and have watched as institutions of power failed to see that act as a step toward justice. Through our scholarship and engagement here, we hope to reimagine the ways that we as scholars can engage with and learn from demands for a different future. The scholars in this volume, and the built communities signaled by the collectives, ask that we deeply consider histories and contexts from which power structures emerge, and that we interrogate our own complicity, proximity, and intimacy within these structures, so that we can disavow and disassemble them. They urge us to reconsider the social skin that connects us, and to refigure and enable the creativity and acts of survival submerged but full of life in sites of violence that include our own institutional spaces, which were never intended for *all* of us.

Authors in this book demonstrate the ways that patriarchal, heteronormative, xenophobic, and racist logics colonize, create, and perpetuate their categories through spatial practices: through gender-policing spaces (Doan and Cofield, Barefoot), through the twinned impositions of capitalism and patriarchal gender formations (Curley and Yazzie), through persistent intergenerational and North-South divides and the challenges of traveling across worlds (Hariharan, Valdivia et al., Zaragocin), and through urban planning that perpetuates masculinist perspectives and plantation logics (Gardner, Gauger, Vasudevan). Among these ruins, as feminist scholars, we often find ourselves in academic institutions that enable our work and constrain it, institutions that become worlds unto themselves, among neoliberal education structures that remake us into less political and more complacent versions of ourselves. We would do well to take seriously the premises of contributors to this volume. Consider what we can learn from Hariharan's engagement with Dalit feminists, who work to create different forms of intergenerational kinship to pass down embodied knowledge, or think of Gardner's tiny house that builds a fugitive and improvisational space in the racialized metropolis of Minneapolis. What can we learn from these forms of intergenerational transmission and small world-making practices?

Our aspiration is that we take seriously our own life within, outside of, and adjacent to academic institutions as an embodied terrain of struggle (Ahmed 2017). We ask what kinds of changes need to be made in order for us to prefigure spaces in which a more abundant form of scholarship and life can emerge, and the ways that these spatial practices have the capacity to transcend bounded spaces (such as the university) through our work with students, activists, and the people we engage with during our research (sometimes these categories will overlap). Through examining the story arcs and timelines of our own discipline, we must locate ourselves in a constellation of power relations and consider what kind of world we prefigure every day. Our task is to enable forms of feminist world-making that maintain political intention, while making space for the translocation and translation of critically important ideas across the borders of nation-states and disciplines. This means a feminist world-making that does the risky work of examining its own weaknesses and insularity through engagement with those in allied justice-oriented fields who have sometimes been excluded from feminist spaces and praxis. In orienting feminist geographies toward radical vulnerability, justice, and solidarity (Dowler this volume), we ask: How are we to understand ourselves situated within the temporalities and spatialities of foundational and ontological violence? What kind of future do we make through the new forms of knowledge, community, and practice that we are making in the present? What kinds of improvisational and vernacular architectures of kinship, relation, and meaning can we intentionally prefigure for a more just world? We have worked to position this book as one step on a path with no end.

REFERENCES

Abu-Lughod, Lila. 2002. "Do Muslim Women Really Need Saving? Anthropological Reflections on Cultural Relativism and Its Others." *American Anthropologist* 104 (3): 783–90.

Ahmed, Sara. 2004. *The Cultural Politics of Emotion*. New York: Routledge.

Ahmed, Sara. 2010. *The Promise of Happiness*. Durham, NC: Duke University Press.

Ahmed, Sara. 2012. *On Being Included: Racism and Diversity in Institutional Life*. Durham, NC: Duke University Press.

Ahmed, Sara. 2017. *Living a Feminist Life*. Durham, NC: Duke University Press.

Alvarez, Sonia. 2014. "Introduction to the Project and the Volume/Enacting a Translocal Feminist Politics of Translation." In *Translocalities/Translocalidades. Feminist Politics of Translation in the Latin/a Américas*, edited by Sonia Alvarez, Claudia de Lima Costa, Verónica Feliu, Rebecca Hester, Norma Klahn, and Milie Thayer, 1–18. Durham, NC: Duke University Press.

Arvin, Maile, Eve Tuck, and Angie Morrill. 2013. "Decolonizing Feminism: Challenging Connections between Settler Colonialism and Heteropatriarchy." *Feminist Formations* 25 (1): 8–34.

Bayoumi, Moustafa. 2009. *How Does It Feel to Be a Problem?: Being Young and Arab in America*. New York: Penguin.

Berlant, Lauren. 2011. *Cruel Optimism*. Durham, NC: Duke University Press.

Berry, Maya J., Claudia Chávez Argüelles, Shanya Cordis, Sarah Ihmoud, and Elizabeth Velásquez Estrada. 2017. "Toward a Fugitive Anthropology: Gender, Race, and Violence in the Field." *Cultural Anthropology* 32 (4): 537–65.

Brickell, Katherine. 2014. " 'The Whole World Is Watching': Intimate Geopolitics of Forced Eviction and Women's Activism in Cambodia." *Annals of the Association of American Geographers* 104 (6): 1256–72.

Butler, Judith. 1990. *Gender Trouble: Feminism and the Subversion of Identity*. New York: Routledge.

Butler, Judith. 2014. "Bodily Vulnerability, Coalitions, and Street Politics." *Critical Studies* 37: 99–119.

Caldwell, Kia Lilly. 2018. "Sexism, Racism Drive Black Women to Run for Office in Brazil, US." *The Conversation*, October 4, 2018. http://theconversation.com/sexism-racism-drive-more-black-women-to-run-for-office-in-both-brazil-and-us-104208.

Cheng, Yi'En. 2014. "Time Protagonists: Student Migrants, Practices of Time and Cultural Construction of the Singapore-Educated Person." *Social & Cultural Geography* 15 (4): 385–405.

Collard, Rosemary-Claire, Jessica Dempsey, and Juanita Sundberg. 2015. "A Manifesto for Abundant Futures." *Annals of the Association of American Geographers* 105 (2): 322–30.

Collins, Patricia Hill. 1990. *Black Feminist Thought: Knowledge, Consciousness, and the Politics of Empowerment*. New York: Routledge.

Crenshaw, Kimberlé. 1989. "Demarginalizing the Intersection of Race and Sex: A Black Feminist Critique of Antidiscrimination Doctrine, Feminist Theory and Antiracist Politics." *University of Chicago Legal Forum* 1: 139–67.

Crenshaw, Kimberlé. 1991. "Mapping the Margins: Intersectionality, Identity Politics, and Violence against Women of Color." *Stanford Law Review* 43 (6): 1241–99.

Da Silva, Denise Ferreira. 2013. "To Be Announced Radical Praxis or Knowing (at) the Limits of Justice." *Social Text* 31 (1 (114)): 43–62.

Daigle, Michelle. 2016. "Awawanenitakik: The Spatial Politics of Recognition and Relational Geographies of Indigenous Self-determination." *The Canadian Geographer/Le Géographe Canadien* 60 (2): 259–69.

Das, Veena. 1995. *Critical Events: An Anthropological Perspective on Contemporary India*. New Delhi: Oxford University Press.

Davis, Heather, and Zoe Todd. 2017. "On the Importance of a Date, or, Decolonizing the Anthropocene." *ACME: An International Journal for Critical Geographies* 16 (4): 761–80.

De Leeuw, Sarah. and Hunt, Sarah. 2018. "Unsettling Decolonizing Geographies." *Geography Compass* 12 (7). https://doi.org/10.1111/gec3.12376.

Denetdale, Jennifer Nez. 2006. "Chairmen, Presidents, and Princesses: The Navajo Nation, Gender, and the Politics of Tradition." *Wicazo Sa Review* 21 (1): 9–28.

Denetdale, Jennifer. 2008. "Carving Navajo National Boundaries: Patriotism, Tradition, and the Diné Marriage Act of 2005." *American Quarterly* 60 (2): 289–94.

Dennison, Jean. 2012. *Colonial Entanglement: Constituting a Twenty-First-Century Osage Nation*. Chapel Hill, NC: UNC Press Books.

Dimpfl, Mike. 2017. "Micro (Bial) Management: Everyday Cleanliness and the Divisive Power of Hygienic Worries." *Cultural Geographies* 25 (1): 201–16.

Dimpfl, Mike, and Sara Smith. 2018. "Cosmopolitan Sidestep: University Life, Intimate Geopolitics and the Hidden Costs of 'Global' Citizenship." *Area* 51 (4): 635–43.Dixon, Deborah P. 2014. "The Way of the Flesh: Life, Geopolitics and the Weight of the Future." *Gender, Place & Culture* 21 (2): 136–51. https://doi.org/10.1080/0966369X.2013.879110.

Doan, Petra L. 2010. "The Tyranny of Gendered Spaces—Reflections from beyond the Gender Dichotomy." *Gender, Place & Culture* 17 (5): 635–54.

Domosh, Mona. 2013. "Geoeconomic Imaginations and Economic Geography in the Early Twentieth Century." *Annals of the Association of American Geographers* 103 (4): 944–66. https://doi.org/10.1080/00045608.2011.653740.

Domosh, Mona. 2015. "President's Column: Why Is Our Geography Curriculum So White?" *AAG Newsletter*. June 1, 2015. http://news.aag.org/2015/06/why-is-our-geography-curriculum-so-white/.

Dowler, Lorraine, and Joanne Sharp. 2001. "A Feminist Geopolitics?" *Space and Polity* 5 (3): 165–76. https://doi.org/10.1080/13562570120104382.

Du Bois, W.E.B. (1903) 1989. *The Souls of Black Folk*. New York: Bantam Books.

Du Bois, W.E.B. (1920) 1999. *Darkwater: Voices from Within the Veil*. Mineola, NY: Dover Publications.

Dyson, Jane, and Craig Jeffrey. 2018. "Everyday Prefiguration: Youth Social Action in North India." *Transactions of the Institute of British Geographers* 43 (4): 573–85.

Eng, David L. 2010. *The Feeling of Kinship: Queer Liberalism and the Racialization of Intimacy*. Durham, NC: Duke University Press.

England, Kim. 1994. "Getting Personal: Reflexivity, Positionality and Feminist Research." *Professional Geographer* 46: 80–89.

English, Daylanne K., and Alvin Kim. 2013. "Now We Want Our Funk Cut: Janelle Monáe's Neo-Afrofuturism." *American Studies* 52 (4): 217–30.

Esson, James, Patricia Noxolo, Richard Baxter, Patricia Daley, and Margaret Byron. 2017. "The 2017 RGS-IBG Chair's Theme: Decolonising Geographical Knowledges, or Reproducing Coloniality?" *Area* 49 (3): 384–88.

Faria, Caroline, and Sharlene Mollett. 2016. "Critical Feminist Reflexivity and the Politics of Whiteness in the 'Field.' " *Gender, Place & Culture* 23 (1): 79–93.

Farris, Sara R. 2017. *In the Name of Women's Rights: The Rise of Femonationalism*. Durham, NC: Duke University Press Books.

Fluri, Jennifer L. 2011. "Bodies, Bombs and Barricades: Geographies of Conflict and Civilian (in)Security." *Transactions of the Institute of British Geographers* 36 (2): 280–96. https://doi.org/10.1111/j.1475-5661.2010.00422.x.

Frazier, Chelsea M. 2016. "Troubling Ecology: Wangechi Mutu, Octavia Butler, and Black Feminist Interventions in Environmentalism." *Critical Ethnic Studies* 2 (1): 40.

Gökarıksel, Banu. 2012. "The Intimate Politics of Secularism and the Headscarf: The Mall, the Neighborhood, and the Public Square in Istanbul." *Gender, Place & Culture* 19 (1): 1–20. https://doi.org/10.1080/0966369X.2011.633428.

Gökarıksel, Banu, and Sara Smith. 2017. "Intersectional Feminism beyond U.S. Flag Hijabs and Pussy Hats in Trump's America." *Gender, Place & Culture* 24 (5): 628–44.

Graff, Agnieszka, Ratna Kapur, and Suzanna Danuta Walters. 2019. "Gender and the Rise of the Global Right: Introduction." *Signs* 44 (3): 541–60.

Gumbs, Alexis Pauline. 2016. *Spill: Scenes of Black Feminist Fugitivity*. Reprint. Durham, NC: Duke University Press Books.

Gumbs, Alexis Pauline. 2018. *M Archive: After the End of the World*. Durham, NC: Duke University Press.

Hage, Ghassan. 2017. *Is Racism an Environmental Threat*. Cambridge: Polity Press.

Haraway, Donna J. 2016. *Staying with the Trouble: Making Kin in the Chthulucene*. Durham, NC: Duke University Press.

Harney, Stefano, and Fred Moten. 2013. *The Undercommons: Fugitive Planning & Black Study*. Wivenhoe, NY: Autonomedia.

hooks, bell. 1981. *Ain't I a Woman: Black Women and Feminism*. London: South End Press.

hooks, bell. 1984. *Feminist Theory: From Margin to Center*. Boston: South End Press.

hooks, bell. 1995. *Art on My Mind: Visual Politics*. New York: New Press.

Hunt, Sarah, and Cindy Holmes. 2015. "Everyday Decolonization: Living a Decolonizing Queer Politics." *Journal of Lesbian Studies* 19 (2): 154–72.

Hyndman, Jennifer, and W Giles, eds. 2004. *Sites of Violence: Gender and Conflict Zones*. Berkeley: University of California Press.

Jacobs, Harriet. (1861) 2000. *Incidents in the Life of a Slave Girl*. New York: W. W. Norton.

Jazeel, Tariq. 2017. "Mainstreaming Geography's Decolonial Imperative." *Transactions of the Institute of British Geographers* 42 (3): 334–37.

Kobayashi, Audrey, and Linda Peake. 2000. "Racism Out of Place: Thoughts on Whiteness and an Antiracist Geography in the New Millennium." *Annals of the Association of American Geographers* 90 (2): 392–403. https://doi.org/10.1111/0004-5608.00202.

Kohl, Ellen, and Priscilla McCutcheon. 2015. "Kitchen Table Reflexivity: Negotiating Positionality through Everyday Talk." *Gender, Place & Culture* 22 (6): 747–63.

Laliberté, Nicole, and Carolin Schurr. 2016. "The Stickiness of Emotions in the Field: Introduction." *Gender, Place & Culture* 23 (1): 72–78.

Lam-Knott, Sonia. 2017. "Understanding Protest 'Violence' in Hong Kong from the Youth Perspective." *Asian Anthropology* 16 (4): 279–98.

Legg, Stephen. 2010. "An Intimate and Imperial Feminism: Meliscent Shephard and the Regulation of Prostitution in Colonial India." *Environment and Planning D: Society and Space* 28 (1): 68–94. https://doi.org/10.1068/d10507.

Longhurst, Robyn. 2000. *Bodies: Exploring Fluid Boundaries*. London; New York: Routledge.

Lorde, Audre. 1984. *Sister Outsider: Essays and Speeches*. Freedom, CA: Crossing Press.

Lowe, Lisa. 2015. *The Intimacies of Four Continents*. Durham, NC: Duke University Press.

Lugones, María. 2010. "Toward a Decolonial Feminism." *Hypatia* 25 (4): 742–59.

Mahtani, Minelle. 2014. "Toxic Geographies: Absences in Critical Race Thought and Practice in Social and Cultural Geography." *Social & Cultural Geography* 15 (4): 359–67. https://doi.org /10.1080/14649365.2014.888297.

Mayer, Tamar. 2004. "Embodied Nationalisms." In *Mapping Women, Making Politics*, edited by Lynn Staeheli, Eleonore Kofman, and Linda Peake, 156–61. New York: Routledge.

McKittrick, Katherine. 2006. *Demonic Grounds: Black Women and the Cartographies of Struggle*. Minneapolis: University of Minnesota Press.

McKittrick, Katherine. 2014. *Sylvia Wynter: On Being Human as Praxis*. Durham, NC: Duke University Press.

McClintock, Anne. 1995. *Imperial Leather: Race, Gender and Sexuality in the Colonial Contest*. New York: Routledge.

Monk, Janice, and Susan Hanson. 1982. "On Not Excluding Half of the Human in Human Geography." *The Professional Geographer* 34 (1): 11–23. https://doi.org/10.1111/j.0033 -0124.1982.00011.x.

Moss, Pamela, and Avril Maddrell. 2017. "Emergent and Divergent Spaces in the Women's March: The Challenges of Intersectionality and Inclusion." *Gender, Place & Culture* 24 (5): 613–20. https://doi.org/10.1080/0966369X.2017.1351509.

Moss, Pamela, Karen Falconer Al-Hindi, and Hope Kawabata. 2002. *Feminist Geography in Practice: Research and Methods*. Malden, MA: Wiley-Blackwell.

Mountz, Alison. 2015. "For Slow Scholarship: A Feminist Politics of Resistance through Collective Action in the Neoliberal University," *ACME: An International Journal for Critical Geographies* 14 (4): 1235–59. https://www.acme-journal.org/index.php/acme/article/view/1058.

Mountz, Alison, and Jennifer Hyndman. 2006. "Feminist Approaches to the Global Intimate." *Women's Studies Quarterly* 34 (1/2): 446–63.

Muhs, Gabriella Gutiérrez y, Yolanda Flores Niemann, Carmen G. González, and Angela P. Harris. 2012. *Presumed Incompetent: The Intersections of Race and Class for Women in Academia*. Boulder: University Press of Colorado.

Muñoz, José Esteban. 2009. *Cruising Utopia: The Then and There of Queer Futurity*. New York: New York University Press.

Nagar, Richa. 2014. *Muddying the Waters: Coauthoring Feminisms across Scholarship and Activism*. Champaign: University of Illinois Press.

Nagar, Richa. 2019. "Hungry Translations: The World Through Radical Vulnerability: The 2017 Antipode RGS-IBG Lecture." *Antipode* 51 (1): 3–24.

Nast, Heidi J. 1998. "Unsexy Geographies." *Gender, Place & Culture* 5 (2): 191–206.

Naylor, Lindsay, Michelle Daigle, Sofia Zaragocin, Margaret Marietta Ramírez, and Mary Gilmartin. 2018. "Interventions: Bringing the Decolonial to Political Geography." *Political Geography* 66: 199–209.

Noxolo, Patricia. 2017. "Introduction: Decolonising Geographical Knowledge in a Colonised and Re-colonising Postcolonial World." *Area* 49 (3): 317–19.

Oberhauser, Ann M., Jennifer L. Fluri, Risa Whitson, and Sharlene Mollett. 2017. *Feminist Spaces: Gender and Geography in a Global Context*. London; New York: Routledge.

Oswin, Natalie. 2012. "The Queer Time of Creative Urbanism: Family, Futurity, and Global City Singapore." *Environment and Planning A* 44 (7): 1624–40.

Oswin, Natalie. 2018. *Society and Space, Here and Now*. London: SAGE Publications.

Pain, Rachel. 2015. "Intimate War." *Political Geography* 44: 64–73.

Pain, Rachel, and Lynn Staeheli. 2014. "Introduction: Intimacy-Geopolitics and Violence." *Area* 46 (4): 344–47. https://doi.org/10.1111/area.12138.

Peake, Linda, and Beverley Mullings. 2016. "Critical Reflections on Mental and Emotional Distress in the Academy." *ACME: An International Journal for Critical Geographies* 15 (2): 253–84. https://www.acme-journal.org/index.php/acme/article/view/1123.

Perry, Imani. 2018. *Vexy Thing: On Gender and Liberation*. Durham, NC: Duke University Press.

Pratt, Geraldine. 2004. *Working Feminism*. Philadelphia: Temple University Press.

Pratt, Geraldine, and Victoria Rosner. 2012. *The Global and the Intimate: Feminism in Our Time*. New York: Columbia University Press.

Puar, Jasbir K. 2012. " 'I Would Rather Be a Cyborg than a Goddess': Becoming-Intersectional in Assemblage Theory." *PhiloSOPHIA* 2 (1): 49–66.

Pulido, Laura. 2002. "Reflections on a White Discipline." *The Professional Geographer* 54 (1): 42–49. https://doi.org/10.1111/0033-0124.00313.

Puwar, Nirmal. 2004. *Space Invaders: Race, Gender and Bodies out of Place*. Oxford: Berg.

Radcliffe, Sarah A. 2017. "Decolonising Geographical Knowledges." *Transactions of the Institute of British Geographers* 42 (3): 329–33. https://doi.org/10.1111/tran.12195.

Rose, Gillian. 1993. *Feminism and Geography: The Limits of Geographical Knowledge*. Cambridge, MA: Polity.

Sharpe, Christina. 2009. *Monstrous Intimacies: Making Post-Slavery Subjects*. Durham, NC: Duke University Press.

Sharpe, Christina. 2016. *In the Wake: On Blackness and Being*. Durham, NC: Duke University Press.

Silva, Kumarini. 2018. "Having the Time of Our Lives: Love-Cruelty as Patriotic Impulse." *Communication and Critical/Cultural Studies* 15 (1): 79–84.

Simpson, Audra. 2014. *Mohawk Interruptus: Political Life Across the Borders of Settler States*. Durham, NC: Duke University Press.

Slaughter, Sheila, and Gary Rhoades. 2000. "The Neo-Liberal University." *New Labor Forum* 6: 73–79.

Smiles, Deondre. 2018. " '. . . to the Grave'—Autopsy, Settler Structures, and Indigenous Counter-Conduct." *Geoforum* 91: 141–50.

Smith, Sara. 2012. "Intimate Geopolitics: Religion, Marriage, and Reproductive Bodies in Leh, Ladakh." *Annals of the Association of American Geographers* 102 (6): 1511–28. https://doi.org/10.1080/00045608.2012.660391.

Spillers, Hortense J. 1987. "Mama's Baby, Papa's Maybe: An American Grammar Book." *Diacritics* 17 (2): 65–81.

Stoler, Ann Laura, ed. 2013. *Imperial Debris: On Ruins and Ruination*. Durham, NC: Duke University Press.

Tadiar, Neferti X. M. 2015. "Decolonization, 'Race,' and Remaindered Life under Empire." *Qui Parle: Critical Humanities and Social Sciences* 23 (2): 135–60.

Tolia-Kelly, Divya P. 2016. "The Landscape of Cultural Geography: Ideologies Lost." *Area* 48 (3): 371–73. https://doi.org/10.1111/area.12288.

Torres, Rebecca Maria. 2018. "A Crisis of Rights and Responsibility: Feminist Geopolitical Perspectives on Latin American Refugees and Migrants." *Gender, Place & Culture* 25 (1): 13–36.

Tuck, Eve, and C. Ree. 2013. "A Glossary of Haunting." In *Handbook of Autoethnography*, edited by Stacy Holman Jones, Tony E. Adams, and Carolyn Ellis, 639–58. New York: Routledge.

Tuck, Eve, and K. Wayne Yang. 2012. "Decolonization Is Not a Metaphor." *Decolonization: Indigeneity, Education & Society* 1 (1).

Vasudevan, Pavithra, and Sara Smith. 2020. "The Domestic Geopolitics of Racial Capitalism." *Environment and Planning C: Politics and Space*. https://doi.org/10.1177/2399654420901567.

Weheliye, AG. 2014. *Habeas Viscus: Racializing Assemblages, Biopolitics, and Black Feminist Theories of the Human*. Durham, NC: Duke University Press.

Whyte, Kyle Powys. 2016. "Our Ancestors' Dystopia Now: Indigenous Conservation and the Anthropocene." In *Routledge Companion to the Environmental Humanities*, edited by Ursula Heise, Jon Christensen, and Michelle Niemann, 206–15. New York: Routledge.

Whyte, Kyle Powys. 2018. "Indigenous Science (Fiction) for the Anthropocene: Ancestral Dystopias and Fantasies of Climate Change Crises." *Environment and Planning E: Nature and Space* 1 (1–2): 224–42.

Wynter, Sylvia. 1971. "Novel and History, Plot and Plantation." *Savacou* 5: 95–102.

Wynter, Sylvia. 2003. "Unsettling the Coloniality of Being/Power/Truth/Freedom: Towards the Human, After Man, Its Overrepresentation—An Argument." *The New Centennial Review* 3 (3): 257–337.

Yaszek, Lisa. 2006. "Afrofuturism, Science Fiction, and the History of the Future." *Socialism and Democracy* 20 (3): 41–60.

Yazzie, Melanie K. 2018. "Decolonizing Development in Diné Bikeyah: Resource Extraction, Anti-Capitalism, and Relational Futures." *Environment and Society* 9 (1): 25–39.

Zaragocin, Sofia. 2019. "Gendered Geographies of Elimination: Decolonial Feminist Geographies in Latin American Settler Contexts." *Antipode* 51 (1): 373–92.

PART I

DISCOMFORT ACROSS ENCOUNTERS

BROWN SCHOLAR, BLACK STUDIES: ON SUFFERING, WITNESS, AND MATERIALIST RELATIONALITY

Pavithra Vasudevan

This chapter is a reflection on how I approach research as a political praxis, a commitment to theorizing the operations of power in collaboration with communities devastated by racial capitalism. I examine three encounters, occurring at various stages of my research process, that startled me and prompted deeper reflection on who I am in the world of my research. The first was a casual conversation with an older white man who spent decades working as a manager in the Alcoa aluminum smelting plant in Badin, North Carolina, the company town that is the subject of my research. Following this interaction, which occurred after I had completed the bulk of my fieldwork with residents of West Badin, the African American section of town, I found myself questioning why I had chosen to ground my study of capitalism in Black experiences. The second encounter occurred during a campus visit while applying for an academic job. During one of the interviews, a white male academic doing quantitative work on social inequality challenged my proximity to my research subjects, and in particular my focus on their experiences of suffering, leading me to consider why I study anti-Black violence. The third encounter reaches back to the start of fieldwork, my first interview in West Badin with a pair of middle-aged Black women who recounted the traumas they have lived through. The paralysis I experienced following this interview pushed me to seriously consider my role in witnessing suffering, and its relationship to research as political praxis.

I stage these encounters here, out of chronological sequence, to address the following questions concerning the relationship between racial identity, research focus, and methodology: *Why am I, a brown immigrant scholar, work-ing in Black studies? What are the implications of focusing my work on anti-Black violence? What are my ethical responsibilities in witnessing Black people suffering?*

I suggest that our intersectional identity, the cards we are dealt, is only part of the game. How we choose to play the game is in equal measure about adopt-ing a *political orientation* to the world, which informs our research praxis and how we negotiate the complexities of power, refracted through, but extending beyond, identities—ours and others' (Chennault, ch. 2 this volume).

My research addresses how waste and race converged in the history of Badin, North Carolina, a company town where aluminum was produced from 1917 to 2007, and the implications of toxicity as a mode of racial oppression for Black life and politics. As "the material of modernity" (Sheller 2014), alu-minum enabled twentieth-century US geopolitical predominance militarily and economically, infused into infrastructures of transport and warfare, everyday built environments, and communication technologies. The aluminum indus-try's teleological imaginary of efficiency, modernization, and progress erases countless localized contestations over environmental and corporeal devasta-tion wrought by the global supply chain (Padel and Das 2010; Sheller 2014). As I argue elsewhere (Vasudevan 2019), Black experiences of living and working in Badin are critical to understanding aluminum production as racial capitalism.

My overarching methodology is critical performance ethnography (CPE), a research approach committed simultaneously to analytical, activist, and aes-thetic production (Conquergood 2013; Madison 2005). This project was collab-oratively formulated with the North Carolina Environmental Justice Network (NCEJN), a statewide advocacy organization, and the Concerned Citizens of West Badin Community (CCWBC), a grassroots group formed in September 2013 to address racial exclusion, ongoing contamination, and health concerns. At CCWBC meetings, I engaged in "observant participation" (Vargas 2008, 175) by sharing insights from fieldwork, supporting strategies for mobilizing community participation, and serving as a liaison to the NCEJN. I conducted fourteen oral history interviews with eighteen Badin residents, former Alcoa workers and their families, five of which were jointly conducted with Naeema Muhammad, NCEJN organizing codirector, who served as a project coinves-tigator. I also interviewed lawyers and environmental advocates involved in contamination lawsuits concerning Badin, gathered documentation from legal processes and congressional hearings, and examined domestic archival materi-als such as scrapbooks.

From the outset, I envisioned the project as activist scholarship "in dia-logue, collaboration, [and] alliance with people who are struggling to better their lives" (Hale 2008, 4). Interview excerpts and ethnographic data were incorporated into a ninety-minute play titled "Race and Waste in an Aluminum Town," performed initially for the local community in April 2016 and restaged twice for broader publics, in October 2016 at the NCEJN annual summit and in February 2017 for the Swain Studio 6 Performance Series at the University of North Carolina at Chapel Hill. Despite my explicit commitment to supporting grassroots organizing, I questioned my suitability for this project throughout the research process. This chapter takes up several of those moments to reflect on the significance of racial identity to research as political praxis.

REFLEXIVITY THROUGH RELATIONALITY

Feminist scholarship aspiring to antiracism and decolonization emphasizes reflexivity in research, a disarmingly simple and necessary intervention: if power shapes knowledge production, then as scholars we must interrogate how *who* we are impacts *how* we work and *what* knowledge we produce. Reflexivity calls for analyzing our structural position (Haraway 2013) within a complex terrain of power relations in order to uncover how our identities inform how we relate to research subjects and are received by them, how we navigate everyday life in fieldwork and the academy, and the choices we make in gathering and interpreting data. Reflexivity recognizes that "all knowledge is produced in specific circumstances and that those circumstances shape it in some way" (Rose 1997, 305). The desire for reflexivity, however, is complicated by the politics of identity. Identity is a "construction-in-process" (Ahmed 1997), produced at the intersections of multiple axes of power (Crenshaw 1991). However, the incorporation of intersectionality into multicultural discourses of neoliberal institutions (Puar 2017) dampens its critical force through an "overly academic exercise of speculative or normative musings" (Bilge 2013, 411), producing feminist genealogies that erase Black feminism's foundational contributions to intersectionality as a concept. In such apolitical contexts, reflexive writing operates as a self-indulgent confessional about one's own privileges, divorced from transformative political praxis (Kobayashi 2003), and reinstantiates the researcher's grasp on power by serving "as a shallow of legitimation and a back door for the god trick claiming to understand not only the lives of our research participants but even our own relations and limitations within the field" (Smith 2016, 137).

This chapter attempts an alternate approach to critical feminist reflexivity (Faria and Mollett 2016) that acknowledges fieldwork as a complex affective terrain in which the significance of racial identity shifts according to circumstances, complicating research relations and outcomes. As my ethnographic account suggests, emotional responses to my bodily presence in the field and academy revealed the unnaturalness and contingency of racial meanings (Faria and Mollett 2016). However, for reflexivity to move beyond self-discovery (England 1994) to serve as a "more meaningful conceptual [tool] that can help us advance transformative politics of difference" (Nagar 2014, 85) requires a reformulation of reflexivity in explicit relation to political praxis. Here, I offer one approach to reflexivity that destabilizes the academic "self" and a focus on positionality, through situated solidarities (Nagar 2014, 85) grounded in materialist relationality.

A relational approach begins with acknowledging how humanity is constituted by racialized suffering; racialized peoples, excepted from legal definitions of personhood or "juridical humanity" (Esmeir 2012), are used to justify the continued dominance of liberalism, even as they are paradoxically excluded from legal protection (Weheliye 2014). In what follows, I suggest that as scholars, we are materially connected to racialized suffering in excess of our identities. Orientations, "how bodies are directed towards things," *matter* for liberatory research—both in terms of what is most significant and in the sense of physical substance (Ahmed 2010b, 234). Within this framework, reflexivity can engender change when we orient toward building solidarity across the oppressive cleavages that unevenly produce suffering (Valdivia et al., ch. 5 this volume).

This analysis reflects two decades of reflexive participation in social justice struggles. I am writing this chapter at a time when the anxieties and fervent desires that radical *desis* in the US have long discussed in private have generalized into a public dialogue. In support of the Movement for Black Lives, Asian and South Asian Americans have called for a "Model Minority Mutiny" (Jung 2014). In open letters to family and community, activists argue that Asian immigrant communities benefit from the excesses of capitalism's violently racial hierarchies (Iyer 2014), and call for subjective rebellion against public and state expectations of Asian Americans to be docile subjects and complicit participants in anti-Black violence (Nair 2016). While such initiatives aspire to mutiny, their tendency to function as "inward-looking moral strictures, rather than explanations for how such disparities came into being" (Pan 2015) reiterates the very narratives through which Asian Americans are positioned as a privileged minority, used to justify and perpetuate ongoing racial violence.[1] Here, I evoke the desire for race mutiny through reflexive analysis rooted in an explicit political orientation that begins with but moves beyond static understandings of one's own identity. When informed by participation in political struggle, identity becomes reformulated through situated solidarities

(Nagar 2014) that challenge racial capitalism's dependence on identification with racial hierarchies. Thus politicized, identity offers a different entry point to reflexivity for activist scholars committed to antiracism.

This piece is a product of "kitchen table reflexivity" (Kohl and McCutcheon 2015), reflecting the many informal conversations through which I processed difficult and awkward fieldwork encounters with academic mentors; graduate colleagues in geography, performance ethnography, and critical race studies; and my partner and friends, many of whom are more concerned with political struggles against heteropatriarchal racial capitalism than the latest academic debates.[2] What seemed like "everyday talk" (Kohl and McCutcheon 2015) led to profound insights about the nature of race, power, and knowledge, pushing me to clarify when my internal strife intersected with operations of power, why emotionally intense encounters with ambivalent meanings may deserve attention, and most important, how to reexamine and refine my political praxis through reflexivity. I have voiced thoughts here that I would rather reserve for women-of-color spaces, in the spirit of reclaiming feminist critique as a generative practice rather than a territorializing maneuver (Nash 2017). In academia and activism alike, the politics of identity require rejuvenation and honest reexamination, if we are to carry reflexivity forward as a tool in the struggle. I begin with exploring the implications and responsibilities inherent to being a brown immigrant scholar studying anti-Black violence.

WELCOME TO AMERICA

Ethnographic Fieldnote

July 24, 2017

Last week, I serendipitously found myself at the hundredth birthday party for the Yadkin dam, a guest of the Yadkin Riverkeeper, a regional environmental advocate. The event was hosted by Cube Hydro, an engineering company that repurposes old dams for "green" hydropower. Ownership of the Yadkin and three other dams that have long supplied energy for Alcoa's smelting operations in Badin has recently been transferred to Cube. After spending eighteen months learning about Badin's history from Black residents, being at the party felt strangely unsettling. The "party" celebrated the technological achievements of the dam and provided Cube with an opportunity to honor Alcoa's commitments to safety and innovation. Guests included former Alcoa managerial staff, several of whom were easing into new positions with Cube, Cube employees who were visiting Badin from their Virginia headquarters, including a surprising number of attorneys specializing in environmental law, and city, county and state economic development stakeholders. Libby McClure, my collaborator on a related health project whispered to me, "I feel like I'm a spy."

I walked outside, joining several guests who were speaking with Jimmy Benson,[3] the former plant manager. A white man in his sixties, Jimmy carries himself as if he is entitled to respect and held the attention of his audience about the marvels of the dam's engineering. During a break in the conversation, I introduced myself to Benson as a PhD student studying Badin and Alcoa. His response floored me. "Welcome to America!" Benson said, at once friendly and condescending. I glibly replied that I had lived in the US for twenty-five years but thanked him nonetheless for the welcome. Having had limited access to white Badin residents and Alcoa management during fieldwork, I saw this moment as a valuable opportunity. I asked Benson what happened to former employees when the plant shut down, to which he replied proudly that they had been offered vocational training to transition to other jobs or retired with generous packages. Unsurprisingly, he did not mention the two hundred plus occupational injury lawsuits involving former workers, or the ongoing environmental contamination contestations following the plant closure. I also learned that Benson's son manages the e-waste processing center occupying the old factory.

I have replayed my ethnographic encounter with Benson multiple times, wondering at the layers of meaning insinuated by his statement. Was it an innocent invitation to join in the celebration of technological and industrial glory that was the underlying narrative of the day? Or was it the drawing of a boundary, a delineation of (white) American greatness that implicitly rendered me forever an outsider to this country? The Yadkin dam's hundredth-birthday party was a lesson in the intimate reproduction of whiteness and how capitalism narrates its own history. In Benson's statement, and throughout the celebration, the invocation of white ancestry as the source of innovation and labor that powered industrial progress offered a glimpse into how white America claims entitlement through capitalism, and in who and what constitutes "America."

For immigrants like me—South Asian, middle-class, highly educated—our desires for and investment in "America" are nurtured through cultural consumption well before we enter the territorial bounds of the state (Grewal 2005). We enter into a *de facto* white historical narrative that justifies the state's existence through ownership of land, modernization, and color-blind multicultural democracy. The imaginary of the US as a blank canvas for dreams of utopia, development, and progress are reproduced through a series of era-sures, in which Indigenous existence is relegated to a historical past, and white guilt is salved through the legal abolition of slavery and the nominal gains of civil rights. In this context, brown immigrants must prove their allegiance through labor and symbolic gestures that disavow their presumed ties to ter-rorism because of skin color, religious affiliation, or national origin (Puar and Rai 2002). Those who accept the terms of whiteness may then conditionally access material benefits denied to Black Americans, further serving whiteness as "model minorities" who uphold the lie of American multiculturalism. Always en route to whiteness (Grewal 2005), we can then live in comfortable suburbs with highly funded public schools and walkable urban neighborhoods with farmers markets, failing to understand how these superstructures are built onto and dependent upon anti-Black violence and Indigenous dispossession (Gardner, ch. 6 this volume).

Despite my general proclivity toward reflexivity, I reflect on the role my ethnic/racial identity plays in research encounters with some hesitance. Being South Asian, an ethnicity that is both valorized and demonized by the US, and having faced both overt racism and subtle microaggressions in interactions with Americans of various races, I occupy a complex racial positionality that is neither transparent in research (Rose 1997) nor clearly captured in discourses of privilege and oppression. Since emigrating to the US at age eleven, I have frequently been asked where I am from and how I learned to speak English so well, misrecognized as a political refugee from Southeast Asia or an undocu-mented border-crosser from Latin America. When registered as South Asian, I have been suspected of affiliations with radical Islam and envied for inheriting Hindu philosophy's ancient wisdom, interpolated alternately into Orientalist narratives of the demonic and exoticizing varieties. Hilariously, one of the only times I have been assigned a US origin was while conducting a different re-search project in the small town of Warrenton in eastern North Carolina, when I was asked by a white man on a tractor what a "Yankee" like me was doing down South—perhaps projecting onto me the threat of an imagined urban (brown, queer, liberal) North encroaching on Southern (white, male, deserving, and increasingly precarious) independence (Silva 2016). As a brown researcher in the US South, working within a largely dichotomous racial landscape in which Indigeneity and immigrant presence alike are consistently erased, I have puzzled over the diverse readings of race assigned to me and the emotions they engender in my research encounters. However, Benson's "Welcome to America" reminded me of the utility in occupying a racially ambiguous positionality in research, particularly as a scholar of race, where my very presence unfixes racism's claims to truth and reveals the unnaturalness of race by destabilizing how bodily markers such as skin color, hair, and voice are interpreted within localized racial scripts that reiterate the global workings of whiteness (Faria and Mollett 2016).

Benson's statement is not the first time that white Americans have sought to educate me, by inclusion or exclusion, in their rendition of history. Liberal white Americans delight in teaching me about their immigrant ancestors who made a home in the US through hard work. Some perceptively note, with an air of tolerance and a whiff of resentment, that they have met many Indian doctors, and ask if my parents are doctors. I sometimes prefer the less sugar-coated unsolicited reaction I receive from those insulted by my presence who spontaneously declare that (brown) immigrants are taking over all their jobs. "You may not know this," all these interactions suggest, "but you are lucky to be here." What I am *not*, for Benson and for many other white people I interact with, is Black. And as a corollary, my political affiliations are unclear. I am more likely read as a student of engineering, as several guests at the dam celebration assumed, than a scholar of Black radicalism or feminism.

Why am I, a brown immigrant scholar, working in Black studies? Centering Black experience in studying racial capitalism is an active rejection of my racial assignation by the US state, which positions me not only as a beneficiary but as a mechanism for furthering anti-Blackness.[4] Beyond acknowledging my structural positionality, I draw on an alternate identity that is oriented (Ahmed 2010b) toward decolonization and solidarity. Submerged within racial capitalism's erasures are histories of Asian immigrants who understood that anti-Blackness functions as a template and justification for other forms of racialized violence within and outside the US. Through activism and scholarship, politicized Asian immigrants have situated themselves in solidarity with Black communities and struggles, a path forged for some in realization of their own disenfranchisement and for others, through re-examination of the lie of American democracy. In the early twentieth century, South Asians who traveled to North America for trade and as a result of British colonialism, discovered that the America that welcomed them was Black (Bald 2013). Embedded within and excluded by the US, "Black is a country" (Singh 2004) whose freedom dreams have long inspired Asian struggles for justice. Flows of solidarity, while emerging from particular contexts, have contaminated mythical imaginations of cultural purity with transnational aspirations (Prashad 2001). Black radicals who linked their racial oppression to global colonization sought out political exchanges with the Muslim Third World (Daulatzai 2012). Communication between political leaders in India and the US redefined how race figured in anti-imperialist struggles (Slate 2012) and inspired Dalit activists to draw on Black Power movements for inspiration and strategy in fighting caste-based oppression (Pandey 2013). Asian-Black solidarity redresses Benson's distorted glorification of white American capitalism: to imagine another world demands scholarly understanding of how modernity is structured through anti-Blackness, implicating us all, and how Black life persists in defiance of racial capitalism (Bledsoe 2017; Weheliye 2014).

PROXIMITY TO PATHOS

A year after my fieldwork was completed, I was invited to interview for a faculty position at a large Southern public university. My research talk discussed the centrality of race to global capitalism, focusing on the political ecology of racialized toxicity in Badin. In one of the small-group faculty interviews that followed the talk, I met with two white male geographers who conduct quantitative analyses of vulnerability, spatial segregation, and social access. As the meeting progressed, one of the professors, Derek (a pseudonym), appeared increasingly uncomfortable. During a pause in the conversation, he asked with sudden intensity, "How do you negotiate your proximity to pathos?" Unsure of what he meant, I asked for clarification. He continued, "Aren't you concerned about positioning yourself so close to people's suffering?"

I was taken aback by his question. Keeping in mind that he focused on quantitative data, I tried to imagine his concerns about my research. While our work theoretically shared an interest in social inequality, my approach differed not only in methodology but in its explicit political commitment. After thinking for a minute, I responded that yes, I have various concerns about the ethics of working closely with those who are vulnerable. And yet there are lessons to be learned from people's experiences of suffering about how structures of power "objectively" operate. He pushed further. "But what have you learned? Won't your closeness to your research subjects influence your findings?"

I was in a difficult position. I did not want to make myself vulnerable to researchers whose insistence on objectivity may preclude reflexive engagement with their own or their subjects' positionalities. What had I learned from West Badin residents' experiences that could not be gleaned from quantitative studies alone? I responded by saying, "Absolutely, focusing on suffering changes my findings. One of the things I learned, and did not expect to going into this

project, is the importance of death. We talk about social reproduction, and the work of maintaining life. But for those who are threatened by toxicity as a form of racial violence, maintaining life is as much about attending to death, what Black studies scholar Christina Sharpe [2016] describes as 'wake work.' "
I explained that in racial capitalism, the premature deaths of racialized peoples are not taken seriously—they are considered incidental, unnecessary, and sad, perhaps, but not significant. To understand racialized deaths as meaningful and fundamental to how our society operates would demand a complete restructuring of current configurations to produce a more just society.

Thinking back on this conversation, I wonder, was it the *pathos* or my *politics* that were disturbing to Derek? While he framed his concern as methodological bias, I intuitively responded to what I sensed beneath his stated question about my proximity to my research subjects: a particular discomfort with my political orientation, framed in affirmation of Black lives devalued by racial capitalism. Many communities of color excluded, ignored, and harmed by allegedly "neutral" research understandably require researchers to demonstrate an explicit political commitment before engaging with them in research (Vargas 2008). When both the researcher and the research site are non-white, claiming methodological bias becomes a tactic by which to delegitimize intellectual integrity and rigor (Vargas 2008). In reference to racialized violence, scholars of color are then blamed for overidentification with negativity, as though "the exposure of violence becomes the origin of violence" (Ahmed 2010a, 68). In my response, I posed a challenge about how research lacking political commitment, whether qualitative or quantitative, may reiterate the violences that enable Black death in the first place.

In retrospect, I am grateful for the opportunity this encounter afforded. Derek's question about my "proximity to pathos" inadvertently pushed me to reflect on an aspect of my research I had struggled to articulate—namely, why I focus on Black suffering in studying racial capitalism. What is gained in studying capitalism through experiences of suffering? Does the study of racialized life express only the particular perspective of marginalized subjects? Are there implicit lessons about how the structure itself functions?

What if we were to reconceptualize the inanimacy of aluminum, its attendant conveniences and cold comforts in our lives, through the violences and excess of Black suffering? I have never lived adjacent to an industrial plant, never had to wonder whether the air I breathed daily or the water or food I consumed were layering lethal toxins into my body, never questioned whether my very existence in a particular place and time were cause for concern. What if we were to reimagine the existential paradox of contaminated life in Badin not simply as an unfortunate exception but as the very condition upon which my ability to live freely, drink clean water, and eat safe food are predicated? How would my distance from suffering be altered if I allowed Badin's sacrificial existence to contaminate my claims to freedom?

Materialist relationality calls for sensuous and compassionate attention "that beholds us to the work of the living that has to always contend with the dead and the not present, and the modes of presence and materiality that the dead and the living share and call each other to" (Abbas 2010, 7). For researchers who study inequality, maintaining distance under the guise of objectivity, even with awareness of one's own privileges, may provoke sympathy and allow us to advocate on behalf of a racialized Other who is less fortunate. However, such a position substantiates liberalism's insistence that suffering is unknowable, producing victims who cannot be agents and a politics premised on injury as exception, thereby upholding imperial and capitalist logics that produce conditions of suffering in the first place (Abbas 2010). My distance from others' suffering allows me as a liberal subject to feel sympathy, to position those who suffer as victims in need of recognition or charity. Unsettling this liberal hierarchy requires a displacement of both victim and agent, and a repositioning of life itself through "claiming and dwelling in the monstrosity of the flesh" (Weheliye 2014, 137). Recognizing the *proximity* of suffering to our lives and humanity, let alone our research, is to understand that if our labor and presence are valued, it is not in contrast with but rather constituted by the devaluation of another as "flesh" to be mined for profit (Spillers 1987).

In Badin, those who have survived carry a tremendous burden of making meaning of generations of Black life forestalled in the name of progress. Attending to "the dead and the not present" (Abbas 2010, 7) involves a range of social reproductive labor, such as bearing witness to unjust and premature deaths in homemade scrapbooks, gathering scientific evidence to prove injustice to a neglectful state apparatus, and fighting for community welfare amid ongoing racial violence (Vasudevan and Smith 2020). Such survival practices "offer pathways to distinctive understandings of suffering that serve as the speculative blueprint for new forms of humanity, which are defined above all by overdetermined conjurings of freedom" (Weheliye 2014, 14). As researchers, our work may not offer any resolution in contexts of generational suffering, despite our best intentions and thoughtful engagement in supporting communities we work with. And yet proximity to pathos allows for the emergence of situated solidarities that collaboratively produce meaning (Nagar 2014), as I describe in the next section.

I REMEMBER THAT, REAL GOOD

I conducted my first interview with sisters Frances McCray Greene and Roberta Simpson, who had grown up in West Badin and live there now with their families. We were sitting in their church basement and the room was silent. Frances, the younger of the two, looked up to Roberta, a strong and outspoken community leader; I did not expect Frances to volunteer to speak first. Following the oral history training I received, I opened with a general question: "Tell me about growing up in Badin. What was it like? What do you remember?" Frances responded that "it was a good life in Badin." She described a close-knit Black community in the segregated town, "a village" where adults shared responsibility for children, who would run through gardens picking fruit. They could not swim in pools, so they would walk to the swimming hole, a secluded part of Badin's lakeshore that Roberta described as "the Black side."

Frances's nostalgic tone continued as she described her father coming home from working at Alcoa, "and we would have to wash his work clothes, and it would be so smutty." In the next instant, she was recalling a day of heavy rains. The deep ditches Alcoa had built around their new construction site had filled with water. Frances's friends had gone out to play in the rain, and four children had drowned. "And the different parents was down in there, you know, just trying to catch the children." I asked how old Frances was then, and she thought she may have been eight or nine. "Yeah, I remember that, real good." She proceeded to stoically inventory a lifetime of tragedies as they occurred to her: the trash pile nearby that burned for months from accumulated chemicals, discovering there was a dump site behind their house, the smut on her father's and then her husband's skin when they returned from long days at work, having to fight daily to survive the newly integrated high school. Roberta joined in then, reiterating "the good life" of childhood in Badin, prior to integration: Black teachers who cared, Black-owned dance halls and cafes, the pleasure of digging around in the trash pile for throwaway toys and scraps. After the drowning, Roberta remembered, "They closed that reservoir up, put dirt in it, and now it doesn't even look like it existed." The interview lasted for close to two hours, and ended with Roberta asking me to turn the recorder off after revealing that a coworker in the factory had tried to kill her for speaking up about racial discrimination.

I sat through the interview, listening and asking clarifying questions, but some open receptive part of me had shut down after hearing about the drowning. Thinking back now, what struck me was the ordinariness of the violence

(Das 2007). The story could have been anyone's tragic memory; I too recall a child in my class dying around that age. Death occurring at a time of youth when one assumes that life will extend indefinitely becomes definitively sedimented into memory. However, Frances's story, recounted as though a memory of human suffering like any other, speaks of a particularity of experience that is not universally shared. Those children, one of them her classmate, died because an industrial company did not consider Black employees worthy of protection, did not value the safety of Black children, who could play in an unsecured construction pit as though it were merely a puddle.

I was incapacitated by the extent of trauma Frances and Roberta revealed. It took me a week to process the interview in an ethnographic fieldnote:

October 15, 2015

I did my first interview last Friday and I've been paralyzed and exhausted since then. I drove back with Naeema till Apex where I picked up my car. As soon as I was alone, I started crying. I cried again when I talked to my friend that night, telling her how wrong it was, how they've been fucked over. It's easy to forget when you study about capitalism that in a way there is nothing abstract about it, that real people are killed all the time, worked to death, poisoned to death; and yet, their deaths and the injustice of it are denied, masked, invisiblized by concrete poured over to rebuild, grass grown to erase any evidence.

I woke up in the middle of the night Friday, overwhelmed, making lists of the logistics I needed to deal with. Until today, I haven't been able to write about it or write any of it down. I cried off and on all day on Saturday, and I'm crying again now remembering the injustice, the violence, the wrongness of it all. The powerlessness I feel, witnessing and feeling unable to do anything. The guilt and anger at myself for having such a low tolerance, such a limited capacity, knowing so many have been fighting for so long. The strangeness of hearing conceptual arguments verbalized so clearly in people's experiences. The unfiltered, untempered rage and pain I heard, that breaks through in moments, and knowing that it's there throughout, that people carry and live with that pain their whole lives, or even for generations.

I wondered why I had chosen this site for my project. What is my ethical responsibility as a researcher, when there is so much suffering and so little I can do to alleviate it? I considered changing projects or altering my methods. I had only done one interview. Maybe I could focus on archives instead of ethnography, or maybe I could shift sites? If I did not return, perhaps they would not notice that I had left.

I revisited my research proposal, browsed writing on engaged scholarship, and reviewed literature on racial capitalism, hoping that one of these would relieve my paralysis. Finally, I returned to my notes from the first CCWBC community meeting I had attended a month earlier. When Naeema and I proposed a project to record oral histories of West Badin residents and Black Alcoa workers, we were met with total silence in the room. I was mentally preparing myself to walk away from the project if the community was not interested, when Roberta stood up and declared, "We cannot remain silent anymore!" With a desperate intensity, she talked about how her father, and all of their fathers and uncles, had worked without knowing that they and their families were being exposed to toxic chemicals. "They were dedicated to their jobs. And *they* were dedicated to killin' them for what they were doing." Roberta's urgent plea catalyzed a revelatory conversation about how racism and toxicity had layered into their everyday lives, profoundly unsettling any sense of comfort or security that is associated with home: uncertainty about swimming in Badin Lake and eating fish, guilt about exposing their families to workplace toxins by taking clothes home, anger and awe at realizing that the community hog pen was located next to an industrial landfill (Vasudevan 2019). By the end of the meeting, those present were strongly committed to breaking the silence, and Naeema and I were encouraged to conduct interviews.

I did not initially understand the silence at the community meeting. I have since learned that few people in West Badin talk to each other or their families about the generational exploitation and devaluation they have experienced with Alcoa. For some, talking about Alcoa betrays their deeply ingrained sense of familial loyalty, while others are concerned about their safety, well aware of how those who speak out have been punished. Yet in the economic and social precarity that has accompanied the closure of the Badin Works plant, there is a growing desire to make sense of the history that led to the present, to share the stories of Black Badin that have been erased from Alcoa's celebratory narrative. In returning to the community meeting, I discovered my role as a researcher in this historical moment. As an outsider to Badin, and to the Black-white racial binary of the South, I could serve as an invested observer, bearing witness to and articulating the suffering experienced by working and living in Badin.

While the community's imperative to share their stories clarified the purpose of my research, playing the role of activist scholar remained complicated. Throughout fieldwork, I questioned what it meant to witness Black suffering. The stories I heard from West Badin counter mainstream US understandings of racism as an unfortunate historical fact without bearing on the present. This teleological narrative was reiterated by many of my interviewees as well, for instance in their insistence that industrial jobs provided relief for Black workers from the brutality of prior sharecropping regimes. In interviews, I witnessed Black residents struggling to acknowledge how anti-Black racism structured their lives, even as they sought to claim Alcoa, Badin, and the US through their own contributions. Participatory research models frequently privilege "community voices" as primary sources of authority, yet I found myself disagreeing with the interpretation of Black industrial labor in Badin as preferable to sharecropping.[5] Was I ethically required to accept people's interpretation of their own life experiences without critique?

I discovered an alternate model of engaged scholarship in how my coinvestigator Naeema approached interviews. Joe Black, a specialist in keeping aluminum production pots running efficiently, nostalgically spoke of a time when "after we got past all the racism and stuff, things got better and we were like a family working down there." I was surprised by his statement that racism had been overcome, and noticed Naeema's slight reaction. After all, Naeema and I were in Badin precisely because racism was ongoing, excluding Black residents from negotiations between the company and the town. Naeema asked Joe, "What do you consider moving past the racism?" Joe responded that Black workers were able to move up beyond manual labor jobs to become technicians. Though Naeema framed her question innocently as a request for clarification, having worked with Naeema for some time, I understood that as a community organizer, she approached every conversation as a learning moment that would strengthen critical analysis through conversation.

Naeema's approach to research as a venue for building solidarity through dialogue reflects critical performance ethnography's emphasis on the intersubjective nature of encounters "in which there is negotiation and dialogue toward substantial and viable meanings that make a difference in the Other's world" (Madison 2005, 9). As a form of "dialogical performance" (Conquergood 2013), critical ethnographic encounters are an embodied interplay between researchers and their interlocutors, producing a situated solidarity through which to collaboratively interpret lived experiences (Nagar 2014). As participant in this interplay, Naeema brings a nuanced awareness of structural conditions from decades working with Black communities in the South, including the complexities of how people interpret and narrate their own subjectivities. I have followed Naeema's lead in approaching research as a processual dynamic that generates possibilities for reexamining lived experiences in relationship to structural forces. My research toolkit includes the radical aspirations and theoretical explorations of the Black studies canon, which I bring into conversation with how my interviewees explain their realities.

Assuming I was not from the South, or from the US, people would teach me about what America was, from a Black perspective. Jason Anderson shared that in the 1920s and 1930s, Black workers, responding to Alcoa's advertisements, migrated to Badin from all over the South. "They gave their blood, sweat, life. Was mistreated and considered less than the other people." Jason's clear statement of Alcoa's exploitation has become increasingly important to my understanding of how anti-Black racism functions through toxic exposure. In Badin, racism has intimately infused life with toxicity, profoundly unsettling Black residents' relations with their white neighbors, with each other, and with their local environments. Conversely, nearly a century of aluminum produced in Badin is suffused with the "blood, sweat, life" of Black labor (Vasudevan 2019) that materially constitute the infrastructures of twentieth-century modernity.

IN CLOSING: WITNESS TO SUFFERING

In interpreting Black life through suffering, I enter into contentious terrain within Black studies. Some argue that narrating Black history through suffering and death performs a secondary violence, pathologizing the Black body "as a suffering object that reinforces the global web of anti-Blackness" (McKittrick 2017, 99). Black suffering is central to racial capitalism not only through material violation but in the ongoing consumption of Black corporeal violence as public spectacle, reinscribing an unharmed white national body and a traumatized Black collective memory rooted in the threat of bodily harm (Alexander 1994). The paradox of Black suffering—where anti-Blackness is foundational to humanness and yet occupies "the position of the unthought" (Hartman and Wilderson 2003, 185)—leads to divergent epistemological positions: Is Blackness a condition of "social death" (Sexton 2011; Wilderson 2010), a state of total nonexistence in modern society, or does Blackness signify an excess to abjection, a "fugitive movement in and out of the frame, bar, or whatever externally imposed social logic" (Moten 2009, 179)?

In analyzing ethnographic data, I found myself trapped by the ideological implications of interpreting Blackness as death or as fugitivity. The insights I was drawing from Badin were murkier, reflecting the complexities of lived experience that resist clear abstraction, but the tension was present in residents' recounting as well. Frances's narrative of lifelong trauma and Joe's nostalgia for an illusory postracial moment signal the profound disjunctures that Black residents and workers face in reconciling their loyalty to the company with the inexplicable injustices they are subject to. Black residents' claims of industrialization as progress are no accident; Alcoa has spent millions producing an image of itself as a progressive company that seeks to minimize harm, a narrative employed to reframe lived realities from the minute workers were recruited, through decades of exploitative and unsafe working conditions, and ongoing today in the portrayal of Badin as a caring company town.

Frances's litany of injustices reminds me of Audre Lorde's (1997, 255) injunction that for those "who were never meant to survive," the "illusion of some safety to be found" in silence is enforced by tactics of fear. Fear has been generationally imprinted into the lives and bodies of West Badin residents by Alcoa, their benevolent patriarch; I can only speculate about how some overcame the intimidation to decide that "it is better to speak" (Lorde 1997, 255). And yet, in interviews and community dialogues, detailed descriptions of everyday life in Badin express an underlying depravity and disposability that conditioned their very existence in industrial life. If I—a temporary visitor to Badin, without generations of fear and bodily insecurity—was to narrate Badin's story as progress, I would be obscuring and denying the unspoken realities of Black suffering I witnessed. Such a project would be "obscene: the attempt to make the narrative of defeat into an opportunity for celebration, the desire to look at the ravages and the brutality of the last few centuries, but to still find a way to feel good about ourselves" (Hartman and Wilderson 2003, 185). Being reflexive in this context required me to move beyond the trappings of my own positionality to face the ravages and violence with integrity.

As the Yadkin dam celebration reminded me, the material devaluation of Black life has been buffeted by a narrative violence that erases Black experience from aluminum's story altogether. Serving as a witness to anti-Blackness in Badin challenges Alcoa's ongoing denial of how racialized trauma forestalls Black futurity (Smith and Vasudevan 2017). However, attending to how Black workers and residents have suffered not only validates the experiences of those most directly impacted but redresses historical erasure by decolonizing knowledge regimes that erase Black life from their explanatory frameworks. Derek's concern about my proximity to pathos reflects a failure to understand how racial violence is our collective legacy. If freedom and oppression are relational, mutiny cannot be reduced to recognition of injustice enacted upon a racialized Other nor to mere acknowledgment of the researcher's privileges. Materialist relationality disrupts these racially determined subjectivities through the realization *that another world, a new possibility of humanity untethered from the grammar of racial capitalism, will emerge from these very lived experiences.*

Is it possible to encounter Black suffering as a non-Black scholar without reaffirming the "racial table" that fixes power in whiteness and pathology in Blackness (da Silva 2013), and without exploiting the Black body as simply a placeholder for justice (Hartman 2016)? What can I offer as witness, if not recognition or resolution? I am left with these questions still, and the possibility that there may be no resolution, actually or theoretically, to make sense of the excess of violence that continually recreates capitalism through Black suffering. To embrace suffering, however, is not to accept defeat; rather, it is to understand "the importance of miniscule movements, glimmers of hope, scraps of food, the interrupted dreams of freedom found in those spaces deemed devoid of full human life" (Weheliye 2014, 12). To witness, document, and reflect back these moments is to make meaning of unjust deaths, an alignment in solidarity with the potential of alternate futures. For scholars of race interpolated into racial capitalism's interstices to prop up whiteness's imagined entitlements to land, labor, and luck, we can choose to desert our assigned posts. However, we must not redirect our decolonizing energies toward reflexive pronouncements of privilege and complicity that perpetuate white fragility. To do so would voluntarily mute our mutiny.

NOTES

1. The narrative of racial complicity simplistically positions South Asians as uniformly privileged, erasing how anti-Blackness reverberates in and intersects with post-9/11 Islamophobic racial surveillance and violence targeting Arabs, Muslims, and South Asians. See DRUM (2016) and Husain et al. (2016) for examples disrupting this narrative.
2. I am particularly indebted to Anusha Hariharan for insights into feminist of color scholarship on reflexivity, transnationalism, and South Asian history; Dr. Helen Orr for her reminders about CPE's dialogical approach to witnessing and suffering; and Dr. Stevie Larson for encouraging me to articulate my discomforts with identity politics with a spirit of radical generosity.
3. All names of research interlocutors are pseudonyms.
4. For a parallel intervention addressing how non-Indigenous people of color and particularly immigrants uphold settler colonialism and Indigenous dispossession, see Lawrence and Dua (2005) and Dhamoon (2015).
5. I thank Dr. Kenneth Janken for highlighting this divergence in historical interpretation and Dr. Neel Ahuja for pushing me to think further about the implications of this ethnographic moment.

REFERENCES

Abbas, Asma. 2010. *Liberalism and Human Suffering: Materialist Reflections on Politics, Ethics, and Aesthetics*. New York: Palgrave Macmillan.

Ahmed, Sara. 1997. "'It's a Sun-Tan, Isn't It?': Auto-Biography as an Identificatory Practice." In *Black British Feminism: A Reader*, edited by Heidi Safia Mirza, 153–67. London and New York: Routledge.

Ahmed, Sara. 2010a. *The Promise of Happiness*. Durham and London: Duke University Press.

Ahmed, Sara. 2010b. "Orientations Matter." In *New Materialisms: Ontology, Agency, and Politics*, edited by Diana Coole and Samantha Frost, 234–57. Durham and London: Duke University Press.

Alexander, Elizabeth. 1994. " 'Can You Be BLACK and Look at This?': Reading the Rodney King Video(s)." *Public Culture* 7: 77–94.

Bald, Vivek. 2013. *Bengali Harlem and the Lost Histories of South Asian America*. Cambridge, MA: Harvard University Press.

Bilge, Sirma. 2013. "Intersectionality Undone: Saving Intersectionality from Feminist Interstersectionality Studies." *Du Bois Review* 10 (2): 405–24. https://doi.org/10.1017/S1742058X13000283.

Bledsoe, Adam. 2017. "Marronage as a Past and Present Geography in the Americas." *Southeastern Geographer* 57 (1): 30–50. https://doi.org/10.1353/sgo.2017.0004.

Conquergood, Dwight. 2013. *Cultural Struggles: Performance, Ethnography, Praxis*. Edited by E. Patrick Johnson. Ann Arbor: University of Michigan Press.

Crenshaw, Kimberlé. 1991. "Mapping the Margins: Intersectionality, Identity Politics, and Violence against Women of Color." *Stanford Law Review* 43: 1241–1300.

da Silva, Denise Ferreira. 2013. "To Be Announced: Radical Praxis or Knowing (at) the Limits of Justice." *Social Text 114* 31 (1): 43–62. https://doi.org/10.1215/01642472-1958890.

Das, Veena. 2007. *Life and Words: Violence and the Descent into the Ordinary*. Berkeley and Los Angeles: University of California Press.

Daulatzai, Sohail. 2012. *Black Star, Crescent Moon: The Muslim International and Black Freedom beyond America*. Minneapolis: University of Minnesota Press.

Desis Rising Up and Moving (DRUM). 2016. "Building Community Safety: Reflections on Our Power in Times of Bigotry." http://www.drumnyc.org/buildingcommunitysafety/.

Dhamoon, Rita. 2015. "A Feminist Approach to Decolonizing Anti-Racism: Rethinking Transnationalism, Intersectionality, and Settler Colonialism." *Feral Feminisms* 4: 20–37.

England, Kim V. L. 1994. "Getting Personal: Reflexivity, Positionality, and Feminist Research." *Professional Geographer* 46 (1): 80–89. https://doi.org/10.1111/j.0033-0124.1994.00080.x.

Esmeir, Samera. 2012. *Juridical Humanity: A Colonial History*. Stanford: Stanford University Press.

Faria, Caroline, and Sharlene Mollett. 2016. "Critical Feminist Reflexivity and the Politics of Whiteness in the 'Field.' " *Gender, Place & Culture* 23 (1): 79–93. https://doi.org/10.1080/0966369X.2014.958065.

Grewal, Inderpal. 2005. *Transnational America: Feminisms, Diasporas, Neoliberalisms*. Durham and London: Duke University Press.

Hale, Charles. 2008. *Engaging Contradictions: Theory, Politics, and Methods of Activist Scholarship*. Berkeley and Los Angeles: University of California Press.

Haraway, Donna Jeanne. 2013. *Simians, Cyborgs, and Women: The Reinvention of Nature*. New York: Routledge.

Hartman, Saidiya. 2016. "The Belly of the World: A Note on Black Women's Labors." *Souls* 18 (1): 166–73. https://doi.org/10.1080/10999949.2016.1162596.

Hartman, Saidiya V., and Frank B. Wilderson III. 2003. "The Position of the Unthought: An Interview with Saidiya V. Hartman; Conducted by Frank B. Wilderson, III." *Qui Parle* 13 (2): 183–201.

Husain, Atiya, Pavithra Vasudevan, and Neel Ahuja. 2016. "Islamophobia & Anti-Blackness: A Call to Action at UNC." *Monsoon*, April 6. http://monsoon.web.unc.edu/islamophobia-anti-blackness-a-call-to-action-at-unc-by-atiya-husain-pavithra-vasudevan-and-neel-ahuja/.

Iyer, Vijay. 2014. "Our Complicity with Excess." The Margins, Asian American Writers' Workshop. http://aaww.org/complicity-with-excess-vijay-iyer/.

Jung, Soya. 2014. "The Racial Justice Movement Needs a Model Minority Mutiny." *Race Files.* October 13, 2014. https://www.racefiles.com/2014/10/13/model-minority-mutiny/.

Kobayashi, Audrey. 2003. "GPC Ten Years On: Is Self-Reflexivity Enough?" *Gender, Place & Culture* 10 (4): 345–49. https://doi.org/10.1080/0966369032000153313.

Kohl, Ellen, and Priscilla McCutcheon. 2015. "Kitchen Table Reflexivity: Negotiating Positionality through Everyday Talk." *Gender, Place & Culture* 22 (6): 747–63. https://doi.org/10.1080/0966369X.2014.958063.

Lawrence, Bonita, and Enakshi Dua. 2005. "Decolonizing Antiracism." *Social Justice* 32 (4): 120–43. https://doi.org/10.2307/29768340.

Lorde, Audre. 1997. *The Collected Poems of Audre Lorde.* New York and London: Norton.

Madison, D. Soyini. 2005. *Critical Ethnography.* Thousand Oaks, CA: Sage Publications.

McKittrick, Katherine. 2017. "Commentary: Worn Out." *Southeastern Geographer* 57 (1): 96–100. https://doi.org/10.1353/sg0.2017.0008.

Moten, Fred. 2009. "The Case of Blackness." *Criticism* 50 (2): 177–218. https://doi.org/10.1353/crt.0.0062

Nagar, Richa. 2014. *Muddying the Waters: Coauthoring Feminisms across Scholarship and Activism.* Urbana: University of Illinois Press.

Nair, Sathvik. 2016. "Letters for Black Lives: South Asian American Version." *Letters for Black Lives.* August 2, 2016. https://lettersforblacklives.com/letters-for-black-lives-south-asian-american-version-f5d8ec9a46ac.

Nash, Jennifer C. 2017. "Intersectionality and Its Discontents." *American Quarterly* 69 (1): 117–29. https://doi.org/10.1353/aq.2017.0006.

Padel, Felix, and Samarendra Das. 2010. *Out of This Earth: East India Adivasis and the Aluminium Cartel.* New Delhi: Orient BlackSwan.

Pan, Jennifer. 2015. "Beyond the Model Minority Myth." *Jacobin.* July 14, 2015. https://www.jacobinmag.com/2015/07/chua-changelab-nakagawa-model-minority/.

Pandey, Gyanendra. 2013. *A History of Prejudice: Race, Caste, and Difference in India and the United States.* Cambridge, MA: Harvard University Press.

Prashad, Vijay. 2001. *Everybody Was Kung Fu Fighting: Afro-Asian Connections and the Myth of Cultural Purity.* Boston: Beacon Press.

Puar, Jasbir. 2017. *Terrorist Assemblages: Homonationalism in Queer Times.* Durham, NC: Duke University Press.

Puar, Jasbir K., and Amit Rai. 2002. "Monster, Terrorist, Fag: The War on Terrorism and the Production of Docile Patriots." *Social Text* 72 (3): 117–48.

Rose, Gillian. 1997. "Situating Knowledges: Positionality, Reflexivities and Other Tactics." *Progress in Human Geography* 21 (3): 305–20. https://doi.org/10.1191/030913297673302122.

Sexton, Jared. 2011. "The Social Life of Social Death: On Afro-Pessimism and Black Optimism." *InTensions* 5 (5): 1–47.

Sharpe, Christina. 2016. *In the Wake: On Blackness and Being.* Durham, NC: Duke University Press.

Sheller, M. 2014. *Aluminum Dreams: The Making of Light Modernity.* Cambridge, MA: The MIT Press.

Silva, Kumarini. 2016. *Brown Threat: Identification in the Security State.* Minneapolis: University of Minnesota Press.

Singh, Nikhil Pal. 2004. *Black Is a Country: Race and the Unfinished Struggle for Democracy.* Cambridge, MA: Harvard University Press.

Slate, Nico. 2012. *Colored Cosmopolitanism: The Shared Struggle for Freedom in the United States and India.* Cambridge, MA: Harvard University Press.

Smith, Sara. 2016. "Intimacy and Angst in the Field." *Gender, Place & Culture* 23 (1): 134–46. https://doi.org/10.1080/0966369X.2014.958067.

Smith, Sara, and Pavithra Vasudevan. 2017. "Race, Biopolitics, and the Future: Introduction to the Special Section." *Environment and Planning D: Society and Space* 35 (2): 210–21. https://doi.org/10.1177/0263775817699494.

Spillers, Hortense J. 1987. "Mama's Baby, Papa's Maybe: An American Grammar Book." *Diacritics* 17 (2): 64–81.

Vargas, João Costa. 2008. "Activist Scholarship: Limits and Possibilities in Times of Black Genocide." In *Engaging Contradictions: Theory, Politics, and Methods of Activist Scholarship*, edited by Charles R. Hale, 164–82. Berkeley: University of California Press.

Vasudevan, Pavithra. 2019. "An Intimate Inventory of Race and Waste." *Antipode: A Radical Journal of Geography*. https://doi.org/10.1111/anti.12501.

Vasudevan, Pavithra, and Sara Smith. 2020. "The Domestic Geopolitics of Racial Capitalism." *Environment and Planning C: Politics and Space*. https://doi.org/10.1177/23996544 20901567.

Weheliye, Alexander G. 2014. *Habeas Viscus: Racializing Assemblages, Biopolitics and Black Feminist Theories of the Human*. Durham, NC: Duke University Press.

Wilderson III, Frank B. 2010. *Red, White, & Black: Cinema and the Structure of U.S. Antagonisms*. Durham, NC: Duke University Press.

CHAPTER 2

THE PATH TO RADICAL VULNERABILITY: FEMINIST PRAXIS AND COMMUNITY FOOD COLLABORATIONS

Carrie Chennault

PROLOGUE

On a summer day in 2016, I met with a small group of gardeners participating in a statewide university-community collaboration: Growing Together Iowa. The partnership works to address the lack of fresh produce in places like food pantries. That morning we sat around a picnic table overlooking the garden while talking about plans for harvest and distribution. Amid conversations, the gardeners wove in questions, stories, and discussions about their rural community and food. Suddenly, two gardeners started conversing heatedly and at length about where to donate the food and whether Latinx community members[1] were food insecure. One gardener wanted to distribute at places like the laundromat, where the gardener's adult daughter drops off clothes for donation to Latinx children. The laundromat might make a good site for food distribution, the gardener reasoned, reporting that the community lacked a designated food pantry. I understood the gardener to believe that if people cannot afford a washing machine, then they probably cannot afford to buy food either.[2] The other gardener refuted the need to distribute food at the laundromat and insisted that not all Latinx community members were food insecure—those who worked at the poultry plant[3] made "good money." The gardener explained that Latinx people who rent homes without washing machines must use the laundromat, despite having jobs and income. Their broader assumptions connecting the laundromat, food insecurity, and the plant were not further elaborated upon and remained unclear to me, an outsider visiting the community for the first time.

At that moment, the first gardener, growing visibly agitated, pointed a finger in my face and said, "Here's something for your research." The gardener's daughter had encountered a child[4] in town who confided, "I don't have food because my mom went and got a tattoo last night." While retelling the daughter's account, the gardener acted increasingly upset and could not get over why the mother would neglect feeding the child. The gardener subsequently characterized the mother as someone who spent limited resources on selfish indulgences. The mother and child were not the only people experiencing food insecurity, according to the gardeners. Children in the community, the other gardener noted, were "unchurched and unfed," and I recalled how earlier the first gardener mentioned that no one at their church was food insecure. The first gardener spoke of "a lot of white families that are druggies" and how those children did not receive enough food either. The two gardeners soon focused on how to feed the children in their community.

INTRODUCTION

Growing Together Iowa is part of the SNAP Education[5] program in Cooperative Extension.[6] The project's name refers to producing, gleaning, and distributing communally grown fruits and vegetables to address food insecurity. Growing Together supports these activities at university research farms and through grants to county extension offices in coordination with Master Gardeners[7] and other partners—including food pantries, food banks, free meal programs, congregate meal sites, schools, organizations serving immigrants and refugees, farmers, gardeners, 4-H, and youth programs.

As a researcher in Cooperative Extension, I located my work within emerging efforts to make equity a core food systems principle and racial equity a top priority (Mosley, Ammons, and Hyden 2015; Pirog, Koch, and Guel 2016; Undoing Inequality in the Food System Working Group 2018). I aspired to develop alliances in Iowa, through which equity principles could take greater root in food systems projects. This collective journey toward equity is challenging because the colonizing history of Extension has shaped and continues to shape the racialized relations of food and agriculture (Collins and Mueller 2016; Firkus 2010a, 2010b; Grim 2015; Harris 2008; Pirog, Koch, and Guel 2016). For instance, when I joined Growing Together, I expected limited opportunities for alliance because the project neither made racial justice and equity foundational to its structure nor included them as goals. In my role, I searched for those limited opportunities to foster ties among allied participants and extend Growing Together's impact beyond donated produce.

Alliance work can begin from an understanding of the everyday as political, from something as seemingly politically insignificant as community gardening. Working within and in tension with Cooperative Extension, I aspired to cocreate alliances that Nagar (2014) terms *radically vulnerable* (see also Nagar et al. 2016; Hariharan, ch. 10 this volume). Radical vulnerability is "an intellectual and political alliance where there are no sovereign selves or autonomous subjects" (Nagar et al. 2016, 511), and requires "trust and critical reflexivity" (513). These alliances are collectively reflexive and work across university-community boundaries to decentralize knowledge production.

The journey of radical vulnerability includes budding opportunities for activist collaborations, but also failed and missed ones (Nagar 2014). Despite mentions of this journey, Nagar constructs radical vulnerability as coauthorship, raising questions of how to do praxis and write in instances of failed, missed, and even impossible alliance. The encounter in the prologue proved to be one of those moments in my continuing journey. Like Vasudevan (this volume), my encounter spurred critical engagement with discomforting fieldwork as a decolonizing mode of feminist geographic inquiry. Physically, I was uncomfortable with the palpable sense of tension and fear I felt during the encounter. Reflexively, I was concerned with the ways in which a focus on moral character can erase the racial foundation and structural unevenness of food insecurity. The silence emanated from my discomfort and concern but also, I recognized, from my complicity in whiteness.

The future encounters with the gardeners that could have deepened understanding were limited due to the logistics of a statewide project, the gardeners' schedules, my embodied discomfort, and an uncertainty about how to bridge divides. Nor did I meet any members of the gardeners' community who were experiencing food insecurity. From the beginning, food-insecure people were positioned in Growing Together not as active partners in cocreating solutions but as recipients of food and of nutrition education.[8] Even if unintentionally, this intervention model arguably casts food recipients as being in need and deficient, not only in terms of food but also in terms of the knowledge, skills, and capacity to be active partners.

Situating coauthorship as a journey, in this chapter I extend radical vulnerability to include the praxis that can develop while in search of alliance. To set the stage for this journey, the following two sections provide the social contexts of agriculture and food security in Iowa. I follow Nagar's (2014, 85) approach to reflexivity—emphasizing context and relational engagement over static notions of a researcher's identity.

The next section introduces radically vulnerable praxis as a mode of political alliance with the potential to disrupt injustices and turns to scholarship on queerness and vulnerability to extend the concept of radical vulnerability in moments of failed, missed, and impossible alliance. Returning to the garden encounter, I then reflect on how I reacted to the discomfort of encountering racism with silence and complicity, and how I have since responded through multiple retellings. The retellings ground me in the *"lengthy duration"* and "stickiness" of confronting racism and other marginalizations (Ahmed 2004, sec. 49, 57, emphasis original), even as my performative politics is future-oriented. Through opening, destabilizing, and angling, each section of analysis reveals types and sources of discomfort. In differentiating and disentangling them, I shed light on the political potentials of engaging discomfort.

Finally, this chapter considers how to build alliances that can transform agrifood systems, land-grant universities, and Cooperative Extension. Challenging the racialized relations within which projects like Growing Together are embedded remains an ongoing effort. In closing, I discuss what steps Extension can take toward allied partnership and accountability.

THE GEOPOLITICS OF IOWA AGRICULTURE

Growing Together is situated within the historical, economic, cultural, political, and ecological contexts of food and agriculture. In Iowa, as elsewhere, commodity agriculture began with the expulsion of Indigenous peoples[9] and has continued through decades of land-grant research and technocratic agricultural modernization that have led to cheap food, destroyed ecosystems, and inequitable social relations (Carter, Chennault, and Kruzic 2018). Agronomic research from US land-grant institutions to modernize global agriculture through the Green Revolution and biotechnology have sowed the foundations upon which more violence, colonization, and inequity have occurred (Patel 2013; Shiva 2016). These marginalizations stand in stark contrast to the ubiquitous patriarchal discourse in Iowa of the productive, independent farmer who feeds the world.

Undergirding modern Iowa agriculture are complex geopolitical relations developed through neoliberal economic and trade policies. I use the term *geopolitical* to identify food insecurity as a process of "state-subject-territory" (Smith 2012, 1515) formation through which bodies in their everyday lives are linked with national and international agrifood policies and politics. Relevant to this chapter, the bodies of Latinx populations have become territories through a geopolitical relationship in which US-dominated policies, such as the flooding of Mexican markets with cheap US corn, have pushed people off land in their country and into the United States as migrant labor (Jarosz 2014). Latinx immigrants in the United States experience high rates of food insecurity; they simultaneously often face unstable employment and dangerous labor conditions coupled with insufficient wages, health care, housing, and social supports, and, for noncitizen immigrants, lack of access to government safety net programs (Greder et al. 2009; Greder, Slowing, and Doudna 2012; Sano et al. 2011). Thus, the (de)territorialization of Latinx bodies occurs through transnational migration and precarious repositioning as laborers—including in poultry plants and livestock facilities but also, as this chapter presents, as mothers navigating the intertwined politics of morality and survival at play in their new communities.

The rise of Latinx agro-industrial labor in the Midwest dates back to the early twentieth century, and in more recent decades occurred as meat processing relocated to lower-wage rural communities in response to heightened global competition and consolidation since the 1970s (Gouveia and Saenz 2000; Saenz 2011; Stanley 1994). The 1980s farm crisis devastated Midwestern rural "family farm" economies, and communities were eager to see agribusinesses arrive (Cantú 1995; Stanley 1994). Consequently, Iowa actively incentivized agro-industry development, resulting in the recruitment of immigrant and minority, including Latinx, laborers to fill worker shortages (Cantú 1995). By 2017, agro-industry growth in Iowa supported, among others, an annual production of 16 billion eggs and 22.8 million hogs (Iowa Department of Agriculture and Land Stewardship 2018). In this era, Iowa's Latinx population[10] rose from 32,647 in 1990 to an estimated 178,249—5.7 percent of the population—in 2017 (State Data Center of Iowa, n.d. a; US Census Bureau 2017). The Latinx population in the rural town in this chapter grew from under 2 percent in 1990 to over 20 percent in 2017 estimates (State Data Center of Iowa, n.d. b; US Census Bureau 2017).

The effects of US agricultural policies are not unique to Iowa. As elsewhere, they resulted in consolidated farms and agro-industries, and transnational migration of agricultural laborers dispossessed of land and livelihood. Yet the scale of Iowa agriculture is practically unthinkable elsewhere. Almost two-thirds of the land is covered with two crops: corn and soybean (Iowa State University Extension and Outreach 2017). From these geopolitical relations arises the contradiction of Iowa having some of the world's richest soils, yet more than one in ten households experienced food insecurity between 2014 and 2016 (Coleman-Jensen et al. 2017).[11] Statewide rates of food insecurity for Latinx households are unavailable for Iowa; however, USDA estimates a national rate of 18.5 percent for 2016 (Coleman-Jensen et al. 2017; see also Sano et al. 2011).

The Rural Families Speak project documented the experiences of food insecurity and related challenges faced by Latinx immigrant mothers in rural Iowa (Sano et al. 2011; Greder, Slowing, and Doudna 2012). Greder, Slowing, and Doudna (2012) recommend that family and consumer science professionals connect immigrant families with their new communities to improve healthy eating and address high rates of food insecurity. Master Gardeners, they argue, might serve a critical role in educating Latinx immigrant mothers to grow vegetables in a new climate. However, community connections and educational programs can also place mothers' bodies and health at risk when broader political clashes over identity, nationalism, immigration, and the impacts of globalization on rural communities surface as regulations on behavior.

The encounter in this chapter demonstrates how well-intended programs focused on the everyday life of raising healthy families become projects of state-subject-territory formation, in this case with injurious consequences. The gardeners I met that day constructed *food insecurity* in relationship to their understandings of agro-industry, Latinx immigration, increasing drug use among non-Latinx rural residents, and motherhood, illustrating the geopolitical tensions that have arisen in rural Midwestern communities.

FEEDING THE WORLD WHILE FOOD INSECURE

"Food security," Jarosz (2014, 169–70) notes, "is embedded in dominant technocratic, neoliberal development discourses emphasizing increases in production and measurable supply and demand." A simultaneous structuring and invisibility of food insecurity plays out through the connections and contradictions of two interrelated discourses: *food security* as Iowa producers feeding the world and *food insecurity* as an individualized problem (Dankbar et al. 2017). In the first discourse, agricultural commodities—along with technologies—increase global food security. To maintain this discourse, food insecurity, in Iowa and throughout the United States, ontologically forms as an individualized phenomenon associated with laziness or immorality. Through unquestioned narratives of racial marginalization and whitened cultural practices—social stigmas, stereotypes, dispossession, and displacement—people who experience food insecurity are situated as deserving of blame for their problems (Dutta, Anaele, and Jones 2013; Minkoff-Zern 2014; Sbicca 2014). Structural causes of food insecurity remain invisible.

In conversations at gardens and pantries, I frequently encountered the expectation that with hard work and thrift, one will not, even cannot, experience food insecurity. After all, the Iowa that many gardeners describe is a place of agricultural abundance. Through participants' ongoing collaboration in Growing Together, new experiences disrupt this narrative. For example, one participant recalled their surprise at a farm family coming to the food pantry for assistance. Farming for this family was not a guarantee of enough income to feed themselves. Yet the assumptions that link food insecurity to laziness and food security to moral behavior invisibilize other people who might receive the produce donations while perpetuating the image of a racialized other.

While contradictions like the farm family encourage a rethinking of food insecurity in some instances, the persistence of global food security discourses—and the geopolitical relations within which they are embedded—impact the potential for decolonial political alliances. Global food security discourses resonate particularly for Iowans because of the state's identity as an agricultural leader through technocratic, neoliberal development. Iowa agriculture is imagined as feeding food to insecure *others* located *elsewhere*. Growing Together emerged within the land-grant university and these discourses.

VULNERABILITY AS PRAXIS

Feminist praxis can disrupt a blaming, moralizing ontology of food insecurity by generating ontologies that account for the "political economy of food insecurity, including the spatial, social, cultural, political, and the emotional aspects of food" (Miewald and McCann 2014, 543). I engage the scholarship of Richa Nagar to explore opportunities for radically vulnerable alliances that can disrupt these narratives through the practices of speaking-with and situated solidarity (Nagar 2014, 85; see also Nagar and Geiger 2007; Routledge and Derickson 2015; Vasudevan this volume). Speaking-with underscores "economic, political, and institutional" contextualization of fieldwork encounters (Nagar 2014, 85), and situated solidarity repositions focus on "the 'fields' that our 'research subjects' inhabit" and encourages academic, institutional, and geographical border crossings that resituate knowledge production in line with political struggles (86–88). Together, these concepts guide scholars in anti-essentialist, decolonial, and relational praxis with activist communities.

Preparing for fieldwork, I considered how to mobilize speaking-with and situated solidarity. For instance, I embraced more relational ways of seeing myself-in-the-world and distanced myself from any notion of Cooperative

Extension as an organization of experts who have the solution. By contextualizing Growing Together within the institutional and social structures of land-grant universities and Corn Belt agriculture, I acknowledged how these *fields* could simultaneously support and constrain radically vulnerable university-community alliances. Still, prior to fieldwork, I did not fully understand the messiness of disjunctures between the PhD proposal and fieldwork (Billo and Hiemstra 2013), nor between the research I sought to do in Extension and Extension as an institution. I would need guidance in navigating the search for alliances in spaces where few partners are working to reconfigure power relations.

Expanding Nagar's praxis, I turned to queer scholarship from Butler (2016) linking vulnerability to political resistance. Broadly, queerness can be described as "a movement of thought and language contrary to accepted forms of authority"—a "deviation" from social norms (Butler 2016, 17). Butler presents queerness as a mode of "agency and resistance" (25) and asserts that "the vulnerability to dispossession, poverty, insecurity, and harm that constitutes a precarious position in the world itself leads to resistance" (12).

Queer praxis acknowledges vulnerability as a "condition of dependency and interdependency" mobilized to resist injustice (Butler 2016, 25–26). The political mobilization of vulnerability contrasts with paternalistic efforts seeking to resist and master vulnerability (Butler 2016). As noted elsewhere in this volume, challenging paternalistic modes of thinking about vulnerability may open productive paths that "dismantle the societal barriers that keep change from happening" (Cofield and Doan, ch. 3 this volume). Utilizing this distinction, a queer analysis of vulnerability enables me to draw on three practices that mobilize vulnerability in resistance: opening, destabilizing, and angling.

Opening emphasizes processes of becoming. It complements Nagar's acknowledgment of praxis as a journey, in which there is room for failure. Gilson (2011, 310) thus characterizes vulnerability as "a basic kind of openness to being affected and affecting in both positive and negative ways." This practice involves opening oneself to discomfort, to "the ambivalence of our emotional and bodily responses and to reflecting on those responses in nuanced ways" (Gilson 2011, 325). Through this chapter, I vulnerably open myself—and my relationship to Growing Together—to being affected and affecting. I explore the discomfort of encountering racism, and my shame in responding with silence. I consider how experiences of discomfort and shame might generate future openings for alliance.

The practice of destabilizing subjectivity can challenge essentialist and fixed forms of embodiment while acknowledging the risks of writing alone.

Mitchell (2018, 196–97) draws upon Butler and Gilson to develop vulnerability as a destabilization of the subject, which involves "the disruption of any kind of stable narratorial 'I'—while exploring qualities of 'interdependence and incompletion.'" Similarly, Adams and Holman Jones (2008, 384) propose autoethnography-as-queer as a destabilizing methodology that "embraces fluidity, resists definitional and conceptual fixity, looks to self and structures as relational accomplishments, and takes seriously the need to create more livable, equitable, and just ways of living" (see also LeFrançois 2013). Adams and Holman Jones's (2008, 374) methodology aligns with Nagar's (2014) grounding of reflexive praxis within economic, political, and institutional contexts.

I borrow the concept of angling from Mitchell's (2018, 197) work on vulnerability, which advises us to "angle ourselves towards it and to see where that angling takes us." Angling within a queer approach means orienting myself and Growing Together toward vulnerability—conceiving of vulnerability as a "constitutive" form of interdependency (Mitchell 2018, 197; see also Butler 2016; Gilson 2011). Angling suggests that vulnerability extends beyond any single encounter while recognizing that the journey is far from certain. It encompasses a lifelong process of working toward alliances of interdependency—not in resistance of vulnerability but in pursuit of its political potential. Recognizing vulnerability as agential and disruptive makes it possible to consider how scholars, activists, and Cooperative Extension can angle projects like Growing Together toward greater accountability to people experiencing injustices and inequities.

Working within a context shaped by strong societal distastes for vulnerability, "becoming otherwise" (Butler 2004, 217) creates openings where it becomes possible to disrupt oppressions—like food insecurity—that are forms of bodily vulnerability emanating through social relations (Butler, Gambetti, and Sabsay 2016, 4; Gilson 2011; Mitchell 2018). While autoethnographic analyses of discomfort can turn the gaze inward by revealing the intimate links between the embodied discomfort of vulnerability and discursive and structural forms of oppression, I endeavor instead to identify pathways for political action.

RESPONDING TO UNCOMFORTABLE ENCOUNTERS

Experiencing discomfort is not unfamiliar territory in feminist and decolonial praxis (Caretta and Jokinen 2017; Kaomea 2003; Laliberté and Schurr 2016; LeFrançois 2013; Smith 2016). When I encountered racism and responded with silence, I experienced the tension between collaboration and embodied discomfort. I questioned how one could dismantle inequities through programs that provide food to community members when those community members become imagined as *others*. I underscore that my retelling of the encounter does not represent the expressed viewpoints and actions of most Growing Together participants, nor does it reveal the full experiences and perspectives of the two gardeners. Yet it reflects a commonly unquestioned discourse that seeped into the project—one in which structural causes of food insecurity are portrayed as individualized problems.

The gardeners that day grappled with labor and food in complex, contested ways that brought in race, ethnicity, gender, heteronormativity, class, age, religion, moral judgment, and individualized perceptions of poverty. For one gardener, a poultry plant job meant enough money for food. For the other, concern centered on personal judgments—of tattoos, drug abuse, and church nonattendance. Their stories about food-insecure children concentrated on how parents could afford to buy food by spending more judiciously—without questioning whether food would be available and adequate had the mother not gotten the tattoo. Good mothering became conflated with being middle class, married, and Christian. I understood the discussed plans for donation as implicitly communicating that certain types of parents are less deserving and even undeserving of assistance. Neither gardener mentioned having relationships with the community members they were talking about, and the discourse linking hard work to food security was not pried open further.

I have considered how responses to such encounters, while firmly antiracist and anticolonialist in messaging, need to account for the complexity of broader relations of power. Yet communication—between me, with a feminist relational ontology, and others, with different ways of seeing the world—stood as a barrier just as I wanted to break barriers down. My discomfort stemmed not only from my understanding of how racism structured the project but from my unpreparedness to respond with feminist principles in a way that would be, and could be, received.

My response would prove critical. Yet in that moment, I remained silent. I sat around the picnic table where the gardeners conversed. I sat listening, uncomfortable, trying to make sense of what was said and to figure out whether and how to respond.

For what reasons did the gardeners join Growing Together? What would happen if I alienated them and the garden failed? How could I build a transformative collaboration without partners interested in equity? Why did Extension not reach out directly to the project's intended beneficiaries as partners? How was my participation reinforcing racism and instituting separations between those deemed worthy and unworthy to receive the food? My silence? In that silence, I reinforced social marginalization, despite potential justifications for my silence. Sudbury and Okazawa-Rey (2016) note the risk of idealizing activist research, calling for scholars to pay attention to power relations and the contradictions that infuse such projects. Despite believing that for people to think, feel, and belong differently in the world, surely we need to collectively "*do* differently" (Carolan 2016, 142, emphasis original), I found myself unable to act, limited by what I could do in that moment.

I recognize that my silence represents a disconnect between working to decolonize our worlds and a complicity in whiteness, a desire to be seen as "good" and "respectful." The discomfort of isolation and fear of losing partnerships pressed against me and won in that moment.

Ahmed (2010, 68–69), in writing on the *feminist killjoy,* has spoken to my feelings in that encounter:

> Power speaks here in this moment of hesitation. Do you go along with it? What does it mean to not go along with it? To create awkwardness is to be read as awkward. Maintaining public comfort requires that certain bodies "go along with it." To refuse to go along with it, to refuse the place in which you are placed, is to be seen as trouble, as causing discomfort among others. There is a political struggle about how we attribute good and bad feelings, which hesitates around the apparently simple question of who introduces what feelings to whom.

In and despite my multiple and fluid relational positionings to the gardeners, some visible and others hidden—as a researcher representing Extension, as someone not from Iowa, as a student, as a younger person, as a lesbian, as a queer person, as a feminist killjoy, as someone who has experienced violence and trauma—I went along with it and internalized the discomfort. The strength and ferociousness of the conversation felt like a hairball lodged deep in my throat. Through taking refuge in my privilege of being silent in that moment, of appearing invulnerable, I avoided causing discomfort to others, and in so doing contributed to the normalization of racism.

I have considered the possibilities and limits of feminist performative knowledge production from this encounter. I stayed within the comfort of passing as semi-insider and denied my accountability to marginalized Iowans. I ignored that the conversation may have offended others in attendance that day. Had I not remained silent, I could have provided leadership and allyship from Extension rather than complicity.

Speaking up also might have impacted the project's ability to deliver fresh produce at this site. I could not ignore the food, and participants were volunteering their labor to produce it. I also could not ignore questions about where the food would go, who would receive it, who would decide, and how those decisions were made.

Being a troublemaker may or may not have led to an emotional connection across difference—to a connection invoking care and paving the way for critically reflective conversations. In that moment I closed off the potentiality of becoming otherwise through vulnerability (Mitchell 2018, 197). Yet, according to Butler (2016, 25), to "bare our fault lines as if that might launch a new mode of authenticity or inaugurate a new order of moral values or a sudden and widespread outbreak of 'care' " is rarely politically effective and risks turning vulnerability into defensiveness. While sharing emotions can serve as a potential basis for solidarity, in this context it as easily could have backfired or been misunderstood.

CONTENDING WITH FIXED DIFFERENCE

In queering autoethnography (Adams and Holman Jones 2008), I wrestle with the contradiction of wanting to draw attention to the racializing effects of essentialism, but in so doing, I find essentialism impossible to escape. In my encounter, for instance, the two gardeners spoke of community members as either "white" or "Hispanic." In fixing social difference, they simultaneously conflated and essentialized race and ethnicity, and situated themselves in relation to an outside Other. Fixed social categorizations are fraught with ontological violence, into which the physical violence of food insecurity is woven. That day, the gardeners derogatorily employed the phrase "the Hispanics" as the sole identifier of an entire segment of the community, which simultaneously was not part of their community.

What do encounters of social categorizations and fixed difference mean for feminist scholars? How do we contend with limits that are brought forth in the very retelling of such encounters? I ask these questions because beyond that moment in the garden, and beyond that community, the violence of fixed difference performatively perpetuates in the writing of this chapter. In retelling this story using fixed categorical descriptors, I am participating in this violence even though I am calling attention to injustice. The limits of language and categories constrain my ability to get beyond essentialist divisions.

Nagar's (2014, 14) description of radical vulnerability, of storytelling as a form of coauthorship outside the university, touches upon these concerns:

The telling of stories must continuously resist a desire to reveal the essential or authentic experience of the subject; instead, every act of storytelling must confront ways in which power circulates and constructs the relationalities within and across various social groups.

By retelling this encounter as autoethnography, I aim to engage in non-essentialist storytelling that makes relationalities visible without reducing Growing Together participants, recipients, or myself to single, fixed categories or autonomous selves. Though I pursue this goal, I worry my retelling will craft not only Latinx people but also the gardeners in a way that forecloses agencies, voices, and perspectives other than my own. In telling this story alone, rather than in coauthorship, I risk perpetuating these violences.

My position in Growing Together and the statewide program structure provided me with limited ability to connect with the gardeners. The encounter took place during an Extension training for Master Gardeners, in which I assisted the trainer while interacting with participants as a researcher. I arrived at the garden not knowing whom I would meet. Following our encounter, I reached out to both gardeners. One gardener had interest in meeting but was unable to participate in a follow-up interview due to family obligations and travel. When I later presented this manuscript for feedback, the gardener expressed concern with representing their community as having drug users and how its mention would risk making the community look negative to outsiders. Sensitive to reductive portrayals of rural America's drug epidemic, I struggled with the choice to leave this part of the chapter intact.

The other gardener pulled back from Growing Together due to a busy schedule, but within our email communications shared another story of mothers buying drugs rather than feeding their children. The gardener was unavailable for a follow-up interview and unable to provide feedback on the manuscript until years later. Drug use among white non-Latinx mothers remained a high concern, as well as the changing demographics of the community within the past fifteen years. The gardener offered that the daughter's story about the mother with the tattoo may have involved a "Caucasian" or "Hispanic" child, and the gardener was uncertain which was the case—which differed with my understanding of the conversation at the garden that day. The gardener did not recall having personally seen any Latinx mothers in the community with tattoos, only "white" mothers. Another point the gardener raised is that because Latinx children are "dressed to the nines," it is hard for many people to realize that their families may be low-income and not have enough food. In a story that I interpreted as a marker of the morality of the Latinx community, the gardener described Latinx families as "Catholics" and "Christians" and spoke of a congregation of fifty to sixty Latinx people attending a baptism service at a nearby lake. After reiterating how Latinx girls are "nicely" and "neatly dressed," "with cell phones," and "clean," the gardener expressed sincere doubt that Latinx families were not feeding their children. I gathered from this statement that the gardener made a distinction between *low-income* families without enough food and *neglectful* families that fail to feed their children. At the same time, in providing feedback, the gardener conveyed senses of approbation for Latinx community members that were different from the strongly negative impressions that I perceived the gardener to hold during our encounter at the garden. Nearly three years had elapsed, and I understand many possible explanations might account for the expressed and perceived differences across these two moments in time.

Our interactions remained limited to the initial encounter and few instances of feedback. Without sustained engagement, the door was closed to future conversations that critically reflected on these exchanges and the broader geopolitics of food insecurity.

RECOVERING RADICAL VULNERABILITY?

Moments of discomfort serve an important purpose. They are not just "undesirable" detours on the path to productive, radically vulnerable alliances. They are part of the work you need to do to "make your screw-ups and your challenges opportunities to become better allies" (Harper 2016). Even though I have made the mistake of not speaking out, I can repurpose uncomfortable encounters as political moments to reengage scholars, activists, and Extension in practices of radical vulnerability.

A commitment to equity should prompt Cooperative Extension to question who is and is not among its institutional colleagues and community partners, and why. New forms of partnership must be deliberate in challenging binary norms of "vulnerability as passive" and "agency as active" (Butler, Gambetti, and Samsay 2016, 3) that have shaped food and nutrition interventions. Otherwise, placing Extension "experts" in positions to "help poor and uneducated others" achieve food security, health, and well-being—no matter how well intentioned—will continue to dismiss mutual interdependency in the world. I imagine Growing Together might be an entirely different project if Extension embraced an approach that begins with the needs and values of food-insecure communities. Through radically vulnerable alliance, Extension can turn to communities to engage with their vast and in-depth knowledges. By decentralizing knowledge production, university-community partnerships can cocreate decolonizing solutions in ways that build trust and harness collective reflexivity (Nagar 2014).

Cooperative Extension is well positioned to resource "situated solidarity" (Nagar 2014, 85; see also Nagar and Geiger 2007; Routledge and Derickson 2015). To reformulate practices and policies, however, it must radically open up which knowledges and perspectives it permits to cross into its academic, expert-driven spaces (Hassel 2004). Extension will need to work against institutional forces that limit the political mobilization of scars and wounds—of vulnerability—in pursuit of equity (Pelaez Lopez 2018). It will need to value the contributions of communities of color, Indigenous people, queer and gender-nonconforming people, people experiencing poverty, and other marginalized people, and not reduce us to head counts or to "diversity management" strategies (Ahmed 2004, sec. 9). In the hiring of a diverse range of people and the inclusion of diverse community partners, Extension must embrace our troublemaking worldviews and acts of resistance, even and especially when they depart from the comfort of normatively white institutional practices.

Developing radically vulnerable relationships will be a necessary foundation for new types of engagement and collective action. Unlearning institutional practices takes time. Forming relationships of alliance within Extension—let alone with communities—can seem like an impossible journey. Underscoring the criticality of challenging oppression in spaces of white privilege, radical vulnerability can start within land-grant universities and Extension through problematizing institutional roles, past and present, in fostering structural inequities.

Though the road ahead is long, Cooperative Extension can restructure the systems that determine who has a say in community food policies, programs, and practices. While I do not minimize my responsibility to speak up, creating institutional spaces for conversations about Extension's approach to diversity hiring and community partnerships is a necessary step in the more difficult structural work of addressing inequities in resource distribution and decision-making. Extension may fear alienating employees and partnerships that have produced important results, such as increasing fresh produce in food pantries. We also stand to strengthen existing partnerships and gain new ones. Greder, Brotherson, and Garasky (2004), through their research on Iowa's immigrant communities, have called for listening to marginalized community voices. Extension can take clear steps to place this goal at the forefront of its mission.

CONCLUSION

Engaging questions of how one speaks for, about, and with another has long been an active area of feminist inquiry (Lugones and Spelman 1983; Nagar 2014). With Growing Together, the path to forming radically vulnerable alliances took an unexpected turn that helped me reflect more fully on these questions. During fieldwork, I experienced uneven power differences flowing in multiple directions that complicated speaking up when I encountered racism within the institutional spaces of Cooperative Extension. Disappointed in my complicity in the production of whiteness as the norm, I have turned to multiple, albeit imperfect, retellings of these encounters. Sourcing vulnerability as an affective opening, in and through these retellings, I have reengaged with experiences of discomfort to strengthen existing alliances and angle myself toward new ones (Gilson 2011, 310; Mitchell 2018).

Feminist and queer concepts of vulnerability are supporting me in a lifelong journey of praxis that will never be completed. They call attention to the necessity for continued discussion of collaborations—which ones we pursue and why, how we form them, navigating different ontologies and commitments, and ways to seek out the feminist political potential even when the path is challenging. The result is a more complex, messy, and uncomfortable practice of radical vulnerability and feminist praxis.

NOTES

1. I wrestle with the discomfort of describing community members referenced in this story without reinforcing colonizing knowledge systems. After much contemplation, I have decided to use the term Latinx—a product of the queer, decolonial, and antiracist mobilizations of Latinx activists (Pelaez Lopez 2018)—and have replaced references to "the Hispanics" in this retelling. Throughout the chapter, I replace instances when the gardeners used the phrases "Hispanic" or "the Hispanics" with "Latinx" or "Latinx community member(s)." My research did not include Latinx participants in the community. The decision to retell the story of this encounter without having them as partners in Growing Together, or as coauthors of this chapter, enacts a colonizing form of authorship: nonparticipants yet again are passively identified, in this case as Latinx.
2. In reviewing the manuscript, this gardener did not remember the conversation about the laundromat but agreed that it would make a good site for distribution. Reflecting on being raised in a middle-class family without a washing machine, the gardener also said that using a laundromat would not mean someone is food insecure.
3. Upon review, the gardener clarified that mention of the "poultry plant" more broadly referred to the egg and hog operations in the community.
4. The story I present is constructed from fieldnotes and my interpretation of the encounter. I originally wrote my account describing the family as Latinx, based on my

understanding of the remarks about the child and mother, which occurred in the midst
of the gardeners' discussing Latinx food insecurity. Later, I include discussion of this
point and the gardeners' other feedback.

5. Supplemental Nutritional Assistance Program (SNAP) Education state-level programs
receive support from the eponymous USDA program to provide education and resources
on nutrition and physical activity for recipients of SNAP (formerly food stamp) benefits.

6. Cooperative Extension, or Extension, refers to the educational outreach and
engagement operations of US land-grant universities. The Smith-Lever Act of 1914
(2006, 7 U.S.C. §§ 342) established Extension to transfer scientific technologies of
agricultural modernization to the "public," historically to rural farming communities
(Gould, Steele, and Woodrum 2014).

7. In 1972, Washington State University Extension created an unpaid volunteer model of
Master Gardeners to handle increasing public requests for gardening advice, education,
and training, a program that now extends across the US (Rohs and Westerfield 1996;
Takle 2015).

8. Within Growing Together, Master Gardeners, as primary partners, have autonomy to
form partnerships with community organizations and members. Some gardening
projects I visited did include people experiencing food insecurity as active partners, yet
Extension did not directly reach out to them as partners.

9. Indigenous peoples living and farming in present-day Iowa and the upper Midwest
during the eras of French, British, and US settlement include, but are not limited to, the
Sisseton-Wahpeton Oyate (Dakota), Sauk and Meskwaki, Winnebago (Ho-Chunk),
Ioway, Oto, Medewakanton, Omaha, and Wahpekuta (US Forest Service 2018;
EagleWoman 2004/2005; Colbert 2008). The US Forest Service (2018) has built an
interactive map that includes Indigenous land cessions through treaties between 1784
and 1896, including for Iowa.

10. US Census Bureau records population estimates for "Hispanic or Latino (of any race)."

11. The 2014–2016 USDA estimates for Iowa are 10.7 percent of households annually, with
1.4 percent margin of error.

REFERENCES

Adams, Tony E., and Stacy Holman Jones. 2008. "Autoethnography Is Queer." In *Handbook of Critical and Indigenous Methodologies*, edited by Norman K. Denzin, Yvonna S. Lincoln, and Linda Tuhiwai Smith, 373–90. Thousand Oaks, CA: Sage.
Ahmed, Sara. 2004. "Declarations of Whiteness: The Non-Performativity of Anti-Racism." *Borderlands* 3 (2).
Ahmed, Sara. 2010. *The Promise of Happiness*. Durham, NC: Duke University Press.
Billo, Emily, and Nancy Hiemstra. 2013. "Mediating Messiness: Expanding Ideas of Flexibility, Reflexivity, and Embodiment in Fieldwork." *Gender, Place & Culture* 20 (3): 313–28. https://doi.org/10.1080/0966369X.2012.674929.
Butler, Judith. 2004. *Undoing Gender*. New York: Routledge.
Butler, Judith. 2016. "Rethinking Vulnerability and Resistance." In *Vulnerability in Resistance*, edited by Judith Butler, Zeynep Gambetti, and Leticia Sabsay, 12–27. Durham, NC: Duke University Press.
Butler, Judith, Zeynep Gambetti, and Leticia Sabsay. 2016. "Introduction." In *Vulnerability in Resistance*, edited by Judith Butler, Zeynep Gambetti, and Leticia Sabsay, 1–11. Durham, NC: Duke University Press.
Cantú, Lionel. 1995. "The Peripheralization of Rural America: A Case Study of Latino Migrants in America's Heartland." *Sociological Perspectives* 38 (3): 399–414. https://doi.org/10.2307/1389434.

Caretta, Martina Angela, and Johanna Carolina Jokinen. 2017. "Conflating Privilege and Vulnerability: A Reflexive Analysis of Emotions and Positionality in Postgraduate Fieldwork." *The Professional Geographer* 69 (2): 275–83. https://doi.org/10.1080/003 30124.2016.1252268.

Carolan, Michael. 2016. "Adventurous Food Futures: Knowing about Alternatives Is Not Enough, We Need to Feel Them." *Agriculture and Human Values* 33: 141–52. https://doi.org/10.1007/s10460-015-9629-4.

Carter, Angie, Carrie Chennault, and Ahna Kruzic. 2018. "Public Action for Public Science: Re-Imagining the Leopold Center for Sustainable Agriculture." *Capitalism Nature Socialism* 29 (1): 69–88. https://doi.org/10.1080/10455752.2017.1423364.

Colbert, Thomas Burnell. 2008. " 'The Hinge on Which All Affairs of the Sauk and Fox Indians Turn': Keokuk and the United States Government." In *Enduring Nations: Native Americans in the Midwest*, edited by Russell David Edmunds, 54–71. Urbana: University of Illinois Press.

Coleman-Jensen, Alisha, Matthew P. Rabbit, Christian A. Gregory, and Anita Singh. 2017. *Household Food Security in the United States in 2016*. ERR-237. U.S. Department of Agriculture, Economic Research Service.

Collins, Christopher S., and M. Kalehua Mueller. 2016. "University Land-Grant Extension and Resistance to Inclusive Epistemologies." *The Journal of Higher Education* 87 (3): 303–31. https://doi.org/10.1080/00221546.2016.11777404.

Dankbar, Hannah, Emily K. Zimmerman, Carrie Chennault, Andrea Basche, Jacqueline Ann Nester, Maritza Pierre, and Gabrielle Roesch-McNally. 2017. "Lettuce Learn: Student Reflections on Building and Sustaining a Community Donation Garden." *Journal of Critical Thought and Praxis* 6 (3): 71–85.

Dutta, Mohan Jyoti, Agaptus Anaele, and Christina Jones. 2013. "Voices of Hunger: Addressing Health Disparities through the Culture-Centered Approach." *Journal of Communication* 63 (1): 159–80. https://doi.org/10.1111/jcom.12009.

EagleWoman, Angelique A. (Wamdi Awanwicake Wastewin). 2004/2005. "Re-Establishing the Sisseton-Wahpeton Oyate's Reservation Boundaries: Building a Legal Rationale from Current International Law." *American Indian Law Review* 29 (2): 293–66. https://doi.org/10.2307/20070732.

Firkus, Angela. 2010a. "Agricultural Extension and the Campaign to Assimilate the Native Americans of Wisconsin, 1914–1932." *The Journal of the Gilded Age and Progressive Era* 9 (4): 473–502. https://doi.org/10.1017/S1537781400004229.

Firkus, Angela. 2010b. "The Agricultural Extension Service and Non-Whites in California, 1910–1932." *Agricultural History* 84 (4): 506–30. https://doi.org/10.3098/ah.2010 .84.4.506.

Gilson, Erinn. 2011. "Vulnerability, Ignorance, and Oppression." *Hypatia* 26 (2): 308–32. https://doi.org/10.1111/j.1527-2001.2010.01158.x.

Gould, Frances I., Douglas Steele, and William J. Woodrum. 2014. "Cooperative Extension: A Century of Innovation." *Journal of Extension* 52 (1).

Gouveia, Lourdes, and Rogelio Saenz. 2000. "Global Forces and Latino Population Growth in the Midwest: A Regional and Subregional Analysis." *Great Plains Research: A Journal of Natural and Social Sciences* 10 (2): 305–28.

Greder, Kimberly A., Mary Jane Brotherson, and Steven Garasky. 2004. "Listening to the Voices of Marginalized Families." In *Family and Community Policy: Strategies for Civic Engagement*, edited by Carol L. Anderson, 95–121. Alexandria, VA: American Association of Family and Consumer Sciences.

Greder, Kimberly A., Christine C. Cook, Steven Garasky, Yoshie Sano, and Bruce C. Randall. 2009. "Rural Latino Immigrant Families: Hunger, Housing, and Social Support." In *Strengths and Challenges of New Immigrant Families: Implications for*

Research, Education, Policy, and Service, edited by Rochelle L. Dalla, John DeFrain, and Julie Johnson, 345–68. Lanham, MD: Lexington Books.

Greder, Kimberly A., Flor Romero de Slowing, and Kimberly Doudna. 2012. "Latina Immigrant Mothers: Negotiating New Food Environments to Preserve Cultural Food Practices and Healthy Child Eating." *Family and Consumer Sciences Research Journal* 41 (2): 145–60. https://doi.org/10.1111/fcsr.12004.

Grim, Valerie. 2015. "The 1890 Land-Grant Colleges: From the New Deal to Black Farmers' Class-Action Lawsuit, 1930s–2010s." In *Service as Mandate: How American Land-Grant Universities Shaped the Modern World, 1920–2015*, edited by Alan I. Marcus, 80–111. Tuscaloosa: University of Alabama Press.

Harper, A. Breeze. 2016. "Uprooting White Fragility: Intersectional Anti-Racism in the 'Post-Racial' Ethical Foodscape." Intersectional Justice Conference, Clinton, WA, March 25–27. YouTube video, 1:11:35. https://www.youtube.com/watch?v=rPWTR h4nng0.

Harris, Carmen V. 2008. " 'The Extension Service Is Not an Integration Agency': The Idea of Race in the Cooperative Extension Service." *Agricultural History* 82 (2): 193–219. https://doi.org/10.3098/ah.2008.82.2.193.

Hassel, Craig A. 2004. "Can Diversity Extend to Ways of Knowing? Engaging Cross-Cultural Paradigms." *Journal of Extension* 42 (2): 1–4.

Iowa Department of Agriculture and Land Stewardship. 2018. "A Look at Iowa Agriculture." Accessed March 1, 2019. https://www.iowaagriculture.gov/quickFacts.asp.

Iowa State University Extension & Outreach. 2017. "Crop and Land Use: Statewide Data." https://www.extension.iastate.edu/soils/crop-and-land-use-statewide-data.

Jarosz, Lucy. 2014. "Comparing Food Security and Food Sovereignty Discourses." *Dialogues in Human Geography* 4 (2): 168–81. https://doi.org/10.1177/2043820614537161.

Kaomea, Julie. 2003. "Reading Erasures and Making the Familiar Strange: Defamiliarizing Methods for Research in Formerly Colonized and Historically Oppressed Communities." *Educational Researcher* 32 (2): 14–23.

Laliberté, Nicole, and Carolin Schurr. 2016. "Introduction: The Stickiness of Emotions in the Field: Complicating Feminist Methodologies." *Gender, Place & Culture* 23 (1): 72–78. https://doi.org/10.1080/0966369X.2014.992117.

LeFrançois, Brenda A. 2013. "The Psychiatrization of Our Children, or, an Autoethnographic Narrative of Perpetuating First Nations Genocide Through 'Benevolent' Institutions." *Decolonization: Indigeneity, Education & Society* 2 (1): 108–23.

Lugones, María C., and Elizabeth V. Spelman. 1983. "Have We Got a Theory for You! Feminist Theory, Cultural Imperialism and the Demand for 'the Woman's Voice.' " *Women's Studies International Forum* 6 (6): 573–81.

Miewald, Christiana, and Eugene McCann. 2014. "Foodscapes and the Geographies of Poverty: Sustenance, Strategy, and Politics in an Urban Neighborhood." *Antipode* 46 (2): 537–56. https://doi.org/10.1111/anti.12057.

Minkoff-Zern, Laura-Anne. 2014. "Knowing Good Food: Immigrant Knowledge and the Racial Politics of Farmworker Food Insecurity." *Antipode* 46 (5): 1190–1204. https://doi.org/10.1111/j.1467-8330.2012.01016.x.

Mitchell, Kaye. 2018. "Feral With Vulnerability." *Angelaki* 23 (1): 194–98. https://doi.org/1 0.1080/0969725X.2018.1435398.

Mosley, Janetty, Shorlette Ammons, and Heather Hyden. 2015. "Implementing Equity in Our Food Systems Work: Considerations for Cooperative Extension." eXtension. https://foodsystems.extension.org/implementing-equity-in-our-food-systems-work -considerations-for-cooperative-extension/.

Nagar, Richa. 2014. *Muddying the Waters: Coauthoring Feminisms across Scholarship and Activism*. Urbana: University of Illinois Press.

Nagar, Richa, and Susan Geiger. 2007. "Reflexivity and Positionality in Feminist Fieldwork Revisited." In *Politics and Practice in Economic Geography*, edited by Adam Tickell, Eric Sheppard, Jamie Peck, and Trevor Barnes, 267–78. London: Sage Publications Ltd.

Nagar, Richa, Özlem Aslan, Nadia Z. Hasan, Omme-Salma Rahemtullah, Nishant Upadhyay, and Begüm Uzun. 2016. "Feminisms, Collaborations, Friendships: A Conversation." *Feminist Studies* 42 (2): 502–19. https://doi.org/10.15767/feministstudies.42.2.0502.

Pelaez Lopez, Alan. 2018. "The X in Latinx Is a Wound, Not a Trend." *Color Bloq*. September 13, 2018. https://www.colorbloq.org/the-x-in-latinx-is-a-wound-not-a-trend.

Patel, Raj. 2013. "The Long Green Revolution." *The Journal of Peasant Studies* 40 (1): 1–63. https://doi.org/10.1080/03066150.2012.719224.

Pirog, Rich, Kaitlin Koch, and Anel Guel. 2016. "Race, Ethnicity, and the Promise of 'Good Food' for Michigan: A Three-Voice Commentary." *Journal of Agriculture, Food Systems, and Community Development* 5 (4): 83–86. https://doi.org/10.5304/jafscd.2015.054 .011.

Rohs, Frederick R., and Robert R. Westerfield. 1996. "Factors Influencing Volunteering in the Master Gardener Program." *HortTechnology* 6 (3): 281–85.

Routledge, Paul, and Kate Driscoll Derickson. 2015. "Situated Solidarities and the Practice of Scholar-Activism." *Environment and Planning D: Society and Space* 33 (3): 391–407. https://doi.org/10.1177/0263775815594308.

Saenz, Rogelio. 2011. "The Changing Demographics of Latinos in the Midwest." In *Latinos in the Midwest*, edited by Rubén O. Martinez, 33–55. Lansing: Michigan State University Press.

Sano, Yoshie, Steven Garasky, Kimberly A. Greder, Christine C. Cook, and Dawn E. Browder. 2011. "Understanding Food Insecurity among Latino Immigrant Families in Rural America." *Journal of Family and Economic Issues* 32 (1): 111–23. https://doi.org/10.1007 /s10834-010-9219-y.

Sbicca, Joshua. 2014. "The Need to Feed: Urban Metabolic Struggles of Actually Existing Radical Projects." *Critical Sociology* 40 (6): 817–34. https://doi.org/10.1177/08969205 13497375.

Shiva, Vandana. 2016. *The Violence of the Green Revolution: Third World Agriculture, Ecology and Politics*. Lexington: University Press of Kentucky.

Smith, Sara. 2012. "Intimate Geopolitics: Religion, Marriage, and Reproductive Bodies in Leh, Ladakh." *Annals of the Association of American Geographers* 102 (6): 1511–28. https://doi.org/10.1080/00045608.2012.660391.

Smith, Sara. 2016. "Intimacy and Angst in the Field." *Gender, Place & Culture* 23 (1): 134–46. https://doi.org/10.1080/0966369X.2014.958067.

Stanley, Kathleen. 1994. "Industrial and Labor Market Transformation in the U.S. Meatpacking Industry." In *The Global Restructuring of Agro-Food Systems*, edited by Philip McMichael, 129–44. Ithaca, NY: Cornell University Press.

State Data Center of Iowa. n.d. a. "Hispanic or Latino Groups in Iowa: 1980–2000." https:// www.iowadatacenter.org/datatables/State/sthispanicgroups19802000.pdf.

State Data Center of Iowa. n.d. b. "Race and Hispanic Origin in Iowa Incorporated Places: 1990." https://www.iowadatacenter.org/datatables/PlacesAll/plracehispanic1990.pdf.

Sudbury, Julia, and Margo Okazawa-Rey. 2016. "Introduction: Activist Scholarship and the Neoliberal University after 9/11." In *Activist Scholarship: Antiracism, Feminism, and Social Change*, edited by Julia Sudbury and Margo Okazawa-Rey, 1–16. London: Routledge.

Takle, Bryn. 2015. "Motivation and Retention of Iowa's Master Gardener Volunteers." Master's thesis, Iowa State University.

Undoing Inequality in the Food System Working Group. 2018. "Racial Equity in Food Systems Work: Beginning the Journey." http://www.canr.msu.edu/resources /racial-equity-in-food-systems-work-beginning-the-journey.

US Census Bureau. 2017. "ACS Housing Demographic and Housing Estimates: 2013–2017 American Community Survey 5-Year Estimates." American FactFinder. http://factfinder .census.gov.

US Forest Service. 2018. "Tribal Connections." https://usfs.maps.arcgis.com/apps /webappviewer/index.html?id=fe311f69cb1d43558227d73bc34f3a32.

CHAPTER 3

TOILETS AND THE PUBLIC IMAGINATION: PLANNING FOR SAFE AND INCLUSIVE SPACES

Rachael Cofield and Petra L. Doan

INTRODUCTION

The recent spate of political posturing over public restrooms has sharpened the debate over inclusion and public safety in these vulnerable spaces. Right-wing and conservative Christian manipulation of the public imaginary about the lurking transgender menace to cisgender women and girls in such spaces has certainly intensified some electoral politics and shifted the conversation about safety (Samek 2016). This can be seen in the legislation debates surrounding the Houston Equal Rights Ordinance of 2015 (HERO) and the 2016 Public Facilities Privacy and Security Act (HB2) in North Carolina. Both laws sought to enhance or limit freedoms based on sexual orientation or gender identity and instigated public conversations about gender, safety, and inclusion. Our chapter seeks to integrate feminist and queer social science and design perspectives into this discussion by asking whose safety needs protecting.

According to a 2016 Human Rights Campaign report, increased transgender exposure has led to forty-four state bills targeting trans people, more than in any previous year. Federal efforts in 2016–2018 include attempts to ban transgender individuals from the military, rescind Obama-era guidance allowing transgender K–12 students to use school bathrooms matching their gender identity, and rescind previous memos indicating that trans workers were protected under civil rights law. More recently, these efforts include a push to define gender as an immutable and biological category determined by genitalia at birth that effectively eliminates gender identity as a protected category. Understanding the source of the animus toward transgender and gender-nonnormative people is a critical first step in countering anti-transgender narratives. In this chapter we draw on Sara Ahmed's (2004) insights about the cultural power of emotions and especially the way that emotion is used in politics to intensify feelings such as hatred and disgust. Ahmed's concern takes as a focus the discourse of conservative groups that is steeped in emotional claims of pain and injury that motivate followers to feel hatred and disgust toward "others." Ahmed (2004, 88–89) suggests that, "Disgust reactions are not only about objects that seem to threaten boundary lines of subjects, they are also about objects that seem 'lower' than or below the subject. . . . Lower regions of the body—that which is below—are clearly associated with both sexuality and with 'the waste' that is literally expelled by the body."

In the context of this chapter the tendency of the nonnormatively gendered to move across well-established gender binaries facilitates the politics of emotions, since such gender boundary transgressors are already easily seen as objects of disgust. Linking these nonnormative bodies to "lower" status functions such as sexuality and bodily waste facilitates the classification of them as disgusting threats to normative subjects who likely have no firsthand experience of harm from them. Such feelings of fear and disgust are then manipulated by a right-wing politics that centers "an ideal masculine, impenetrable, normalized and heteronormative white male body" (Gökarıksel and Smith 2017, 339) and "others" the nonnormative, making them the object of derision. This political othering is the hallmark of the Trumpian strategy that "relies on an embodied nationalism that places women, and here, LGBTQ people, as passive objects of male control, protection, and sexual violence" (Gökarıksel and Smith 2016, 80).

The uneven access to public restrooms is reasonably well acknowledged. For instance, Anthony and Dufresne (2007, 270) argue that "although access to American public restrooms has been constrained by discrimination among genders, classes, races, levels of physical ability, and sexual orientations, only issues of race and physical ability have been addressed through federal legislation." The authors suggest that the persistence of discrimination on the basis of class, gender, and sexual orientation makes the availability of public restrooms highly contingent on identity. Recent political rhetoric has inflamed debate over this access to public restrooms, by zeroing in on transgender use of bathrooms, with commentators from both the conservative right wing as well as trans-exclusionary radical feminists (TERFs) suggesting that women and especially young girls are in grave danger from the degendering of public toilets (Jeffreys 2014). In fact, the TERF perspective is exemplified by Jeffreys's (2014, 43) insistence on using the terminology "men who transgender" to refer to trans women, thereby refusing to acknowledge that these individuals could ever be real women and thus should be precluded from using facilities intended for women. Right-wing supporters of HERO and HB2 echo Jeffreys's language as they exaggerate anxieties, threats, and fears of men pretending to be women and entering restrooms. However, no evidence is presented to document this perspective, most likely because there is no such evidence. Szczerbinski (2016) argues strongly that there has only been a single case, in Canada, of a sexual predator pretending to be a woman to gain access to the women's bathroom. On the contrary, the greatest harm linked to public toilets is the lack of access and threat of violence experienced by transgender and gender-nonconforming individuals (Browne 2004; Herman 2013; Lucal 1999). This chapter integrates more recent efforts to examine restrooms from a queer and inclusive perspective (Cavanaugh 2010; Gershenson and Penner 2009; Greed 2016; Molotch 2010) in light of recent events in Houston and North Carolina that have politicized the issue of transgender inclusion in bathrooms.

Public bathrooms serve an important role in daily life while simultaneously contributing to exclusionary gendered practices such as gender policing and perpetuation of harmful heteronormative logics about where one can and cannot reside (Bender-Baird 2016; Browne 2004; Castrodale and Lane 2015; Spain 1992). Our chapter seeks to better understand this gendered segregation through the use of gender-separated bathrooms. We are interested in these locations as public spaces of marginalization and potentially as points of intervention for making spaces more inclusive. Examination of everyday spaces is critical for feminist geography and planning, gesturing at how we must be reflective on the everyday, which is both political and politicized. In keeping with the themes of *Feminist Geography Unbound*, we challenge the taken-for-granted and assumed authority of material space, clarifying ideas about how discomfort in sites of intimacy is harnessed for harmful political ends and how gender disruption in these sites may be useful in combating patriarchy. Our goal is to understand how sex-segregated bathrooms reinforce binary conceptions of gender, who they harm and in what ways, who benefits from their continued use, and what potential lies in their discontinued use.

We analyze the public discourse regarding bathroom laws in places such as Houston, Texas, and North Carolina. In this process we conducted a media review of the prominent newspaper coverage of the bathroom debates, scoured local newspapers, and engaged with various media and propaganda produced by proponents of fear. Houston and North Carolina are useful bathroom debate cases because they are both early examples that influence other potential legislation. Houston was prescient, demonstrating the capacities of a right-wing evangelical and anti-LGBTQ neoconservative coalition to capture public outcry in a post–gay marriage United States. In Houston, their tactics worked, setting the stage for other potential rulings to enforce stricter bathroom usage. In North Carolina, another neoconservative coalition pushed for a similar bathroom law, which was initially successful. Yet the state's HB2 inevitably failed, due to public outcry and financial losses, halting similar legislation in other places.

These are the showcase pieces of legislation regarding bathrooms, one successful, one not, that serve as some of the first salvos in a continued culture war against LGBTQ individuals, particularly transgender people. Our work identifies the themes of public safety and gender to discover the arguments for and against the gender desegregation of bathrooms. Often, the argument against gender desegregation revolves around protecting women from a perceived transgender threat. However, it becomes clear, considering the lack of data about such a threat, that this argument is only superficially about paternalistic concerns of protecting women and children. Instead, it serves as a smoke screen for an unspoken fear that gender nonconformity might lead people to question the perceived naturalness of gendered bodies and destabilize patriarchy. We argue that gendered toilets are a means of controlling public space to maintain gender normativity and keep women and transgender individuals in "their place" within the supposed gender binary. Overall, gender-segregated bathrooms are a patriarchal means of control that can result in significant harm to marginalized and gender-nonconforming individuals. Sex-segregated bathrooms indicate neoconservative politics about gender, seeking to preserve patriarchal dominance while simultaneously pushing against the increasingly visible numbers of people who are transgender or gender nonconforming.

We position bathrooms as part of a lineage of binary gendered spaces that compound gender norms and harm transgender individuals. Sex-segregated bathrooms reinforce binary conceptions of gender, serving as a means of maintaining and enforcing gender norms by forcing people to choose between men's and women's rooms. Adherence to binary public bathrooms is reflected in the debates on new legislation seeking stricter enforcement of binary bathrooms. We demonstrate the politicized nature of binary bathrooms by exploring the narratives surrounding these legislation debates in both Houston and North Carolina. In both cases, neoconservative anti-LGBTQ coalitions sought to police nonbinary use of bathrooms, presenting transgender individuals as predators and proponents of violence, demonstrating their strict adherence to binary gender norms and creating a language of fear surrounding the breaking of norms. We suggest that such fearmongering and politicized manipulation of disgust serve as barriers to change, in which the difficulty of modifying public bathrooms spaces is difficult for not only financial and physical reasons but social and cultural reasons as well.

BATHROOMS AS GENDERED SITES

While sex-segregated bathrooms existed in the United States before the end of the nineteenth century, the first law to mandate this separation was enacted in 1887 in Massachusetts (Kogan 2010). According to Kogan, this was part of a larger move to address public health concerns that came about as a result of the cholera epidemics, rampant disease, and death during the Civil War. Yet it also served to control the influx of women into the city to work in factories and maintain the Victorian idea of separate spheres for men and women (Nirta 2014). Bathrooms today are not simply sites for the bodily act of waste disposal; they serve as visible reinforcers of a fairly rigid gender dichotomy. Municipal codes for public buildings often specify precisely the number of separate toilets/urinals required for men and women. Signage to make these separate spaces visible is highly gendered and reinforces traditional understandings of gender roles. A review of photos of gendered bathroom signs posted by users on Pinterest is instructive. Some simply say "men" or "women" while others use "gents" and "ladies" (adding a class dimension); some use stick figures suggesting that people wearing dresses should use a particular bathroom; others use an image of a pipe, a moustache, or a necktie to indicate men's rooms and a high-heeled shoe or full lips for women's rooms. Others use stick figures with an inverted triangle to suggest men's broader shoulders in contrast to an opposite triangle to suggest women's broader hips, and still others use more explicit signs to mark how patrons are likely to approach a toilet, sometimes using tongue-in-cheek language ("pointers" and "setters") or more explicit reference to the flow generated by urinating in different positions.

The interior layout of public restrooms also adds to the gendering of these spaces. Restrooms designed for men have a bank of urinals and a few closed stalls. Restrooms designed for women have only closed stalls, but they also typically include a diaper-changing station since it is assumed that women are mothers and should be the caregivers of children. Of course, bathrooms also serve as spaces for changing clothes, adjusting contact lenses, blowing noses, brushing teeth, putting on makeup, and many other personal acts (Castrodale

and Lane 2015). They are essential to our daily lives. Plaskow (2008, 52) de-
clares that access to toilets is a "prerequisite for full public participation and
citizenship." For Plaskow, contemporary plans for bathrooms in public space
function to perpetuate gendered inequalities, failing to adequately provide
enough facilities for women and neglecting women's comfort and needs in specific bathroom planning and design. "Potty parity," wherein men have greater
bathroom access, is evidence of continued gender discrimination, serving to
harm not only women's access but also their health (Anthony and Dufresne
2007; Greed 1995, 2016). From a pragmatic standpoint, not having access to
preferred facilities limits everyday activities, affecting what people can and
cannot do on a very basic level that many cis people never encounter as a problem. Urban planners must better understand social norms and gender acces-
sibility in order to fulfill all people's needs for a more just public space. Feminist
geographers must actively engage these sites of vulnerability, pushing back
against the idea that sites are settled, comfortable, or already complete.

Finally, the design of US public restrooms is based on only limited privacy
for both men and women, resulting in various acts of policing by users. Greed
(1995) argues that not considering the physical differences between women
and men in the design of facilities constitutes a type of gender discrimination.
Urinals vary but may have either a very small screen or none at all between
each one to maximize space and efficiency. Most closed stalls in both types of
restrooms have walls for each stall that are not floor to ceiling, allowing one
person to view at least the shoes of another person in the neighboring stall,
and in the case of very tall individuals to view over the top of the usual six-foot
stall height. The stall doors rarely close tightly, allowing a person on the outside
to glimpse another person using the stall. These privacy limitations also create
a sense of vulnerability, making the informal "policing" of such spaces an important element. Boys are trained at a young age to look straight ahead when
using a urinal, since to cast a sideways glance might be misconstrued. Girls,
trained by the patriarchy to be fearful of violence by unknown others, do their
policing by "reading" the gender presentations of other patrons with a wary
eye for intruders who do not meet the gendered standard. Such "trainings"
are often rooted in fear of transgressing normative gender and sexuality, and
the underlying threat of violence maintains patriarchal norms. Lucal (1999)
describes the problems she has encountered as a large woman as a result of
this intrusive reading that assumes any tall woman must be a man in the wrong
place. For transgender individuals this excessive attention to gender policing
can result in negative consequences.

As space and gender are co-constitutive, segregated bathrooms are one avenue to investigate gendered space. Interested in the ways that the design and construction of urban space normalize patriarchy, Spain (1992, 2014) argues that "gendered spaces" separate women from the technical knowledge of urban planning used by men to reproduce their power and privilege in society. She traces this lineage from the Victorian era, in which women were intentionally restricted and only able to navigate the spaces designed specifically for them. This meant that women could only utilize certain spaces, greatly restricting their mobility in the city. Spain (2014, 585) argues that the man-made environment is "just that: the material manifestation of a patriarchal society." Public bathrooms are some of the most visible examples of patriarchal constructions of space. Even as bathrooms are a necessary part of daily life, catering to natural bodily functions, they are still not above reproach or analysis on how they are shaped by gendered hierarchies and power.

Part of the difficulty in crafting equitable policy in this area is that what happens in bathrooms is often constructed as unmentionable (Molotch 2010), creating effective spatial barriers due to real-world power relations. The construction of bathrooms as taboo and women's limited access to planning knowledge work hand in hand to reinforce patriarchal exercises of power and prevailing male advantages. In this chapter, we extend Spain's (1992) argument about the patriarchal gendering of bathrooms as reinforcing male advantages by highlighting that the physical construction of such highly gendered spaces reifies and codifies the social construction of the gender binary. This dichotomous fabrication has powerful consequences for over half the population, with even more injurious consequences for gender nonnormative individuals from both sides of the binary. Thus, rallying for change in this aspect of life that is often considered dirty or taboo can potentially help ameliorate problems that lead to distress in people's lives.

BINARY BATHROOMS AND NONBINARY POPULATIONS

Binary conceptions of gender underscore the way bathrooms have been designed and used in public spaces, reinforcing separate spheres and the implicit "need" for space based upon different cultural habits. Molotch (2010) agrees that there are cultural differences in how men and women interact with and view bathrooms and the toilet, such as length of time it takes to use the bathroom. Yet these cultural differences are rarely presented with empirical evidence, as it can be difficult to gauge and get responses from interviewees about matters often considered taboo. Overall, binary thinking does impact one group more frequently in the bathroom segregation debates. Transgender individuals are often subject to regulatory practices based upon the binary constructions of gender, both internally and externally (Hines 2010). The way bathrooms are designed serves as both a public and private space in which these regulations play out.

Public restroom spaces are specifically and intentionally designed to be gendered. This fits with the argument of many scholars who argue that space is gendered and heteronormative, both explicitly (as with bathrooms) and implicitly (Doan 2010; Oswin 2008). The division of bathrooms and the idea that gender is provable assumes that sex and gender are synonymous and thus interchangeable (Butler 2006; Weinberg 2010). This has been assessed in regards to legality, as defining males and females based upon biology reinforces gender norms and furthers gender binaries (Weinberg 2010). Bender-Baird (2016) argues that sex-segregated bathrooms are technologies of disciplinary power that reinforce the gender binary by forcing people to choose between men's and women's rooms. This connects well to Browne's (2004) argument that sexed spaces exist through continual maintenance and enforcement of gendered norms, meaning that people impact the spaces around them. The idea that gender binaries are reified and perpetuated by the built environment is evocative, as it suggests that the built environment is malleable and could evolve to be indicative of another construction of gender. In other words, the matter is still unsettled, leaving room for further destabilizing of borders between bodies and genders.

CONSEQUENCES OF BINARY PUBLIC BATHROOMS

The binary constructions of gender and their influence on bathroom construction directly contributes to marginalization and problems for transgender individuals and women. These constructions of gender are pervasive and the limits to inclusion and safety are reinforced by the everyday symbols in our lives. Castrodale and Lane (2015) note that bathroom signage, in particular, is often exclusionary and marginalizing. Typical bathroom signage relies on binary images of men and women as discussed earlier. Such symbols and signs mediate behaviors and movement, and their meanings are contingent on and mediated through discursive meaning and social understandings. These serve as another means of demonstrating who is and who is not accepted in certain spaces, similar to the labeling system under Jim Crow meant to keep racial groups separate (Abel 1999). Although the legacies of Black and transgender discrimination carry with them complex and variegated histories, under both systems such groups encounter literal signifiers that reinforce their segregation.

It is not simply the visual indicators of belonging that matter. People who are transgender also police their movement in and decisions to use or not use public bathrooms based on their own understandings of public safety and the actions of others. Transgender individuals recognize that because their existence may challenge normative gender binaries, they are susceptible to violence from other individuals who may be deeply offended or, in Ahmed's (2004) terminology, disgusted by their presence. Accordingly, a type of self-surveillance emerges. Political ideologues manipulate this fear and disgust through their discourse that citizens must "protect women and children" from transgender individuals. The rhetoric of anti-HERO and pro-HB2 proponents is a clear example of such discourse that provokes public concern and fear, even though there is no data supporting this threat. This means there exists a potential of forced removal by security guards or vigilante citizens (Cavanagh 2010). Such fear is even a concern for trans-friendly bathrooms, as some people falsely identify trans individuals as threats themselves. These ideas turn bathrooms into sites of violence and gender policing, allowing some to mislabel trans persons as deceivers (Bender-Baird 2016). Thus, dressing as their preferred gender and simply living their lives puts trans individuals in a vulnerable position where their actions may be critiqued unnecessarily. In a survey of trans people in Washington, DC, Herman (2013) found that 68 percent experienced verbal harassment in sex-segregated restrooms and 9 percent had been physically assaulted. Another nationwide survey of trans people found that more than 25 percent had been denied access to bathrooms at work or in school settings (Grant et al. 2011). This form of individual policing of transgender bodies predates both HERO and HB2 but signaled to right-wing operatives that the "bathroom issue" might be usefully manipulated.

Yet it is not just physical violence that is problematic. Trans individuals are vulnerable already, often encountering microaggressions (or just outright aggression) in their everyday lives. Being unable to use restrooms without fear increases that vulnerability in a harmful way that could be mentally damaging, altering their ability to feel a sense of safety even in an area that should be safe (like a bathroom). Herman (2013) argues that gendered restrooms contribute to the stress of transgender people. The mental side effects of sustained fear and continued mistreatment are other aspects of public safety that must be considered. Nemoto et al. (2005) argue that research indicates that ecological and psychosocial factors, such as discrimination, stigma, health service barriers, and poor social support, contribute to many other health risks. This is an example of how gendered space plays a role in both physical and mental damage to trans people.

POLITICIZING NONBINARY USE IN THE PUBLIC NARRATIVE

In many ways, heightened awareness of transgender and nonbinary populations has been damaging to these groups, leading to increased gender policing and discourses of fear regarding bathrooms, as noted by the 2016 Human Rights Campaign report. Anti-trans sentiments can be seen in public narratives and legislation surrounding trans-friendly bathrooms and updating sex-segregated bathrooms into all-gender bathrooms as well. In the wake of the failed efforts to block same-sex marriage, Chris Johnson (2016) of the *Washington Blade* reported that the "Republican National Committee encourages state legislatures to enact laws that protect student privacy and limit the use of restrooms, locker rooms, and similar facilities to members of the sex to whom the facility is designated." The intent here was clearly to exploit widespread lack of understanding and uncertainty about transgender issues and identities, leading to what Westbrook and Schilt (2014, 34) refer to as "gender panics" wherein "people react to disruptions to biology-based gender ideology by frantically reasserting the naturalness of a male–female binary." Decisions to capitalize on this panic can be seen in targeted campaign strategies that used false ideas about transgender populations being predators and of gender nonconformity leading to sexual deviancy and violence upon women. Manipulation of public fears and lack of understanding of transgender issues can be seen in the narratives surrounding such legislation as HERO and HB2.

HERO, known by some as the "bathroom ordinance," was an antidiscrimination ordinance specifically banning businesses that serve the public, private employers, housing, city employment, and city contracting from discriminating based on sexual orientation, gender identity, sex, race, color, ethnicity, national origin, age, religion, disability, pregnancy, genetic information, family, marital, and military status. The ordinance was passed by the Houston City Council but quickly received intense backlash in the form of a petition signed by fifty thousand people. Although the petition was debunked as containing forgeries and following improper procedures, the Texas Supreme Court granted the petition and ruled that HERO must be repealed or included as a referendum on the November 2015 ballot. In the November elections that followed, 61 percent of voters voted against HERO (on the ballot as Houston's Proposition 1).

Absent from the above story is the role that bathrooms played in the public debate. Opponents of the bill used fearmongering tactics about transgender individuals entering women's bathrooms, portraying women and children as populations vulnerable to assault in sex-segregated spaces, arguing that men might pretend to be transgender women to enter such spaces to cause harm (Moyer 2015). Groups such as the conservative Campaign for Houston led the attack, accusing the ordinance of undermining traditional family values by adding two new protected classes—sexual orientation and gender identity—to the human rights ordinance. On their official website, they argued that "the ordinance gives new special privileges to two special interests, neither of which qualify as true 'minorities' requiring special legal protection." Additionally, they perpetuated the bathroom predator myth, playing on voters' fears that their daughters, wives, sisters, or mothers would be forced to share public restrooms with "gender-confused men." Their slogan—"No men in women's bathrooms!"—was used in a large media campaign and became a rallying cry for protestors against the bill. Campaign for Houston produced advertisements on multiple platforms challenging HERO. One commercial stated, "Any man at any time could enter a women's bathroom, simply by claiming to be a woman that day" and urged viewers to "protect women's privacy, prevent danger, vote 'no' on the Proposition 1 bathroom ordinance" (Campaign for Houston 2015). Other groups allied with Campaign for Houston included the Conservative Republicans of Texas (CRT), whose prominent leader, Steve Hotze, referred to HERO and transgender people as "a satanic movement on our country promoting evil of every kind" (Quinn 2015). These groups claim to worry about women's safety, but they do not include transgender women in that group, using coded language like "gender-confused men" to refer to trans individuals. The language of Campaign for Houston, Conservative Republicans of Texas, and other anti-LGBTQ groups like Texas Values Action is clear—they do not view transgender identity as legitimate, instead pathologizing any identity that does not respect the gender binary. Indeed, to them, trans women are not allowed to exist, let alone have rights.

The public outcry surrounding the proposal to allow access to bathrooms based upon gender identity demonstrates the direct influence of binary thinking on legislation. The refusal to accept gender nonconformity means that the Campaign for Houston and supporters of Proposition 1 continue to delegitimize anyone who might not fit within the presumed traditional binary categories of man and woman. Yet their insistence that "men" might use the excuse that they are women in order to assault women and children in bathrooms is not backed by any factual information, and it is unclear whether they mean "men" or transgender women (Fitzgerald 2016).

The overtly political nature of this campaign can be seen from a decision at a Republican National Committee strategy session in January 2016 (two months after the Houston vote) to press for similar bathroom legislation across the country (Johnson 2016). Legislation was introduced in a number of states, but it only passed in North Carolina, in response to a local ordinance in Charlotte that resembled HERO. In North Carolina, House Bill 2 not only removed local governments' ability to pass human rights ordinances but explicitly specified that bathroom access would only be permitted based on sex listed on birth certificates. The large-scale negative response of groups and businesses to HB2 may have cost North Carolina more than $3 billion in lost revenue (Dalesio and Drew 2017). This backlash may be linked to the narrowness of the Republican appeal to disgust and fear in localities such as Houston regarding transgender people, but also to a significant shift in acceptance toward LGBTQ people generally. In addition, transgender individuals and allies mustered a number of arguments against HB2. Such arguments point to the ways in which HB2's adherence to biological sex and not gender identity also unsettled transgender people in North Carolina. James Parker Sheffield, a transgender man, famously tweeted an image of himself as a self-proclaimed "grumpy hillbilly" with the words "It's now the law for me to share a restroom with your wife" with the goal of using the binary rhetoric to point out the ridiculousness of gendered restrooms. Additionally, he argued, "Often facilities are not laid out in a way where there is a choice of gender neutral space and it is unreasonable to think we (trans people) should just not be in those spaces" (Sheffield 2016). These sorts of arguments emphasize the importance of bathrooms and everyday inclusion of space for transgender people. Transgender activist Hunter Schafer explains that while the fight for bathroom equality matters, "the core issue is the deep-rooted transphobia that lies beneath." Schafer continues, "Transphobia resides at the heart of HB2, a bill which appeals to a public still clinging to the gender binary and fearful depictions of those who reside outside of it" (Schafer 2017). For such individuals, the perpetuated rhetoric of fear is notably political, and the gender binary reinforces a harmful stigma.

Nearly a year after the passing of the law, the NCAA announced that unless HB2 was changed, all college championship events would be moved out of North Carolina. Under this pressure, the state acted to adjust its legislation (NCAA 2016). On March 30, 2017, the portion of the bill regarding bathroom use based on gender assignment at birth was repealed and replaced by House Bill 142, which prohibits local government from passing nondiscrimination ordinances until 2020. While the NCAA lifted its ban, its officials noted that North Carolina had only "minimally achieved a situation where we believe the NCAA championships may be conducted in a nondiscriminatory environment" (NCAA 2017). It appears that public outrage and economic sanctions convinced the state legislature to soften HB2, but in some regard the matter is still unresolved. For example, transgender activist Lara Americo describes a continued fear for her own well-being and for other transgender people living in North Carolina even after the implementation of House Bill 142, stating that "transgender people are in even more danger now . . . Our state government made it clear that they put profit and sports ahead of our safety, and that mentality trickles down. We still don't have the protections we need—all we have is a spotlight on us" (Americo 2017). Such a mentality points to the effectiveness of the right-wing narrative against transgender individuals.

Ideas of social acceptability and protection of women and children also played into the HB2 debates. In favor of the bill were groups such as Mark Creech's Christian Action League, the NC Values Coalition, and Ron Baity's Return America. Both Creech and Baity are known for their inflammatory comments regarding the LGBTQ community.[1] In an opinion piece on the Christian Action League's website, Creech alluded to the sullied reputation of North Carolina by liberal news media calling out HB2 as bigoted. Instead, he argues, "the new law in North Carolina is not discriminatory" and claims that "the ordinance, barring all common sense, allowed an individual, regardless of his or her biological anatomy, to use any restroom, locker room, shower, or changing room, with whichever gender he or she subjectively identified. Such an ordinance created a loophole that sexual predators could exploit, making women and children vulnerable to situations of danger" (Creech 2016). Other groups, such as the Institute for Faith & Family, secured a six-figure advertising campaign railing against the repeal of HB2. In this broadcast, a concerned young woman claims, "I'm worried about the Charlotte bathroom ordinance . . . It's not just about privacy, it's safety, too. Charlotte's ordinance gives men access to what should be a very private place." The video goes on to say that "HB2 protects the safety and privacy of women and children in bathrooms and locker rooms" (Jarvis and Campbell 2016). Again, the rhetoric conflates trans women with men and perpetuates patriarchal notions of fear and safety for women. These discourses lend credence to male-female binarism, further naturalizing the idea that women are weak and men are dangerous.

Yet there is still some positive movement on the bathroom front, with some large municipalities adopting very progressive ordinances. At least for single-stall restrooms, many laws have been passed that allow for use based on gender identity, not sex at birth. Legislation in Seattle, Portland, Austin, Philadelphia, and New York City points to changing thoughts about bathroom use as well as increased gender acceptance. However, the vehemence of these debates in both these progressive cities and in states like Texas and North

Carolina demonstrate the caustic nature of binary conceptions of gender and how they play out, showing that further work must be done to push against these ideas and bring about equality in public space.

CONCLUSION

Bathrooms remain contested sites where social and political issues play out and are central to struggles over civil rights today. The rhetoric used by right-wing pundits during Houston's HERO and North Carolina's HB2 debates preyed upon the people's fears, depicting women and children as vulnerable and gender nonconforming and transgender people as predators. Although there is no evidence supporting this discourse, it is still powerful, and as argued by Ahmed (2004), it sticks to trans bodies as they navigate space in ways that lead to more gender policing and conflict. This discourse of fear serves patriarchal ends by positioning some men as protectors, paternalistically labeling women as needing protection, and denigrating transgender individuals as impostors in public space, as "gender-confused" and deviant. We argue that recent political and legislative focus on the perceived transgender threat and the upholding of bathroom access in accordance with assigned sex at birth instead of performed gender identity demonstrates a direct attempt to reinforce the gender binary.

Public narratives seeking to protect binary gender and maintain the bathroom status quo further reduce access to basic human rights for those not easily categorized. Adherence to rigidly binary politics has serious consequences for those who do not fit within narrowly dichotomous categories. In this chapter, we have explored current contestations over gender in space by focusing on popular debates regarding public bathrooms. It is possible that through more exploration of this topic, people's understanding of gender and transgender identities could change. Clearly, creating more gender-neutral toilet options is a useful step. However, this may not be sufficient, given the embedded bias in our patriarchal system against violators of gender normativity. Sheila Cavanaugh (2010, 5) suggests that more fundamental change is needed:

> The institutionalization of gender-neutral toilet designs is an urgent and important political project to ensure access for all who depart from conventional sex/gender body politics. But it is equally important to think creatively about how we may build gendered architectures that prompt

people to think about gender, sexed embodiment, desire, and our relations to others in new and ethical ways.

There is potential in conceptualizations of bathrooms that might yet cause disruption and challenges to patriarchal gendered sites. Yet the full solution is not yet clear, especially when gendered bathrooms continue to marginalize and keep people separate. Perhaps as Herman (2013) argues, the task of ameliorating harmful gendered space is within the purview of public policymakers and administrators to correct. For Spain (1992), it is women themselves who must be able to influence policy, planning, and architecture. By this logic it is necessary for transgendered individuals to more fully engage with these professions in order to dismantle the societal barriers that keep change from happening. There is no simple solution, but a critical first step is the need to deconstruct the ways that gender is considered as a binary and to examine the struggles of trans and gender-nonconforming individuals in space and public life. Once the weakness of this dichotomy has been recognized, the task of dismantling unequal access to bathrooms can be undertaken. Public toilets emerge as sites of visible power relations and social inequalities that continue to plague anyone who does not fit within the perceived gender norms (Faktor 2011; Plaskow 2008). They are public spaces in which misogyny plays a large role and benefits patriarchal interests while clearly harming nonnormative others, as well as gender-conforming individuals. It is necessary to look at the means of how gender has been formed and conceptualized (and continue to be thought about in the public imagination) in order to counter the negative impacts they have on human lives.

NOTES

1. In response to a federal court judge striking down a gay marriage ban in North Carolina, Baity preached against the blasphemy of such rulings, declaring: "You think Ebola is bad now, just wait. If it's not that, it's going to be something else. My friends, I want you to understand, you can't thumb your nose at God, and God turn his head away without God getting your attention" (Mazza 2014).

REFERENCES

Abel, Elizabeth. 1999. "Bathroom Doors and Drinking Fountains: Jim Crow's Racial Symbolic." *Critical Inquiry* 25 (3): 435–81.
Ahmed, Sara. 2004. *The Cultural Politics of Emotion.* Edinburgh: Edinburgh University Press.
Americo, Lara. 2017. "I'm a Trans Woman of Color, and I've Never Been More Scared to Live in North Carolina: Reflections on the State's Recent 'Compromise.' " *Mother Jones.* April

9, 2017. https://www.motherjones.com/politics/2017/04/im-trans-womancolor-north
-carolina-heres-how-hb20-affects-me/.

Anthony, Kathryn H., and Meghan Dufresne. 2007. "Potty Parity in Perspective: Gender and Family Issues in Planning and Designing Public Restrooms." *Journal of Planning Literature* 23 (3): 267–94.

Bender-Baird, Kyla. 2016. "Peeing under Surveillance: Bathrooms, Gender Policing, and Hate Violence." *Gender, Place, & Culture* 23 (7): 983–88.

Browne, Kath. 2004. "Genderism and the Bathroom Problem: (Re)Materialising Sexed Sites, (Re)Creating Sexed Bodies." *Gender, Place & Culture* 11 (3): 331–46.

Butler, Judith. 2006. *Gender Trouble: Feminism and the Subversion of Identity*. New York: Routledge.

Campaign for Houston. 2015. "Campaign for Houston TV commercial." Posted on October 12, 2015. YouTube video, 0:30. https://www.youtube.com/watch?v=WYpko86x6GU.

Castrodale, Mark A., and Laura Lane. 2015. "Finding One's Place to Be and Pee: Examining Intersections of Gender-Dis/ability in Washroom Signage." *Atlantis* 37 (1): 70–83.

Cavanaugh, Sheila. 2010. *Queering Bathrooms: Gender, Sexuality and the Hygienic Imagination*. Toronto: University of Toronto Press.

Cavanaugh, Sheila. 2012. "Response from the Author." *Gender, Place & Culture* 19 (4): 549–51.

Creech, Mark. 2016. "The Smearing of a State." *Christian Action League*. April 16, 2016. https://christianactionleague.org/news/the-smearing-of-a-state/.

Dalesio, Emery P., and Jonathan Drew. 2017. "Price Tag of North Carolina's LGBT Law $3.76B." Associated Press. March 27, 2017. https://www.apnews.com/fa4528580f3 e4a01bb68bcb272f1f0f8.

Doan, Petra. L. 2010. "The Tyranny of Gendered Spaces—Reflections from beyond the Gender Dichotomy." *Gender, Place & Culture* 17 (5): 635–54.

Faktor, Alex. 2011. "Access and Exclusion: Public Toilets as Sites of Insecurity for Gender and Sexual Minorities in North America." *Journal of Human Security* 7 (3): 10–22.

Fitzgerald, Erin. 2016. "A Comprehensive Guide to the Debunked 'Bathroom Predator' Myth: Here's The Evidence Refuting the Myth about Trans-Inclusive Bathrooms." *Media Matters for America*. Blog post, May 5, 2016. https://www.mediamatters.org/sexual
-harassment-sexual-assault/comprehensive-guide-debunked-bathroom-predator-myth.

Gershenson, Olga, and Barbara Penner (eds.). 2009. *Ladies and Gents: Public Toilets and Gender*. Philadelphia: Temple University Press.

Gökarıksel, Banu, and Sara Smith. 2016. "Making America Great Again?: The Fascist Body Politics of Donald Trump." *Political Geography* 54: 79–81.

Gökarıksel, Banu, and Sara Smith. 2017. "Intersectional Feminism beyond U.S. Flag Hijab and Pussy Hats in Trump's America." *Gender, Place & Culture* 24 (5): 628–44.

Grant, Jamie M., Lisa A. Mottet, Justin Tanis, Jack Harrison, Jody L. Herman, and Mara Keisling. 2011. *Injustice at Every Turn: A Report of the National Transgender Discrimination Survey*. Washington, DC: National Center for Transgender Equality and National Gay and Lesbian Task Force.

Greed, Clara. 1995. "Public Toilet Provision for Women in Britain: An Investigation of Discrimination Against Urination." *Women's Studies International Forum* 18 (5/6): 573–84.

Greed, Clara. 2016. "Taking Women's Bodily Functions into Account in Urban Planning and Policy: Public Toilets and Menstruation." *The Town Planning Review* 87 (5): 505–24.

Herman, Jody L. 2013. "Gendered Restrooms and Minority Stress: The Public Regulation of Gender and Its Impact on Transgender People's Lives." *Journal of Public Management & Social Policy* 19 (1): 65–80.

Hines, Sally. 2010. "Queerly Situated? Exploring Negotiations of Trans Queer Subjectivities at Work and within Community Spaces in the UK." *Gender, Place & Culture* 17: 597–613.

Human Rights Campaign. 2016. *Unprecedented Onslaught of State Legislation Targeting*

Transgender Americans. https://www.hrc.org/resources/unprecedented-onslaught-of
-state-legislation-targeting-transgender-american.

Jarvis, Craig, and Colin Campbell. 2016. "Religious Group Launches Pro-HB2 TV Ad Drive."
News & Observer. October 6, 2016. http://www.newsobserver.com/news/politics
-government/politics-columns-blogs/under-the-dome/article106149197.html.

Jeffreys, Sheila. 2014. "The Politics of the Toilet: A Feminist Response to the Campaign to
'Degender' a Women's Space." *Women's Studies International Forum* 45: 42–51.

Johnson, Chris. 2016. "RNC Endorses Anti-Trans Bathroom Bills." *Washington Blade.*
February 25, 2016. http://www.washingtonblade.com/2016/02/25/rnc-approves-anti
-trans-resolution/.

Kogan, Terry S. 2010. "Sex Separation: The Cure-All for Victorian Social Anxiety." In *Toilet:
Public Restrooms and the Politics of Sharing,* edited by Harvey Molotch and Lauren Noren,
145–64. New York: New York University Press.

Lucal, Betsy. 1999. "What It Means to Be Gendered Me: Life on the Boundaries of a
Dichotomous Gender System." *Gender and Society* 13 (6): 781–97.

Mazza, Ed. 2014. "Ron Baity, Baptist Preacher, Claims God Will Send Something Worse Than
Ebola as Punishment for Gay Marriage." *Huffington Post.* October 15, 2014. https://
www.huffpost.com/entry/ron-baity-ebola-gay-marriage_n_5987210.

Molotch, Harvey. 2010. "Learning from the Loo." In *Toilet: Public Restrooms and the Politics of
Sharing,* edited by Harvey Molotch and Lauren Noren, 1–20. New York: New York
University Press.

Moyer, Justin W. 2015. "Why Houston's Gay Rights Ordinance Failed: Fear of Men in
Women's Bathrooms." *Washington Post.* November 4, 2015. https://www
.washingtonpost.com/news/morning-mix/wp/2015/11/03/why-houstons-gay-rights
-ordinance-failed-bathrooms.

National Collegiate Athletic Association (NCAA). 2016. "NCAA to Relocate Championships
from North Carolina for 2016–2017." NCAA. September 12, 2016. http://www.ncaa
.org/about/resources/media-center/news/ncaa-relocate-championships-north-carolina
-2016-17.

National Collegiate Athletic Association (NCAA). 2017. "NCAA Board of Governors' Position
on HB2 repeal." NCAA. April 4, 2017. http://www.ncaa.org/about/resources/media
-center/news/ncaa-board-governors-position-hb2-repeal.

Nemoto, Tooroo, Don Operario, JoAnne Keatley, Hongmai Nguyen, and Elko Sugano. 2005.
"Promoting Health for Transgender Women: Transgender Resources and Neighborhood
Space (TRANS) Program in San Francisco." *American Journal of Public Health* 95 (3):
382–84.

Nirta, Caterina. 2014. "Trans Subjectivity and the Spatial Monolingualism of Public Toilets."
Law Critique 25: 271–88.

Oswin, Natalie. 2008. "Critical Geographies and the Uses of Sexuality: Deconstructing Queer
Space." *Progress in Human Geography* 32 (1): 89–103.

Plaskow, Judith. 2008. "Embodiment, Elimination, and the Role of Toilets in Struggles for
Social Justice." *Crosscurrents: The Journal of the Association for Religion and Intellectual
Life* 58 (1): 51–64.

Quinn, Dan. 2015. "Houston Hate-Monger Steve Hotze: Transgender People Are Promoting a
'Satanic Movement.' " *Texas Freedom Network.* December 17, 2015. http://tfn.org
/houston-hate-monger-steve-hotze-transgender-people-are-promoting-a-satanic
-movement/.

Samek, Alyssa. 2016. "Marginalizing the Queer Vote Post-Marriage: The Challenges of
Visibility." *Women's Studies in Communication* 39 (4): 361–65.

Schafer, Hunter. 2017. "Trans Activist Hunter Schafer on Why She's Fighting for Much More
Than Bathrooms." *iD:Vice.* March 31, 2017. https://id.vice.com/en_us/article/43wwzq
/trans-activist-hunter-schafer-on-why-shes-fighting-for-much-more-than-bathrooms.

Sheffield, J. P. 2016. "Civilities: The ACLU, GLAAD, and a Trans Man Talk about NC's Sweeping Anti-LGBT Law." *Washington Post*. March 29, 2016. https://live .washingtonpost.com/civilities-with-steven-petrow-20160329.html.

Spain, Daphne. 1992. *Gendered Spaces*. Chapel Hill: University of North Carolina Press.

Spain, Daphne. 2014. "Gender and Urban Space." *Annual Review of Sociology* 40: 581–98.

Stone, Clarence. 1993. "Urban Regimes and the Capacity to Govern: A Political Economy Approach." *Journal of Urban Affairs* 13 (1): 1–28.

Szczerbinski, Katherine. 2016. "Education Connection: The Importance of Allowing Students to Use Bathrooms and Locker Rooms Reflecting Their Gender Identity." *Children's Legal Rights Journal* 36 (3): 153–55.

Weinberg, Jill D. 2010. "Transgender Bathroom Usage: A Privileging of Biology and Physical Difference in the Law." *Buffalo Journal of Gender, Law & Social Policy* 18: 147–56.

Westbrook, Laurel, and Kristen Schilt. 2014. "Doing Gender, Determining Gender: Transgender People, Gender Panics, and the Maintenance of the Sex/Gender/Sexuality System." *Gender & Society* 28 (1): 32–57.

INTERVIEW WITH KUMARINI SILVA, OCTOBER 2018

Editors: In your opening remarks at the 2017 Feminist Geography Conference, you spoke of how popular feminist movements—at the time represented by the Women's March, pink pussy hats, Pantsuit Nation, and the Day Without Women—potentially depoliticize feminism, flattening its complexities for a comfortable white femininity. Since the conference, we have witnessed this popular feminism emerge as a key point of resistance to masculinist politics, manifesting in forms of political organizing ranging from the #MeToo movement to a record number of women running for political office. Do you see these recent movements continuing the "comfort feminism" you spoke of—with a desire for quick solutions and swift change—or are there stirrings of more complex interventions in this activism? How do you see the role of the feminist killjoy within these popular feminist movements? What does "breathing in the spaces that cause us discomfort" mean to you in this particular moment?

Silva: It seems so long ago that I was upset with the Women's March and pink pussy hats because there is so much more to be upset about now! But I'll start there as a way to answer the question: I certainly was not the first person to point out that the Women's March was white-feminist-centric, but I had my own reasons for reaching that conclusion. At the conference, I shared that for those of us who grew up in the tropics, and therefore were never taught to knit (why would we, when the temperatures hover around eighty-eight all year round?), those of us whose vaginas aren't various hues of pink, or those who don't have vaginas but identify as women were left out of that conversation even though we were and continue to be among the most vulnerable since the 2016 elections. Racially othered bodies are essentialized through originary geographies that we are never able to leave behind, so the knitting communities, the pink color, the exchange of knitted hats between (largely white) women were intense moments of alienation for many of us who couldn't participate in that kind of community building. While the march was well intentioned, and I'm not denying that, for me it highlighted how a one-size-fits-all feminism—one that is represented by objects and corresponding subjects of an appropriately comfortable anger—is the default mode of mainstream feminist politics in the United States. This comfortable anger, devoid of nuance, is what I identified as "comfort feminism." The way that hat, and its anatomical specificity, was seen as such a transgressive act exemplifies the ways that we become caught up in the moment of generalizable inequality without moving to the structural or the systemic in any meaningful way. And I do see, to some extent, the same thing happening with the #MeToo movement, but it's more complicated than the comfort feminism of the Women's March. There is no way that we would have uncovered the political machinations of or seen the fragility of the US judicial system without the popularity of the #MeToo movement. And to know that is invaluable for social justice movements moving forward. At the same time, I have tremendous reservations about the confessional mode of #MeToo, especially the one popularized by the actor Alyssa Milano. Much like the symbolism and shared meaning of the hat, when Milano mainstreamed Tarana Burke's decades-long work with the hashtag, there was an unspoken expectation that every good feminist would share their own #MeToo story on social media or, failing that, would at least write #MeToo in their feed. This expectation of public confessionals, much like the pink pussy hats, assumes a particular ethos of shared participation. But, again, we all come from different places/cultures/spaces where such public confessions are complicated and tied to geographies that have different storytelling practices than the public confessional mode from which (largely) white women tell their stories.

But, in spite of these reservations, I do acknowledge that the movement has been remarkable in calling attention to the myriad ways violence is practiced and perpetuated. We saw that most recently in the Brett Kavanaugh Supreme Court nomination hearings in September 2018. That kind of public outcry (regardless of the outcome) would never have happened without the #MeToo movement. I don't know if I can actually comment on the role of feminist killjoy in these movements, because I could never do justice to the beautiful complexity of that term coined by Sara Ahmed. But I do think criticism is necessary for the success of any social justice movement, even if we support them, and even when we don't have solutions to the problems we're identifying. So often we are unwilling to call out problems because we feel that we should produce a solution alongside the problem, but I've become increasingly comfortable also sitting in the discomfort of not having some perfect solution, and recognizing that the longer I sit with that discomfort, the more clarity I have about the problem I'm grappling with. I think capitalist democracies tells us that if we identify a problem that is getting in the way of productivity, we must fix it immediately and move onto the next problem. It's such hubris. We all buy into this fiction even if we absolutely know it's false. I've started realizing that everything can't be fixed immediately, but that speaking the problem gets started toward some sort of productive action.

Editors: Similarly, you have spoken of how these popular movements are characterized by a "misguided patriotism" animated by nationalist discourses that position women-as-nation. How do these discourses serve as a form of gatekeeping in these popular movements? How does such a misguided patriotism work to obscure historical relations of trauma in service to comfort feminism?

Silva: In her essay "Mama's Baby, Papa's Maybe: An American Grammar Book," Hortense Spillers writes that " 'family,' as we practice and understand it 'in the West'—the vertical transfer of a bloodline, of a patronymic, of titles and entitlements, of real estate and the prerogatives of 'cold cash,' from fathers to sons and in the supposedly free exchange of affectional ties between a male and a female of his choice—becomes the mythically revered privilege of a free and freed community" (Spillers 1987, 74). For me, this summarizes beautifully what I think you are asking here. Women's labor and identity, whether black or white or any other racialized, essentialized category, has always been in the service of a white patriarchy. Because our societies are organized around maintaining the supremacy of this white heterosexual patriarchy, it obscures the ways that its specter looms over even our organizing, protests, activisms, and collaboration. And that specter makes some of us more complacent and more willing to try and find a "comfortable" middle ground from which to speak back. But that's a very privileged position, and one that rarely gets results for those who are more vulnerable or on the margins. While I do know that there are women in these privileged positions who do, there are still many more who feel like it's not really affecting them or their families right this minute, so there's no need to "get involved" beyond casting a vote or signing an online petition.

Editors: Your participation in the 2017 conference was only possible because the Trump Administration's travel ban made international travel perilous for you and your family. This same ban prevented several registrants from attending the conference. In the time since the conference, crossing the United States border has only become more difficult and dangerous for people of color. In your book *Brown Threat: Identification in the Security State*, you discussed how the post-9/11 security state worked to identify the brown body as a threat to the nation and responded with efforts to confine, contain, and keep the border ever present in the lives of anyone deemed threatening to the United States. Since the election of Donald Trump and the implementation of these travel bans, how have these practices changed? What discourses about the nation are emerging in these travel bans and the increasing securitization of brown bodies, and how can feminists respond?

Silva: A lot of what I talked about in the book has intensified and become more widespread since the elections in 2016. White supremacy and its political and social manifestations are no longer covert or at the margins, but front and center masquerading as patriotism. One of the recent headlines (in fall 2018, at the time I'm doing this interview) is the president's desire to challenge the Fourteenth Amendment and intervene in birthright citizenship. Every reasonable person knows that this is actually impossible to do through an executive order as he claims he can; it's not as simple as dismissing his racist naiveté but recognizing the significance in his desire to create a "nationalist" space. And senators like Lindsey Graham support him. At the same time that this is in the news, a caravan of immigrants is moving toward the US–Mexican border, and the president has deployed more than seven thousand soldiers to that border, claiming that the migrants (who are fleeing violence, poverty, and death) are "invading" the United States. Those are just two examples of where we are today. And these are indeed feminist issues— biopolitics always are. I think feminists can respond by demanding justice and being allies or reaching out to allies, not just in larger national movements (though that is important, too) but also within their own communities. I'm lucky enough to live in a town (Durham, North Carolina) that has this kind of intersectional, diverse, and yet somehow convergent feminist community that is really amazing and makes one feel secure. I wish that for everybody.

Editors: Your own background in communication and cultural studies has spanned a wide range of interests, from your work on securitization for *Brown Threat* to research on Sri Lankan romance novels. What are the threads from feminist theory that connect your projects? What emerging themes in feminist studies broadly do you find most animating in this moment? And how has your engagement with feminist geography and geographers shaped your unfolding work?

Silva: While researching for and writing *Brown Threat,* I decided that my next book was going to be something that was a little less visceral and didn't unfold in real time. I started working on this manuscript about the global circulation of romance novels, and the ways that they functioned as social disciplining in postcolonial spaces. But, since 2016, I've seen a much stronger connection between the work started in *Brown Threat* and the more explicit feminist focus of the romance work. Because of this, I've started thinking through the term "love-cruelty" that I started presenting and publishing on more recently. I use the term to describe how affective relationships animate regulatory practices that are deeply cruel and alienating under the guise of love. While the overall project looks at different manifestations of this—migration, denaturalization, containment, and the carceral state—I also extend love-cruelty to the #MeToo movement and popular narratives of romantic love, mapping the dysfunctional relationship between love, violence, and coercion. I turn to popular narratives of heterosexual romance—like *Beauty and the Beast* and romance novels from companies like Harlequin and Mills and Boon—and connect it to the #MeToo movement to argue that love, violence, and coercion are institutionalized on an everyday romantic level to bolster the politics of patriarchy, race making, and social disciplining. What I'm (re)turning to, in this project, and for pleasure and sustenance during these times are the writings and work of feminists of color. I think the resurgence of black feminist theory in the academy and beyond is a good indication of the kinds of struggles we are facing right now, their deeply historical roots, and whose voices are able to articulate that history while also directing us toward a more just future. There is so much value to (re)reading the work of people like Hortense Spillers and Christina Sharpe to understand how and why we are where we are today. Because they always frame their sociopolitical observations through movement, geography, and space, their work spans the breadth of history but is also deeply embodied and personal. I find a similar resonance in the work of feminist geographers. I am especially appreciative of the ways that feminist geographers extend that relationship between space and embodiment to understand politics and political activism. It's the kind of nuanced feminism we need right now, and I'm immensely grateful that it exists both as an area of study and also as a community of scholars.

REFERENCES

Silva, Kumarini. 2016. *Brown Threat: Identification in the Security State*. Minneapolis: University of Minnesota Press.

Spillers, Hortense. 1987. "Mama's Baby, Papa's Maybe: An American Grammar Book." *Diacritics* (17) 2: 64–81.

PART II

GENDERED BODIES AS A TERRAIN OF POLITICAL STRUGGLE

"REAL" AND "MYTHICAL" BODIES WEAVING SOCIAL SKIN: TWO WAORANI WOMEN DISRUPTING GENRES OF AMAZONIAN HUMANITY

Gabriela Valdivia, Kati Álvarez, Alicia Weya Cawiya, Manuela Ima Omene, Dayuma Albán, and Flora Lu

INTRODUCTION

I recommend to women of color in the US that we learn to love each other by learning to travel to each other's "worlds."
—Maria Lugones (1987, 4)

Alicia Weya Cawiya and Manuela Omari Ima Omene, two well-established Waorani leaders from the Ecuadorian Amazon, attended the Feminist Geography Conference (FemGeog) at the University of North Carolina at Chapel Hill in May 2017 to speak about the Waorani of Ecuador. Along with Ecuadorian scholars and activists Kati Álvarez and Dayuma Albán, who brokered Alicia and Manuela's visit, they participated in a panel organized by Flora Lu and Gabriela Valdivia that was sponsored by a National Science Foundation–funded collaborative project on oil and citizenship in Ecuador. Alicia and Manuela's visit to North Carolina and our collective participation in the conference was an opportunity to speak to a global audience about the injustices that the Waorani face.

In this chapter, we outline some of the lessons learned from how our engagement at FemGeog mediated Alicia and Manuela's effort to make Waorani humanity legible to non-Waorani (*cowori* in Waotededo). We claim that our bodies and embodiments became a "social skin" (Turner [1980] 2012) or common language for translating our humanity to each other, "partially connecting" (Strathern 2004) Waorani and non-Waorani worlds and experiences. Turner introduces the term "social skin" to describe how the Kayapó of Brazil manifest subject formation and socialization through bodily expression and adornment, covering themselves in a metaphorical fabric of social meanings and signifiers. He proposes that the surface of the body works as a biological *and* psychological boundary for communicating personhood among and within kin and community. Conventionalized modifications of the body can signal diverse categories of *being human*, for example, marriage, leadership, seniority, age, or sex. Other Amazonian scholars refer to similar processes as the "interpenetration of essences," as identities and experiences connect and form collectivities through the form and language of bodies (Seeger, da Matta, and Viveiros de Castro 1979). While Turner was concerned with tracing the social skins that make personhood legible within a group, we bring together our voices—as academics, activists, and allies—to extend this idea to examine how social skin stretches to connect across Waorani and *cowori* worlds, albeit imperfectly.

Our first lesson is that our weaving of social skin was simultaneously a work *of* and *about* translation. Weaving social skin together at times meant subsuming another's world into our own—interpreting and staging each other within our own worlds. Alicia and Manuela represented the Waorani using cultural and symbolic capital that connected an international audience to their communities. Kati, Dayuma, Gabriela, and Flora participated in this extension of Waorani social skin, sometimes explicitly interpreting Waorani language, clothing, and performance and thus weaving our personal social skin to Waorani worlds. However, our mutual translations had uneven seams, and we cannot claim to *know* each other's worlds. Despite numerous experiences together over the years, our extended social skin bunches up and gathers. Unevenness shapes our extended skin, challenging us to write and rewrite about how we weave—and translate—together. As this chapter demonstrates, our common experience of FemGeog is alive with vibrations that make us feel strange within our own skins.

Second, the social skin that we weave together is imperfect. We might not share the same territories, political horizons, intellectual projects, or feminist approaches, but participating in FemGeog allowed us to share a common project of wishing to make Waorani humanity legible in *cowori* spaces. At times, we narrate our experiences using an ethnographic lens to document what we do, where, and how. As Viveiros de Castro writes, ethnography is translation: "To translate is to situate oneself in the space of the equivocation and to dwell there; it is to communicate by differences" (2013, 7). This might make it look like we speak in a single theoretical voice, which facilitates academic comprehension. At other times, we highlight the uneven seams of this social skin. We make these "duplex" approaches (Strathern 2005) explicit in the constitution of this chapter. At FemGeog (and in this chapter), Kati, Dayuma, Flora, and Gabriela, as ecologists, anthropologists, and geographers, offered a background *about* the Waorani because they thought it necessary to persuade *cowori* to recognize Waorani worlds. They also refused to curate Alicia and Manuela's contributions, which appear in this chapter as they were offered at FemGeog, translated and lightly edited. Kati, Dayuma, Flora, and Gabriela then translate Manuela and Alicia's worlds into *cowori* terms. This duplex practice aims to make translation work strange so that we see each other as (in)dependent selves "grafting" (Lugones 1987) ourselves onto each other to make an imperfect, bunched-up, misaligned social skin.

Finally, weaving social skins together to communicate Waorani humanity requires dwelling in equivocation. We use the term "Waorani humanity" in the sense that Alexander Weheliye (2014) suggests: to see people not as objects of study (ready to be mapped and consumed as knowledge) but for the ways in which their struggles to maintain and protect socialities can disrupt the categories of their subjection. We struggle with the realization that seeing our humanity at moments involves objectifying each other—subjects subjecting each other in order to make us knowable to the collective. For example, Alicia and Manuela sometimes appear to perform an "Indigenous role" to capture the interest of an international *cowori* audience; they travel to *cowori* worlds, in the sense that Lugones (1987) proposes. Kati, Dayuma, Flora, and Gabriela also traveled, experiencing and interpreting them without fully knowing Waorani humanity. At other times, Alicia and Manuela moved between worlds and categories, defying a divided *cowori* and Waorani humanity, and inviting us to see them as traveling subjects, even when subjected.

We speak from these lessons to examine how Alicia and Manuela's visit disrupted both Amazonian genres and the (feminist) *cowori*. The next section follows two methods of translation. First, we narrate a brief political economy of Waorani territorial transformations and settlement. Then, Gabriela, Kati, Dayuma, and Flora weave together scholarly advocate worlds with Alicia and Manuela's presentations at FemGeog to make the conditions of Waorani humanity legible in *cowori* terms. The subsequent section uses an event ethnography approach to explore how Alicia and Manuela embodied different forms of being Waorani—a movement we propose engages "real" and "mythical" bodies through which they (partially) interrupted being contained by hegemonic *cowori* codes of Indigeneity. We conclude with observations on how these exercises in translation are futile but necessary. We work with imperfect collective social skin if only for its potential to produce an *other-politics* that accommodates "relations among divergent worlds as a decolonial practice . . . with no other guarantee than the absence of ontological sameness" (de la Cadena 2015, 281).

WAORANI TRANSLATIONS

The Waorani are a Native Amazonian group from northeastern Ecuador, renowned for their hunting prowess and ecological knowledge, and whose territory encompasses one of the most biodiverse forests in the world. According to the 2010 national census, there are approximately 2,462 Waorani living in fifty-two communities distributed in three Amazonian provinces: Napo, Pastaza, and Orellana. Many of these villages lie along navigable rivers. Some are alongside roads while others are more distant, accessible only by foot or landing strip. The total number of villages changes often, due to abandonment and fission, reflecting a traditional Waorani seminomadic settlement pattern. However, communities are increasingly sedentary due to state and corporate provisioning of services, infrastructure, and resources, which vary significantly.

Waorani life and social reproduction changed drastically in the twentieth century (Albán 2015; Álvarez 2009). In the 1930s, Waorani territory included 20,000 km^2 and was home to approximately 500 Waoranis. In the 1950s, Protestant missionaries, invited by the Ecuadorian state, urged the Waorani to move into a much smaller Protectorate on the western edge of their territory. By the 1970s, sustained peaceful contact was established, and many families agreed to relocate and convert to Christianity, though many also fled the Protectorate to return to their original territories. Many of these returning families found their previous territory already settled by agricultural colonists, oil companies, loggers, and other Amazonian peoples. Waorani families who refused to accept missionaries and the Ecuadorian state in their lives relocated deep into the forest, becoming peoples living in voluntary isolation. The Tagaeri and Taromenane, some of whom are believed to be related to the Waorani, are among these.

Throughout the twentieth century, roads for petroleum exploration and extraction opened up Waorani territory to settlers, who caused deforestation and defaunation, and to loggers, who changed forest community structure. The Auca Road, Pompeya-Iro Road, and a recently opened road close to oil block 33 (also known as the ITT block) fracture Waorani territory. Today, oil activity exists within and outside of Waorani communities, undermining subsistence activities, promoting integration into the market, and transforming Waorani worlds (Albán 2017; Lu 2007). Pipelines and wells are ubiquitous, sometimes adjacent to schools and homes. In addition, Western commodities such as alcohol, cell phones, television, and rifles have changed the lives of many Waorani (Lu 2007; Lu et al. 2016).

Biodiversity conservation also reorganized Waorani territory and lifeways (Holt 2005). In 1979, the Ecuadorian government declared more than one million hectares from Waorani territory as the Yasuní National Park (YNP), and in 1989 UNESCO recognized the park as a Man and Biosphere Reserve. In 1990, the Ecuadorian government reduced the size of YNP in order to permit oil extraction, and two years later enlarged the YNP to its current size and shape and created the Waorani Ethnic Reserve, covering 679,220 hectares. In 2007, under pressure from Indigenous and conservation organizations, the Ecuadorian government established the Intangible Zone Tagaeri and Taromenane, with 758,000 hectares.

Alicia and Manuela's lives are bound to these territorial and cultural shifts. They are both from worlds of settled Waorani, which means they were born into and continue to live a history of pacification, conversion, sedentarization, and extraction. Their lives are shaped by state-created categorizations of Waorani land (as reserves, parks, biospheres) and the categories of humanity associated with these: settled Waorani, Waorani in voluntary isolation, and *cowori*. Both have childhood memories of living under missionary influence while also feeling connected to their grandparents through living together as kin, or "shared substance" (Rival 2005) as a *nanicabo* (intergenerational family house). And both deeply value alliances beyond their *nanicabo*, though they weave these into their leadership positions in distinct ways. Next, we include translated transcription of their presentations at FemGeog, where they elaborate on how their own lives have unfolded between Waorani worldviews and *cowori*-led transformations.

Alicia: Strengthening Our Voices

My name in Waorani is Alicia Weya Cawiya and I am a Waorani woman from the Ecuadorian Amazon. My territory used to be between the Napo River and the Curaray River. It was an immense territory; the Waorani were happy, lived well, and they enjoyed the territory freely, without contamination. This forest was intact so that we could have energy and be strong. Without the roads, the Waorani way of life was very happy. The Taromenani also were happy with this territory we had; also the birds, the animals, the forest of the Waorani was better. Without these roads, we lived well. Later on, the oil companies came to destroy our forest, our medicines, our way of life. To destroy with the contamination of the rivers, too. We are born from this forest and we are living these changes today.

Oil companies entered this territory to take out oil without consulting us, without prior informed consent from the communities. When the oil company entered, it destroyed the forest, the things that were sacred: our pathways, the spirits we have; we have the spirit of the jaguar. They do not respect this forest and they leave us large platforms instead. The Waorani way of life is now sickness, new illnesses.

In this forest, we used to have pure air. When the oil company arrives, it leaves us a large flare in the forest. How are we going to breathe? The ants that we consume, ants that we eat, those ants die in the fire. The jaguars have to step on the mud and they will die. The birds, guacamayos, and these feathers that I am wearing, they are in danger, because all birds are contaminated. We are worried that this territory used to be healthy but now that we have platforms, and the contamination of land and water, the water that comes from upstream. And our Taromenani and Tagaeri brothers that live deep in the forest are also in danger, because they are consuming this water.

And this river also goes downstream. The children, because they are expert forest children, our children, our families, we all bathe in the river. Even just getting into the water, fungus appears on the skin from this contaminated water. Too much sickness has come with this oil, and the Waorani have not benefited from this. It is killing Waorani way of life; our life used to be better before.

In this forest, you see small houses. These are the Taromenani. They live deep inside, in the Yasuní National Park and in Waorani territory, and in the intangible zone that is inside the Waorani territory. But they are also living from the same forest, from the contamination of rivers. When it rains, the contamination goes downriver; they drink this water and they can die. The Taromenani are at risk. This is why Waorani women are defending the forest, so that our children and the Taromenani can live. In the future, they are going to suffer. Maybe tomorrow we won't be at the frontlines, but they are going to suffer from those contaminated waters, those waters going through the Amazon and the Yasuní.

We have founded, along with other Indigenous nationalities, a voice to face the state and the politicians, so that they can hear the voice of the women from the forest. We are the living forest. We take care of the forest, we maintain this forest of the wise jaguar and of the sacred lakes. We take care of it as the Waorani. But the government does not listen to us. This is why we have come together. We have left the Amazon, trekked to Quito, so that they respect our right as a people that are living. Our Waorani comrades have protested the oil company Petrobell, against a road built next to our communities, where we live. But they were put in jail because they protested. In the Indigenous world, we are not used to being punished with jail. It is our right, this is our house. We have placed a complaint against the oil company. They have not respected our rights as a people. We are aboriginal people. We are ancestral people living in this forest. Now we give our voices of women to the world, because the Yasuní forest is not only for our children. We are giving the Yasuní forest to the world, so that humanity can have it, so that it can serve to save the world.

We take care of the forest and are sharing this message so that you can understand. This is our house. We want oil companies and logging companies to respect us because this is our house. Our grandparents left this forest for us. This is my message. You are welcome to come visit our forest. See with your own eyes so that you can understand that our forest is very old. My grand-parents fought to defend this forest for many years. It made me angry that in this forest, this sacred place of mine, where my grandfather is buried, when the roads came, they threw away my grandfather's body! This made me mad and I said, "No! This is where the oil companies need to stop. This is my house and they need to respect it." This is why the women have come together, to defend our right as Waorani. With his spear, my grandfather defended. But us women, with our voices, we defend so that future generations of Waorani and the world, can have the Yasuní forest. Thank you.

Manuela: Strengthening Our Sharing Economies

Hello! Wake up! I am here!

My name is Manuela Ima and I am happy to be here. As women, we have to be strong and defend and fight! I would love to be able to speak in my language, but if I do, you will not understand me. We have to be strong women. We have to fight next to the men and fight for the future. We have life from the water, land, and air. These are all important. We are kin and human beings.

Today you are going to hear about many things that my Waorani relatives have said. First, we are Waorani, and we have Waorani chocolate. It is called *wao*! We have a store in Puyo. You have to come; the purpose of our store is to strengthen Waorani culture. We also are working. We are the association of Waorani women (AMWAE), which we created in 2005. This was very difficult because it was hard to understand Spanish. We speak Waoterero. But thanks to God, we also learned Spanish. This is us, the first women trained. My mother, my aunt, my sisters—we are all fighters. It is very important to hear Waorani, to understand Waorani, to know what happens in the forest. This is where we started. We train women.

A long time ago, it was typical for Waorani men to go hunt with a blowgun. But now they have learned to kill with a shotgun. They go hunting, searching. Women also go hunting and foraging. But it worries us because it is different. Women are strengthening the management of the Waorani culture, through weaving and Waorani chocolate. This is what we are doing to strengthen the Waorani community. A long time ago, we always took care of the forest. But now we are here to tell you what is happening. There were no roads before. There was nothing before and the Waorani took care of the forest. But when the roads came and entered the three provinces of the Amazon, they saw that the Indigenous peoples were there. So outsiders tried to negotiate how they could get animal meat. The Waorani were hunters, not agriculturalists, and they didn't negotiate meat. But later they saw and learned, and their friends taught them, and they learned how to sell and negotiate meat in the market. So the Waorani negotiated. But one day we said, "You can't do this! This is our family, you have to keep the forest for your children." One day we talked and decided it is not possible to negotiate anymore. No more! I am talking about this very quickly because it is important to the topic of handicrafts and chocolates. These things will strengthen us. This is going to be education, this is going to be health; everybody will benefit from this, not just a few. This is why I am so happy to be here. To take care of the future, of what we have for the future.

Since 2005, we have a store in Coca, province of Orellana, a small store. We go to the communities and train women. We teach them about our culture and how to do tourism for the communities. We have strengthened through the Waorani store. The Waorani are in three big provinces, we need stores in these. It is very important to maintain the culture; to keep the communities together to continue maintaining the culture. To have a guide that serves them.

We train women in different forms of weaving: colorful bands, earrings, hammocks, bracelets, all sorts of things. The Waorani look for the natural fiber. We have brought these with us here. As you can see, I am dressed in chambira. I need to bring something back because this is going to serve the schools. This is strengthening the children. This is very important to me because we are improving ourselves.

The women come from each of their communities to be trained, in their own language, to continue working in their own communities. Women that come from the forest are teaching how to manage the natural fiber. They manage the seeds, the leaves, the roots. How to use the different natural colors. This is all very important to me because they teach us when we observe them. One day, when we look for them and they are gone, we can make these things. They are teaching the children and grandchildren. These fibers of different colors are very important to us, to maintain our own culture and to continue learning.

We work with chocolate, from the Yasuní. Some people live deep in the forest and it is difficult for them to come outside. So we go into these communities and teach them how to strengthen their education. We go outside searching for opportunities, in the market, to sell their products. Then, we return to these communities with what we were able to gather. We also search for small foundations or small stores, or weekend fairs. This is why I am here. Even when small things are bought, they are very grateful. I am happy that even if it is small, this is a way to strengthen my people.

We also do reforestation projects. When a woman plants the seeds, the plant grows and helps her children. This is good wood. The same with cacao. The woman needs to manage the cacao: keep the land clean, dry the cacao, and ferment it. We are teaching women how to do this so that when the seed is ready, it can serve the community. Also the chambira plant; the women are working together with the weavings to work with the communities. We won a prize in New York; the Waorani chocolate won a prize from the United Nations. There were twenty-five projects sponsored. We competed and only four won; we were one of these. The Waorani community was very happy. When I presented this information to them, they were happy and said that we would continue doing this, helping, sowing, and strengthening our family. We will continue sowing seeds and growing, like you. We are sowing the future. It is important that you continue visiting us and continue fighting with us. Thank you for inviting me. Let's be together until we are no longer. Now I would like to sing a song that serves to strengthen our spirit, the women, and nature. We are all going to sing now, because I am here.

COWORI RECOGNITION

At FemGeog, Alicia and Manuela translated their respective fights into a language that *cowori* can understand, as Manuela explained. In this section, Kati, Dayuma, Flora, and Gabriela weave *cowori* interpretations into Alicia and Manuela's work. Alicia became politically active at the age of thirteen, inspired by her grandmother, who told her that men and women should fight together in the struggle to keep oil companies away from their territory. Alicia's political personhood flourished through her connections with environmental organizations, within and beyond Ecuador, particularly through her fight against the presence of oil companies in the YNP. In 2005, with other community leaders, she founded the Association of Waorani Women of Ecuador (AMWAE for its acronym in Spanish), recognized by the Ecuadorian state through Decree 825 of the National Council of Women (CONAMU). For Alicia, territory is necessary to preserve Waorani humanity, as it allows people to "freely collect for life, not with money . . . we need the forest to live freely . . . not to be caged within a territory" (Vera 2013). Alicia is often portrayed as an Indigenous woman who fights the "oil patriarchy" (Etchart 2017) and self-identifies as a *lidereza* (woman leader) (Eco Amazónico 2014). Alicia also acknowledges the trade-offs of this political activism; *liderezas* often have to leave their communities, families, and children (some choosing not to have children) and move to urban areas, or travel internationally to represent the Waorani.

At the core of Alicia's claims as a leader is the demand for an ethic of reciprocity with the Ecuadorian state. For her, there is a rupture in the social skin between the Waorani and the Ecuadorian state, as the state denies the Waorani their full humanity by hollowing out their ability to thrive. In her presentation at FemGeog, Alicia told of a relationship of neglect and exploitation by the Ecuadorian state, where the state takes from the original free peoples, the Waorani, without giving back (e.g., the state has not compensated for loss of life, the contamination of water, the reduction of territory, or the dislocation of her grandfather's grave). The state's lack of reciprocity is a denial of relationship, an abnegation of sociality, and a way in which life becomes exhausted. She believes the state is indebted to the Waraoni because it has allowed roads to reduce the abundance of their territory, limiting the life of freedom and movement that is at the base of Waorani social reproduction. The state thus needs to provide both the resources that are no longer available and the things that improve Waorani quality of life (e.g., access to education, health, and urban services, and the general structures required for living a dignified life). "For 40 years, the Waorani people have not benefited from oil exploitation. We have not been valued. We are affected by contamination . . . we want to live freely . . . the state needs to pay what it owes us . . . we should live the way we want to live . . . they have destroyed us, our territory, our houses" (Eco Amazónico 2014).

Alicia has joined the chorus of women's voices to denounce state abandonment and to demand compensation, "If the government does not help, the Waorani will keep dying" (Acción Ecológica 2016). In December 2012, she was recognized by Ecuadorian environmental organizations as a "guardian of life" because of her strong stance against oil activities. In 2013, in a famous speech at Ecuador's parliament, Alicia demanded a cessation of oil activities in the YNP, a stand that defied a script given to her by a well-known Waorani figurehead who condoned oil drilling in Waorani territory. In 2015, after Alicia continued to oppose oil activities, she received death threats (OAS 2015). The InterAmerican Commission on Human Rights urged the Ecuadorian government to set protection provisions for Alicia.

Manuela's story offers a different reading of Waorani humanity. She was born in 1969, in what is now the Intangible Zone Tagaeri and Taromenane, close to the border with YNP. Her mother took her to live within the Waorani Protectorate, but her family abandoned this location because of a devastating polio epidemic. Among her cherished childhood memories are the celebrations that brought extended Waorani kin together. She sees these as fundamental to Waorani ways of life because they symbolize sharing happiness, and are tied to the Waorani ability to access the bounty of the flora and fauna of the rainforest. Her young adult life was marked by integration into the Ecuadorian nation, a time when the Waorani were "attentive to the codes of this relationship" (Omene 2013, 53). At this point, she accepted the call to become a *lidereza*. Manuela describes this transformation as a radical change coming upon her: while having to give up Waorani traditions of living among close kin, she also felt her personal relationships and network of external allies grow, which allowed her to contribute to and build projects *of* and *for* the Waorani. In 1990, Manuela became a representative in the first Waorani federation, the Organización de la Nacionalidad Huaorani de la Amazonía Ecuatoriana (ONHAE), and in 2008 she was elected president of the AMWAE.

Manuela sees the Waorani having different opinions about what their struggle entails and believes she needs to design projects that bring them together under a common voice (Omene 2013). In 2010, the AMWAE asked Waorani communities to stop selling bush meat, which had reached unsustainable levels and was threatening Waorani food security, and instead produce naturally dyed handicrafts and organic cacao to make chocolate for the market to secure monetary income (Omene 2014). These more sustainable ventures support their organization and nurture their common voice. Today, the AMWAE oversees over thirty hectares of cacao trees. Women participating in the chocolate cooperatives earn anywhere between USD $30 and $150 a month, which they invest in improving the quality of life in Waorani communities, through better access to health, education, and housing. Under Manuela's leadership, the AMWAE sought to lessen pressures on resources and to protect the spaces used by peoples living in voluntary isolation.

Manuela sees the AMWAE working for the future: "with all our farms run by women, our new role in the community is inspiring the next generation of both young women and men to take on leadership to broaden our community development and build a bridge between our former way of life with the contemporary world" (Omene 2014). A second flagship project of the AMWAE is the management of chambira forests (*obogenkawe* in the Waorani language and *Astrocaryum chambira* in scientific nomenclature), from which women make the handicrafts—bags, jewelry, and hammocks—that diversify household income sources and finance ecotourism and permaculture projects. Manuela views the AMWAE's transnational connections through chocolate and chambira as a product of the work of women who strengthen Waorani humanity. Over 400 women in thirty-five communities currently participate in these projects, developing resource use and conservation plans that nurture community-based production and strengthen access to health and education. In her presentation at FemGeog, Manuela wove Waorani economies of gathering and sharing with the capitalist market: producing and selling handicrafts and chocolate to outsiders to bring back money to the communities. Her approach stressed strengthening Waorani procurement practices and sharing the goods gathered with each of the participating women and *nanicaboiri* (groups of extended kin). For her, the market, and the need to turn to the market, reflect how the social skin is warped; reciprocity between families and kin is now usurped to a certain degree by a need to produce for and consume from the market.

Alicia and Manuela's formal narratives are powerful and recognizable expressions of their political fight. Next, we examine aspects of their visit, within and beyond FemGeog, that broaden our understanding of how their political fight crosses worlds.

TRAVELING ACROSS WORLDS

Alicia and Manuela's suitcases were heavy and full when they arrived in North Carolina. Traveling over 2,500 miles from the Amazonian city of Puyo, they carried necklaces, bracelets, belts, baskets, placemats, and a hammock, all woven by Waorani women from the fiber of the Amazonian chambira palm. Waorani women weave chambira into everyday artifacts, such as the *yoo* (hammocks) upon which they sleep and give birth, *shigras* (bags), or into handicrafts for sale (Omene 2012). The material made from *A. chambira* is a labor-intensive process of turning thin, almost wispy parts of pinnae (the upper or adaxial side of the individual leaflets that make up a palm leaf or frond) into a strong, twisted braid for making bags and hammocks capable of bearing 100 or more pounds of weight. The pinnae parts are boiled, dried in the sun, and rolled against the thigh (Jensen and Balslev 1995) to produce the seamless braid. The processed fibers are then naturally dyed with achiote (*Bixa orellana*), sisa (*Arrabidae* spp) and guisador (*Curcuma longa*). The weavings that Alicia and Manuela brought had colorful geometric shapes with encrusted Huayruro (*Ormosia coccinea*) and other forest seeds; others had feathers, claws, and teeth from Amazonian animals. Alicia and Manuela requested to have a sales table at FemGeog, something they often do when visiting *cowori* spaces. No other group had asked for vending space, and shoppers flocked to their table. Manuela and Alicia recognized resemblances between shoppers and people they knew back home, tailored chambira belts to their size, and gave them Waorani names stressing endurance, strength, and fierceness. As they worked the sales table and connected with conference attendees, Alicia and Manuela continued to weave unruly chambira fibers into their own items for sale.

According to Amazonian scholars, Waorani humanity involves the tying together—weaving—of people into a "shared substance" built from the routines and sensual processes of living well together (Rival 2016). The word *Waorani* means "true humans" in *Waoterero* or *Waotededo*, the Waorani language, and signals the recognition and celebration of fully embodying living well together. Those who are wild, uncontrolled, and disembodied from the shared substance of their *nanicaboiri* are no longer true humans (Rival 2005). To live well together, individuals are expected to be expert gatherers and hunters of forest products; procuring independently is highly admired as a social trait. Fulfillment as "good" Waorani comes from nurturing sociality through the sharing of abundance—of items gathered or made—with the *nanicabo*. The sale of Waorani crafts and the presentations at FemGeog could fall under this ethic of sharing Waorani abundance with others (who also have abundance, in the form of money and connections) to expand Waorani sociality.

Cowori, in this ethics of existence, are outsiders who do not share substance and can prey upon the Waorani, seeking to rob them of their life (Rival 2012). Describing these sorts of prey-predator dynamics, Viveiros de Castro (2013) proposes that, in Amerindian societies, each species sees others as nonhumans who prey upon them, "everything happens as in a great trophic chain . . . we all consume something different from us or are consumed by another" (58). Moreover, humanity is corporeally sensed through the social skin. A jaguar, for example, when alone in the forest, takes off its "jaguar clothes" and shows itself as a human. Its jaguar body is a sort of clothing that hides its human form. Thus, "when an animal speaks to you, do not respond . . . you have to gaze at the animal first, before it gazes at you. If it gazes at you first . . . you will be captured by its subjective power, and you will lose your sovereignty. It will own you" (Viveiros de Castro 2013, 57).

At FemGeog, Alicia and Manuela's representation of Waorani humanity tied together this predator-prey dialectic with Waorani social skin to make their political fights legible. When Gabriela and Kati met them in Waorani territory and Quito, Alicia and Manuela both wore Western-style clothing: pants, blouses, and sneakers. In preparation for our panel, they asked Gabriela to go shopping, to look for *huito* (*Genipa americana*) to paint their bodies, a natural plant dye, which we were not able to find in Chapel Hill. Instead, we secured black markers and black henna. A few minutes before the panel started, Alicia and Manuela underwent a metamorphosis: they exchanged their clothing for bark skirts, chest wraps made of chambira, feathered crowns, and bracelets, anklets, and necklaces decorated with peccary teeth and seeds. Gabriela and Dayuma helped them paint their bodies with markers and henna, drawing black zigzag lines that resembled anacondas on their arms and legs, a marker of Waorani origin myths of women fighters born from the head of the anaconda. They painted red masks on their faces with achiote—red is the color of life and well-being. Alicia painted black dots on her stomach—the spots of the jaguar, she explained. Manuela wore a jaguar tooth pendant and earrings. A superficial reading could risk rendering these events as commercialized, opportunistic performances and, worse, as moments of objectification that strip away their political ontology. A deeper reading suggests that, with these corporeal transformations, Alicia and Manuela crossed worlds and *cowori* crossed theirs, heightening our mutual sensing of Waorani humanity. These "clothes," gathered by their *nanicabo* kin, are markers of Waorani sovereignty in the face of the *cowori* settler state. These clothes *are* the human forests, woven chambira fibers, and hunted animals sustaining Waorani sociality. These are the best products that the forest can offer, explained Manuela and Alicia; their fathers and grandfathers, among the best hunters of the forest, gathered them, and they wore them at the conference to heighten *cowori* perception of their humanity.

Anthropomorphizing (wearing or weaving the parts of others onto the human body to acquire the qualities of others) are mechanisms of *self-transformation* that influence how others see the self (Álvarez 2011)—a sign of social skin authorship. In everyday life in the *nanicabo*, women do not typically transform their bodies with theriomorphic marks or paint. They show themselves as "real" humans. Their bodies are living humans that gather, collect, and share substance. When Manuela visits Waorani communities or leads cacao workshops, she wears her "real" body. However, in the political fight, a "cosmic body" is reconstituted from grafting various others to put together a body whose presence reorders differences and inequalities. This political body gazes back at governmental and nongovernmental organizations, oil companies, and feminist scholars. Whether inhabiting *cowori* categories or exceeding them, Alicia and Manuela's categorical ambiguities are playful and "survival-rich" (Lugones 1987, 14). Donning their mythical bodies to engage the *cowori* audience and providing items for sale, they invited FemGeog participants to consume Waorani culture, *under Waorani terms of relationality.*

Differences in interpretation notwithstanding, what emerges from these observations is that to recognize the Waorani political fight, Alicia and Manuela both participated in their own objectification through the *cowori* gaze *and* refused to be completely translated by it. Indeed, oftentimes Waorani leaders have expressed their frustration when environmental organizations and governmental representatives, or even singular Waorani, speak in the name of all Waorani. "How can one person stand in for all of a nationality?" Manuela asks, pointing to how the *cowori* use their own genres of Amazonian Indigeneity to capture and consume Waorani life. For Manuela, Waorani women wish to be the ones gazing first (taking the photographs, narrating the stories, coding their bodies), as authors of their humanity. Authorship is about mixing, exchanging, and "grafting" (Lugones 1987) parts of others onto the self, even those seen as nonhuman/enemies.

REAL BODIES BEYOND FEMGEOG

Manuela's questioning of how Amazonian peoples are represented and by whom echoes what Sylvia Wynter (Wynter and McKittrick 2014) calls the disruption of hegemonic genres of humanity. For Wynter, genres of the human, such as class, place, race, and gender, have complicated, deep roots in domination, subjection, and complicity that organize how we inhabit the world (as women, Indigenous, nonwhite, etc.) and how we "auto-institute" ourselves within this hegemonic grid of human kind (Wynter and McKittrick 2014, 31). It is not that Alicia and Manuela are "inventing" forms of being Indigenous; the critique of state abandonment and adopting capitalist market ethics are hardly radical options in and of themselves. What is different is *how they claim authorship* over their specific forms of representation. Baring their mythical, composite bodies, they understood they would be intelligible to *cowori*, comprehended and consumed through the value of Indigenous difference to grow their networks of support for the Waorani.

Some of the moments that allow grasping the complexity of these political fights for life took place outside of the conference, when Alicia and Manuela's mythical clothes were off, so to speak. In the Quito airport, Alicia and Manuela handled their large suitcases and time with an expertise that comes only with frequent traveling, blending into the anonymity of the crowds. No feathers, no jaguar teeth, no chambira; no difference. On the way back to Ecuador, Alicia calmly explained that the Raleigh-Durham airport is small compared to the New York and Morocco airports, places that she has visited as a representative of the Waorani. In the airport, she told Kati that they had plenty of time to window-shop and admire the bountifulness. Kati was equally struck by how easily Manuela disappeared into the crowds of Ecuadorians at the bus terminal, becoming one more Indigenous woman going home.

In Chapel Hill, Dayuma and Gabriela showcased "their territory" as their real bodies: the pine forests of North Carolina waking up with flowers, hawks, frogs, and small rodents and the outdoor venues where various groups of people gathered and ate together. Our "shared forests" prompted both Alicia and Manuela to invite us to their homes so that we too could admire their abundance. We shared our homes with Alicia and Manuela. We helped them collect items they needed, for example, Western clothes and shoes for men, women, and children of all ages; goods that ended up filling the suitcases now emptied of weavings. We selected and gathered the right sizes, colors, and models to be shared with their kin. Manuela happily exchanged information about Wao chocolate with the owner of a local coffee shop, drawing yet another market connection through which to strengthen the Waorani. Cacao cultivation might not be "traditional" among the Waorani, but weaving connections that strengthen the *nanicabo* is.

Sharing embodied substance with Alicia and Manuela wove proximity with *cowori* lifeways too. Alicia made *chucula* (sweet mashed plantain drink) in Gabriela's kitchen and shared it while we discussed and storied maps of Waorani territory. We broke into Waorani chants while talking about *nanicaboiri* and identifying the contents of *monito ome* (roughly, "our land/forest" or "homeland"), a joint Waorani-NGO project to recognize collective ownership of Waorani territory. Alicia and Manuela told Gabriela's children about the feats of their fathers and grandfathers, such as Kemperi, who transformed into a jaguar to warn his people of the dangers of territorial dispossession. Alicia and

Manuela approved of the ways in which Gabriela's partner procured and cooked meat to share with all.

These gatherings and outings were moments of social skin weaving, of turning the fibers of intimacy into braids of alliances. These were moments of intentional, purposeful observing and sharing, of assessing the details by which individual projects to protect Waorani life, or parts of it, succeed or fail. Alicia conveyed her worry that, by downsizing Waorani territories and allowing oil activities in the YNP, the Ecuadorian state is pitting settled Waorani against their brethren in voluntary isolation, the Taromenani and Tagaeri. She is advocating a personal fight informed by the increasing killings between Waorani and Taromenane. Many *nanicaboiri* have followed oil companies, relocating closer to oil camps, wells, and roads, because these companies provide goods in exchange for being in their territory. According to Kati, who has worked with one of these companies, companies observe and learn about Waorani sociality and incorporate reciprocity ethics into their community relations practices. And, as Waorani communities grow, they consume resources from the YNP, where people live in voluntary isolation. During one of our conversations about the almost two dozen communities surrounding the YNP, Alicia reflected, "I tell those communities who have settled on the borders of the Yasuní: you have to plant more forests, more resources to share with the Taromenane . . . plant more yucca, more *chonta*, more food to share." For Alicia, this is the Waorani humanity that needs to be strengthened: sharing substance to live well together, or else resource competition leads to violence and bloodshed. The state needs to provide for these peaceful relations to develop.

Manuela shared her concerns, too, expressing a worry that integration into the market leads to inequalities and differentiation among the Waorani. Younger generations, who are quick to learn weaving patterns, produce weavings that are more aesthetically pleasing to the *cowori*. Indeed, the weavings brought to FemGeog were mostly produced by younger women, who have learned Western aesthetics. Flora reflected on how weavings by elders tend to be thicker and less colorful, meant not for decoration but for everyday use and for gathering forest wealth. As Manuela described, younger women have an easier time picking up the new weaving trends they learn at the workshops that *cowori* women teach. Generational differences are also evident in the cultivation of cacao. Cacao cultivation requires sedentary agricultural practices: planting, nurturing, pruning, and the correct harvesting and fermentation methods, which involve different practices than the minding of forests of *chonta* palm (*Bactris gasipaes*) planted by ancestors. While people are excited about the possibility of exchanging cacao for money for health and education, the cultivation practices are foreign. Only those open to shifting their ways tend to be successful in these projects.

CONCLUSIONS

How do our experiences at FemGeog expand *cowori* understanding of Waorani humanity? Alicia and Manuela do not perform the masculinist tropes of bravery, hostility, and autonomy with which the Waorani are often identified. Their political tools are not the blowguns, spears, or rage epitomized by well-known books and films such as *Savages* (Kane 2012) and *End of the Spear* (Hanon 2005), or in the widely circulated images of oil workers, agricultural colonists, and loggers speared by Waorani and people living in voluntary isolation. Alicia and Manuela do not use a lexicon of structural oppression either. Instead, they identify their political ontology as female. It is "playful" (Lugones 1987), moving between their political and real bodies to weave a common embodied language that disrupts hegemonic codes of humanity, at times "taken" by the category "Indigenous woman," other times intentionally donning it, as if by consuming Indigeneity others can join their fight, though not necessarily know it. Their cosmopolitanism is strong and marginalized; they consume and are consumed.

Alicia and Manuela's visit was multifaceted. It was an opportunity to speak truth to a global audience about the injustices that the Waorani face. Income, employment, housing, and access to basic services, including health and infrastructure is limited in Waorani communities. Poverty and dispossession are directly tied to the erosion of territorial sovereignty, a corporeality that Alicia and Manuela, among many Indigenous leaders, are worried about. Alicia and Manuela donned a "social skin" steeped in cultural and symbolic capital and brought items for exchange and display to connect these concerns about their communities. We hope that this chapter disabuses the reader of a cynical stance that wearing feathers and chambira is superficial and performative. Recognizing these practices as forms of crossing worlds, and using them to weave extended social skins of connection, is intensely Waorani.

Extending social skin is political because it points to the shifting ontology of Waorani life. The Waorani thrive in bounty and abundance, not scarcity, yet the disappearing wealth of their homelands undercuts their subsistence. Alicia and Manuela recognize there is wealth in the US, and they are eager to partake in it. They also seek reparations from the settler state to meet resource obligations. Extending their social skin, through sharing substance at FemGeog (e.g., the sale and display of human forest items, gifting, and sharing of stories), Alicia and Manuela weave others onto the social skin that make them stronger and that they actively author. This is Alicia and Manuela's fight.

We struggle with the possibility that this chapter serves to "other" Alicia and Manuela. Talking about the difficulties of creating a common social skin that translates Waorani humanity is one strategy to address this concern, though it is not sufficient. Alicia and Manuela deploy their mythical bodies— how their Waorani being is captured by *cowori*—as a political and ethical web that stands in contrast to the desire to have one's distinctiveness as a people recognized. Kati, Dayuma, Gabriela, and Flora were complicit in these acts of translation. As *cowori* enmeshed in Alicia and Manuela's social skin, they used an ethnographic approach to foster engagement through the same narratives of conservation, resistance, and subject singularity. We struggle with how to disrupt the coloniality of these entanglements, which reify Indigenous difference. Dayuma, Kati, Flora, and Gabriela believe that their role is to continue developing playful ways to support Alicia and Manuela's extended social skin, even when they recognize that their own individual efforts are imperfect. This social skin weaving is feminist and possible through the affirmation of the plurality in each of us and in our collective work (Lugones 1987).

Our translation practices are not free of the ills of Western colonialism. And we cannot ignore the power relations that condition how our voices come together to produce knowledge *about* the Waorani. Putting ourselves on display and analyzing how Alicia and Manuela interacted with *cowori* (including Kati, Dayuma, Flora, and Gabriela) at FemGeog is an imperfect way of representing Waorani humanity, and risks objectifying our Waorani coauthors. Moreover, using a dominant language of representation that narrows down the possible trajectories of our engagements and performances can amount to a form of betrayal, as the Italian proverb *tradurre e tradire* (loosely translated as treason and translation) suggests (Valdivia 2018). No single language can fully capture the politics and poetics of our FemGeog encounters. That is not our intention either. Our weaving of extended social skins is an exercise in "world traveling" to break down the categories that divide and erase our humanity. Our reflections are one possible rendering of a critique of how Amazonian Indigeneity is produced and consumed, an intervention that we hope contributes to the ongoing development of a collective consciousness "motivated by the shared sense of obligation to preserve the collective being" (Robinson 1983, 245).

REFERENCES

Acción Ecológica. 2016. "Alicia Cahuilla Nacionalidad Huaorani." YouTube video, February 2, 2016. https://www.youtube.com/watch?v=h3QsEcpanrw.

Albán, Dayuma. 2015. "Teen Pregnancy on the Oil Road. Social Determinants of Teen Pregnancy in an Indigenous Community of the Ecuadorian Amazon." Master's thesis, Anthropology, UNC Chapel Hill.

Albán, Dayuma. 2017. "Huao Onquiyenani." *Terra Incognita* 47 (May–June). http://www .terraecuador.net/revista_47/47_huao_onquiyenani.html.

Álvarez, Kati. 2009. "El Efecto del Contacto de la Sociedad Nacional en las Prácticas Culturales Entorno a la Muerte en los Waoranis." Master's thesis. Quito: FLACSO Sede Ecuador.

de la Cadena, Marisol. 2015. *Earth Beings: Ecologies of Practice across Andean Worlds*. Durham, NC: Duke University Press.

Eco Amazónico. 2014. "Alicia Cawia, vicepresidenta de la nacionalidad Wao, del taller de mujeres." YouTube video, October 24, 2014. https://www.youtube.com/watch?v=e8Bb CXGnyoE.

Etchart, Linda. 2017. "One Woman against Big Oil and Patriarchy." *New Internationalist*, March 1, 2017. https://newint.org/features/2017/03/01/one-woman-against-big-oil -and-patriarchy.

Hanon, Jim. 2005. *End of the Spear*. Rocky Mountain Pictures.

Holt, Flora Lu. 2005. "The Catch-22 of Conservation: Indigenous Peoples, Biologists, and Cultural Change." *Human Ecology* 33 (2): 199–215.

Kane, Joe. 2012. *Savages*. New York: Vintage.

Lu, Flora. 2007. "Integration into the Market among Indigenous Peoples: A Cross-Cultural Perspective from the Ecuadorian Amazon." *Current Anthropology* 48 (4): 593–602.

Lu, Flora, Gabriela Valdivia, and Néstor L. Silva. 2016. *Oil, Revolution, and Indigenous Citizenship in Ecuadorian Amazonia*. New York: Springer.

Lugones, Maria. 1987. "Playfulness, 'World'-Travelling, and Loving Perception." *Hypatia* 2 (2): 3–19.

Jensen, Ole Holm, and Henrik Balslev. 1995. "Ethnobotany of the Fiber Palm *Astrocaryum Chambira* (Arecaceae) in Amazonian Ecuador." *Economic Botany* 49 (3): 309–319.

OAS. 2015. "Comisión Interamericana de Derechos Humanos: Resolución 38/2015." Accessed October 6, 2018. https://www.oas.org/es/cidh/decisiones/pdf/2015/MC530-15-ES.pdf.

Omene, Manuela Omari Ima. 2012. *Saberes Waorani y Parque Nacional Yasuní: Plantas, Salud y Bienestar en la Amazonía del Ecuador*. Quito: Iniciativa Yasuní ITT.

Omene, Manuela Omari Ima. 2013. "Manuela Ima: Una Lidereza Waorani Habla sobre su Cultura y la Explotación Del Yasuní." YouTube video, September 13, 2013. https://www .youtube.com/watch?v=fCVvk6pyBlE.

Omene, Manuela Omari Ima. 2014. "Chocolate Is Saving My Jungle." *Huffington Post*. September 22, 2014. https://www.huffingtonpost.com/entry/chocolate-is-saving-my -ju_b_5861894.html.

Rival, Laura. 2005. "The Attachment of the Soul to the Body among the Huaorani of Amazonian Ecuador." *Ethnos* 70 (3): 285–310.

Rival, Laura. 2012. *Trekking through History: The Huaorani of Amazonian Ecuador*. New York: Columbia University Press.

Rival, Laura. 2016. *Huaorani Transformations in Twenty-First-Century Ecuador: Treks into the Future of Time*. Tucson: University of Arizona Press.

Robinson, Cedric J. 2000. *Black Marxism: The Making of the Black Radical Tradition*. Chapel Hill: University of North Carolina Press.

Seeger, Anthony, Roberto da Matta, and Eduardo Viveiros de Castro. 1979. "A Construção da Pessoa nas Sociedades Indígenas Brasileiras." In *Sociedades Indígenas e Indigenismo no*

Brasil, edited by João Pacheco de Oliveira Filho, 11–39. Río de Janeiro: UFRJ, Editora Marco Zero.
Strathern, Marilyn. 2004. *Partial Connections.* Walnut Creek, CA: AltaMira Press.
Strathern, Marilyn. 2005. *Kinship, Law and the Unexpected: Relatives Are Always a Surprise.* Cambridge: Cambridge University Press.
Turner, Terrence. [1980] 2012. "The Social Skin." *HAU: The Journal of Ethnographic Theory* 2(2): 486–504.
Valdivia, Gabriela. 2018. "Translations of Indigeneity: Knowledge, Intimacy and Performing Difference in Ecuador." *Development and Change* 49 (5): 1347–58.
Vera, Christian. 2013. "Secretos del Yasuní: La Mujer de la Selva." YouTube video, October 4, 2013. https://www.youtube.com/watch?v=Cy-RZm-jNZ0.
Viveiros de Castro, Eduardo. 2013. *La Mirada del Jaguar. Introducción al Perspectivismo Amerindio.* Buenos Aires: Tinta Limón Ediciones.
Weheliye, Alexander G. 2014. *Habeas Viscus: Racializing Assemblages, Biopolitics, and Black Feminist Theories of the Human.* Durham, NC: Duke University Press.
Wynter, Sylvia, and Katherine McKittrick. 2014. "Unparalleled Catastrophe for Our Species?: Or, to Give Humanness a Different Future: Conversations." In *Sylvia Wynter: On Being Human as Praxis,* edited by Katherine McKittrick, 9–89. Durham, NC: Duke University Press.

CHAPTER 6

(TINY) HOUSES AND BLACK FEMINIST GEOGRAPHIC PRAXIS: BUILDING MORE HUMANLY WORKABLE GEOGRAPHIES

Tia-Simone Gardner

I learned to see freedom as always and intimately linked to the issue of transforming space.

—bell hooks (1995, 147)

Black women's geographies open up a meaningful way to approach both the power and possibilities of geographic inquiry. I am not suggesting that the connections between black women and geography are anything new—indeed, I assume a legacy of black women's geographies and geographic knowledges. Rather, I am suggesting that the relationship between black women and geography opens up a conceptual arena through which more humanly workable geographies can be and are imagined.

—Katherine McKittrick (2006, xii)

In 2016, I built a house, a tiny house, in Minneapolis. This tiny house potentially gives me access to affordable housing as a single Black woman doctoral student living on an annual salary of around $15,000 to $18,000. As a practicing artist, it simultaneously affords me work space and serves as a mobile artist residency, allowing me to move as needed. I named the project, which I adaptively refer to as a prototype, an intervention, or an experiment, *Inhabitation*. It is a flexible space in that its interiors can be changed to accommodate a range of programs. This tiny house is an ongoing engagement in a Black feminist geographic praxis of building, writing, and expressing the problems of what Katherine McKittrick calls humanly workable geographies. McKittrick argues that the relationship between Black women and geography assumes a true and unquestioned connection between Black womanhood and landscapes of death, trauma, and disloca- tion. That is, the spaces allocated to Black women's lives—socially, politi- cally, economically—vis-à-vis the kitchen, the field, "the space between the legs" have created a connection between Black women and geography that is so thickly antihuman that it would appear to be indissoluble (McKittrick 2006, 46). This link between Black women and geography is one of bare life, rather than a connection that could bear life (Agamben 1998; Williamson 2016). McKittrick, however, lays out a poetic Black feminist geography that speaks to different critical geographic theories and is highly imaginative and more habitable for Black life.

I approach human workability here as praxis and praxis as human work- ability, particularly as the occupation of space/place and an ongoing political struggle with architecture and the geography of cities. I define human work- ability as a process of collaboration, of teaching and learning with others, and of teaching oneself through the building of this improvised house, also known as a tiny house. I use the lowercase tiny house to refer to this alternative way of thinking about these structures as Black feminist possibilities and capitalize Tiny House to refer to market-driven housing projects that dominate popu- lar culture and are products of intentions very different from those of Black feminists. I build on Black feminisms to theorize and place myself into archi- tecture as an architectural subject, that is, an agential body-mind-spirit who comprehends and exercises the power and necessity of shaping built space for and around the needs of her particular self. Architecture is a cultural practice, and living smaller, I argue, may be a necessity for survival as it makes living in urban areas, where there is greater access to work, education, transportation, and kinship networks, possible. It also creates new political possibilities.

Both the Tiny House and the tiny house, I argue, allow us to see the violent workings of the state. As a derivation of the shotgun house, which I discuss below, the tiny house is a product of a vernacular architecture that emerges out of the lived experiences and diasporic knowledges of Black folks to meet their needs and reflects their experiences.[1] This gap between need and the city's plan is where tiny houses like mine and others' are instructive. As vernacular, self-built homes, they reflect an aesthetic interest in objects but also the cre- ative ways that the Black women and women of color I interview in this essay have *tried* to make cities work for them, even while knowing that sometimes cities will not work for them, and may even actively work against them. In some cases, the tiny house materializes as a refusal to participate in a housing economy that depends on growth and displacement and the trend of houses growing bigger and bigger (Sparshott 2016).

In this essay, I investigate the house as a site of power or a "matrix of domination" through an intersectional Black feminist lens (Collins 2002, 23), and I embrace the creative imagination of living small and the problem and potentiality of tiny houses. The house, as a racial, sexual, classed, ableist political site in the US, is an ontological and epistemic problem that contributes to the humanly unworkable geographies of the city. I focus on the relationship between spatial improvisation and spatial knowledge, analyzing how the projects and actors that I examine in this essay reflect a Black feminist geographic praxis. The tiny house, usually self-built by the women I interview, is not solely an object of utility but an object of critical thinking about one's ecology, self-expression, and relation to place. Pushing beyond the current popularity and uncritical celebration of these small mobile homes as adorable and a new niche market, I am interested in how Black women and other women of color use these homes to mobilize the political potential of the tiny house to escape techniques of control, to transform space, and to form more humanly workable geographies. I draw on the writing of bell hooks and Katherine McKittrick, connecting traces of their work to the experiences and thoughts of these experimentally housed women. I theorize and address the idea of architectural subjectivity and how Blackness is often dislocated from geographic and architectural place. I use interviews with Black women and women of color who live in tiny houses as well as discourse analysis from blogs and online journals in order to understand what the Tiny House movement has come to mean in the US, why it is fraught, and for whom and where it might be made useful.

I began this project with the desire to situate the Tiny House movement within the larger context of housing and urban design in the US. As part of a Black feminist praxis, I use the object of the tiny house as a way to interrogate and trace the relationship of architecture to spatial injustice and the operation of state power. Rather than locate the beginning of the Tiny House movement with late-1990s white middle-class attempts to "go tiny," I trace an alternative genealogy of the tiny house through the Black vernacular architecture of the shotgun house. I end with an analysis of the tiny house as a Black feminist project based on my interviews with Black, Latinx, and other research participants, as well as my own experience. In this way I show the production of a more humanly workable Black geography into practice by creating and imagining different architectural arrangements through Black feminist praxis.

HOUSING AND RACIAL JUSTICE IN US CITIES

The Black feminist praxis I engage through the intentional design of my tiny house responds to the architectural and urban injustices inscribed into housing and spatial organization in Minneapolis, Minnesota. The physicality of a city reveals much about its socio-racial histories and visions for the future. The planning and paving of streets, sidewalks, lampposts, and building design speak to multiple processes of valuation. When a city evaluates which areas are worth investment, which districts and neighborhoods present revenue-generating opportunities through development, and which areas should be leveled or obliterated, economic lines are drawn. In the US, these borders historically and contemporarily follow an anti-Black geographic logic (Gotham 2000; Haynes 2001; Hernandez 2009; Long and Johnson 1947; Waring 2008; Zenou and Boccard 2000). Whether we term this process redlining, urban renewal, redevelopment, or gentrification, Black space continues to move through these cycles of devaluation, effectively making it worth less.

Minneapolis is not an exception. The city, just like other US cities, functions as a space of anti-Black devaluation. In this city, a drive from south to north or west to east quickly reveals intentional patterns of uneven development, a landscape that bears visible scars of a history of restrictive covenants and zoning restrictions that strategically targeted or negatively affected the economies and infrastructures of Black communities. For example, the Rondo neighborhood in St. Paul, a once predominantly Black community, like many Black neighborhoods in the US, was plowed through, in the name of urban progress and connecting the nation, in order to make room for the US interstate system. These patterns of displacement are co-constituted by ongoing spatial matters that seek to cultivate and/or dismantle other ethnic enclaves including Native American, Hmong, Latinx, and Somali communities. Thus, a part of the violent injustices of the present involve the purge, or segregation, of nonwhite bodies from the city through the planning and designing of dwelling space. Architecture and urban planning at the hands of the professional architects and planners are governing technologies of the state (Crysler 2003; Crysler, Cairns, and Heynen 2012; McKittrick and Woods 2007; Smith 2005; Woods 1998). In Minnesota in general, and Minneapolis and St. Paul in particular, de facto and de jure spatial segregation have an ongoing impact on the lives of people from these groups. There are major barriers to wage earning and education that leave these communities vulnerable to city policy and development. There are numerous examples, from the uprooting of Hmong farmers in the May Township to the most recent example by the city of Minneapolis to close its last public housing complex, the Glendale Homes (Du 2016; Walsh 2012). The house, then, does not only provide shelter but becomes a mechanism of control, surveillance, and taxation on the population, specifically targeting the nonwhite and the poor (Chapin 1938; Du 2016; Goetz 1993; Long and Johnson 1947; Vlach 1993).

A recent report on the rise of segregated housing in Minneapolis states, "Out of the nation's predominantly white metropolitan regions, the Twin Cities area is now the nation's most starkly segregated, with severe impacts in both neighborhoods and schools" (Institute on Metropolitan Opportunity 2016, 5). The report meticulously outlines the ways that the federally subsidized housing market has been utilized to create this immense social inequity, displacing whole communities of color from city centers. In a more widely read article for *The Atlantic* titled, "The Artist Loft: Subsidized Housing for White People," journalist Alana Semuels (2016) further outlines aspects of the report, detailing how the market for federally subsidized housing contributes to urban economic and housing segregation, particularly white-segregated housing, via the invention of below-market-rate artist lofts—housing units that can also be used as workspace that are restricted to renters who can prove through credentials and portfolios that they are artists. ArtSpace, a Minneapolis developer that focuses specifically on these kinds of mixed-income multifamily buildings, has done a number of prominent renovations in the Twin Cities, with four projects alone exceeding costs of $460 million. This was possible because of an exemption, lobbied for by ArtSpace, in the IRS Low-Income Housing Tax Credit program. Until 2008, there were no exceptions for artists under the Low-Income Housing Tax Credit program.

In July 2008, ArtSpace, with members of Congress, the Local Initiatives Support Corporation, the National Equity Fund, and others, worked to "add clarifying language" to the Housing and Economic Recovery Act of 2008, HR 3221. They wanted artists to constitute a special constituency of housing-vulnerable people, along with individuals with special needs and groups who qualify for federal/state housing support. The language that was ultimately added to the bill stated that under the general public use, people "who are involved in artistic or literary activities" could be favored as tenants and developers could use federal tax dollars from the Low-Income Housing Tax Credits to provide subsidies for this new special group.[2] In this way we can see a direct relationship between the economic crisis of 2008 and the opening up of what some might call a loophole in the Fair Housing Act. One that, like other civil rights legislative measures, is being used to undermine equity measures in favor of de jure inequality.[3]

The report terms these units Politically Opportune Subsidized Housing (POSHs). As a nonwhite artist and scholar working at the intersection of cultural production, community-based practice, and urban planning, I was not surprised by the article; rather, it provided valuable evidence of harming low-income families of color while making "winners of developers, politicians, and neighborhoods. Instead of helping the struggling urban poor escape poverty and segregation, the region's most celebrated housing projects appear aimed at helping white, moderate-income 'creatives' live comfortably in Minneapolis and St. Paul's most exclusive urban quarters" (Institute on Metropolitan Opportunity 2016, 6). Thus, the report reveals a social phenomenon that remains largely disavowed and sublimated beneath layers of passive conservatism known by the colloquial phrase "Minnesota Nice."

BUILDING AND INHABITING MY TINY HOUSE

I began thinking tiny, as many do, as a way to make life not just more manageable but more livable. In Minneapolis, I paid nearly $800 a month for rent. Why, you may ask, would I live alone? Roommates are not a constant and leave one at the mercy of the decisions of others. Being an unpartnered Black woman who lives alone and wants to live in a city but with limited income means that my housing options are constrained not only to what I can afford but also where I would be most safe, in all its measures and meanings. A Black female body like mine is less likely to feel psychically safe in a majority-white neighborhood near the university, for example, where there is increased police presence, or where a sense of audible and visual ownership of public space is given over to young white men and fraternal orders. Where and how might I situate myself in a nonwhite neighborhood with this odd little house? How do I avoid becoming a conduit of the new urban plan of creative economies and artist-gentrifiers that have reshaped the housing market in Minneapolis with live/work spaces called artist lofts (Semuels 2016)? How might I build trust and intimacy in a neighborhood with people who look like me, who are around or in most cases above my income level, and for whom I share a sense of time and place while also being a recent migrant to the city? I had to consider all of these questions through a Black geographic and intersectional feminist lens.

Safety has a number of meanings for the Black body's relationship to the city. Thinking about this house brought a form of tangibility to questions of where houses and their inhabitants are situated in the Twin Cities as I needed to think about safety in terms of physical and psychological well-being. I have the privilege to have a car and drive, which many people do not, so this opens up options for me to live outside of the city, and not just in suburbs but in rural areas of Minnesota and Wisconsin. The possibility to live in a rural area with fewer regulations on housing types came up, but this meant choosing to live in predominantly white space. I still needed to think just as strategically, if not more so, about where I place myself, who my neighbors are, and how I will time my comings and goings for my safety (there would be fewer people of color around who could theoretically quell my feelings of isolation and vulnerability). So, like many people, I continued to face the rental market in Minneapolis, which was in second place on *Forbes*'s annual list of the worst cities for renters in 2012 (Brennan 2012), until I could make something else. This renting-vs.-buying paradigm is further complicated by the problem of anti-Black financial markets that make it harder for Blacks to buy a house even if they have the resources because of higher interest rates and fraught lending processes.

My interest in tiny housing is not tied to the idea of participating in "going tiny" or sizing down from large living. I had nothing to size down from. Likewise, I was not invested in "the American Dream." Being a landowner, which historically is tied to matters of personhood, race, and being accounted for in the nation, has never been a path to American citizenship for Black women. My interest in the tiny house as an improvised architecture is in itself a critique of the settler colonial logic of land possession. In Minneapolis, where it is cheaper to have a mortgage than to rent, those who lack the resources, or interest, in buying a home are placed at a political, economic, social, and geospatial disadvantage. My tiny house was a praxis of being more intentional about how I operate in a political awareness of my location, of attempting to build spatial justice.

The small mobile house that I imagined was neither an American Dream nor a Tiny DIY Dream, but rather a way to question the problem of the inhumane unjustness of cities. It was a way to find a human workability within the historical and present problems that linger in our built environments. One journalist states, "living tiny is literally about as close to a grassroots movement as one can get, and proponents are actively engaged in advocacy with local governments to realize their vision of decentralizing materialism" (Carberry 2017). These are the tiny house dwellers that this project is in dialogue with, not the consumer market of the tiny house as spectacle. As this project moved/moves forward, it is increasingly important to acknowledge that entering into even this quasi-oppositional market still poses particular risks.

Kathryn Schenk (2015, 2) writes, "Tiny houses provide a solution to a number of growing issues including sustainability, urban density, affordable housing and wastefulness, but the stigma associated with the movement results in a missed opportunity in the US." The stigma that Schenk mentions might seem to come from the house-dwelling population but in fact comes from a collage of agents across time. That is, the house and the process of housing people has always been a site from which to produce sociopolitical, spatial, and economic inequalities. Institutions like Housing and Urban Development, the Federal Housing Authority, and the whole commodification of the house itself constitute "the housing market." City governments have been invested with authority over building and zoning codes, determining what is and is not, what can and cannot be, a house. These policies create barriers for me and for many other would-be homeowners.

My experience is illustrative of the problems many face. I work in North Minneapolis, where housing types are limited; apartments and multifamily housing are cheaper, but it is rare to find studio or one-bedroom apartments. In this area, there are disproportionately more vacant lots than in the rest of Minneapolis as a result of historical, "natural," and imposed land traumas, including histories of white flight, urban redevelopment, predatory lending, and a tornado that flattened a line of city blocks in a matter of minutes, as well as the City of Minneapolis's own policies regarding procedures for razing vacant houses. The landscape in and around North Minneapolis is racially affected through *deep space,* that is,

> the *production* of space intensified and writ large, ideological and political shifts that impact upon and organize the everyday in multiple contexts and scales—within and across homes, factories, streets, local and world banks, social services, military invasions, developing and overdeveloped nations, resistance tactics, gentrification projects. (McKittrick 2006, 14)

This is similar to other parts of the city that, over the last fifty years and even back to the nineteenth century, have been repopulated by majority nonwhite groups. The river, the interstate, and the railroad tracks mark the entrance and exits to these parts of the cities that one has to pass over, and yet not fully be aware of in order to do so. The city has actively bulldozed more housing in North Minneapolis than in any other part of Minneapolis, leaving more vacant lots to be redeveloped in this area.

In 2017, there were approximately 246 vacant lots in North Minneapolis, while the city as a whole had approximately 459 lots, meaning more than half of the vacant lots for the entire city of Minneapolis can be found in this small area. North Minneapolis is also home to the not-for-profit arts organization Juxtaposition Arts, where I teach in the Contemporary Arts Lab. At this nexus, working in a neighborhood that is economically and racially similar to the one that I grew up in, as an artist, I started to think about interventions.

I considered buying a vacant lot in this neighborhood. Even though land is affordable, the requirement to prove to the city authority that one can build a house heavily favors developers and makes it extremely difficult for people like me to purchase land. More importantly, I was concerned about the politics of owning land in the US, and in Minneapolis specifically, with its particular violent settler colonial past of land dispossession and population replacement. As a matter of spatial justice and human workability, the praxis of my project demanded that I approach land in relation to a justice-oriented feminism. Through purchasing land, I did not want to contribute to or become a complicit actor of settler colonialism. I had to consider whether my work would be for "reconnection, invasion or exploitation" (Boyce Davies 1994, 17). The tiny house, because of its mobility, smallness, and relative affordability, provided a way to think differently with the problem of land owning and the lack of housing diversity. The tiny house also carried deeper meanings about the temporalities, or overdetermined stasis, of architecture and the threatening idea of flight that is connected to a mobile house.

BLACK FEMINIST GEOGRAPHY AND ARCHITECTURE

In her essay "Architecture in Black Life: Talking space with Laverne Well-Bowie," Black feminist theorist bell hooks writes, "Mine is a geography and architecture that grows out of the experience of racial apartheid and class exploitation" (hooks 1995, 159). Feminist architectural scholars have written on relationships between race, the body, and the built world, and hooks (1995) takes up architecture and geography in her work, giving us a point of entry into understanding the ways that the built environment contributes to spatial injustice, particularly in relation to Black folks (see also Colomina 1992; Morton 2003). hooks (1995, 149) writes, "My grandmother's house was not unlike the small shacks that were the homes of many Southern black folks. Her place was just a bigger, more elegant shack." Her words are instructive to the way I want to see the distinction between the Tiny House, the recent, adorable market commodity, and the tiny house; her ideas about architecture allow us to have a conversation about the intersection of cities, race, and spatial control. Not only is hooks thinking about how the Black body can be situated into architecture through the production of a Black architectural subjectivity, but she is also thinking about scale. hooks articulates a necessity of smallness that grew out of sociospatial and geopolitical disenfranchisement that has its legacies in the geographies and architectures of slavery.

Katherine McKittrick (2006, xxviii) uses the narrative of Harriet Jacobs, the pseudonym for the enslaved author Linda Brent, to theorize the garret of Jacobs's grandmother's house, an attic adjacent to the plantation from which she fled, as "usable and paradoxical space." The small hold of the garret was a tiny space, "the last place [anyone seeking to find her] thought of" (Jacobs [1861] 2000, 116–17). It allowed Brent to see the geographies of slavery from a different location of struggle in which she was both free and unfree, to see both the "possibilities and limitations of space" simultaneously as experienced through her racial-sexual body (McKittrick 2006, 52). I do not want to conflate the conditions of my life or those of the women I discuss below with those of Brent, because while the states of unfreedom that impede and disrupt our lives are ultimately chained to white supremacist spatial disciplining of our bodies, our unfreedoms are ultimately not the same. I do want to draw on this conception of the garret as usable and paradoxical by asking how building tiny houses represents a different and contemporary "loophole of retreat" from unafford-able housing markets, capitalism, and unjust cities (Jacobs [1861] 2000).

One interviewee told me that before she was able to get her tiny house built, she was paying approximately 80 percent of her income to try to keep up with the costly rental market in Los Angeles, after having been priced out of New York and San Francisco (Moody 2018). Her tiny house was the last place she would think of, not an apartment, not a tent, but not quite a house either. As a form of garreting that both constrains and offers escape, the tiny house is also a paradoxical space, not an easy site to deal with, and must be understood, just as a house is understood, as a commodity object, one that for some wields economic, social, and cultural capital only marginally differently than a to-scale house.

In cities with dense populations that often struggle to meet housing needs, these small dwellings are often policed, regulated, and deemed illegal. This illegality stems from both the matter of their scale and the mobility that this scale enables. In Minneapolis, as with most US cities, tiny houses fall below the spatial requirements of what is legally recognized as a house, 500 square feet with eight-foot ceilings for bedrooms and specific object distances required for appliances and waste in kitchens, bathrooms, utilities, etc. Likewise, their wheels disallow them from being legal houses, as under building code a *house* must be static and on a foundation. As a Black feminist theorist, I argue that creating errant, criminal, improper subjects of individuals out of those who make use of improvised houses is tied to how cities build and plan around Blackness and (im)mobility. "Blackness," write Stefano Harney and Fred Moten (2013, 51), "operates as the modality of life's constant escape and takes the form, the held and errant pattern, of flight." All of these problems, in urban spaces and the built environment, can be tied to Blackness, if we understand Blackness as Moten and Harney do, as spatially and biopolitically enacted. A house, then, that disallows the possibility of determination of where, when, and how Black folks live, also therefore disallows the possibility of this modality of life, of Black mobility, to exist within cities. Moten and Harney's provocation allows me to see how a problem between blackness and flight is being actively produced around Tiny Houses and destabilizes the idea of the tiny house as purely a "loophole of retreat." The connection between Blackness and flight, or that flight becomes a threat, makes visible why spatial-temporal problems arise for both myself and for other landless women and Black women. That is, in cities that see their major concerns of growth and sustainability being deeply connected to forms of permanency that can be built into the landscape, things that are small and movable become undesirable because they can easily, and quickly, become undetectable, untaxable, and ungovernable.

Like Brent's garret, the tiny house allows seeing and understanding a range of power negotiations in urban settings. Having more space, such as the fixed space of a large immobile house, is traditionally connected to accessing power. The detached single-family dwelling is a political site that continues to fix people to capitalism and to city formations that work against more humane, more workable modes of life. The social production of scale and aesthetics are being meted out in cities to determine the geotemporalities of our lives. Where, how, and for how long we should be placed more and more determines what we can call a legal dwelling. As developer William Levitt humorously said in the post–World War II development boom, "No man who owns his own house and lot can be a communist. He has too much to do" (Beauregard 2006, 156). However, more and more, those living under the conditions of capitalism in the US are seeking and building ways out. Embracing smallness and temporariness may be yet one way that will be aestheticized differently as it is taken up across space and across time. In this terrain, then, the tiny house can tell us much about matters of justice and injustice in a city. Over the course of this project, I interviewed two founders of Tiny House Trailblazers, an online network of people of color who have an altogether different architectural genealogy for why and how they built their tiny houses, which I explore below. They shared that in spite of all of the work they have done over the last ten-plus years to intervene in the whitewashed history of the Tiny House movement, they continue to combat open racism and passive antagonism in their work.

This antagonism is one reason why these houses are productive political sites to examine race and cities.

A BRIEF HISTORY OF THE (WHITE) TINY HOUSE AND AN ALTERNATIVE GENEALOGY OF LIVING SMALL

What we might call the Tiny House movement is often credited to the work of Jay Shafer, who in 1999 built a 110-square-foot mobile house on a trailer that he then lived in for the next five years (Shafer 2009; Wilkinson 2011). Tiny House by Tiny House, the proponents of the Shafer genealogy argue, the movement has grown, and currently there are a number of television shows, web series, and blogs devoted specifically to Tiny House adoration. There are also a growing number of websites and blogs devoted to advocacy and sharing information on navigating design, construction, home organization, and zoning laws. There is, however, another history that can and should be considered when thinking about living small. That is, that people with limited incomes and resources have lived small as a strategy to carve out livable space in cities for as long as cities have existed. Locating the contemporary Tiny House movement with individuals like Jay Shafer negates the material function of the house and its history. As a new niche market for people with unlimited housing choice, the Tiny House creates "new vocabulary to gentrify living in a small space" (Shafrir 2016). Said differently, the very language of Tiny Houses—as opposed to the mobile home, shed house, or tent city—makes the idea of living in what bell hooks referred to above as a shack charming to a group of largely white, middle-class, and young or retired people who would otherwise spend their income on larger, more static dwellings. Tiny Houses on wheels are indeed mobile homes, yet "mobile homes" carry particular classed and geographic baggage. Until the Tiny House became associated with a particular kind of white desirability and choice, this type of living was unremarkable. Doree Shafrir (2016) states it this way:

> "Going tiny" implies that the person who is moving into a tiny house is doing so to escape their previous life of excess: They are coming from one place and going to another. This has made it, by definition, a middle-class movement, one that eschews identification with people who have lived in "tiny" homes for decades—whether that "tiny" home is a mobile home, an RV, or just a really small apartment. And so the tiny house movement has an inherent privilege built in: Going tiny is a *choice*. If you're coming from a more abundant place, in which you *could* live in a 2,000-square-foot

house but you *choose* to live in 200 square feet, then you can be part of the community. If not, well, you're just poor.

An alternate genealogy for the Tiny House movement, however, allows the project to participate in this push for spatial justice with a Black feminist intention. That is, it is important to think about the necessity of living small as something that predates the heightened visibility and new marketability of these small dwellings. Living small is a mode of spatial improvisation and invention that Black people and people of color the world over have engaged, and continue to engage, for a number of reasons, including unaffordable housing markets, houselessness, homelessness, and poverty. The desire, and perhaps the necessity, to live tiny and not just small has now garnered enough determined advocates that it is now called a movement. While smallness is a livable scale that has in many ways been available in cities for some time through studios, efficiency units, and garage apartments, tininess as I position it here carries with it a connotation of not just scale but new unanchored space-time possibilities that facilitate mobility should it become necessary (Abraham 2017; Edwards 2009; Helstein, Towles, and McFerren 1960; Maharidge 2011; Serapião 2016). Tiny housing has steadily grown in the US and Canada since 2014, but it has a longer legacy that is tied to the history of a vernacular architecture colloquially called the shotgun house. One of the women I interviewed, Dominique Moody, states that this history is at times eclipsed by the novelty of the new popular movement. She says, "It's such a shame because . . . because if they had acknowledged that there is this precursor, I think it just would've opened it up more . . . why be frightened or ashamed of a model that is so significant that it's coming back?" (Moody 2018).

The Tiny House on wheels is in many ways a smaller, more custom finished mobile home; however, as hooks points out, the way we make meaning of architecture is shaped by our material experiences of space. The way we make meaning, and the history, of Tiny Houses is also shaped by sociogeographic conceptions of the house. Specifically, what differentiates a Tiny House from a mobile home from an RV? Likewise, what differentiates a neighborhood from a trailer park from a backyard? These questions are matters of geographic and architectural discourse: discursive differences of scale, discursive differences of space. These geographic and architectural discourses provoked the women I interviewed to design and think small as both a matter of necessity and as a radical spatial imagination. These matters predate and even nullify some interests of the contemporary Tiny House movement, which still rely on having access to capital, the skilled labor of others, and, above all, infinite choice about where and how to build a home. This modern Tiny House movement should be understood within the political and temporal context from which it emerged—that is, through the desires of young, largely white, often financially unburdened men with time and resources. Though increasingly there are young couples, even couples with children, and retirees who are embracing these alternate housing models, the issues of where and how we live in relation to other people shift depending on how we are marked by race, class, ability, and age. I understand the tiny house within this framing of an alternate genealogy.

TINY HOUSE AS HUMANLY WORKABLE SPACE

I turn to my experience in the Tiny House movement in Minneapolis and interviews with Dominique Moody and Aurora Levins Morales to understand the tiny house as a form of vernacular architecture. I interrogate how self-built or improvised dwellings create a different history and potentially a different future for reading this traditional approach to architecture. It is within this context, the confluence of the tiny house and the Tiny House movement, that a new architectural subject emerges working to build more humanly workable geographies.

Writing specifically about space, place, and architecture, bell hooks calls on her memory of the spaces of her childhood to theorize herself into architecture, and in so doing allows us to imagine the production of a new architectural subject. She does so by thinking particularly about matters crucial to Black geographies and spatial justice—(small) scale, space, and materiality:

> I can still remember the way [my grandfather] and my father would sit on the porch and have deep discussions about that house; their talk evoked a poetics of space, the joy of thinking imaginatively about one's dwelling. I can recall my disappointment when I finally saw the small square brick house that he built. In my childhood imagination this space seemed so utterly closed and tight. Had I understood the interconnected politics of race, gender, and class in the white supremacist South, I would have looked upon this house with the same awe as I did my favorite house. (hooks 1995, 148–49)

hooks is literally re-membering a new architectural subjectivity for herself, one that she failed to perceive as a desirable and habitable subjectivity as a child. Elsewhere she states, "Growing up in a world where black working-class and 'po' folks, as well as the black well-to-do, were deeply concerned with the aesthetics of space, I learned to see freedom as always and intimately linked to the issue of transforming space" (hooks 1995, 147). The "interconnected politics of race, gender, and class in the white supremacist South" distorted her ability to perceive the modality of life that her father and grandfather saw in the house that he would eventually build. But her remembering allowed her to access an architectural past that was there all along. In this other genealogy, it is important to contextualize the impetus to think and live small within the historical inaccessibility of housing or, as hooks demonstrates, the very ability to imagine a house otherwise.

While Jay Shafer and those who have followed his model of 100-to-300-square-foot houses on wheels are certainly one example of tiny living, this is not the only one. This contemporary HGTV/DIY Network-worthy movement is in many ways premised on the architectural spectacle of adorability. The Tiny House is a scaled-down version of a "real house," like a dollhouse or a gingerbread house or a playhouse. In this formation, as hooks articulates, it only disappoints the fantasy of the "real" thing, a real house. This sleight of hand, performed by the likes of Shafer and HGTV, makes this version of smaller housing acceptable only because it is very cute. It is a sharp contrast from the corrugated metal–clad structures that may come to mind when we think of a mobile home, a trailer home, or an RV. This discourse of tininess also distances these structures from another of its other architectural precursors, the "shotgun" house.

"I always kind of quote around 'shotgun' because I feel it is not its true name" (Moody 2018). Dominique Moody is an artist residing primarily on the West Coast, but I caught up with her in New Orleans while she was an artist in residence at Xavier University.

If a popular genealogy of the Tiny House traces it through white yuppies like Jay Shafer, Moody locates the tiny house's origins in the shotgun house and a distinct Black tradition. Moody is a tall, soft-spoken woman in her sixties who is legally blind. Moody is one of a number of Black women and women of color who live and perform Black geographies and vernacular architecture through a direct engagement with the economic and spatial design problem of the house through the tiny house. In the wake of the 2008 financial crisis, Moody began imagining a house for herself that she could afford. Having grown up in a family of artists and carpenters, Moody understood architectural systems and structural systems of inequality that over time created cycles of renting and improving a living space that would lead to her and her family's displacement from those improved dwellings as the owners of those properties sought to profit from their craft and labor.

Moody has a sharp understanding of architecture and geography, and the collisions that have happened and continue to happen between Black women and the new Tiny House movement. Moody sees the tiny house as a derivative architecture that draws on the long, narrow design of the vernacular architecture colloquially termed shotgun houses. She states: "And [the Tiny House movement folks] are actually afraid to acknowledge [it]. It is astonishing to me because that is the precise model that Tiny Houses on wheels are replicating" (Moody 2018). Because of the obvious architectural and aesthetic ties between shotgun houses and tiny houses, Moody did a lot of research on this particular form of vernacular architecture before and during the design of her house, as she wanted it to reflect a spiritual social history of her ancestral legacy. The weaponizing, as Moody puts it, of an Africanist housing model is significant, as it works to erase the contemporary white Tiny House's connections to a historically Black form of architecture. As early as 1936, we see the discipline of geography thinking about this model of the shotgun house and trying to understand its migration but without examining its connection to the migration of Free Black populations and certainly not anti-Blackness (Kniffen 1936). This omission contributes to the production of misfit architectural subjects, namely the free Black body (Edwards 2009; Vlach 1993). Moody traces the house's name, and its subsequent disavowal from the Tiny House movement, through anti-Black violence.[4] She states:

> After emancipation and the fact that the freer movement of Black people put people in places that they had not been before, certainly free . . . when that happened, white folks had a particular way of addressing that. And that is if you see any evidence of *those* people, and what is the evidence of those people? Those houses. When you see those houses show up, you shoot into them to dissuade them from being there. And it's the shooting into these houses as a threat that became the coinage for the name. It's not a term we wanted; it was a term put on it.

The name "shotgun" is thought to derive from the arrangement of its rooms that fall in line, with one passing into the next in such a way that would allow the pellets of a shotgun to pass through the house without hitting anything. Its roots are contested, but architectural and Black studies scholars agree that the migration of this architecture to the Americas was at least in part due to movement of Black populations from western Africa, such as Yoruba peoples, to the French-colonialized Caribbean, and then to the southeastern United States.

I use "shotgun house" here cautiously, as Moody pointed out that the history of violence that saturates this phrase is still present each time we speak its name. The phrase is steeped in producing a misfit architectural subject. Moody states that it is an African-derived vernacular form and, importantly, "vernacular housing is the predominate architecture of the globe. Architecture in its formal terms is something else. And it's usually political and economic and . . . about privilege." She continues, stating that this kind of common dwelling is "truly the architecture of the globe." Moody understands architecture as "the single largest collective expression that any group of people can have. . . . Each group, tribe, culture, creates its own architecture in line to that collective thought, and aesthetic." She adamantly states that there is a cruel anti-Black subtext to the naming of the shotgun house, in that "there isn't another culture on the planet that would name *that* expression off a weapon" (Moody 2018).

The shotgun house, and its erasure in a historically inaccurate white genealogy of the adorable Tiny House, allows us to see anti-Blackness manifest as a problem in the built environment. As a signifier of free Black mobility, the shotgun house marked socio-racial space. Aware of this connection between Black mobility, space, and design, Moody created a plan for her own home that intentionally embraced the design principles of this vernacular expression. The "errant patterns of flight" that arise from both Moody's articulation of the shotgun house's genealogy and her own genealogy open up a space to see the Black body as both subject and subjection of architecture (Harney and Moten 2013, 51). That one's freedom of movement could be aesthetically mapped onto one's shelter is not necessarily a surprise; we easily understand this phenomenon when a tent or a box become one's living space. Yet it is evoked every time we use the word "shotgun" to describe a house. Moody's life has taken her from New York to San Francisco to Oakland and then to Los Angeles, some of the most expensive housing markets in the United States. What she knows and articulated clearly over the course of our conversations is that as a Black woman, as an artist, her work and labor have consistently been devalued. By creating her tiny house, poignantly named the NOMAD, first as a vision and now a living space and demonstration space, she has been able to create a "loophole of retreat" and a freer mobility for herself within the violent mechanisms of US capitalism and its racial, gendered sociospatial control.

As a discipline, architecture has been largely made inaccessible to folks without formal architectural or building science training. The fraught spaces of tiny houses may yet allow us to unbind the discipline of architecture from idealized subjects and bodies and reconnect it to matters of geography and justice. As it has gained popularity, the Tiny House phenomenon has become synonymous with young white yuppies and aging white retirees, who are financially secure but want to be liberated from the burdens of consumption. The brief writing hooks (1995) does in "Black Vernacular" is important for connecting place, time, and the built environment to race, gender, and freedom. hooks's work offers us a different genealogy and an alternate political terrain to think about scale and space, allowing us to conceptualize how the tiny house represents the production of a new vernacular architecture and architectural subject.

CONCLUSION

> The kind of critical work I envisage moves to redefine our geography to recreate and remove the lines of impossibility in which we exist. . . . In redefining the critical and creative landscape, it is necessary to foreground whether one's work is for reconnection, invasion or exploitation. (Boyce Davies 1994, 17)

The Black feminist imagination that Carol Boyce Davies relays is deeply linked to space and critical invention. In trying to understand what Black feminist geographic practice might do within the Tiny House movement, I also interviewed Jewel Pearson, another African American woman who built and lives in a tiny house. Together, Pearson and Moody created the online community Tiny House Trailblazers, whose mission is to tell "stories of tiny house living and the movement from the lens of people of color. "Our purpose," they continue, "is never to be exclusive, instead our purpose is to ensure we're always included" (Tiny House Trailblazers, n.d.). Pearson is from the East Coast/ Southeast and worked the majority of her life in the financial sector. Pearson and Moody were introduced by geographer Lee Pera, who also built and lives in a tiny house. The three bonded over experiencing different forms of passive alienation, exclusion, or outright racism within the Tiny House movement. Their work performs the problem of human workability where the body of the Black, nonwhite, or physically or chemically injured subject with limited economic resources is a misfit, an untaxable, unsurveillable, uncontrollable problem-body for an architecture that relies on body normativity to rigidly dictate house size, layout, design, and materiality. bell hooks, writing in 1995, points to the need to think intersectionally about human ecologies, scale, and architecture. "Acknowledging that the world we are living in is one where space is becoming smaller and smaller really calls for a rethinking of architectural cultural practices" (hooks 1995, 159). Understanding the tiny house through a Black feminist perspective allows us to think about the mobility and smallness that tiny houses provide as part of a larger struggle to imagine a wider range of architectural subjectivities.

To inhabit an architectural subjectivity for whom there is no architectural plan has meant to live adaptively with the built environment, to make it more humanly workable, as one who thoughtfully engages improvisation, as in improvising a shelter, and the vernacular. This chapter traces the connections between the praxis of Black feminism, architecture, and the political possibility the tiny house may contain.

These are matters of not only geography and housing but Black feminist geography and architecture. With a generic idealistically healthy body in mind, space can be produced in gendered, ableist, classist, and racist ways. In my interviews with Black small and tiny house dwellers, they talk about needing spaces they can inhabit safely, for both the health of their bodies and the health of their minds. This is not safe space, but architectural and geographic space. These spatial thinkers have outlined the perimeters of their work, and it is clearly for the reconnection that Davis points to rather than for "invasion or exploitation" (Boyce Davies 1994, 17). In relation to this project, I see a necessary intervention and convergence of Black feminist thought, architecture, and geography in order to think about the house—not housing, but the house as a material, more humanly workable antagonist to an anti-Black urban plan.

"In white supremacist capitalist patriarchal Western culture neocolonial thinking sets the tone for many cultural practices. That thinking always focuses on who has conquered a territory, who has ownership, who has the right to rule" (hooks 2014, 44). The physical site of the house is a political assemblage of power that furthers capitalism, white supremacy, and settler colonialism. The house itself is a "matrix of domination" (Collins 2002, 23). There is a phenomenology and materiality to this place called a house that goes beyond a feminist theory of space that only understands individual rooms—the kitchen, the dining room, or the bedroom—or the nation space outside of the house as zones of racial-sexual subjugation (Colomina 1992; Domosh 1998, 278; Lupton and Miller 1996). It is difficult at this juncture to know what the future of my tiny house is. They are still illegal in Minneapolis, although as the small structures gain popularity across the US, the city is beginning to ease some of its housing regulations. I continue to believe that if we approach the tiny house through a subversive architectural genealogy I outlined above, then we can exercise our decisions around house planning and cities to stand in opposition to the Master's House, or "the big house" that has bound the Black body to an oppressive sociogeography. "When I visit huge mansions," writes Sterling Plumpp, "I run around to the back, looking for the house behind the house behind the Big house where my origins begin in this republic" (Woods 1998, vi). This relationship to architecture and geography is an altogether different relationship with landscape and is often, unfortunately, obscured by the nomenclature tiny house or Tiny House movement. The geographies and architectures of the past, of the big house, live alongside us in our cities, in our urban plans. Thinking about habitable space differently, the "Big house" continues to design our cities and streets and shape family relationships, implementing unjust forms of social control.

Building more humanly workable geographies is a process that grows out of a Black feminist praxis. For me and the women that I interviewed in this project, humanly workable space-making is not just in the building of the tiny houses themselves, but a process. They didn't build their spaces alone but with friends, designers, and ancestors, collaborating, thinking, working with others, teaching themselves. Tiny houses are fraught, and alone they cannot address the centuries of injustice that have deeply wronged Black folks and people of color who inhabit cities across the US. It is not my goal to pose the tiny house as a radical political object that can eradicate poverty or homelessness. They can, however, allow us to revisit the small and/or mobile architectural models that we once knew but have abandoned. They can help us see the exclusion of nonwhite people's living needs from the planning and development of houses in cities. They also allow us to revisit those alternate scales and densities of smallness as a way to live more humanly. Tiny houses present one possible praxis for building a just city.

NOTES

1. Vernacular architecture is often defined as "informal, usually domestic, architecture that is rooted in local traditions and is generally produced by craftsmen with little or no formal academic training, whose identity is unrecorded" (Alcock et al. 1996).
2. 26 US Code § 42, Low-Income Housing Credit, LII / Legal Information Institute, https://www.law.cornell.edu/uscode/text/26/42, accessed January 23, 2017. Since the writing of this essay, the 2017 Tax Cuts and Jobs Act proposed to replace artists with veterans under the section 42 subclause. While this proposed reform did not ultimately pass conference, the future of this clause remains uncertain.
3. In 2013, parts of the Voting Rights Act that held states with histories of voter suppression accountable to federal oversight were overturned. In 2016 the Supreme Court heard but ultimately upheld an affirmative action case brought on by the denial of admittance of a white student, Abigail Fisher, to the University of Texas at Austin.
4. The shotgun is no longer the most contested house in America. Tents and tent cities are causing municipalities to rethink their housing laws and practices using health and safety as legitimating forces to stage wholesale removals of families from the only

housing they may be able to afford. A recent lawsuit filed in Akron, Ohio, states that tent homes are functioning like "a campground." We could ask discursively what, other than time, is the difference between a campground and a neighborhood. Activists see these as contentious sites where the fight for more just urban housing plans may emerge. In cities like São Paulo, Brazil, planners have had to find ways to incorporate the space-time of favela builders and dwellers into the city's infrastructure because the speed with which these informal architects could move and rebuild their homes and neighborhoods continued to frustrate the city's attempts to eliminate them.

REFERENCES

Abraham, Amani. 2017. "Tent City in Akron Faces Lawsuit, Uncertain Future." *WKYC* (blog), November 20, 2017. http://www.wkyc.com/news/local/akron/tent-city-in-akron-faces -lawsuit-uncertain-future/493398395.

Agamben, Giorgio. 1998. *Homo Sacer: Sovereign Power and Bare Life*. Stanford, CA: Stanford University Press.

Alcock, N. W., et al. 1996. "Vernacular Architecture." *The Grove Dictionary of Art* online. http://www.oxfordartonline.com/subscriber/article/grove/art/T088875.

Beauregard, Robert A. 2006. *When America Became Suburban*. Minneapolis: University of Minnesota Press.

Boyce Davies, Carole. 1994. *Black Women, Writing, and Identity: Migrations of the Subject*. New York: Routledge.

Brennan, Morgan. 2012. "The Best and Worst Cities for Renters." *Forbes*. June 14, 2012. http://www.forbes.com/sites/morganbrennan/2012/06/14/the-best-and-worst-cities -for-renters-2/.

Carberry, Maegan. 2017. "HGTV Loves a Tiny House; You Do Too, but in the Communities That Need Them Most They're Outlawed." *Salon*. January 8, 2017. http://www.salon .com/2017/01/07/hgtv-loves-a-tiny-house-you-do-too-but-in-the-communities-that -need-them-most-theyre-outlawed/.

Chapin, F. Stuart. 1938. "The Effects of Slum Clearance and Rehousing on Family and Community Relationships in Minneapolis." *American Journal of Sociology* 43 (5): 744–63.

Collins, Patricia Hill. 2002. *Black Feminist Thought: Knowledge, Consciousness, and the Politics of Empowerment*. New York: Routledge.

Colomina, Beatriz. 1992. *Sexuality and Space*. Princeton Papers on Architecture. Princeton, NJ: Princeton Architectural Press.

Crysler, C. Greig. 2003. *Writing Spaces: Discourses of Architecture, Urbanism and the Built Environment, 1960–2000*. New York: Routledge.

Crysler, C. Greig, Stephen Cairns, and Hilde Heynen. 2012. *The SAGE Handbook of Architectural Theory*. Thousand Oaks, CA: Sage.

Domosh, Mona. 1998. "Geography and Gender: Home, Again?" *Progress in Human Geography* 22 (2): 276–82.

Du, Susan. 2016. "The Fight over the Minneapolis Housing Project That Sits on Gold." *City Pages*. July 6, 2016. http://www.citypages.com/news/the-fight-over-the-minneapolis -housing-project-that-sits-on-gold-8409176.

Edwards, Jay D. 2009. "Shotgun: The Most Contested House in America." *Buildings & Landscapes: Journal of the Vernacular Architecture Forum* 16 (1): 62–96.

Goetz, Edward Glenn. 1993. *Shelter Burden: Local Politics and Progressive Housing Policy*. Philadelphia: Temple University Press.

Gotham, Kevin Fox. 2000. "Urban Space, Restrictive Covenants and the Origins of Racial Residential Segregation in a US City, 1900–50." *International Journal of Urban and Regional Research* 24 (3): 616–33. https://doi.org/10.1111/1468-2427.00268.

Harney, Stefano, and Fred Moten. 2013. *The Undercommons: Fugitive Planning & Black Study.* Wivenhoe, NY: Minor Compositions.

Haynes, Bruce D. 2001. *Red Lines, Black Spaces: The Politics of Race and Space in a Black Middle-Class Suburb.* New Haven, CT: Yale University Press.

Helstein, Ralph, Shephard Towles, and John McFerren. 1960. "Tent City . . . Home of the Brave: Pamphlet." AFL-CIO. Industrial Union Department.

Hernandez, Jesus. 2009. "Redlining Revisited: Mortgage Lending Patterns in Sacramento 1930–2004." *International Journal of Urban and Regional Research* 33 (2): 291–313.

hooks, bell. 1995. *Art on My Mind: Visual Politics.* New York: New Press.

hooks, bell. 2014. *Feminism Is for Everybody: Passionate Politics.* New York: Routledge.

Institute on Metropolitan Opportunity. 2016. "The Rise of White-Segregated Subsidized Housing." University of Minnesota Law School. https://www.law.umn.edu/sites/law .umn.edu/files/metro-files/imo-white-segregated-subsidized-housing-5-18-2016.pdf.

Jacobs, Harriet [Brent, Linda]. (1861) 2000. *Incidents in the Life of a Slave Girl.* New York: W. W. Norton.

Kniffen, Fred B. 1936. "Louisiana House Types." *Annals of the Association of American Geographers* 26 (4): 179–93.

Long, Herman H., and Charles Spurgeon Johnson. 1947. *People vs. Property; Race Restrictive Covenants in Housing.* Nashville: Fisk University Press.

Lupton, Ellen, and J. Abbott Miller. 1996. *The Bathroom, the Kitchen, and the Aesthetics of Waste.* Princeton, NJ: Princeton Architectural Press.

Maharidge, Dale. 2011. *Someplace like America: Tales from the New Great Depression.* Berkeley: University of California Press.

McKittrick, Katherine. 2006. *Demonic Grounds: Black Women and the Cartographies of Struggle.* Minneapolis: University of Minnesota Press.

McKittrick, Katherine, and Clyde Adrian Woods. 2007. *Black Geographies and the Politics of Place.* Cambridge, MA: South End Press.

Moody, Dominique. 2018. Interview by Tia-Simone Gardner. Audio.

Morton, Patricia. 2003. "The Social and the Poetic: Feminist Practices in Architecture, 1970–2000." In *The Feminism and Visual Culture Reader,* edited by Amelia Jones, 277–81. New York: Routledge.

Schenk, Kathryn. 2015. "Flex House: Prefabricating the Tiny House Movement." Master's thesis, University of Cincinnati.

Semuels, Alana. 2016. "The Artist Loft: Affordable Housing (for White People)." *The Atlantic.* May 19, 2016. https://www.theatlantic.com/business/archive/2016/05/affordable -housing-for-white-people/483444/.

Serapião, Fernando. 2016. "Linking the Formal and Informal: Favela Urbanisation and Social Housing in São Paulo." *Architectural Design* 86 (3): 70–79.

Shafer, Jay. 2009. *The Small House Book.* Sebastopol, CA: Tumbleweed Tiny House Company.

Shafrir, Doree. 2016. "Who Benefits from the Tiny House Revolution?" *BuzzFeed.* July 5, 2016. https://www.buzzfeed.com/doree/who-is-the-tiny-house-revolution-for.

Smith, Neil. 2005. *The New Urban Frontier: Gentrification and the Revanchist City.* New York: Routledge.

Sparshott, Jeffrey. 2016. "U.S. Houses Are Still Getting Bigger." *Wall Street Journal* (blog). June 2, 2016. https://blogs.wsj.com/economics/2016/06/02/u-s-houses-are-still -getting-bigger/.

Tiny House Trailblazers. n.d. "Who We Are." Accessed March 18, 2018. http://tinyhousetrail blazers.com/who-we-are/.

Vlach, John Michael. 1993. *Back of the Big House: The Architecture of Plantation Slavery.* Chapel Hill: University of North Carolina Press.

Walsh, Kaitlyn. 2012. "Dust-up over Hmong Gardens." *Star Tribune.* July 31, 2012. http:// www.startribune.com/dust-up-over-hmong-gardens/163773516/.

Waring, Emma. 2008. "Modification and Discharge of Restrictive Covenants: The Housing Act of 1985." *The Cambridge Law Journal* 67 (2): 249–52.

Wilkinson, Alec. 2011. "Let's Get Small." *New Yorker*. July 18, 2011. http://www.newyorker .com/magazine/2011/07/25/lets-get-small.

Williamson, Terrion L. 2016. *Scandalize My Name: Black Feminist Practice and the Making of Black Social Life*. Oxford: Oxford University Press.

Woods, Clyde Adrian. 1998. *Development Arrested: The Blues and Plantation Power in the Mississippi Delta*. New York: Verso.

Zenou, Yves, and Nicolas Boccard. 2000. "Racial Discrimination and Redlining in Cities." *Journal of Urban Economics* 48 (2): 260–85.

CHAPTER 7

DECOLONIZING DEVELOPMENT, CHALLENGING PATRIARCHY: COLONIALISM, CAPITALISM, AND GENDER IN DINÉ BIKEYAH

Melanie K. Yazzie and Andrew Curley

INTRODUCTION

Colonialism and capitalism gained influence in Diné life partially through the transformation of Diné genders, identities, and relations. This was accomplished by instituting patriarchy, establishing binary gender roles, and hardening boundaries between Diné masculinity and femininity while denying other genders that were a part of historic Diné social life. Through colonial structures and practices, Diné masculinity evolved into forms of "public" labor, such as political representation, blue-collar work, and military service, while Diné femininity shifted into "private" or "domestic" forms of labor like child-rearing, cooking, and cleaning. In this chapter, we argue that labor practices, as well as ideas about what counts as labor, have been reorganized through the enforcement of gender binaries and, specifically, the idealization of Diné binary gender roles that embrace capitalist development and US political supremacy.

Drawing from feminist geography and Indigenous feminism, we historicize two new social roles in Diné life, the politician and the male wage earner, to show how the new energy economies of the postwar period required a gendered division of labor in Diné society consistent with the crisp binaries between public and private work we outline above. We examine in particular

Annie Wauneka's work in Diné health and welfare and demonstrate the function of gender binaries in the logics of "development" that came to dictate Diné social and political life during this period. We conclude by drawing from Indigenous feminists to provide provisional thoughts about decolonizing labor and development through an intersectional framework informed by decolonial and nonheteronormative values. This concluding section builds on the insights of Marxist feminists writing about Diné women who have encouraged scholars to see their "hidden" histories of agency, adaptation, and resistance to capitalism (McCloskey 2007; O'Neill 2005; Voyles 2015). Finally, we advocate for a political project that targets the structures of power, capitalism, and colonialism, which operate cunningly through the gendered guise of development to perpetuate our people's exploitation and elimination.

GENDERED DIVISION OF LABOR IN DINÉ BIKEYAH

In the early-morning hours of Monday, April 29, 2013, dozens of Diné men in jeans, windbreakers, and baseball caps boarded two chartered buses in a grocery store parking lot in the remote northern Diné community of Kayenta. The men on the bus were Diné union workers associated with the United Mine Workers of America (UMWA). In the darkness, they started a trip to Window Rock, the capital of the Navajo Nation, where yet another group of Diné men, elected tribal officials, were set to debate and decide on the future of the Navajo Generating Station and Navajo Mine, the last remaining coal infrastructures in the reservation. Coal work had been in rapid decline since 2006, when the first power plant and mine shut down, resulting in the layoff of hundreds of workers. By April 2006, the tribal government and workers' union had collaborated to salvage the remaining two coal mines in order to preserve the tribal coal economy. This event and mobilization were expressions of values that confirmed not only narratives of development and modernization within the Navajo Nation but also the role of "men" and "women" in Diné society. The "jobs" that were salvaged, albeit temporarily, were not simply sources of work and livelihood but a function of public and domestic roles in the Navajo Nation. These roles were not historic from time immemorial; they were mechanically conditioned through colonial structures.

Fifty years earlier, in 1963, Annie Wauneka, the celebrated daughter of the tribe's first (and equally celebrated) chairman, Chee Dodge, served as the first and only female council delegate in the Navajo Tribal Council, renamed Navajo Nation in 1968 (see Lister 2017). The tribe had just signed its first coal leases, ushering in a form of Diné sovereignty that was expressed through a coal-dominant economy (Iverson and Roessel 2002). By that point, Wauneka had been in office for more than ten years. As a council delegate, she advocated a form of Diné sovereignty that prioritized Diné public health and welfare through advancements in hospitals, medicine, and science. Wauneka was famous for home visits she performed in the course of her work on promoting "Western" medicines among sick Diné people (Niethammer 2004). Her care for everyday Diné people and willingness to demonstrate domestic forms of labor in Diné homes as a Diné leader made her beloved among people. However, this distinct approach also signaled a new politics of care that reflected changing notions of gender and labor in the Navajo Nation, binaries of gender with concomitant notions of work, care, patriarchy, and capitalism in the region.

Wauneka's politics of care, particularly as it was expressed through her labor to eradicate tuberculosis and trachoma, garnered her national and international acclaim at a time when "the predominant motif" in international public health campaigns was the eradication of mass disease in "underdeveloped" nations, which were commonly depicted through gendered logics of backwardness and irrationality that feminized underdevelopment and masculinized development.[1] Diné political and social relations were simultaneously tied to the capitalist exploitation of coal (and uranium). Images of strong, masculine Diné coal workers and tribal leaders gave legitimacy to a new Diné national economy based on the extraction of resources for development. Development, with its masculine overtones, was celebrated as the promise of Diné futurity. Diseases of the home like tuberculosis and trachoma were seen as feminized and pejorative, evidence of underdevelopment and therefore in need of redress. Women of the developing world, like Wauneka, received acclaim and heightened political legitimacy for ushering the Diné people into a masculine age of development through crusades to eradicate a mass disease that was feminized and considered the dominion of women in the domestic household.

Development in the Navajo Nation has historically and structurally relied on extractive industries. The state-sponsored Bureau of Indian Affairs (BIA) established the first form of centralized governing authority in 1922 with a business council whose purpose was to expedite mineral leases within the reservation (Curley 2018a). This business council was exclusively comprised of men. One dominant personality, Jacob C. Morgan, was a Christian who advocated for the assimilation of Diné people into mainstream US society. One of his primary methods for assimilation involved promoting regional independence for northern Diné communities in an effort to speed up development (Iverson and Roessel 2002; Kelly 1968). He was an early proponent of an emergent assimilationist ideology among male leaders in the Navajo Nation. As has been well documented, his viewpoints dominated Diné politics for most of the tribe's subsequent political history (Wilkins 2013). Although the business council was quickly disbanded, its legacy serves as an example of the patriarchy inherent in the tribe's first modern political institutions.

Following iterations of the council reflected changes in federal Indian policy that began in 1934 with the Indian Reorganization Act (IRA). The IRA jettisoned the idea of regional autonomy and created for the first time in Diné history a central government that controlled all of Diné lands (Curley 2014). BIA agents selected regional headmen to the tribe's first council, repeating the patriarchal assumptions of the previous council and excluding women from representing Diné interests in the newly forming political sphere. Once these roles were defined and enforced through voting mechanisms completely new to Diné people, the secretary of the interior invested all remaining power not already reserved to the federal government into this new "elected" tribal council comprised entirely of men (Wilkins 2013).

Diné headmen turned council "delegates" quickly set the Navajo Tribe's agenda toward modernization, Christian morality, assimilation, and economic development through the extraction of natural resources. For the first half of the twentieth century, the Diné Tribe developed oil (Chamberlain 2000) and uranium (Voyles 2015). Revenues from these activities funded the tribal government and expanded services provided to the people (Curley 2018a). Oil and uranium sales, however, were not nearly enough to maintain a cohesive nation, and the BIA still focused on assimilation. The BIA partnered with soil scientists to attack and destroy the Diné sheep economy, the source of remaining economic and political independence for the Diné people (Weisiger 2011). Destruction of the Diné sheep economy became what Karl Marx famously called "original" or "primitive" accumulation (1967). It had the impact of destroying and replacing the matrilineal material basis for the social reproduction of Diné life. The Diné people now had to earn money in the form of wages and labor to survive.

In the 1940s, prospectors found uranium in abundant supply in and around the Navajo Nation (Brugge, Benally, and Yazzie-Lewis 2006). Until coal opened up in the 1960s, uranium mining was one of the most lucrative forms of work for many Diné men. Others were construction, railroad work, and seasonal agriculture (Adams and Ruffing 1977). It would be many years before the Diné people realized that working conditions for Diné men in the mines were deadly. A "slow violence" of exposure to uranium ore without proper ventilation, clothing, or education resulted in hundreds of cancers in Diné men years after they stopped working at the mine site (Eichstaedt 1994). The Navajo Nation first placed a moratorium on uranium mining in 1983 and fully banned it in 2005 with the passage of the Diné Natural Resource Protection Act (Curley 2008; Smith and Frehner 2010).

During the 1960s, the tribe agreed to multiple coal leases and power plants. Coal became a vital part of the expansion of cities in the US Southwest (Needham 2014). Much of this coal was discovered in the Black Mesa region of the Navajo and Hopi Nations (Ambler 1990; Benally 2011; Nies 2014). The Navajo Nation subsequently exploited coal under this new understanding of nature that interpreted the elements of earth as a repository of "resources" rather than part of the earth and its ecosystems (Powell 2017; Powell and Curley 2008).

Between 1877 and 1934, the US government enacted policies that were blatantly racist and meant to destroy Indigenous life and incorporate all Indigenous lands into the expanding United States (Dunbar-Ortiz 2014). In 1934, at the height of the progressive movement in the United States, Congress passed the IRA. The IRA replaced Indigenous systems of leadership with notions of liberal representative democracy and, as we note above, concentrated political power into tribal council systems led entirely by men (Deloria 1985). The official demarcations and boundaries of reservations, as determined by the US government, became the dominion of the Navajo Tribal Council. These were political arrangements imposed onto Diné people from the United States.

Tribal governments made Diné political leadership legible to settler colonists who governed on behalf of the federal government (Curley 2014). As Jennifer Nez Denetdale has pointed out, this transition brought with it colonial ideologies about gender, leadership, and sexuality (Denetdale 2009). Political control over reservation territory was concentrated into a group of men, called a tribal "council," who nominally represented different geographical regions of the nation and who could speak to the majority interest of the people in these regions. Through these mechanisms, the US federal government exclusively empowered male leadership to conform to a colonial project of assimilation. The goal was to make Christianization and gender binaries permanent features of Diné life. BIA officials actively recruited complicit Diné men for roles in leadership and undermined those who challenged federal supremacy and authority. As we note above, women were written out of their roles in political leadership altogether (Denetdale 2006). Tribal sovereignty, as it is understood and practiced today, continues to prioritize the role of men in patriarchal institutions that comport with capitalism and colonialism (Barker 2005, 2011).

At the same time, the BIA pressured Diné people to assimilate at the lowest rungs of an emerging regional capitalist economy, which included work in railroads, construction, and mining (Hosmer, O'Neill, and Fixico 2004). The BIA funded programs that would bring Diné men to work camps in nearby border towns (O'Neill 2005). The BIA encouraged Native men and women to work as seasonal migrants in the once vibrant agricultural economies of the West and Southwest. Eventually, large agribusiness replaced Indigenous labor with that of migrants from nearby Mexico, who could be more easily exploited (Robinson and Santos 2014). For the rest of the twentieth century, Indigenous men worked as labor for the development of infrastructure in the incorporated southwestern states. Alongside the merging of Diné political authority and expression with patriarchy, wage labor produced a gendered division of labor. Women assumed (and, in some cases, continued) the work of traditional subsistence while men earned money. The duties of subsistence fell almost exclusively on women as men sought out "formalized" work in emerging industries. Through a dependence on money, men gained complete control of the household, and despite their relative control over continued subsistence practices like sheepherding, women, too, became largely dependent on the ebb and flow of income that men could earn through wage labor (Albers 1983; Albers and Medicine 1983).

In the 1940s, the United States funded an extensive "relocation" program that moved Indigenous families from reservation communities into urbanizing cities. For Diné people, this included distant cities such as Los Angeles, Phoenix, and Denver (Fixico 1986, 2000). The 1961 documentary *The Exiles* captured this transition as it happened, focusing on families and their daily struggles in the Bunker Hill district of Los Angeles. This documentary chronicles efforts to assimilate Indigenous peoples into a city foreign and hostile to Indigenous cultures. Importantly, the film depicts how Native men and women conformed to the dominant gender roles of the 1950s, with men serving as workers and women remaining at home to take care of children and perform household labor. The BIA and Christian institutions cooperated to encourage this transformation in household and gender roles, which empowered men over women by allowing men to monopolize control over the means of production in almost all facets of daily life, regardless of distinctions between public and private activities (Mojab 2015). They also helped solidify support for patriarchal political leadership by extending male dominance in all spheres of life.

Relocation also intensified poverty, which effectively cemented the gender binaries and divisions of labor by rendering Indigenous peoples dependent upon wage work and unequal social relations premised on unequal terms of trade and exploitation (M'Closkey 2008; Mauer 2014). Settler colonial policies like relocation worked with capitalist labor structures to transform matrilocal kinship relations into nuclear families dependent upon men's wage labor and the subservience of women performing social reproduction at home. Both capitalism and colonialism worked in tandem to separate Indigenous communities from their land. The subordination of women to men within the private and public spheres was accomplished through the expansion of patriarchy and the dissolution of land-based relationality.

DEVELOPMENT, THE POLITICS OF CARE, AND ANNIE WAUNEKA

During the rise of the modern Navajo Nation in the 1950s, Annie Wauneka, the tribe's second (and at the time only) female tribal delegate, was elected to the Navajo Nation Tribal Council and quickly was elected chair of the Council's Health and Welfare Committee—a committee tasked with overseeing the political implementation of gendered domesticity. With her commanding presence and drive for improving Diné health, Wauneka had considerable influence over health and welfare improvement across the Navajo Nation. She brought unwavering support for the paradigms of development and progress that her father, Chee Dodge, had championed during his long tenure as a political leader starting in 1883. In a speech titled "The Diné and His Future" that she delivered to a roundtable conference at El Morro Theatre in Gallup, New Mexico, on August 10, 1951, Wauneka outlined her approach, "The last great Diné leader, Chee Dodge . . . knew that only through education would his tribe be a productive people. . . . I am here for the same purpose, to stress the need for more and bigger schools; the essential needs in hospitals and sanatoriums."[2]

As a child, Wauneka spent most of her time with her father, acquiring political training early on by following him to meetings with important political figures. Wauneka, who credited her famous father with inspiring her to become a political figure, was deeply committed to continuing his work to make the Diné people "productive" through the development of institutions of progress like education and public health. Arguably the most powerful leader in early modern Diné history, Dodge was selected and groomed by US Indian agents in the late nineteenth century to usher the Diné people into an era of development and improvement. He became the first chairman of the 1922 business council and later served as the chairman of the tribe from 1942 to 1946, after which he was elected as the vice chairman just prior to his death in 1947.

Dodge's influence on this important era of twentieth-century Diné history, which brought livestock reduction, the centralization of Diné government in concert with US colonial and capitalist interests, and the introduction of resource extraction, cannot be overstated.

As both an elected official and trusted advisor, Dodge shaped tribal policy for more than fifty years. But he also labored to secure an economic empire for his family at a time when most Diné were suffering from poverty. Dodge was a consummate entrepreneur who created new markets in Diné jewelry, high-end livestock sales, and other profitable opportunities opened up by the construction of railroads—a key technology of settlement and US territorial expansion—through Diné territory. Dodge was quite possibly the first Diné entrepreneur. As Richard Van Valkenburg noted in a June 1943 profile of Dodge that appeared in *Arizona Highways*,

> With the coming of the Atlantic and Pacific R.R. . . . Diné blankets and silver started to develop into a new income source. Recognizing the possibilities for his tribesman, Chee took great interest. Sponsoring the greatest of all Diné silversmiths, Atsidih Sanih, Chee had the old silversmith make him the first turquoise set Diné ring ever wrought from silver.[3]

Dodge and his daughter were also notoriously extravagant, collecting high-quality consumer goods like new vehicles, thoroughbred horses, and diamond jewelry. Dodge was reportedly one of the first Diné to ever own a wagon and, later, a vehicle. In a letter dated April 19, 1884, Navajo agent Denis Riordan highlighted how "Chee was a great one for fine clothes—the best in horses, and everything. You knew he was something when you looked at him!" And like his daughter, who was awarded the Presidential Medal of Freedom in 1963 "for performance of a meritorious act or service in the interests of the security of the United States," Dodge was also recognized for his loyalty to the US government. In the same letter, Riordan states that "Chee's loyalty remains ever steadfast to Washington Sita'ih, the Eternal Chief, who sits in a hogan under a white dome that shines like the sacred white shell in the land east of the sunrise."[4]

Dodge's ability to accumulate both political and monetary capital garnered him the attention and admiration of white Indian agents like Riordan. Decades later, his daughter's accomplishments would be lauded in similar fashion. White politicians, businessmen, journalists, and academics used similar terminology of productivity, progress, and development to celebrate and commend Wauneka's fidelity to the values of capitalist and colonial expansion underwriting US nationalism. Over the cumulative span of one hundred years, Dodge and Wauneka influenced an entire epoch of Diné history by implementing development programs like livestock reduction, resource extraction, and health care delivery. In this sense, Wauneka's legibility as a Diné woman political leader was a direct extension of her father's leading role in defining a modern gendered division of labor. The compound histories of gender, capitalism, and settler colonialism that defined her father's life also conditioned Wauneka's, resulting in a brand of Diné women's leadership that consolidated these histories into an archetype that persists to this day in Diné tribal politics.

Although it would be unfair to claim that Wauneka's father overdetermined her politics and eventual legacy, it is important to point out that her contributions were shaped by class privilege that granted her unusual power (for a woman) and legibility within the emerging gendered division of labor. Like other powerful men holding political office, her father played a major role in normalizing the gendered division of labor in Diné social relations. He also benefited immensely from these changes by literally capitalizing on the economic and political power that the new patriarchy conferred onto him.

These biographical details help to explain part of Wauneka's success as a Diné woman in the public sphere: her gender performance was agreeable to the paradigm of development that extended capitalist and colonial interests (Yazzie 2018).[5] But in other ways she was subject to prevailing gendered logics of labor and value. A review of newspaper and magazine stories about her career demonstrates that her success as a female public figure depended on how well she made "domestic" issues like health, tuberculosis, and child welfare politically relevant by framing them through development idioms like productivity, progress, and improvement. Journalists and political leaders were particularly captivated by her early work to eradicate tuberculosis in the 1950s and her later campaigns in the 1980s to address alcoholism. Articles that focused on her many accomplishments in these areas frequently framed her work in terms of the improvement of Diné life, often citing her as the single most important figure in the history of Diné progress. In a November 1, 1970, article in *Empire Magazine*, Paul Friggens wrote, "White doctors and health officials freely credit Annie with spearheading the greatest improvement in general conditions among the tribe in nearly a century."[6] In an *Arizona Republic* story about Wauneka's legacy following her death in 1997, former Navajo Nation president Albert Hale praised Wauneka as "one of the great Diné leaders" who led the transition of the Navajo Nation from "farming and sheepherding to the modern mixed economy of today."[7] An article in the June 10, 1970, issue of the *Navajo Times* wrote:

Through the efforts of Dr. Wauneka, tuberculosis which was at one time in just about every Diné home has just about been eradicated on the reservation. She has also [sic] much work in the area of environmental health (living standards), in the area of improved housing from the round house to the square house with more windows, improved water wells, better food and eating habits.[8]

Collectively, these accounts portray Wauneka's legacy as a leader who ushered her people into an era of progress through improvements in health, education, welfare, housing, and labor.

As we note in the introduction, Wauneka achieved legibility and power in the public sphere primarily through performing labor like caretaking and self-help advocacy typically considered to be the work of women conducting domestic labor, or care, for their families and homes in the private/domestic sphere. However, private/domestic matters—as well as Wauneka's own labor as a woman—could only be intelligible within the public sphere of Diné politics if Wauneka translated caretaking into a politics consistent with (masculine) ideologies of development. Indeed, it seems that, as a woman, Wauneka was granted access to the Diné public sphere precisely because she embodied and reproduced this politics of care in her political work. Her focus on eradicating biological diseases of the home in the name of developmentalist notions like productivity and improvement speaks powerfully to this. As Wauneka herself boasted later in her life, "I'm forever disappointed with something," implying that her drive to "go and do more" (which is the title of her biography by Carolyn Niethammer) required a commitment to the ethos of improvement and progress that federal lawmakers, Indian agents, and anthropologists had been espousing since the beginning of the reservation period. By all accounts, Wauneka surpassed her male (and female) counterparts by fostering development and perfecting the gendered division of labor.

THE ENFORCEMENT OF PATRIARCHY IN DINÉ BIKEYAH

The enforcement and reproduction of gender binaries like public/private, and political/domestic during this period of Diné history points to how capitalism required gendered logics of heteronormative patriarchy to do its literal and metaphorical work. Indeed, one need only pick up a copy of the Navajo Nation's largest newspaper, *Navajo Times*, in 1963 to find a picture of Wauneka receiving the Presidential Medal of Freedom from then-president Lyndon B. Johnson alongside advertisements from Arizona Public Service, a private utility reliant on Diné coal, extolling the social benefits of the coal industry for Diné people. The visual and narrative coupling of Wauneka's achievements in caretaking with the promise of a coal-driven livelihood secured through the wage labor of Diné men shows how gendered expressions of wage and domestic labor in Diné Bikeyah originate from this key aspect of capitalist expansion across reservation lands.

Yet these binaries also reproduced other structures of power that intersect with capitalism to shape Diné life according to the overarching interests of US nationalism. Gender binaries facilitated the larger project of settler colonialism, as Mark Rifkin points out, and required Native peoples to conform to the hierarchies of value inherent to heteronormative patriarchy (Rifkin 2010). Heteronormative patriarchy, and the hierarchical gender binaries that animate it, were key methods of Indigenous elimination (Simpson 2014; Wolfe 1999). They facilitated the dispossession of land, the destruction of preexisting political and legal structures based on decentralized and matrilineal structures, and the assimilation of Native people into economies of dependency by destroying economic and political independence, which was customarily controlled by women (Denis 2007). In other words, gender binaries facilitated the separation of Diné families from values that prioritized communal responsibility, matrilineal authority, and the caretaking of human and other-than-human relations. These were all key tactics of US settler colonialism.

It is common knowledge among the Diné that prior to the introduction of wage labor, Diné society was matrilineal. Men married into the wife's family and lived and worked among her relatives. Wealth and labor were derived from relationality with land and livestock, practices and values that descended through the mother's line (M'Closkey 2008). The advent of state-sponsored programs euphemized as "livestock reduction" during the 1930s and 1940s changed this (Reed 2005). Land-based structures of labor and sources of wealth, also seen through gendered logics as backward, irrational, or inefficient, were systematically targeted for destruction or improvement by state policies (Shepardson 1982). The destruction brought on by livestock reduction completely transformed the Diné world and facilitated the introduction of and complete dependence on wage economies based on the extraction of resources like coal and uranium (Iverson and Roessel 2002; Weisiger 2011; White 1983). While this transition effectuated the dissolution of Diné gender, labor, kinship, ceremonial, and subsistence practices, it also enforced heteronormative patriarchy to eliminate Diné lifeways and force the Diné to assimilate to Anglo-American nationalist values and practices. This was achieved by attacking the very fabric of Diné social relations—human bodies, lands, temporalities, epistemologies, other-than-human relatives, family and labor structures, and political and individual independence achieved through subsistence economies (Eldridge 2014).

Today the Navajo Nation considers coal, oil, and other extractive industries the backbone of the tribal economy. In 2013, coal workers from Kayenta Mine and Navajo Mine assembled at the Navajo Nation Tribal Council to ask the tribe to renew coal leases and their livelihoods (Curley 2018b). The conditions for masculine public performance, both from the Navajo Nation Council delegates and the coal workers, were conditioned by more than one hundred years of colonial transformations. As this chapter demonstrates, institutions of Indigenous governance and notions of development and gender worked together to produce patriarchal forms of power across Indigenous homelands. Diné coal work, which benefited male wage earners first and foremost, was prioritized over any future subsistence or energy alternatives (Powell 2015). There is even a symbolic metaphor at work in the masculine penetration of the earth, which is often gendered as feminine. At the same time, the nature of capitalism is also changing, moving toward neoliberal development realities that undermine patriarchal roles in welfare states and have led to nativist, racist backlash across the globe (Gökarıksel and Smith 2016). In the Navajo Nation, neoliberalization in the future of coal or energy development has destabilized patriarchal households and has stymied "green" energy alternatives (Curley 2018a). Such a destabilization creates new opportunities and new risks for the decolonization of gender and development. In the final section, we consider future possibilities led by Indigenous feminists.

INDIGENOUS FEMINISM AND FUTURE POSSIBILITIES

Thus far, we have argued that capitalism and settler colonialism do their work through the reproduction of gender binaries and the normalization of gendered labor hierarchies. In this concluding section, we explore how Indigenous feminists challenge the fiction of hierarchical gender binaries, and the capitalist and colonial social relations that rely on them. We follow Albers (1983, 178), who argues that Marxist feminists need to consider "the resistance and challenge of those who labor under capitalism," including women and colonized nations. We look to the labor of Diné women engaged in activism—itself a form of labor typically considered public/political—to examine how these women use their public platform to uncover, challenge, and abolish the violence inherent to exploitation and devaluation. Simultaneously, these women advance a queer and Indigenous politics of care that disrupts gender binaries and labor hierarchies by envisioning and implementing forms of labor premised on horizontal accountability, reciprocity, mutual aid, and kinship.

Although she may never have self-identified as a feminist, Wauneka represents one type of feminist intervention into the gendered division of labor that capitalized on the public/private distinction to politicize domesticity and improve the welfare of her people. However, as her receipt of the Presidential Medal of Freedom implies, the larger political project to which she contributed conformed to developmentalist ideologies, which ultimately resulted in the further incorporation of Diné people into social relations dictated by capitalism, colonialism, and heteropatriarchy. In other words, Wauneka's politics neither acknowledged nor challenged the violence underlying these social relations. Her type of feminism therefore lacked the anticolonial and anticapitalist foundation that other Indigenous feminists—including other Diné women— have identified as central to the project of feminist and queer liberation (Yazzie 2018). Indeed, Indigenous feminists argue that heteronormative patriarchy cannot be abolished without also abolishing capitalism and settler colonialism, for the social relations and constructs (like public/private, political/domestic) that bind these three structures of power are intersectional and therefore deeply intertwined.

Yazzie has argued that gender and sexual violence profoundly condition Indigeneity, as well as the basic elements of agency, subjectivity, and common sense that illuminate its many dimensions (Yazzie 2016). One need only perform a simple Google search of the phrase "missing and murdered Indigenous women," or MMIW, to find almost two and a half million results addressing this issue, including countless news stories, scholarly articles, blog entries, interviews, legislative proceedings, court cases, websites, conference presentations, artistic projects, and activist campaigns. The sheer volume and variety of sources on MMIW demonstrates how profoundly the discourse and material reality of gender and sexual violence have shaped our collective political consciousness as Indigenous feminists and, indeed, as Native people more broadly. As such, we might follow the lead of Indigenous feminists to consider violence as a fundamental mode of exchange in capitalist and colonial societies, and thus one of the principal lenses through which to understand the historical and material dimensions of Native life, including resistance (Yazzie 2016).

Recent movements within Diné Bikéyah have formed to address related forms of violence that attack land (resource extraction) and bodies (gender and sexual violence against Diné women and LGBTQ2[9] relatives). Examples include the women-led Nihígaal Bee Iiná action that sought to draw connections between the environmental violence of resource extraction and gender violence against Diné womxn, femmes, and LGBTQ2 relatives. The K'é Infoshop, which is in the capital of the Navajo Nation, Window Rock, Arizona, hosts "Matriarch Mondays" and has a women- and femme-led collective that espouses Indigenous feminism as one of their guiding principles. Leaders of the collective engage in alternative forms of community building and political discourse that directly challenge capitalism, settler colonialism, and heteropatriarchy in the heart of the very tribal institutions that deliver these ideologies to Diné people.

Others have produced similar campaigns to politicize violence that is typically marked through gendered logics as "domestic" and therefore not political (i.e., not structural). Not surprisingly, this violence is often met with silence and dismissal because it targets bodies, lands, and relatives who have been relegated to a feminized and devalued status as domestic or underdeveloped. Navajo Nation Tribal Council delegate Amber Crotty's advocacy for Ashlynne Mike, an eleven-year-old Diné girl who was raped and murdered by an older male relative in 2016, and Radmilla Cody's decades-long work to stop domestic violence are key examples. The multigender Bordertown Justice Coalition, which has been challenging the 2016 police killing of Diné mother Loreal Tsingine in the border town of Winslow, Arizona, has tied its #Justice4Loreal campaign into the larger movement for MMIW justice. These public efforts, led mostly by prominent Diné women, have not only politicized an issue considered to be private and relegated to the domestic sphere but also raised uncomfortable questions about how gender and sexual violence are perverse forms of gendered labor performed primarily by men to reproduce and enforce relations of exploitation and elimination.

The politicization of gender and sexual violence has made connections between the inequalities, exploitations, dispossessions, and extractions that animate settler colonial and capitalist social relations, and the lived and embodied experiences of Diné women (Million 2009). Ultimately, neither labor nor gender roles can operate according to a logic of patriarchy, which is a violent ideology of gender that simply reinforces the violent ideologies of settler colonialism and capitalism. Diné women have entered political discourse and participation with different expectations that challenge the intersection of these ideologies. These Diné women are carving out new, decolonized definitions and material configurations of women's labor that blur the boundaries between public/private and political/domestic that maintain the patriarchy.

The framework of decolonization that Diné feminists like Yazzie are actively producing is based on what Indigenous feminists call "relationality," or generations of unbroken Indigenous relationships with land, water, and other-than-human kin (Goeman and Denetdale 2009; Yazzie and Baldy 2018). Although some of the most celebrated scholarship on Native liberation is masculine and written by Indigenous men (Alfred 2005; Coulthard 2014; Estes 2019), Indigenous feminists—most of whom are cis women, trans women, gay or lesbian, or gender nonconforming—are drawing from these works but recentering and revaluing forms of political and ontological arrangement that have been silenced, violated, and devalued by the capitalist and colonial gendered division of labor. They are envisioning and enacting decolonial social relations premised instead on land and water protection and caretaking (Goeman and Denetdale 2009; LaDuke 1999).

Kim TallBear (2016) argues that caretaking is an expression of "obligations of human kin with our other kin." However, TallBear advances a queer Indigenous ethics of caretaking that is not attached to specific bodies. For TallBear, caretaking does not presume a natural link to the biological imperative of reproduction (i.e., natalism) that often defines cis hetero Indigenous womanhood and motherhood (Yazzie and Baldy 2018). For example, within the larger tiospaye kinship system that TallBear grew up in as a Dakota woman, biological mothers are not the only caretakers. Likewise, those who choose not to (or cannot) have biological children can be mothers and caretakers within the expansive view of kinship and relationality tiospaye names. Extending from this definition of kinship is a theory and practice of relationality-as-caretaking that regenerates and reproduces life wherever it is practiced. The distinction between natalist and non-natalist definitions of kinship is important; while the former excludes all LGBTQ2, disabled, and gender-nonconforming womxn from the web of caretaking (as both caretakers and those who deserve to be caretaken) because of their perceived biological failure and deviancy, the latter envisions an expansive practice of kinship in which all relatives—regardless of their gender or ability—are included in the circle of caretaking so long as they abide by an ethics of responsibility, respect, and reciprocity that binds kin together.

The queer Indigenous feminist politics of care that extends from TallBear's definition of caretaking is markedly different from the liberal politics of care that Wauneka was expected to perform in her role as a tribal leader. Where the former rejects both hierarchy and normative gender roles in its politics of care, the latter reinforces them to keep capitalist and colonial social relations in place. What is at stake in these different approaches is the possibility for imagining and practicing a politics that might shape decolonial futures. We need to upend the capitalist economic order, which depends on gender binaries, patriarchy, and violence, in our communities in order to decolonize our collective futures.

NOTES

1. See https://www.unicef.org/sowc96/1950s.htm, accessed June 8, 2018.
2. Box 2, Folder 16, Carolyn Niethammer Collection, Arizona State University Libraries Labriola Center, Arizona State University, Tempe, AZ.
3. Box 2, Folder 26, Carolyn Niethammer Collection, Arizona State University Libraries Labriola Center, Arizona State University, Tempe, AZ.
4. Box 2, Folders 25 and 26, Carolyn Niethammer Collection, Arizona State University Libraries Labriola Center, Arizona State University, Tempe, AZ.
5. Although much of her impact on Diné history can be explained through her acceptance of capitalism, settler colonialism, and heteronormative patriarchy, it is important to highlight the ways in which Wauneka resisted one of the key arbiters of colonial control over her people's destiny: the US government. Wauneka took a unique position on the issue of self- determination, arguing that federal superintendence minimized true self-determination and that federally sponsored demonstration programs ought to lead to full Diné control over all matters of administration, economic policy, and governance. Her comment about the 1868 treaty speaks to this view, as do other comments she made during the same speech. She proclaimed, "We don't want the Indian Service to be pestering us forever . . . the Dinés must put forth all their efforts to rid Window Rock of incompetent and useless officials and get Dinés into as many jobs there as possible. Otherwise we will be like monkeys in a cage for the rest of the Americans to look at." However, despite her disapproval of federal superintendence, Wauneka nevertheless championed a form of Diné self-determination predicated on prevailing notions of development at the time. Box 2, Folder 16, Carolyn Niethammer Collection, Arizona State University Libraries Labriola Center, Arizona State University, Tempe, AZ.
6. Paul Friggens, "Annie Wauneka: Great Lady of the Diné," *Empire Magazine*, November 1, 1970. Box 2, Folder 13, Carolyn Niethammer Collection, Arizona State University Libraries Labriola Center, Arizona State University, Tempe, AZ.
7. Mark Shaffer, "Diné Activist against TB Dies: 'Legendary' Annie Wauneka, 89," *Arizona Republic*, undated, Box 2, Folder 16, Carolyn Niethammer Collection, Arizona State University Libraries Labriola Center, Arizona State University, Tempe, AZ.
8. A.L. Roland, "Annie Wauneka, A True Humanitarian," *Navajo Times*, June 10, 1976, Box 2, Folder 12, Carolyn Niethammer Collection, Arizona State University Libraries Labriola Center, Arizona State University, Tempe, AZ.
9. Lesbian, gay, bisexual, transgender, queer, two-spirit.

REFERENCES

Adams, William Y., and Lorraine T. Ruffing. 1977. "Shonto Revisited: Measures of Social and Economic Change in a Navajo Community, 1955–1971." *American Anthropologist* 79 (1): 58–83.

Albers, Patricia. 1983. "Sioux Women in Transition: A Study of their Changing Status in Domestic and Capitalist Sectors of Production." In *The Hidden Half: Studies of Plains Indian Women*, edited by Patricia Albers and Beatrice Medicine, 175–234. Lanham, MD: University Press of America.

Albers, Patricia, and Beatrice Medicine. 1983. *The Hidden Half: Studies of Plains Indian Women*. Lanham, MD: University Press of America.

Alfred, Taiaiake G. 2005. *Wasa*se: Indigenous Pathways of Action and Freedom*. Peterborough, Ontario: Broadview Press.

Ambler, Marjane. 1990. *Breaking the Iron Bonds: Indian Control of Energy Development*. Lawrence: University Press of Kansas.

Barker, Joanne. 2005. *Sovereignty Matters: Locations of Contestation and Possibility in Indigenous Struggles for Self-Determination*. Lincoln: University of Nebraska Press.

Barker, Joanne. 2011. *Native Acts: Law, Recognition, and Cultural Authenticity*. Durham, NC: Duke University Press.

Benally, Malcolm D. 2011. *Bitter Water: Diné Oral Histories of the Navajo-Hopi Land Dispute*. Tucson: University of Arizona Press.

Brugge, Doug, Timothy Benally, and Esther Yazzie-Lewis. 2006. *The Navajo People and Uranium Mining*. Albuquerque: University of New Mexico Press.

Chamberlain, Kathleen P. 2000. *Under Sacred Ground: A History of Navajo Oil, 1922–1982*. Albuquerque: University of New Mexico Press.

Coulthard, Glenn Sean. 2014. *Red Skin, White Masks: Rejecting the Colonial Politics of Recognition*. Minneapolis: University of Minnesota Press.

Curley, Andrew. 2008. *Dóó nal yea dah: Considering the Logic of the Diné Natural Resource Protection Act of 2005 and the Desert Rock Power Plant Project*. Tsaile, Navajo Nation: Dine Policy Institute. https://www.dinecollege.edu/wp-content/uploads/2018/04/DNRPA-and-Desert-RockII.pdf.

Curley, Andrew. 2014. "The Origin of Legibility: Rethinking Colonialism and Resistance among the Navajo People, 1868–1937." In *Diné Perspectives: Revitalizing and Reclaiming Navajo Thought*, edited by Lloyd Lee, 129–50. Tucson: University of Arizona Press.

Curley, Andrew. 2018a. "A Failed Green Future: Navajo Green Jobs and Energy 'Transition' in the Navajo Nation." *Geoforum* 88 (1): 57–65.

Curley, Andrew. 2018b. "T'áá hwó ají t'éego and the Moral Economy of Navajo Coal Workers." *Annals of the American Association of Geographers* 109 (1): 71–86.

Deloria, Vine. 1985. *American Indian Policy in the Twentieth Century*. Norman: University of Oklahoma Press.

Denetdale, Jennifer. 2006. "Chairmen, Presidents, and Princesses: The Navajo Nation, Gender, and the Politics of Tradition." *Wicazo Sa Review* 21 (1): 9–28.

Denetdale, Jennifer. 2009. "Securing Navajo National Boundaries: War, Patriotism, Tradition, and the Diné Marriage Act of 2005." *Wicazo Sa Review* 24 (2): 131–48.

Denis, Verna St. 2007. "Aboriginal Education and Anti-Racist Education: Building Alliances Across Cultural and Racial Identity." *Canadian Journal of Education/Revue Canadienne de L'éducation* 30 (4): 1068–92.

Dunbar-Ortiz, Roxanne. 2014. *An Indigenous Peoples' History of the United States*. Boston: Beacon Press.

Eichstaedt, Peter H. 1994. *If You Poison Us: Uranium and Native Americans*. Santa Fe, NM: Red Crane Books.

Eldridge, Dana. 2014. *Diné Food Sovereignty: A Report on the Navajo Nation Food System and the Case to Rebuild a Self-Sufficient Food System for the Diné People*. Tsaile, Navajo Nation: Dine Policy Institute.

Estes, Nick. 2019. *Our History Is the Future: Standing Rock Versus the Dakota Access Pipeline, and the Long Tradition of Indigenous Resistance*. London and New York: Verso.

Fixico, Donald L. 1986. *Termination and Relocation. Federal Indian Policy, 1945–1960*. Albuquerque: University of New Mexico Press.

Fixico, Donald L. 2000. *The Urban Indian Experience in America*. Albuquerque: University of New Mexico Press.

Goeman, Mishuana R., and Jennifer N. Denetdale. 2009. "Native Feminisms: Legacies, Interventions, and Indigenous Sovereignties." *Wicazo Sa Review* 24 (2): 9–13.

Gökarıksel, Banu, and Sara H. Smith. 2016. "Making America Great Again?: The Fascist Body Politics of Donald Trump." *Political Geography* 54: 79–81.

Hosmer, Brian C., and Colleen O'Neill, and Donald L. Fixico. 2004. *Native Pathways: American Indian Culture and Economic Development in the Twentieth Century*. Boulder: University Press of Colorado.

Iverson, Peter, and Monty Roessel. 2002. *Diné: A History of the Navajos*. Albuquerque: University of New Mexico Press.

Kelly, Lawrence C. 1968. *The Navajo Indians and Federal Indian Policy, 1900–1935*. Tucson: University of Arizona Press.

LaDuke, Winona. 1999. *All Our Relations: Native Struggles for Land and Life*. Cambridge, MA: South End Press.

Lister, Majerle. 2017. "Considering a Navajo Name Change: Self-Identification, Land, and Liberation." *The Red Nation*. July 31, 2017. https://therednation.org/2017/07/31/considering-a-navajo-name-change-self-identification-land-and-liberation/.

M'Closkey, Kathy. 2008. *Swept Under the Rug: A Hidden History of Navajo Weaving*. Albuquerque: University of New Mexico Press.

Marx, Karl, and Friedrich Engels. 1967. *Capital: A Critique of Political Economy*. New York: International Publishers.

Mauer, Kathryn W. 2014. "Landscapes of Disadvantage: The Structure of American Indian Poverty from the Reservation to the Metropolis in the Early 21st Century." PhD diss., Cornell University. http://hdl.handle.net/1813/37089.

McCloskey, Joanne. 2007. *Living through the Generations: Continuity and Change in Navajo Women's Lives*. Tucson: University of Arizona Press.

Million, Dian. 2009. "Felt Theory: An Indigenous Feminist Approach to Affect and History." *Wicazo Sa Review* 24 (2): 53–76.

Mojab, Shahrzad. 2015. *Marxism and Feminism*. London: Zed Books Ltd.

Needham, Andrew. 2014. *Power Lines: Phoenix and the Making of the Modern Southwest*. Princeton, NJ: Princeton University Press.

Nies, Judith. 2014. *Unreal City: Las Vegas, Black Mesa, and the Fate of the West*. New York: Nation Books.

Niethammer, Carolyn. 2004. *I'll Go and Do More: Annie Dodge Wauneka, Navajo Leader and Activist*. Lincoln: University of Nebraska Press.

O'Neill, Colleen. 2005. *Working the Navajo Way: Labor and Culture in the Twentieth Century*. Lawrence: University of Kansas Press.

Powell, Dana E. 2015. "The Rainbow Is Our Sovereignty: Rethinking the Politics of Energy on the Navajo Nation." *Journal of Political Ecology* 22 (1): 54–78.

Powell, Dana E. 2017. *Landscapes of Power: Politics of Energy in the Navajo Nation*. Durham, NC: Duke University Press.

Powell, Dana E., and Andrew Curley. 2008. "K'e, Hozhó, and Non-governmental Politics on the Navajo Nation: Ontologies of Difference Manifest in Environmental Activism." *World Anthropologies Network* 4 (1): 109–38.

Reed, Maureen E. 2005. "Mixed Messages: Pablita Velarde, Kay Bennett, and the Changing Meaning of Anglo-Indian Intermarriage in Twentieth-Century New Mexico." *Frontiers: A Journal of Women Studies* 26 (3): 101–34.

Rifkin, Mark. 2010. *When Did Indians Become Straight?: Kinship, the History of Sexuality, and Native Sovereignty*. Oxford: Oxford University Press.

Robinson, William I., and Xuan Santos. 2014. "Global Capitalism, Immigrant Labor, and the Struggle for Justice." *Class, Race and Corporate Power* 2 (3). https://doi.org/10.25148/CRCP.2.3.16092122.

Shepardson, Mary. 1982. "The Status of Navajo Women." *American Indian Quarterly* 6 (1/2): 149–69.

Simpson, Audra. 2014. *Mohawk Interruptus: Political Life across the Borders of Settler States*. Durham, NC: Duke University Press.

Smith, Sherry L., and Brian Frehner. 2010. *Indians & Energy: Exploitation and Opportunity in the American Southwest*. Santa Fe, NM: School for Advanced Research Press.

TallBear, Kim. 2016. "Making Love and Relations beyond Settler Sexualities." Talk at Social Justice Institute Noted Scholars Lecture Series and the Ecologies of Social Difference Research Network at the University of British Columbia. YouTube video, February 24, 2016. https://www.youtube.com/watch?v=zfdo2ujRUv8.

Voyles, Traci Brynne. 2015. *Wastelanding: Legacies of Uranium Mining in Navajo Country*. Minneapolis: University of Minnesota Press.

Weisiger, Marsha. 2011. *Dreaming of Sheep in Navajo Country*. Seattle: University of Washington Press.

White, Richard. 1983. *The Roots of Dependency: Subsistence, Environment, and Social Change among the Choctaws, Pawnees, and Navajos*. Lincoln: University of Nebraska Press.

Wilkins, David E. 2013. *The Navajo Political Experience*. Lanham, MD: Rowman & Littlefield.

Wolfe, Patrick. 1999. *Settler Colonialism and the Transformation of Anthropology: The Politics and Poetics of an Ethnographic Event*. London and New York: Cassell.

Yazzie, Melanie. 2016. "Contesting Liberalism, Refusing Death: A Biopolitical Critique of Navajo History." PhD diss., University of New Mexico. https://digitalrepository.unm.edu/amst_etds/52.

Yazzie, Melanie K. 2018. "Decolonizing Development in Diné Bikeyah: Resource Extraction, Anti-Capitalism, and Relational Futures." *Environment and Society* 9 (1): 25–39.

Yazzie, Melanie K., and Cutcha R. Baldy. 2018. "Introduction: Indigenous Peoples and the Politics of Water." *Decolonization: Indigeneity, Education & Society* 7 (1): 1–18.

CHAPTER 8

WOMEN-ONLY SPACES AS A METHOD OF POLICING THE CATEGORY OF WOMAN

Abigail Barefoot

Who has the authority to claim the identity "woman"? Who and what defines what a woman is and is not? For some feminists, woman is shaped by socio-historical and cultural forces, and cannot be tied simply to female biology. In the United States, the questions of what makes a woman and if the definition extends to trans women are contested within "women-only" spaces. While many women-only organizations open their membership to trans women, there remain groups of feminists who limit their constituents to cisgender women. I wondered why these feminists would willingly create spaces that shut out trans women and state their policies of exclusion in the name of women's liberation. Why does there continue to be a debate over trans women participating in women-only spaces? Why do some feminist groups experience discomfort or hostility toward trans women?

To answer these questions, this chapter examines how discourses on gender and feminism are used to control the category "woman" within feminist organizations that actively exclude trans women from membership. Through a content analysis of two trans-exclusionary feminist organizations' websites, this chapter examines how discourses on gender and feminism are used to police the category "woman" as it relates to women-only spaces in the United States. I analyze two feminist women-only groups in the US that exclude trans women: Women's Liberation Front (WOLF), a group challenging gender identity's inclusion in Title IX, and Deep Green Resistance's Women's Caucus (DGR), a radical feminist environmental organization. WOLF and DGR deny trans women access to space and question the legitimacy of their identities. In particular,

I explore why trans women represent a threat to the category of woman as constructed by WOLF and DGR, and what political consequences occur from trans women's exclusion from these spaces. I argue trans-exclusionary feminists' refusal to let trans women enter women-only spaces stems from the fear that inclusion will lead to an instability of the category of woman in which the concerns of cisgender women will become irrelevant and their lived realities ignored. To trans-exclusionary feminists, trans women upset the so-called definitive boundaries of men and women in which women are no longer tied to biology, muddling perceived clear differences between men and women based on sex. However, WOLF and DGR are not only regulating who can claim to be a woman within their space but reinforcing a rigid gender binary through a feminist praxis that works to erase transgender experiences and oppression and responds primarily to cisgender women's needs.

In addressing these issues, this chapter responds to the call for an unbound feminist geography by grappling with the tensions within feminist theory and addressing the discomforts and subsequent exclusions by feminist scholars and activists in creating spaces for women. By seeking to expose some of the reasons why trans-exclusionary feminists challenge the validity of transgender identities, I demonstrate how these tensions are used to further exclude trans individuals beyond feminist spaces. To better understand the politics of WOLF and DGR, I first provide an overview of several debates centering on trans women's inclusion in women-only spaces and contextualize WOLF and DGR's grounding in radical feminism and gender abolition, before exploring how these groups' membership policies work to exclude trans women.

OVERVIEW OF WOMEN-ONLY SPACES

During the 1970s, women-only spaces provided an opportunity for women to separate from men to construct and dismantle their understanding of womanhood through consciousness raising, organizing, and developing places of healing. Constructing sex-segregated spaces included a spectrum of decisions ranging from modes of organizing to entirely separatist communities (Frye 1984, 96). While some of these spaces, such as separatist communities, may be long-term alternative communities of women, other spaces, such as lesbian bars, may be temporary, created for a momentary reprieve from male-dominated spaces. Women-only spaces operate under the foundation of separatism in which women exclude men from entering certain locations to allow women to organize. For example, sex-segregated spaces such as women's shelters allow women to find community and safety from trauma caused by men in a space designed for healing (Mackay 2015; Sweeney 2004). In other networks, women-only spaces became centers for activism and women's culture, where women's power and creativity could thrive. Separation was necessary for women to develop their sense of self and reassess their knowledge separate from male-dominated assumptions and values (Frye 1984).

As separatist spaces, women-only communities develop political meanings, even if the organization's mission lacks a political goal. Marilyn Frye argues that by excluding men, these spaces challenge the gendered structure of power by depriving men of the privileges of inclusion (1984, 103). Creating a space for women denies access to others by creating limitations of membership. Rather than seeing this as inherently problematic, Frye argues it can be empowering by giving women control through the ability to limit access to the space. However, Frye's article was primarily referring to the exclusion of men, rather than the policing of other women.

Despite their goals, women-only spaces often face the challenge of creating a space for women while acknowledging that there are no "real" women as the category is a social construction. Yet something must make women women. In this way, women-only exclusionary spaces often promote essentialism and recreate many of the same gender stereotypes feminists try to dismantle (Henrickson 2004; Serano 2013). Kath Browne (2009), writing about the Michigan Womyn's Music Festival's exclusionary policies, argues that to create women's spaces, there must be a definition of woman that has to be policed and enforced. Trans women in particular are susceptible to control within women's spaces, as their bodies and gender expression are used to judge against what defines the norm. As transgender activist Julia Serano (2013, 28) states, "When you're a trans woman, you are made to walk this very fine line, where if you act feminine you are accused of being a parody, but if you act masculine, it is seen as a sign of your true male identity." Regardless of presentation, trans women challenge and transform the definition of woman rooted in sex essentialism in which trans women can never embody womanhood. Serano argues that an anti-trans definition of womanhood has roots within traditional sexism, particularly the fetishization of trans individuals' genitalia, particularly the penis, regardless of surgery. The fixation on genitalia obscures how trans women face similar oppression to cisgender women, although it may not always manifest in identical ways (Serano 2013, 235–37).

Echoing second wave feminists' fears about men forcing their way into women's spaces, trans-exclusionary radical feminists interpret trans women's efforts of inclusion as "male" dominance and desire for control of the space, in which males feel entitled to everything. Access to spaces becomes reinterpreted as a quest for power rather than inclusion and an affirmation of identity, re-inforcing essentialist notions of masculinity. However, trans-exclusionary radical feminists put trans women in a double bind, where if they were "really women" they would not demand access to women-only space. Jennie Ruby and Karla Mantilla stated in response to trans women's demands to be welcomed into the Michigan Womyn's Music Festival that "if these wannabe 'women' had any understanding of what it is to be a woman in patriarchy they would have respected, not violated, women's space" (Ruby and Mantilla 2000, 1). Trans women must put their concerns of inclusion aside to show their understand-ing of the feelings of cisgender women or else be labeled as men. Any attempt by a trans woman to be included as a woman is read by exclusionary feminists as not respecting cisgender women's boundaries, and proof that trans women have male entitlement. Trans-exclusionary feminists frame the debate over inclusion in such a way that it removes any chance for trans women's genuine concerns to be legitimate. Trans-exclusionary feminists label any critique of exclusion as evidence of trans women's male dominance and thus not a real concern. Regardless of what they do, cisgender women are seen as real women, while trans women, no matter what they do, are seen as inauthentic.

However, Judith Butler (1990) argues woman itself is an unstable category as it interacts with race, class, and sexuality. She argues that trying to constrain woman into rigid set boundaries to create a unified identity will only lead to the exclusion of those who do not fit within limits established by the group. Similarly, recognizing that "men" and "women" are socially constructed groups, Kate Bornstein (1994) argues that due to our overlapping identities and rigid expectations of gender, there are no "real" men or women, as the categories are unattainable and fictitious; even those who see themselves as men and women fail to live up to gender expectations. As no one can embody true womanhood, the identity of "woman" can be freely claimed and reconstructed by individu-als regardless of sex. Gender then becomes a messy, intricate process that one engages with, rather than an oppressive, suffocating force as believed by WOLF and DGR. Despite these critiques, WOLF and DGR use the framework of ex-clusionary feminists to argue that trans women cannot be allowed in women's spaces as they are inherently men.

WHO ARE THESE EXCLUSIONARY RADICAL FEMINISTS?

The politics of radical feminism are central to understanding WOLF's and DGR's exclusionary positions as articulated on their websites. Radical femi-nism is often used as an all-encompassing term lacking concrete definitions, or strict boundaries between what is or is not radical. Broadly, radical feminism refers to a specific branch of feminism that believes women constitute a sex class, and thus the relationship between men and women needs to be theorized in political terms (Mackay 2015; Rowland and Klein 1996). Rather than working for equality within a male-dominated structure, like liberal feminism, radical feminism pushes for an overhaul of institutions such as marriage, the family, and law (Echols 1989; Tong 2013). Many radical feminists see sex as the primary oppression that acts as a model for other forms of oppression (see Echols 1989; Rowland and Klein 1996). Critics see radical feminism as essentialist and reinforcing a universal experience of woman based on biology (Echols 1989). Contemporary radical feminist groups do utilize intersectional analysis to discuss difference among women, but argue that women, regardless of other identities, are all subordinate to men. In this way, women occupy a political class based on the shared universal experience of being oppressed based on their sex (Mackay 2015,122). Yet, as seen with WOLF's and DGR's websites, the groups nod to an analysis of race and class but provide little engagement or theorizing of the differences among women.

Most important to radical feminism is its women-centeredness in which women's experiences are the foundation to theorizing and action. Robyn Rowland and Renate Klein state, "Radical feminism's revolutionary intent is expressed first and foremost in its woman-centeredness: woman's experiences and interests are at the center of our theory and practices. It is the only theory by and for women" (Rowland and Klein 1996, 10). If women are the foundation of radical feminism in both theory and practice, then "women" must be clearly defined and maintained. WOLF and DGR both operate within this grounding of radical feminism. Often, the politics of radical feminism leads to a disavowal of trans women altogether as it centers on the experience of being assigned female at birth, though Cristan Williams argues that radical feminists are not inherently anti-trans and have a long history of inclusivity as trans women experience sexism regardless of sex (2016, 257). Despite Williams's acknowledgment that radical feminism does not fundamentally have to be an exclusionary force, the dominant rhetoric of radical feminism often becomes linked to transexclusionary practices, as demonstrated by WOLF's and DGR's websites.

WOLF and DGR explain their exclusionary practices using gender abolition scholarship, particularly the work of Sheila Jeffreys, a feminist scholar who is highly critical of transgender identities. Echoing Jeffreys, WOLF and DGR argue women's oppression originates from their sex, with gender being the vehicle of oppression. Gender acts as a hierarchical system that is forced upon men and women to uphold male dominance and female submission (Jeffreys

2014, 2). Radical feminists believe the process of turning females into women allows for females to be placed in the same political class based on their shared biology and subordination in relation to men. For women to be a unified class, WOLF and DGR believe that biological sex, rather than gender, must provide the grounding for unification. In addition, both WOLF and DGR believe that to achieve women's liberation, gender must be abolished. Gender abolitionists such as Jeffreys believe that gender cannot be redeemed by making it less rigid or more flexible; it must be eliminated, as the hierarchy between women and men can still exist even as gender norms shift. Abolitionists seek to create a genderless society in which gender is an irrelevant category for social life. Gender abolition is challenged by feminists and queer theorists who argue for other solutions such as breaking down the gender binary, challenging gender norms, and expanding what it means to be a woman, man, or other genders (Bornstein 1998; Halberstam 1998). Judith Butler challenges gender abolition, arguing sex cannot be easily detached from gender, as both construct each other so that gender and sex are not fixed, stable categories but something regularly performed and reshaped (1990; 2014). WOLF and DGR disagree and do not believe that challenging gender is enough; instead, they seek to abolish it, leading to transphobic and discriminatory feminist praxis.

Radical feminism and gender abolition have become less popular since the 1990s, partly due to critiques that claim feminist essentialism reinforced a universal experience of women based on biology and ignored factors of race and gender, as well as to the broader cultural and political backlash against feminism (Echols 1989). In addition, the 1990s saw the rise of postmodern thought and of Judith Butler's work challenging previous constructions of gender and sex. These new forms of feminism are at odds with radical feminism, which sees the focus on the malleability of gender and the current trajectory of the waves of feminism as the antithesis to the liberating goals of feminism (Kiraly and Tyler 2015). Trans-exclusionary feminists are trying to uphold a particular feminist vision of the future, in a time in which they see a depoliticization and a weakening of "true feminist values." For exclusionary feminists, women-only spaces are both a place of feminist theorizing and a site of struggle against different articulations of gender that do not align with their beliefs.

WOLF and DGR are adamant about their exclusion of trans women in their women-only spaces and explain their stance in detail through their "About Us," "Statements of Principles," and "Frequently Asked Questions" web pages. As the organizations' websites would be one of the first locations potential members would look for information about the group, their websites offer one way to examine how the politics of trans-exclusionary feminism are articulated to outsiders. Using a content analysis of the policies and guidelines listed on their websites, I reviewed word choice, citations, and constructions of feminist theory to examine how these groups define "woman," discuss transgender identity, and explain their exclusion of trans women. By looking at the construction of their arguments for trans exclusion, one can see how trans women represent a threat to the category of woman constructed by radical feminism, and what steps are taken to construct boundaries around the definition to exclude trans women and invalidate their identities.

I focus on WOLF and DGR because they are two of the most well-known feminist trans-exclusionary activist organizations in the United States. Their elaborate and forceful defense of women-only spaces and trans exclusion make them vital to the debates surrounding transgender inclusion. In addition to LGBT and feminist media covering their politics, mainstream news sources such as the *New Yorker* and the *New York Times* have also interviewed members of the groups about transgender issues, giving them a bigger platform to discuss their politics (Goldberg 2014; Schulevitz 2016). Created in 2014, WOLF organizes around four main areas from a radical feminist position: women's reproductive autonomy, the elimination of porn and prostitution, ending male violence, and gender abolition. However, it is most well-known for suing the US government over including gender identity in Title IX, which will be discussed at length later in this chapter. In addition, WOLF collaborates with conservative women through the Hands Across the Aisle Coalition, a bipartisan group that challenges pro-transgender policies (Hands Across the Aisle n.d.). Through this partnership, WOLF is gaining considerable support within the religious right and conservative organizations.

DGR, which was established in 2011, explores the interconnections between patriarchy and environmentalism. Like WOLF, its anti-transgender policies often gain more attention than its mission. While DGR does not directly engage in lobbying or take legal action on transgender issues, members participate in environmental and anarchist coalitions, with their beliefs impacting not only feminist spaces but other communities engaging in social justice issues. WOLF and DGR are not the only exclusionary feminist groups, but both groups significantly add to the national discourse on transgender civil rights through their media presence and their direct and indirect activism against trans individuals.

The groups' logistics are shrouded in secrecy. While both claim to have chapters throughout the United States, the locations of their headquarters and meeting spaces are not listed on their websites or social media. Additionally, membership numbers for WOLF and DGR remain unknown, as do the demographics of group members. The groups are anonymous, and membership must be earned rather than freely given out. In response to having their needs unmet in other spaces, many groups that include marginalized peoples may create exclusionary policies to limit membership to a shared identity for the possibility of a space of escape and healing from an oppressive society while sharing experiences and building community (Browne 2009). For WOLF and DGR, their exclusionary policies allow them to focus on exploring women's needs, developing interventions on women's oppression, and empowering women while not being hindered by having to teach men how to unlearn sexism or respond to men's microaggressions. WOLF's and DGR's exclusionary policies also respond to the reality that trans-exclusionary groups face harassment for their stance on transgender issues. WOLF and DGR have experienced digital stalking, harassment, and threats of violence (Deep Green Resistance 2013; Women's Liberation Front 2017a, 2017b). Due to these threats, the groups need to work in private to continue the goals of their organizations. DGR also needs secrecy, as some of their members may participate in unlawful activities such as trespassing and sabotage, even though DGR as an organization does not engage in illegal behavior. To protect their members from further attacks and to continue their activism, both WOLF and DGR have an extensively selective membership process.

The groups also try to protect their members by operating within the parameters of private space and meeting in places whose physical location is known only by members. While the groups do appear in public to participate in protests, attend conferences, and appear on news segments, much of the actual activism happens behind the scenes. Thus, both online and physical spaces represent gatekeeping of gender identity and what counts as feminist practice. These women-only spaces are produced through anti-transgender beliefs and exclusionary practices based on sexual difference. By creating feminist spaces that exclude trans women, they locate feminism and feminist activism in cisgender women's bodies and ignore trans women's needs. At the same time, these spaces invalidate trans women's identity as women and do not allow for a more nuanced discussion of sexism that includes trans women's experiences.

To become a member in WOLF, one must go through a two-step interview process. First, prospective members must fill out an online form that includes basic demographics, essay questions on gender and other radical feminist issues, and the names of any personal connections who can vouch for them. After submitting the application, prospective members may be contacted via Skype, phone call, or in person to further assess if they fit well into the organization. The two-step process allows for a vetting process in which WOLF decides if an individual fits the membership requirements and its political orientation. This process is exclusionary not only toward trans women but to other feminists who may have different opinions about how to approach feminism, such as disagreeing with gender abolition or the groups' anti-prostitution and anti-pornography stances. The questions asked of potential members are specifically chosen to reinforce radical feminism as the correct way of doing feminism, and these beliefs are rigidly enforced through the membership process. By creating a membership policy based on sex and certain feminist beliefs, dissent and disagreement are downplayed in favor of agreement on key tenets of the organization, allowing them to devote more time to activism rather than in-fighting. This is not to say disagreement does not happen in WOLF and DGR, as WOLF's decision to collaborate with conservative groups led to severe disagreements and several members leaving the organization, and DGR's anti-transgender politics lead to a decline in members (Deep Green Resistance 2013; Women's Liberation Front 2017a). DGR's and WOLF's membership processes recreate boundaries of what beliefs are representative of radical feminist activism, with correct answers leading to membership.

WOMEN'S LIBERATION FRONT

WOLF is best known for its efforts in pursuing a legal battle against the US Departments of Justice and Education in 2016 to challenge their "joint guidance" requiring schools and universities that receive Title IX funding to interpret sex to include "gender identity" or lose that funding. While WOLF's case was dismissed by the court later that year, it continued to legally challenge gender identity inclusions at a state level and file amicus briefs in Supreme Court cases involving gender identity. With its homage to the women's liberation movement of the 1960s, WOLF grounds its politics within the radical feminism of the second wave in which women constituted a political class. As an organization serving in the battle for women's liberation, WOLF argues in favor of women-only spaces as a means to empower women to organize as a political class. However, as this political class is based on being assigned female at birth, trans women are excluded and denied the ability to claim the identity of woman.

With their tagline, WOLF makes it very clear which women it advocates for: "females who survived girlhood" (Women's Liberation Front n.d. a). The connection between survival and girlhood is twofold. First, WOLF sees girls and women as constantly struggling against male supremacy and exploitation.

From this perspective, survival in a male-dominated society becomes an act of resistance for women. This exploitation is based on both female anatomy and gender expectations. WOLF argues "patriarchy is organized around the extraction of resources from female bodies and minds in the service of men, including reproductive, sexual, emotional, and labor resources" (Women's Liberation Front, n.d. a). For members of WOLF, having a vagina alone does not make one a woman. Instead, women are made through the unfair socialization process that occurs because one possesses a vagina rather than how one is socialized when they have a penis.

WOLF's motto of "females who survived girlhood" also ties into trans-exclusionary arguments that trans women are socialized as boys, and no matter when they transition, they can never embody womanhood. Trans women, in WOLF's analysis, never had to survive girlhood, and therefore cannot identify as women. Thus, womanhood can only exist through the combination of biology and socialization of females, and is not something that can be constructed or claimed by transgender women. WOLF's focus on biology-based socialization echoes Jeffreys's work, as WOLF does not view trans women as "real" women, even if trans women go through sex reassignment surgery. Having a vagina is not enough to be a woman, as exclusionary radical feminists think that after surgery trans women are still men due to their supposedly irreversible socialization as men. Regardless of how long trans women live their lives as women, WOLF believes trans women can never know what true womanhood feels like and therefore can never be "real women."

There is a noticeable tension between biology and socialization in WOLF's analysis. As biology moves beyond a two-sex system with the inclusion of intersex, and as sex reassignment surgery becomes more accepted, biology is not enough to be a woman. While WOLF pushes for a simplistic view of biology, it also cannot deny the complexities of sex. For example, one of WOLF's frequently asked questions is about the role of intersex individuals as it relates to their analysis of gender. In response, WOLF tries to reaffirm its position by refusing to engage with the intersex question and instead argues that the intersex community is too diverse for any specific policy about gender identity and at the same time, too small of a population to challenge the fact that humans are sexually dimorphic (Women's Liberation Front, n.d. b). While the question of intersex in WOLF's gender analysis remains unclear, it represents the slippage in WOLF's supposedly concrete definition of woman. For WOLF, only a woman who is assigned female at birth is considered a woman. By framing "woman" around both biology and socialization, WOLF maneuvers around the question of trans women who have undergone sex reassignment surgery being seen as women simply for having the "correct" set of genitals. By not reducing womanhood to having female genitalia, WOLF can police who counts as women without having to deconstruct the role hormones, surgery, and gender expression play in the spectrum between trans women and cisgender women, allowing WOLF to maneuver around the complexities of when gender is valid and when it can be disentangled from normative understandings of sex.

Trans individuals and allies refute the argument that gender socialization is concretely tied to the sex assigned at birth. Trans women often argue that despite being seen as boys when they were children, they were socialized as trans women. As such, some trans women point out that they were labeled as boys by their families and faced pushback from friends and family when behaving in a more feminine way. Instead of having male privilege, trans women experienced cis sexism. To say that all trans women were socialized as men ignores the complexities of socialization and lumps all transgender histories into a universal narrative. Similarly, critics argue gender socialization is not a universal process, but rather our understanding of gender is shaped through individual and community experiences (Mackay 2015, 248). Assuming one's socialization as a girl or woman defines "women's experience" as something shared downplays the differences among women. This common socialization framework fails to account for women's different lived experiences, since women are not a universal group and are simultaneously impacted by their other identity factors such as race, class, and nationality. While WOLF's statement of principles recognizes that misogyny is enmeshed with white privilege, colonialism, and other forms of oppression, it fails to include an intersectional analysis in their discussion of gender socialization, which reinforces an essentialist view of "woman" (Women's Liberation Front, n.d. a).

Rather than seeing the similarities between cisgender and trans women's experiences of sexism, WOLF argues trans women infringe on women's rights, as constructions of gender identity ultimately disenfranchise women. This means that transgender rights and women's rights cannot coexist because the needs of one infringe on the experiences of the other, creating an unequal balance of power. WOLF claims that it engages in legal battles over gender identity's inclusion in Title IX because of this inequality. An achievement of feminist activism passed in 1972, Title IX prohibits discrimination on the basis of sex in any education program or activity that receives federal funding. Key areas covered under Title IX include athletics, admissions, sex-based harassment, and sexual assault. Title IX represents a focal area to challenge gender identity as WOLF sees Title IX as a landmark achievement in helping cisgender women attain equality—and the inclusion of gender identity as stripping away those achievements. WOLF provides a seventeen-point argument in defense of their position and their trans-exclusionary policies. Inclusion of gender identity in Title IX, WOLF argues, will favor trans women's need for inclusion, whereas cis women's concerns or calls for sex-specific spaces will be labeled transphobic. As WOLF states, "Girls' rights to personal privacy and freedom from male sexual harassment, forced exposure to male nudity, and voyeurism have thus been eliminated" (Women's Liberation Front, n.d. b). WOLF conflates trans women being allowed into sex-segregated spaces such as bathrooms with sexual harassment, as cisgender women are unable to seek redress if they feel uncomfortable being in a space where they might encounter male genitalia. However, this analysis ignores how trans women are often fearful of experiencing sexual harassment and violence in sex-specific spaces. The National Center for Transgender Equality found that almost 60 percent of transgender Americans have avoided using public restrooms for fear of confrontation, saying they have been harassed and assaulted (2015, 228). WOLF argues transgender women's inclusion infringes on cisgender women's claim to equal protections based on sex while ignoring how trans women are also worthy of protection.

For WOLF, gender identity and sex are not equal markers of identity, and therefore are not of similar weight when it comes to justice from oppression. By including gender identity in Title IX, sex loses importance at the expense of cisgender women as the two become conflated within the law. WOLF and others fear that if the two terms are conflated, the category of woman becomes muddled, and "real" women's concerns are ignored yet again by the legal system. WOLF, then, sees gender as creating another layer of hierarchy in which gender trumps biological sex: "When sex-based legal protections do not necessarily refer to any material state of being male or female, but instead to an internal feeling of 'gender identity,' the category of sex becomes meaningless" (Women's Liberation Front, n.d. b). Sex no longer becomes a way to gain retribution for inequality, which for WOLF means women lack the means to fight for their own liberation or challenge their systemic mistreatment because *anyone* can claim to be a woman regardless of biology at the expense of female-born individuals.

In addition to not allowing trans women into their organization, WOLF works toward erasing the category of transgender altogether. On its website's "Frequently Asked Questions" page, the word "transgender" appears only three times and only when quoting someone else. When referring to trans women, WOLF calls them "males" or "males who use the name . . ." (Women's Liberation

Front, n.d. b). Trans individuals are reduced to "those claiming gender identity." In the rare occasion transgender is mentioned elsewhere on the website, it is dismissed as "transgenderism," an offensive term originally used in the fields of medicine and psychology to pathologize transgender identity and mark transgender individuals as abnormal and deviant. (Women's Liberation Front 2016, 2020). "Transgenderism" reinforces the perception of transgender individuals as mentally ill and dangerous. WOLF frequently invokes stereotypes of the transgender sexual predator, providing stories of trans women as rapists or displaying voyeuristic tendencies. In arguing against housing transgender women with cisgender women in prison, WOLF states, "The housing of male [trans women] wife-murderers, rapists, and child molesters in women's prisons is an inevitable result of ending the legal distinction between male and female persons" (Women's Liberation Front 2019). Trans women are portrayed as dangerous men who, if given access to women's spaces, will continue to harm women. In this way, the desire for trans women to be acknowledged as women is rendered as a danger that will harm "real" women.

At the same time, WOLF downplays why individuals would want to transition, blaming it on socially held gender roles rather than how transgender individuals articulate their experiences of gender dysphoria or understandings of their trans identity. For example, WOLF argues that "most reasonable people likely agree that castration, chemical or surgical, is a disproportionately harsh consequence for being a little boy who likes to play with dolls and costumes that Disney and Mattel decided to market only to girls" (Women's Liberation Front 2017b). WOLF challenges the complex and varying experiences of transgender individuals' stories of gender identity and transforms them into a simple narrative that blames gender stereotypes for the creation of trans women. This ignores the agency of trans women in self-defining who they are and denies their experiences of their gender identity (Koyama 2016, 251). WOLF's position rejects trans women's right to assign their own sex and gender identity and relies on pathology to paradoxically argue that trans women are both dangerous men and easily swayed by gender stereotypes.

Through its discursive strategies and exclusionary practices, WOLF actively tries to invalidate the construction of trans women identities and to uphold the binaries of sex/gender and woman/man. Trans women challenge a definition of womanhood based on biological sex and push up against the boundaries of woman set by WOLF. WOLF fears that if society legitimates trans women's claims of womanhood, it will hinder the progress of the feminist movement. By including transgender issues within feminist politics, WOLF argues that the needs of cisgender women will be decentered and ignored.

DEEP GREEN RESISTANCE

Deep Green Resistance (DGR), based in Santa Barbara, California, with chapters across the United States, defines itself as a radical feminist environmental group. DGR understands industrial civilization to be unsustainable and suggests it must be dismantled in order to secure a livable future for the planet (Deep Green Resistance, n.d. a). While DGR's anti-civilization stance is highly criticized by environmental groups, in recent years its anti-transgender policies have also caused a backlash from environmental and feminist groups alike, leading many environmental groups, as well as past DGR members, to disassociate with DGR (Earth First! 2013).

Though DGR has both men and women as members, it sees itself as women-centered and women-led (Deep Green Resistance, n.d. b). To address the needs of oppressed groups and amplify their voices within the organization, DGR has two caucuses: the people of color caucus and the women's caucus, which defines itself as women-only. The policies created within the women's caucus have a direct impact on the organization as a whole. For example, the women's caucus created the "rules for men in the organization." Failure to follow the rules can lead to members being expelled from the organization (Deep Green Resistance, n.d. c). Women-only spaces within DGR, such as the women's caucus, do not allow trans women and erase trans identity within the organization as a whole. Activists have documented numerous incidences of DGR placing trans women in men's housing or not respecting their pronouns (Scofield 2013). In response to accusations of transphobia, DGR states, "Radical feminists also believe that women have the right to define their boundaries and decide who is allowed in their space. . . . We have been called transphobic because the women of DGR do not want men—people born male and socialized into masculinity—in women-only spaces" (Deep Green Resistance, n.d. e). Like WOLF, DGR believes trans women have been socialized as men and therefore cannot be women.

Emerging from the women's caucus and a radical feminist grounding, DGR's definition of gender resembles that of WOLF, where gender becomes inherently problematic:

> Gender is not a binary: it's a hierarchy, global in its reach, sadistic in its practice, murderous in its conclusion, just like race, just like class. Gender is the ideology that underlies the material conditions of women's lives: rape, battering, poverty, prostitution, and gynocide [sic]. Those conditions could not exist without the creation of social categories "men" and

"women"—and those violent, violating practices are in turn are [*sic*] what create people called women. (Deep Green Resistance, n.d. f)

Deep Green Resistance argues gender is socially constructed for the purpose of upholding patriarchy and power inequalities between men and women. Its embodiment of what it means to be a woman develops through violence, particularly gender-based violence. Ultimately, DGR states, "We see nothing in the creation of gender to celebrate or embrace" (Deep Green Resistance, n.d. e). This paints a bleak picture of what gender does, as DGR constructs women as victim to men's violence. For example, DGR emphasizes violence and victimhood when describing the socialization process that turns girls into women: "Female socialization in patriarchy is a process of psychologically constraining and breaking girls—otherwise known as 'grooming'—to create a class of compliant victims. Femininity is a set of behaviors that are, in essence, ritualized submission" (Deep Green Resistance, n.d. e).

In its analysis of gender, DGR equates womanhood with victimhood, which is a subtle difference when compared to WOLF's portrayal of survival as a central aspect of being a woman. Both groups recognize how male violence harms and molds women's experience, making women women. However, WOLF uses "surviving girlhood" as a way to exclude trans women, while DGR uses victimhood as a way to critique alternative feminist constructions of gender that see it as positive. However, this victimhood only applies to cisgender women, not trans women, as DGR sees trans women's discrimination as a choice as discussed below. In responding to what DGR calls a "disagreement of what gender is," DGR compares its perspective on gender with nonradical feminists, which it refers to as "genderists," a common term used by trans-exclusionary radical feminists. After defining gender, DGR provides an extreme, unsourced, and highly problematic example of violence against women: villages in India where women only have one kidney because their husbands have sold the other one (Deep Green Resistance, n.d. e). The organization argues that patriarchy, and its use of gender, allows for human rights abuses such as this. DGR then provides an overly simplistic analysis of genderist views, stating:

Genderists think gender is an identity, an internal set of feelings people might have. Radical feminists think gender is a caste system, a set of material conditions into which one is born. Genderists think gender is a binary. Radical feminists think gender is a hierarchy, with men on top. Some genderists claim that gender is "fluid." Radical feminists point out that there is nothing fluid about having your husband sell your kidney. (Deep Green Resistance, n.d. e)

Setting aside for a moment DGR's appropriation and simplification of Indian women's experiences, this dichotomy presents other feminists as not taking gendered power structures seriously and reinforcing violence against women. DGR, on the other hand, demonstrates that gender is a detriment to women's well-being and thus needs to be eradicated. Gender is not allowed to be nuanced with both positive and problematic aspects; instead, it must be narrowly constructed to present all cisgender women as victims of gender.

This unification of all cisgender women through the trope of woman as victim is problematic, as it ignores the differences among women and reinforces other systems of oppression and, in the case of DGR's India example, reinforces imperialism and histories of colonialism. DGR uses women in developing countries as examples of the reach of patriarchal violence while reinforcing an ahistorical and universal analysis of "culture as violence" (Jibrin 2017; Piedalue 2017). In DGR's analysis, Indian women become racialized and othered, and DGR fails to address the economic, political, and structural context of the violence that lead to husbands selling their wives' organs. While DGR argues that seeing women as a political class does not erase the differences between women of differing racial and economic classes, it does not engage in how these differences impact women's oppression (Deep Green Resistance, n.d. e). The group fails to discuss how issues of race and class also shape gender socialization in which all women do not occupy the same place in a gender hierarchy, and thus simplifies and distorts women's experiences with violence and as women.

Similarly, in using these examples, DGR ignores its own complicity in upholding structural violence. As bell hooks argues, using victimization as a form of unification for women disguises and shields the fact that many white women exploit and oppress other women (hooks 2000, 46). Similarly, Eli Green argues that by portraying women as victims, exclusionary feminists then see only their own oppression, ignoring their role in the oppression of trans women (Green 2006, 241). Not only does the depiction of women as victims of men's violence mean women must be separated from men through clear-cut boundaries for the categories to make sense, but trans women's oppression must be downplayed or ignored to uphold cisgender women as the ultimate victims. In this way, DGR uses victimization and violence against women as proof of sex-based oppression while engaging in acts of violence against women in the developing world and trans women by reducing them to simplistic caricatures.

Unlike WOLF, DGR directly discusses its opinions of transgender individuals. Within a "Radical Feminism Frequently Asked Questions" page, DGR asserts that members' beliefs about trans women and their exclusionary practices stem from DGR's understanding of gender: "Gender is not natural, not a choice, and not a feeling: it is the structure of women's oppression. . . . As radicals, we intend to dismantle gender and the entire system of patriarchy which it embodies" (Deep Green Resistance, n.d. e). When responding to the claim that gender abolition leads to a denial of individuals' identity, particularly for transgender individuals, the group states, "To assert that questioning the legitimacy of gender can be equated with denying the existence of a person is implying that humans cannot exist without gender. We do not accept this. We do not accept that gender, or any oppression, is inevitable or natural" (Deep Green Resistance, n.d. e).

DGR does not recognize either the gender identity of transgender individuals or the category of transgender itself, as it reinforces a need for gender, which pushes against its abolitionist stance. To uphold this abolitionist stance, DGR erases the experiences of trans individuals and invalidates their identities. For example, DGR argues that without gender people would be "free to dress, behave, and love others in whatever way they wished, no matter what kind of body they had" (Deep Green Resistance, n.d. e). As DGR sees gender as an oppressive force for everyone, its arguments belittle the experiences of trans individuals by arguing that because gender acts as an oppressive force, no one feels comfortable in their gender. DGR conflates cisgender women's experiences of being pressured into gender roles with the gender dysphoria often experienced by transgender individuals being assigned the wrong gender at birth. However, DGR believes that gender abolition would lead to the eradication of the categories of men and women, and therefore there would be no more gender norms and transgender identities would be irrelevant. However, this analysis misunderstands trans identities and the experiences of trans women. DGR reinforces the belief that trans women are not "real women" but men.

Another example can be found in a question about the legitimacy of two-spirit individuals, or Indigenous populations who have gender categories beyond a binary. DGR sidesteps the issue by simply stating, "Non-indigenous people have no right to an opinion on this issue" (Deep Green Resistance, n.d. e). DGR shuts down any acknowledgment of culturally specific variations to the two-sex system and how it fits within the group's definitions of gender and power, or anything that might open dialogue about the validity of transgender identities. By failing to address the question, DGR upholds a Western ethnocentric view of sex and gender. In this refusal to accept transgender identities, the category of woman remains tied to biology and materially grounded.

DGR's failure to include trans women in its space helps to uphold the category of woman that must be maintained for its definition of power and male supremacy to make sense. If women are the victims of male violence, then both men and women must clearly be defined and separated. Trans women disrupt this by challenging the belief that womanhood can only be constructed out of violence, and only individuals assigned female sex at birth can become women. For DGR's understanding of women's oppression to be valid, sex and gender must match correctly upon the female and male body.

CONCLUSION: BEYOND THE BOUNDARIES OF WOMEN-ONLY SPACES

WOLF's and DGR's articulations of womanhood reflect how the gender binary and hegemonic gender norms are upheld spatially and work to oppress trans individuals. In the creation of their exclusionary spaces, WOLF and DGR create a border between acceptable and unacceptable categories of women in which only those meeting the group's criteria are allowed entry. As borders are constructed through "the capacities of bodies and their relationship to others and space," they relegate bodies into recognizable identities (Gieseking 2016). Meaning is given to space through individuals' identities and relationships with one another, leading these policies to produce a discourse of who belongs in a women-only space and what makes a woman. By focusing on cisgender women, WOLF and DGR render trans experiences of womanhood illegible and recast them as male. Trans women are not only denied entry, but their identity as women is scrutinized and invalidated. Petra Doan (2010) refers to this policing as the "tyranny of gender," which occurs when individuals, such as those in the trans community, challenge hegemonic gender norms. The tyranny of gender shapes how trans individuals perceive specific spaces and to what extent they feel comfortable displaying certain behaviors in the specificities of the space (Doan 2010, 635). Often, the ability to be accepted and the question of safety spatialize the limit of self-expression (Gieseking 2016, 264). Thus, the ability for transgender women to be visible, and to what extent they perform their gender expression, depends both on the location and the individuals within the space. WOLF and DGR, through their fixation on a rigid sex/gender binary, reinforce a feminism that is impossible for trans women to participate in as it denies their identities and instead keeps trans women locked in a gender-binary system that they seek to dismantle.

However, exclusive feminist groups are not isolated territories cut off from society but permeable places in which ideas flow beyond the space. Jack Gieseking argues lesbian and queer spaces are not always fixed or cohesive physical places but can be produced through the body's interaction with "specific, temporal, fragmented, fleeting, and unstable elements" (2013, 196). WOLF and DGR, while not as well known as larger feminist organizations like the National Organization for Women or EMILY's List, cannot be written off as fringe groups. The exclusionary practices of WOLF and DGR are not only tied to the space of their specific organization but reinforced and made visible in other spaces, as their members interact with the broader public and engage in activism. WOLF and DGR push their analysis of gender into other spaces, reflecting a tyranny of gender that limits and prevents alternative configurations of sex and gender from becoming visible, forcing queer identities to the margins (Elliot 2004, 17). By promoting women-only spaces as sites of feminist organizing and prioritizing the needs of cisgender women and girls, WOLF and DGR uphold sex-segregated spaces such as bathrooms and women's shelters and seek to refocus feminism to address primarily cisgender women's experiences. WOLF and DGR's arguments for cis women-only policies are not limited to the space of their organization but are helping to shape national discourses on gender that limit transgender equality and support transgender discrimination.

Conservative groups are beginning to support and rearticulate the ideas of WOLF and DGR. Members of WOLF were invited to speak at the Heritage Foundation, a conservative think tank, to develop a framework to better challenge pro-transgender policies. They have since partnered on several anti-transgender campaigns, such as sending a joint amicus brief to the Supreme Court with the Christian fundamentalist group Family Policy Alliance (Family Policy Alliance 2017; Heritage Foundation 2017). Despite these conservative organizations creating policies that would negatively impact access to abortion and hurt the livelihoods of lesbians and gay individuals, as well as racial minorities, WOLF argues that the issue of "transgenderism" is too important to not accept alliances with those on the right (Women's Liberation Front 2017b). By trying to protect women, WOLF is further harming women by collaborating with these groups. While DGR, as an organization, does not collaborate politically to limit transgender rights, numerous environmental organizations allege DGR's leaders have publicly outed transgender individuals, forced transgender allies out of their organization, and harassed individuals both online and off, causing their feminist politics to spill into other activist spaces (Scofield 2013; Earth First! 2014). The discourses and practices of DGR and WOLF have political implications beyond their organizational spaces and become part of the wider denial of trans women's womanhood, transphobia, and the maintenance of sex/gender binary in US society at large.

To respond to the harmful discourses produced by these groups, I echo Cofield and Doan's (ch. 3 this volume) call to open up spaces of solidarity. While the needs and experiences of cisgender and transgender women may vary, these differences allow for a more robust analysis of feminist theorizing and more holistic approaches to issues facing women today. Trans women do not nullify cisgender women's experiences and needs, as trans-exclusionary feminists would believe, but rather amplify and add to these discussions. When addressing the issue of women's spaces, whether they be feminist spaces of organizing, bathrooms, or shelters, feminists should pay careful consideration in how the term "woman" is defined and how it can reproduce exclusions, for both cisgender and transgender individuals. Part of this process is moving beyond mere acceptance into feminist spaces and instead thinking about how to restructure these spaces to be more inclusive in both our theorizing and our actions. By addressing both the similarities and differences among women, feminists can counter policies that challenge gender identities and harm trans women.

REFERENCES

Bornstein, Kate. 1994. *Gender Outlaw: On Men, Women, and the Rest of Us*. New York: Routledge.

Browne, Kath. 2009. "Womyn's Separatist Spaces: Rethinking Spaces of Difference and Exclusion." *Transactions of the Institute of British Geographers*, 34 (4): 541–56. https://doi.org/10.1111/j.1475-5661.2009.00361.x.

Butler, Judith. 1990. *Gender Trouble: Feminism and the Subversion of Identity*. New York: Routledge.

Butler, Judith. 2014. *Undoing Gender*. New York: Routledge.

Deep Green Resistance. n.d. a. "About Deep Green Resistance." Accessed July 12, 2017. https://deepgreenresistance.org/en/who-we-are/about-deep-green-resistance.

Deep Green Resistance. n.d. b. "Deep Green Resistance Caucuses." Accessed July 12, 2017. https://deepgreenresistance.org/en/who-we-are/our-structure/deep-green-resistance-caucuses.

Deep Green Resistance. n.d. c. "Deep Green Resistance Bylaws." Accessed July 12, 2017. https://deepgreenresistance.org/en/who-we-are/our-structure/deep-green-resistance-bylaws.

Deep Green Resistance. n.d. d. "Guiding Principles of Deep Green Resistance." Accessed July 12, 2017. https://deepgreenresistance.org/en/who-we-are/guiding-principles-of-deep-green-resistance.

Deep Green Resistance. n.d. e. "Radical Feminism Frequently Asked Questions." Accessed July 12, 2017. https://deepgreenresistance.org/en/who-we-are/faqs/radical-feminism-faqs.

Deep Green Resistance. n.d. f. "Frequently Asked Questions of Deep Green Resistance." Accessed June 14, 2020. https://deepgreenresistance.org/en/who-we-are/faqs/deep-green-resistance-faqs.

Deep Green Resistance. 2013. "Protect Women, Feminism, and Free Speech." *Blog.* May 16, 2013. Accessed July 12, 2017. https://deepgreenresistance.blogspot.com/2013/05/.

Doan, Petra L. 2010. "The Tyranny of Gendered Spaces—Reflections from beyond the Gender Dichotomy." *Gender, Place & Culture* 17 (5): 635–54. https://doi.org/10.1080/09 66369X.2010.503121.

Earth First! 2013. "Deep Green Transphobia." *Earth First! Newswire.* May 15, 2013. http://earthfirstjournal.org/newswire/2013/05/15/deep-green-transphobia/.

Earth First! 2014. "A Toxic Culture of Violence and Shame: How DGR's Denial of Transphobia Exposes Worse Tendencies." *Earth First! Newswire.* February 23, 2014. http://earthfirstjournal.org/newswire/2014/02/23/a-toxic-culture-of-violence-and-shame-how-dgrs-denial-of-transphobia-exposes-worse-tendencies/.

Echols, Alice. 1989. *Daring to Be Bad: Radical Feminism in America, 1967–1975.* Minneapolis: University of Minnesota Press.

Elliot, Patricia. 2004. "Who Gets to Be a Woman?: Feminist Politics and the Question of Trans-Inclusion." *Atlantis: Critical Studies in Gender, Culture & Social Justice* 29 (1): 13–20.

Family Policy Alliance. 2017. "Unlikely Allies for Privacy and Safety: A Radical Feminist Group & Christian Pro-Family Group." January 9, 2017. Accessed December 10, 2019. https://familypolicyalliance.com/issues/2017/01/09/unlikely-allies-privacy-safety/.

Frye, Marylin. 1984. *The Politics of Reality: Essays in Feminist Theory.* Berkeley: Crossing Press.

Gieseking, Jen Jack. 2013. "Queering the Meaning of 'Neighbourhood': Reinterpreting the Lesbian-Queer Experience of Park Slope, Brooklyn, 1983–2008." In *Queer Presences and Absences,* edited by Yvette Taylor and Michelle Addison, 178–200. New York: Palgrave Macmillan.

Gieseking, Jen Jack. 2016. "Crossing Over into Neighbourhoods of the Body: Urban Territories, Borders and Lesbian-Queer Bodies in New York City." *Area* 48 (3): 262–70. https://doi.org/10.1111/area.12147

Goldberg, Michelle. 2014. "What Is a Woman?: The Dispute between Radical Feminism and Transgenderism." *New Yorker.* August 4, 2014. https://www.newyorker.com/magazine/2014/08/04/woman-2.

Green, Eli R. 2006. "Debating Trans Inclusion in the Feminist Movement: A Trans-Positive Analysis." *Journal of Lesbian Studies* 10 (1–2): 231–48.

Halberstam, Judith. 1998. *Female Masculinity.* Durham, NC: Duke University Press.

Hands Across the Aisle. n.d. "Who We Are." Accessed June 14, 2020. https://handsacrosstheaislewomen.com/home/.

Henrickson, Heidi Allene. 2004. "Feminisms and Femininities: Gendered Processes in Women-Only Groups." PhD dissertation, University of York. http://etheses.whiterose.ac.uk/11003/1/437599.pdf.

Heritage Foundation. 2017. "Biology Isn't Bigotry: Why Sex Matters in the Age of Gender Identity." YouTube video, December 17, 2017. https://youtu.be/Rt9DW4e1Cvw.

hooks, bell. 2000. *Feminist Theory: From Margin to Center.* London: Pluto Press.

Jeffreys, Sheila. 2014. *Gender Hurts: A Feminist Analysis of the Politics of Transgenderism.* New York: Routledge.

Jibrin, Rekia. 2017. " 'Ain't I a Feminist?': The Politics of Gender Violence, Anti-Violence, and Education in Oakland, CA." *Gender, Place & Culture* 24 (4): 545–62. https://doi.org/10.1080/0966369X.2017.1335289

Kiraly, Miranda, and Meagan Tyler. 2015. *Freedom Fallacy: The Limits of Liberal Feminism.* Brisbane: Connor Court Publishing.

Koyama, Emi. 2016. "The Transfeminist Manifesto." In *Catching a Wave: Reclaiming Feminism for the 21st Century,* edited by Rory Dicker and Alison Piepmeier, 244–59. Boston: Northeastern University Press.

Mackay, Finn. 2015. *Radical Feminism: Feminist Activism in Movement.* New York: Palgrave Macmillan.

National Center for Transgender Equality. 2015. "The Report of the 2015 Transgender Survey." Accessed March 15, 2019. https://www.transequality.org/sites/default/files /docs/USTS-Full-Report-FINAL.PDF.

Piedalue, Amy. 2017. "Beyond 'Culture' as an Explanation for Intimate Violence: The Politics and Possibilities of Plural Resistance." *Gender, Place & Culture* 24 (4): 563–74. https:// doi.org/10.1080/0966369X.2016.1219323.

Rowland, Robyn, and Renate Klein. 1996. "Radical Feminism: History, Politics, Action." In *Radically Speaking: Feminism Reclaimed*, edited by Diane Bell and Renate Klein, 9–27. North Melbourne: Spinifex Press.

Ruby, Jennie, and Karla Mantilla. 2000. "Men in Ewes' Clothing: The Stealth Politics of the Transgender Movement." *Off Our Backs* 30 (4): 5–12.

Schulevitz, Judith. 2016. "Is It Time to Desegregate the Sexes?" *New York Times.* October 15, 2016. https://www.nytimes.com/2016/10/16/opinion/sunday/is-it-time-to-desegregate-the-sexes.html.

Scofield, B. 2013. "How Derrick Jensen's Deep Green Resistance Supports Transphobia." *Decolonizing Yoga.* May 24, 2013. Accessed May 10, 2017. http://www.decolonizingyoga .com/how-derrick-jensens-deep-green-resistance-supports-transphobia/.

Serano, Julia. 2013. *Excluded: Making Feminist and Queer Movements More Inclusive.* Emeryville, CA: Seal Press.

Sweeney, Belinda. 2004. "Trans-Ending Women's Rights: The Politics of Trans-Inclusion in the Age of Gender." *Women's Studies International Forum* 27: 75–88.

Tong, Rosemarie. 2013. *Feminist Thought: A Comprehensive Introduction.* New York: Routledge.

Williams, Cristan. 2016. "Radical Inclusion Recounting the Trans Inclusive History of Radical Feminism." *Transgender Studies Quarterly* 3 (1–2): 254–58. https://doi.org/10.1215/232 89252-3334463.

Women's Liberation Front. n.d. a. "Women's Liberation Front: Statement of Principles." Accessed July 12, 2017. http://womensliberationfront.org/document-statement-of -principles/.

Women's Liberation Front. n.d. b. "Women's Liberation Front: Wolf V. U.S. Frequently Asked Questions." Accessed December 12, 2019. http://womensliberationfront.org/wp-content/uploads/2019/02/WoLF-v-US-FAQ-final-1.pdf.

Women's Liberation Front. 2016. "Thinking Differently Conference." July 25, 2016. Accessed June 1, 2020. http://womensliberationfront.org/thinking-differently-conference/.

Women's Liberation Front. 2017a. "Statement on Malicious Rumors." April 12, 2017. Accessed December 10, 2019. http://womensliberationfront.org/statement-on -malicious-rumors/.

Women's Liberation Front. 2017b. "Statement on Working with Conservatives." May 4, 2017. Accessed December 10, 2019. http://womensliberationfront.org/wolf-statement-on -working-with-conservatives/.

Women's Liberation Front. 2019. "Declaration of No Confidence in LGB Movement Leadership." January 30, 2019. Accessed June 1, 2020. http://womensliberationfront .org/declaration-of-no-confidence-in-lgb-movement-leadership/.

Women's Liberation Front. 2020. "Gender Dysphoria and Mental Health." February 28, 2020. Accessed June 1, 2020. http://womensliberationfront.org/gender-dysphoria/.

CHAPTER 9

INTERVIEW WITH PETRA DOAN, JULY 2018

Editors: It's been around a decade since you wrote two of your landmark articles in *Gender, Place & Culture*, "Queers in the American City" and "The Tyranny of Gendered Spaces." In these years, we've seen both a broadening of representations of people who are transgender and a simultaneous entrenchment of laws that work to maintain a gender binary (like North Carolina's HB2). Looking at this past decade, what developments do you see as hopeful or promising for transgender issues? Are the questions at stake the same ones you addressed in these articles, or has the conversation shifted?

Doan: The state of transgender people has certainly shifted remarkably over the past twenty years since my official transition and especially over the past eleven years since the publication of "Queers in the American City" (Doan 2007) and the past eight years since "The Tyranny of Gendered Spaces" (Doan 2010). In the late '90s, there were still continuing debates about whether trans should even be include in the LGBTQ alphabet soup. Most national-level gay and lesbian rights groups had moved to embrace trans issues, but there were still a number of lingering issues. For example, the debate over the Employment Non-Discrimination Act (ENDA) in the US Congress [introduced in 2013], and especially comments by one of its sponsors, former Rep. Barney Frank, who refused to countenance the inclusion of trans folks in the bill on the grounds that doing so would kill the bill, undermined the status of trans individuals as legitimate members of the queer community. Even national organizations such as the Human Rights Campaign (HRC) continued to waffle about whether to throw trans people under the bus (they did, then they said they wouldn't, and then they did again, and finally they invited us to sit in the bus—but please tone it down, OK?).

The '90s also saw the expulsion of Nancy Burkholder in 1991 from the Michigan Womyn's Music Festival (MWMF) for the "crime" of being transgender, which sparked a series of protests called Camp Trans and Son of Camp Trans outside the front gate of the music festival (Williams 2013). These anti-trans policies were celebrated by a small group of feminists sometimes called trans-exclusive radical feminists (TERFs). Eventually, public outcry from the trans community and trans allies led to a boycott of the MWMF in 2013, which sadly may have contributed to the eventual collapse of the MWMF in 2015. While I mourn the passing of this important space for women, I still fail to understand how allowing trans women to participate would have been worse than shutting down the festival. I recognize that the increasing support from many feminist and trans allies is one of several very encouraging trends over the past decade.

Other areas of significant progress over the past ten years include the broadening of nondiscrimination ordinances and increasing recognition of trans vulnerability. Many institutions, including my home county (Leon County, Florida) and my workplace (Florida State University) have adopted anti-discrimination ordinances inclusive of gender identity and appearance. These much-needed protections have been added by many jurisdictions and organizations across the country, providing a measure of protection for often highly vulnerable trans individuals. The collection of formal data on hate crimes against transgender people mandated by the Matthew Shepard and James Byrd Hate Crimes Prevention Act of 2009 also begins to provide some baseline data for assessing what appears to be a spiraling increase in hate crimes against trans women, and especially against trans women of color.

A more significant, and I believe, positive change (though controversial in some places) is the rapid rise in visibility of gender-nonconforming individuals, who may or may not identify as trans but often use terms like gender queer, third gender, or a wide variety of other highly creative terms (Harrison, Grant, and Herman 2012). It is difficult to make a precise count of how many people are identifying as gender nonnormative and using alternate pronouns, but most concerned observers suggest that among young people the numbers are substantial. My recent article in *WSQ: Women's Studies Quarterly* (Doan 2016) discusses the difficulties of making these kinds of estimates but highlights the importance of recognizing this as a growing trend toward much greater gender fluidity.

The controversy surrounding this proliferation of genders lies in the inability of a patriarchal system deeply invested in a binary gender system to come to terms with gender nonconforming threats to this long-established dichotomy. Whether this turmoil is the last gasp of a failing system or the harbinger of a new era of anti-trans activism remains to be seen. Certainly, measures to restrict transgender access to bathrooms have gained recent notoriety (see Cofield and Doan, ch. 3 this volume), and it is possible that Trumpian autocrats may increase the invective against transgender and gender-nonconforming people, creating convenient scapegoats as a distraction from their own ineptitude.

Editors: In an article in *Gender, Place & Culture,* you shared a transcript of your speech to the Tallahassee women's march in 2017, where you spoke of how your own struggles with identity twenty years ago changed your activism and your relationship to academia (Doan 2017). How do you see feminist geographers engaging with activism and social movements in this moment of political "darkness"? What potential do you see in connecting personal experience to activist and academic lives? And how do you think spatial strategies and analyses can be effectively mobilized to disrupt gendered, sexualized inequalities and heteronormativity and create new spaces?

Doan: I think to answer these questions we have to consider the groundwork needed for feminist activism. It seems to me that the point of feminist standpoint analysis is to reflexively analyze the position from which we view the world because it makes such a difference in our understanding and interpretation of what we are experiencing. Before engaging in any feminist analysis, we must take into account both the physical location and social spaces of our own subjectivity. Sara Ahmed (2004) reminds us that in taking stock of our positionality we must also confront the ways that various events have created deep impressions on our bodies. For women, these emotions are often linked to events that have caused us great pain or have made us deeply angry, and it is in making these connections that a deeply grounded feminism emerges. This process is elaborated by bell hooks, who described the movement of feminism into politics as connected to our experiences of pain and anger that must be linked to the "overall education for critical consciousness of collective political resistance" (hooks 1989, 32; cited by Ahmed 2004).

For feminist academics, connection to the #MeToo movement is certainly one path into greater activism. The pent-up anger and pain of so many women can be both a powerfully motivating force for individuals but also the means to connect with the broader experiences of others who have experienced similar life-changing mental and physical abuse. In my own case, the fear and pain of coming out in a fairly hostile and deeply patriarchal world left me emotionally and physically shredded to the point where suicide seemed an easy solution. However, in my case, connecting with that pain and the anger that accompanied these scars provided me with the impetus to simultaneously explore the intellectual underpinnings of hatred and violence, but also to reach out to other trans women (and men) who were experiencing similar conditions and seek ways to respond to that violence. My work in analyzing both the potential and the frustration of creating queer safe spaces has emerged from that dual focus. Connections through emotional experiences shared with others can be incredibly empowering and enable significant changes. For example, shortly after I came out as trans I attended an annual gathering of unprogrammed Quakers who in general were supportive of difference but not very clued in about trans issues. After one meeting for worship, a Friend rose to invite women to attend a moonlight gathering the next day hosted by the women's support center. As a newly out trans woman seeking to connect with other women, I approached the woman who made the announcement afterwards and quietly asked if these gatherings would welcome trans women. She was initially unsure and promised to "get back to me" later that day. After checking with the committee that ran the center, she informed me sadly that the committee had discerned that trans women were *not* welcome at this women-only gathering. I took in this deeply upsetting news for a while, trying desperately not to care and failing badly in the effort. The next day at our daily meeting for worship, the dam broke and I rose to share my deep pain and was overwhelmed with wave after wave of tears. I sat back down sobbing uncontrollably. I soon felt first one hand gently on my back, then another, and then there were some disconnected rustlings. Finally, one Friend whispered to me, "Petra, look up," and what felt like half the room of more than one hundred Friends had moved in semicircle around me, holding me in the Light as I sobbed. At the rise of that meeting, one Friend rose to say that he was on the central committee (organizing committee for the entire gathering) and would take this matter up with them. By suppertime that evening, the central committee had convened and discerned that while it was fine for the women's center to hold a women-only gathering, it was not up to the center to determine whether an individual's gender identity measured up to some standard. My tears and sharing had opened a pathway for transformation. Many women came up to me after dinner to be sure that I knew that they welcomed my participation.

I think that this kind of open sharing of our pain as well as our anger is a vital first step in changing the ways that narratives are understood. If I had made a dispassionate plea for inclusion, special committees would have been formed to study the matter, and within a year or two an answer would have been provided. But the immediacy of my pain opened others' hearts and made connections to their own pain. As a result, I think that feminist scholars must find ways to write their own pain and suffering caused by patriarchal structures and actions in ways that enable a broader understanding and recognition of the painful yet different experiences of others. From this understanding of difference can come what Paulo Freire termed "conscientization" or what bell hooks called the development of critical consciousness, which is essential as the underpinning of activism.

Editors: We read with interest the recent exchanges on the feminist geography (femgeog) listserv about transgender terminology. A graduate student had asked a question about a textbook section on transgender issues in Southeast Asia, and you responded with a generous reflection on the terms and implications. We appreciated the academic and emotional labor you put into your response, including a reflection on your own subjectivity.

You wrote,

> My own current pet peeve on this topic is when people use the term transgenders to describe two or more transgender individuals. I am a blue-eyed person, but please don't call me a blue eye. Or lump me with other blue-eyed people and call us blue eyes. Because the term transgender is an umbrella term that includes a range of different subjectivities my identity is not as a transgender. If truth be told the best self-description I have used is something like a bisexual transsexual lesbian woman who tried but failed miserably at being gay. Some would call me greedy for trying to claim all of the LGBT letters in one subjectivity. Others would critique my use of bisexual and lesbian in the same phrase, but nearly all my attractions are to women and especially to the woman to whom I now married. But as a Quaker I believe in speaking truth and I acknowledge the truth of a broader attraction in my early years, so adopt the term bisexual into my own assessment of my complex subjectivity. It is my subjectivity so I get to name it. Subjectivities are not always stable so I always resist people putting others into neat boxes. Hence don't call me a transgender.

This kind of frankness is refreshing and can do so much to help others "get" the experience of being a person who doesn't identify with the sex they were assigned at birth. You are also speaking to the limitations of identity categories to capture complex identifications and subjectivities and pointing to how categories change individually, socially, and politically over time. What do you see as possible productive responses to the limitations of identity categories? What work do these identities do or fail to do? What would a feminist geographical approach to identity look like given the important political work identity categories do, even as they always fail to fully express the subject in her entirety/multiplicity of subjectivity?

Doan: I think that in the case of the ongoing evolution of trans and gender-nonconforming identity categories the most productive response is to embrace the creativity of an individual's self-selected/created identity. The category "transgender" itself has evolved from the rather narrow transgenderist term used by Virginia Prince to refer to cross-dressers like herself who lived full-time in a gender role different than that assigned to her at birth but who eschewed surgery (Williams 2014). Over time the category has been expanded to include cross-dressers, transsexuals, and a range of gender-queer individuals who challenge gender stereotypes in some manner.

The growing edges of this category are people who adopt gender-neutral pronouns but who otherwise show little signs of outward gender nonconformity. It is these people who really push the edges of transgender subjectivity. It is certainly possible that their adoption of gender-neutral pronouns may be an honest attempt to be a trans ally and live in solidarity with their more overt trans brothers and sisters. It may also be that they are simply doing the hard, internal work of sorting out their individual subjectivity in the face of deeply embedded dichotomous categories and will be ready to be more open at some future point. Finally, it is possible that the wider acceptance of lesbian and gay subjectivities has made those identities seem a bit tame, and so young people looking for an edgier subjectivity may be experimenting with an explicitly nondichotomous category. While some of these possible subject positions might not naturally also identify as trans, I feel strongly that gatekeeping is quite unproductive. Accordingly, I am happy to keep expanding the trans umbrella, although I recognize that the metaphor may be a bit frayed at the edges. The point is that the sheltering nature of the category is still useful for a wide range of subjectivities.

The trans umbrella is by now a well-recognized component of the even wider LGBTQ acronym that itself keeps expanding—some groups now use LGBTQ+ or LGBTQQI. Finding community in the largest possible group is extremely valuable for the purposes of political lobbying for nondiscrimination, social services, and other needs that may be provided by elected representatives. The LGBTQ community has come to represent an important group that increasingly has a voice in political decision-making and is certainly a voting bloc that some candidates reach out to. However, it is important to note that some trans issues are quite different than other LGB issues and need to be highlighted. For example, medical benefits for many trans individuals are often contested—whether this includes hormones, gender affirmation surgery, or mental health care needs. Other trans-specific needs include updated birth certificates, driver's licenses, and passports. I fully recognize that not all gender-nonconforming individuals wish to undergo medical procedures or receive therapy, and some may have no intention of changing their legal paperwork. However, the issue of access to public accommodations broadly, and specifically to bathrooms, affects nearly all of the trans community, and the need for protection from discrimination in employment and housing is fairly universal for trans and nonconforming individuals.

The work of feminist geography that pertains to these evolving categories is to recognize the need for continued exploration of the dimensions of gender in all its complexities. The rate of change in this area has been very swift over the past decade, requiring fairly nimble category formations. Simple language modifications when asking about gender in surveys and qualitative work can be rich and enormously productive. Rather than asking an individual's sex, it is probably more helpful to ask "What sex were you assigned at birth?" Rather than presenting gender as a dichotomy, it is better to be sure to ask an open-ended question, such as "What gender do you identify as now?" Changes like these are likely to add some complexity to subsequent analysis, but they will add much greater depth and richness to the resulting work.

Editors: Your work has engaged feminist and queer theory while also developing theories for trans geographies. Do you see trans geographies as a separate field with little intersection or dialogue with feminist geographies? What do you wish feminist and queer theory would pick up from trans geographies? What new questions and insights are trans geographies developing that you see as important for contributing to feminist geography and more broadly to geography as a discipline and perhaps even academia as a whole?

Doan: I don't really see a huge gulf between feminist and queer theory and the work I am doing to develop more theory related to trans geographies. My reading of feminist and queer geography (especially Gavin Brown, Michael Brown, Kath Browne, Phil Hubbard, Lynda Johnston, Larry Knopp, Robyn Longhurst, Natalie Oswin, Gillian Rose, Gill Valentine) was foundational to my work on understanding gay and lesbian spaces and the way that trans folks intersect with those spaces. Reading those authors was also enormously helpful to me as I reflected on how to describe my own experiences of gender.

I think that adding the trans perspective to existing theory really adds several types of insights. The first is an elaboration of the embodied nature of gender, building on the work of Robyn Longhurst and Lynda Johnston but adding a focus on the fluidity of gender that in many cases challenges dichotomous views of the gender binary. I recognize that not all trans people consider themselves as outside the binary (after they have transitioned anyway), but many trans women with deep voices and large bodies (such as myself) and certainly trans men who decide to become pregnant or need continuing gynecological care simply push the gender binary by the fact of their existence. The increasing gender fluidity and nonconformity shown more recently by increasing numbers of young people also undermines dichotomous ways of thinking in profound ways.

The second area where I think trans perspectives may add to existing theory is in the interaction between gender performativity (à la Judith Butler) and the external environment. Gregson and Rose (2000) suggest that gender performance can have an effect on the surrounding environment, but in "The Tyranny of Gendered Spaces" I argue that these influences go both ways. My gender performance in any given location partly reflects my own sense of gender but is also intimately connected to the ways that observers in the external environment are perceiving me and are in turn changed by my performance as my performance also morphs in response. I think this mutually co-constitutive nature of gender and performance remains a growing edge for theoretical development.

Finally, I feel that the one area in which trans geographies may make a useful contribution lies in the intensely personal and immediate experience of gender and especially the negative consequences of "violating" the gender binary. While trans folks "do" theory in an intellectual sense, the intensity of our experiences and all too frequently the extremely negative effects of those interactions with the patriarchy make that theory all the more immediate and, in many cases, urgent. While some might argue that this is also true for women in general, and hence most feminist scholars, my position is that living in the gendered borderlands or even just transitioning through the gendered barrier provides a uniquely intense and embodied experience of patriarchal power that is etched deeply into our consciousness. Certainly, victims of rape and sexual abuse also carry deep trauma from that event or series of events, especially if the system succeeds in persuading them that they are in any way to blame for this experience. However, if these unfortunate victims are able to rise above their trauma and speak out against the perpetrators, they may gain a measure of healing as they name the individuals who have harmed them and perhaps see justice done. Trans people frequently experience similar kinds of traumatic abuse, but only infrequently are able to experience the healing of naming and seeing justice done. The widespread shaming of all victims is highly problematic, but when the victim is also "guilty" of being trans, there is little public forgiveness and even less justice, especially for trans women of color. Furthermore, on a day-to-day level trans and gender-nonconforming people are so routinely misgendered, mispronouned, and misidentified in ways that deny our very identity that all too often we are thrust into virtual "outcast" status. It is from these experiences that I believe trans perspectives can provide useful insights into the fragility of gendered embodiment that may help us to reimagine ways to conceptualize the gendered nature of society.

REFERENCES

Ahmed, S. 2004. *The Cultural Politics of Emotion*. Edinburgh: Edinburgh University Press.

Doan, P. L. 2007. "Queers in the American City: Transgender Perceptions of Urban Areas." *Gender, Place & Culture* 14 (1): 57–74.

Doan, P. L. 2010. "The Tyranny of Gendered Spaces—Reflections from beyond the Gender Dichotomy." *Gender, Place & Culture* 17 (5): 635–54.

Doan, P. L. 2016. "To Count or Not to Count: Queering Measurement and the Transgender Community." *WSQ: Women's Studies Quarterly* 44 (3-4): 89–110.

Doan, P. 2017. "Coming out of Darkness and into Activism." *Gender, Place & Culture* 24 (5): 741–46.

Gregson, N., and G. Rose. 2000. "Taking Butler Elsewhere: Performativities, Spatialities and Subjectivities." *Environment and Planning D: Society and Space* 18 (4): 433–52.

Harrison, J., J. Grant, and J. L. Herman. 2012. *A Gender Not Listed Here: Genderqueers, Gender Rebels, and OtherWise in the National Transgender Discrimination Survey*. Los Angeles: University of California Los Angeles, Williams Institute Working Paper. http://escholarship.org/uc/item/2zj46213.

hooks, bell. 1989. *Talking Back: Thinking Feminist, Thinking Black*. London: Sheba Feminist Publishers.

Williams, C. 2013. "Michigan Womyn's Music Festival." *TransAdvocate*. April 9, 2013. http://transadvocate.com/michigan-womyns-music-festival_n_8943.htm.

Williams, C. 2014. "Transgender." *Transgender Studies Quarterly: TSQ* 1 (1–2): 232–34. https://doi.org/10.1215/23289252-2400136.

PART III

TEMPORALITY AND FEMINIST FUTURES

CHAPTER 10

MAKING MEMORY: CARE AND DALIT FEMINIST ARCHIVING

Anusha Hariharan

It was a breezy, soporific afternoon in Arakkonam, a town in Tamil Nadu, in southern India. After my first year of graduate work in the US, I was back home—a place that was now becoming a "field site"—for the summer. I was in the office of an activist collective that I call the Dalit Women's Movement (DWM),[1] a space I had previously occupied over the years as a volunteer and Tamil-English translator. That summer, I had returned to conduct ethnographic research, a changing role that I was slowly familiarizing myself with; a process, I am sure my collaborators, the activists of the DWM, shared. White plastic chairs were strewn around, recently emptied by thirty activists who had come in for the DWM's weekly check-in meeting. Occupying chairs next to me were Gloria and Arasi, DWM activists and my research collaborators. The three of us fought the urge to take a nap. We had come together to talk about a collaboratively curated digital archive of DWM's activist history, a medium that would bring together activists' memories of being part of a movement.

DWM is among a number of vital grassroots movements in the Tamil-speaking region that works toward social justice for Dalit communities. Dalit is an umbrella term to denote the politicized identity of those who belonged to erstwhile "untouchable" castes in India. India's constitutional guarantee of freedom from untouchability is one of the hard-won successes of Dalit political activism. These successes are due to Babasaheb Dr. B. R. Ambedkar's leadership in the twentieth century. He was one of the first—and most prominent—pioneer Dalit leaders in India, and many contemporary Dalit movements have modeled themselves on his thoughts and ideals, be it politics around inequality or Buddhist practice toward a more just social world. Dalit movements today address issues of social justice that have to do with structural inequality, violence, and atrocity against culturally, politically, and economically disempowered communities.

Concurrently, in their struggle for social justice, Dalit activists have produced a vast array of materials and artifacts that relate to Dalit social and cultural life. These materials account for centuries of erasure—of "Dalit voices"—from dominant social and political discourses in India. With this ideal in thought and practice, Dalit communities have produced a robust body of writing, speeches, art, activist literature and material, films, songs, poetry, testimonials, and life narratives that foreground the experience of *being* Dalit (Guru 2011; Rawat and Satyanarayana 2016). How would a digital archive represent what it means to inhabit the world and live life by a set of ethics that challenges inequality and oppression and, in doing so, upholds a different political vision for society (Guru 2011)? The DWM's effort to construct an archive of activist history, to bring together activists' narratives and material produced over thirty years, emerges from this commitment to address historical elisions by powerful groups in India. In this chapter I trace how memory-work is fundamental to a sense of place rooted in care for past and future generations, through the ways that activists work to sustain alternative forms of kinship. Simultaneously, this chapter engages with Richa Nagar's "radical vulnerability" by tracing the institutional commitments and experiences that are enmeshed with my traversal through feminist spaces in Delhi and Tamil Nadu (Nagar 2014, 3–5).

In the years before I started graduate school, Beulah *Akka*,[2] an older activist in the DWM, often spoke of finding a way to tell the history of the Dalit women activists of Arakkonam: their stories of working together, the many obstacles they had overcome to address issues of caste and gender-based violence, and more importantly, the ways in which they had found faith in each other and through that, within themselves. To understand the DWM's histories through affective ties, embodied experience, and the productive tensions that animate Dalit women's struggles requires a brief foray into how this movement emerged, and the forms it has taken through the years.

The DWM has a trajectory similar to many grassroots movements fighting for social justice through Dalit women's rights in India. In their trajectory, the famous Beijing Conference—a metonym for the 1995 United Nations' World Conference on Women held in Beijing—serves as a temporal marker. Like many other grassroots movements that emerged from structurally disempowered communities in the 1980s, the DWM became a robust candidate for international donor funding. This necessitated certain changes in the structure and form of the movement: the DWM acquired an "organizational front," an office space to conduct meetings and the concurrent funds to run campaigns, manage programs, hire the forty or so activists engaged in the movement as full-time employees, and pay them for the campaign work they performed (Alvarez 2009). The ethos and thrust of their work remain the same—raising awareness on sexual violence against Dalit women, livelihood issues of Dalit communities, challenging caste-based violence in Tamil Nadu, land redistribution, and domestic violence—as they continue to respond to the various challenges that have emerged in the last two decades. These challenges emerge from shifts in the sociopolitical landscape of India since the 1990s that speak to neoliberal reforms and restructuring, which will be discussed later in this chapter.

An archival history of a movement such as the DWM requires careful navigation of this terrain: of Dalit struggles, grassroots women's movements, their organizational fronts, the changing sociopolitical landscape of Tamil Nadu, and more importantly, how these shifts relate to the affective changes between activists over time. Which brings us back to that summer afternoon, when Arasi, Gloria, and I began to address what this archive would mean to the DWM activists, and why such an endeavor is necessary. As discussions such as this one often meander, Gloria stated that an archive such as this could further their legacy, and the legacy of Ambedkar. To this, Arasi retorted: "Ambedkar did great things, but where has that left us? This [endeavor] should be about what *we* did, and how *we* can use this to do what we want to do . . . demand policy change, talk about our experiences . . . young Dalit women should know what their mothers, grandmothers, aunts have fought for."

Arasi's words animate some of the concerns that shadow the DWM, and possibly other Dalit women's struggles today. In telling microhistories of Dalit struggles—that are rooted in *place*, as caste dynamics are specific to spatial and temporal geographies—Dalit activists and scholars hope that these plural histories can speak to each other and across generations. The attempt is to consolidate a broader genealogy of Dalit experience and history through appreciating the multiplicity of these microhistories while methodologically challenging metanarrative history. This attempt recognizes that to honor the richness and granularity of these histories, they have to be grounded in place and speak to linguistic and geographical specificities of caste: the experiences it produces and the dynamics it generates. The "we" and "us" that Arasi's words emphasize speak to these aspirations to narrativize place-based microhistories of *their* Dalit community; that is, to tell the history of DWM's struggles, the various emotional and affective journeys that activists share, would require this history to stand on its own. Arasi's insistence on a narrative that is about their experience—as opposed to one that is meant to further Ambedkar's legacy—upholds this intent.

I start this chapter by laying out the specific feminist commitments that pushed each of us—the different activists and myself—toward conceptualizing an archive as the means to uphold the DWM's legacy. I draw on Richa Nagar's theorizing and suggested practice of "radical vulnerability" to explore the shifting relationship between activists and researcher, each arriving at a collaboration through feminist political labor (Nagar 2014, 3–5). The section that follows discusses memory and archiving to Dalit movements, foregrounding the DWM activists' engagement with these notions of legacy, care, inheritance, and aspiration. In creating an archive with intent, Dalit feminists are in the process of self-narration and of making their everyday life, experience, and activist labors identifiable within a larger history of Dalit politics. In doing so—as I discuss in the subsequent section—they are forging a legacy, a past worthy of passing on to future imaginaries and aspirations. This raises the question of *who* can lay claim to the past, to enact future aspirations. In exploring these concerns, I delve into the circulation of kinship idioms, vocabularies of indebtedness, and intergenerational notions of care as binding an activist community together. The following section provides a brief ethnographic interlude that illuminates the anxiety precipitated through the breakdown of activist care networks, opening us up to a longer discussion of anxiety in my last section, demonstrating intergenerational shifts in forms of organizing and changes in spatialities of labor that Dalit women inhabit. By drawing a link between memory, place-making, spatialities of labor and organizing, and aspirations for the future, I conclude with notes on what necessitates an archive of activist history.

FEMINIST COMMITMENTS

Gloria and Arasi were coming to this conversation about the archive as activists who had engaged in this movement for years, and as women who belong to the Dalit communities that this movement works with. Aspiration for Gloria and Arasi is an affectively charged object. Their affects are drawn from a combination of the past and the present, and oriented toward potential futures, for the longevity of the movement. Here, activist legacy and memories that surround them function as resources that can be drawn on to labor toward an aspirational future. These affects have "movement" (Ahmed 2004, 120), as they travel in a specific direction: the future. I, however, come to this conversation from a different place: I spent several years traversing feminist activist spaces in New Delhi, the capital city of India. As a place, New Delhi is defined by its conceptual proximity to the nation-state. Due to its status as the national capital, it is meant to "rise above" or "depart" from regional particularities. Delhi's activist spaces are defined by the assemblage of persons who inhabit the place and the specific commitments they identify for themselves at any given point in time. Delhi's proximity to ideas, metaphors, and imaginaries that are associated with the postcolonial nation-state shapes the forms of political engagement possible in the city: for one, it seeks to obliterate markers of regional particularity, requiring its inhabitants to fashion themselves as liberal secular political subjects. For example, in the years that I inhabited the city, I experienced a tacit persuasion within activist communities to transcend the regional, linguistic, and cultural specificities that marked my own subjectivity.

I came to live in New Delhi as an immigrant from Chennai, a city rooted in its regional particularity of being Tamil, where the culture of Tamilness is tied to the politics of language and place. In Tamil Nadu, as in many regions in India, caste—and its politics—is tied to the notion of place. As a structure, identity, embodied practice and affect, caste varies across different places in India, and its political inflections differ as well. I found that activist spaces in New Delhi were unable to offer what I had fervently been seeking: an engagement with feminist politics that is grounded in regional specificity through the lens of caste. I found myself in search of a political space that centered caste in its articulation of feminist politics, as opposed to one that acknowledged caste as one among many intersecting identities that had to be analyzed through a feminist lens.

Sharmila Rege, a feminist scholar from India, writes about this process as illustrative of the tension between caste-Hindu feminist activism and Dalit feminist activism (Rege 1998). Within a caste-Hindu feminist rhetoric, argues Rege, there exists an imaginary that posits the *ideal* feminist subject as having transcended community and broken off any ties to caste or communal groups, thereby giving rise to the homogeneous category of "woman" (Rege 1998, 40). When I first started interacting with the DWM activists in 2012, I was struck by how their enactment of feminist politics was refracted through the lens of caste. I had also moved back to Chennai and begun interacting with other Tamil Nadu–based feminist activists and scholars who came to the question of caste through a similar struggle. This was a significant departure from how I had engaged with feminist politics in New Delhi. Thus, by working with the DWM, I am in the process of trying to understand how my own feminist political praxis and scholarship could engage caste, both as intimate identity and as politics. As part of this endeavor, and building on years of shifting relationships with the DWM activists, I am in the process of articulating what it would mean to practice Richa Nagar's (2014, 3–5) notion of "radical vulnerability."

Nagar posits "radical vulnerability" as a process by which the researcher approaches the work she does—whether it is academic/scholarly or activist or a combination of the two—through careful interrogation of the intricate ways in which power indexes her interactions with people in the process of ethnographic work. She speaks of this process in the context of doing feminist ethnographic fieldwork with communities that are historically and/or structurally disempowered. She observes that ethnographic work often posits a challenge to the feminist researcher and her location in power structures. She also discerns an emergent tension that arises when the researcher engages with the field in an embodied manner. Further, she recognizes that this tension could be wielded as a site of creative work that implicates both researcher and her interlocutors (Nagar 2014).

Elsewhere—and in relation to what I am interested in exploring—Nagar has argued that conversations centered on the researcher's "positionality" that occur within institutionalized academic spaces in the global North often stand in for a more nuanced and challenging engagement with power. She says: "Reflexivity in US academic writing has mainly focused on examining the identities of the individual researcher rather than on the ways in which those identities intersect with institutional, geopolitical and material aspects of their positionality" (Nagar 2002, 182). I see the two arguments Nagar makes as interconnected: often, an acknowledgment of our own identities vis-à-vis our interlocutors becomes a placeholder for the nitty-gritty details of negotiations feminist scholars are constantly making throughout their careers.[3] Conversations regarding "positionality" also limit the possibility of both researchers' and interlocutors' notions of themselves being constructed intersubjectively, and as constantly shifting within the space of the field.

Drawing on these insights, I work to practice "radical vulnerability" in this process of archive building with the DWM. This requires the researcher to embrace discomfort and allow it to become productive. When the DWM and I first started conceptualizing this archive, I was caught up with questions about whether it would be an archive about an organization or a movement, and what form of collective the DWM self-define as. It became clear over time, by observing the amount of discomfort I felt about my own lack of clarity with regard to this question, that it actually did not matter how they self-define. It is also evident that identifications such as these are not rigid and unchanging—they are shaped by the audience that the DWM engage with at a given point of time. Further, I recognized that my discomfort emerged from my early feminist training, which had me believe that a movement loses its radical edge when it acquires an organizational form. This experience opened up new lenses through which I could understand feminist political practices.

Similarly, I engage in an ongoing reflexive exercise that interrogates how my interlocutors' and my locations (within and outside of academic institutions, and more importantly, within a caste hierarchy in Tamil Nadu) shape the ways in which this archive assumes the form that it will in the future. I realize that the intent(s) we bring to the process of archiving from the multiple feminist practices and politics we feel committed to will shape this archive over time. It will also require constant navigation of how caste is embodied and the ways in which it structures interactions and power equations. Last, it requires caution to never posit an unequivocal "we" in feminist politics or assume that all feminists have the same commitments at a given point in time.[4] I hope that future writings on this archival process will continue to animate and articulate what radical vulnerability in this context could look like.

This chapter aims to understand how Dalit feminist activists at the DWM think of legacy as something they inherit. It explores how they see themselves as forging a path otherwise untrammeled, and what they would like to bestow upon the next generation of Dalit women who choose to continue these struggles. This exploration centers on the anxieties that activists experience within a shifting sociopolitical and economic landscape. I contend that these anxieties emerge from the need to rearticulate activist tools in these rapidly changing landscapes. "Memory-work" (Till 2012, 7)—or the political labor performed by activists and community members to claim authority and legitimacy to represent their own pasts in a public sphere—becomes crucial for encouraging younger generations to continue the feminist struggle of the previous generations. The performance of this kind of political labor, or "memory-work," will consolidate what Karen Till calls a "place-based ethics of care" (Till 2012, 8): a mode of caring for place through caring for those who inhabit place and in allowing yourself to be cared for.

In the context where I work, the everyday lived experience of caste and caste-based struggles is grounded in the notion of place. Functioning through logics of pollution and purity, caste suffuses landscapes, constructs spatialities, and delineates group access to places. Gloria and Arasi's relationship with Arakkonam as place is precipitated by their caste membership. As women from Dalit communities, they have to lay claim to place-making as a political struggle. A place-based ethics of care would involve nurturing or caring for the work and legacy that allowed any of these women to lay claim over place. I argue that the idea of political legacy as something that can be inherited is tied to notions of intergenerational care that are rooted in a "sense of place," or people's experience of place through the changing relationships they have with the past and present (Kuusisto-Arponen 2009). To lose a sense of place would also mean an erasure of the memory of struggles that enabled these women to stand up to caste normativity and violence. Without a legacy that future generations could potentially inherit, activists are anxious that a network of care (for each other, for older activists, for activist "kin") they established through the 1980s and 1990s would be dismantled. Legacies assemble a narrative where legendary figures/activists and leaders—who have spent their entire lives performing activism as an "ethic of care" (Tronto 1993 in Till 2012, 11)—are rendered visible and, in turn, become recipients of care. As Gloria once rationalized, "If legacy were to be understood as 'collective' inheritance, the labor of care that is called upon should also be collective." Emergent within this rationale is the anxiety to be cared for, by each other and by future generations, as conduits of history. It demands that narratives of legacy invoke a sense of responsibility in younger generations of activists, cementing a notion of duty and care enmeshed in each other and across generations of women. In order to propel a place-based ethic of care as tied to memory and legacy of the movement, the DWM want to use an archive of activist history as the tool that would enable this intent. The archive, then, accords legitimacy to their collective memories within a public sphere.

THE DWM, MEMORY, AND AN ARCHIVE

The digital archive of activist history that the DWM and I are co-curating will trace activists' journeys and intimate narratives against the broader arc of the social and cultural landscape of caste and feminist politics in India. The act of bringing memories together as a counternarrative to hegemonic political histories is a central feature of Dalit activism. The origins of *Dalit* activism as we recognize it today (petitioning, public protest and marches, awareness building, and demanding legal redressal) can be traced back to the late nineteenth or early twentieth century in Maharashtra (Rao 2009).[5] Through the 1970s and 1980s, Dalit women's issues have been addressed within other movements as well, such as worker's movements, peasant movements, and Communist party organizing.[6] Dalit women's organizing underwent shifts in the early 1990s with a proliferation of independent and autonomous movements, collectives, and organizations. Movements that chose to adopt organizational fronts channeled donor funding into programs that addressed violence against Dalit women, Dalit women's rights over land and other resources, and gender and sexuality. Simultaneously, the 1990s witnessed the popularizing of "Dalit feminism," articulated as a political position that emerges from challenging an upper-caste rendition of Indian feminism based on elisions of "difference" that marks Dalit women's subjectivities (Rege 1998, 40).

Over the past decade, discussions on Dalit feminism have not been restricted to physical places of organizing where activist organizers and community members come together in meetings, rallies, and conferences. Social media and the blogosphere have allowed for dialogue and debate regardless of physical proximity. They have also managed to bring together different generations of Dalit ideologues and activists in conversation, tending to Dalit futurities. Blogs such as *Dalit Camera* and *Saavari* interweave scholarly analyses of Dalit life and politics with a public political discourse. Work on Dalit popular culture and "remembrance" has also emerged as a result of pedagogic exercises within the Krantijyoti Savitribai Phule Women's Studies Centre in the University of Pune in Maharashtra.[7] Graduate students in the department have self-published two works, *Youth Cultures: Defamiliarizing the Familiar* (2011) and *Plundering Popular Culture* (2010), which are both results of graduate coursework engaging oral histories and collective memory within Dalit communities. Literary sources offer the possibility of analyses as cultural artifacts, as well as knowledge-products that convey Dalit social histories (Purushottam, Ramaswamy, and Shyamala 2016; Ravikumar and Azhagarasan 2012; Satyanarayana and Tharu 2011, 2013). Y. S. Alone has conducted a similar analysis on Dalit caste narratives and visual representation (2017). Alone and other scholars of visual cultures ground their empirical detail in Dalit art and photography (also see Jain 2010; Tartakov 2012), calling attention to the manner in which Dalit artists have repurposed conventional and hegemonic visual narratives, particularly in print and sculpture art, to foreground a Dalit lens in reshaping extant narratives.

For artists and activists, as well as the DWM, the creation of art and the construction of memory is itself an act of resistance, asserting claim over nationalist and other hegemonic narratives and forming a Dalit counterpublic. In the context of DWM's efforts to create an archive, memory must be understood as processual: memory is forged in the process of creating an archive, as opposed to the archive and its material contents performing the labor of substantiating a preexisting historical narrative (Raiford 2009). The curation of this archive, then, is not just a product but the enactment of ethical labor where "memory-work" denotes care (Till 2012). I argue that this particular act of care is embedded and is contiguous with other forms of care rooted in place. The landscape of Arakkonam, for the DWM activists, is constructed through everyday forms of resistance and in reclaiming spaces they stand to lose easily. To care for the movement, their legacy, and for each other would also mean caring for Arakkonam. The DWM's intent to curate this archive lies at the intersection of memory-work and place-based ethic of care (Till 2012, 7–8).

Through the process of building this archive, activists navigate anxieties on an everyday basis: *who* would inherit the legacy of their movement? The negotiation of anxieties is moored in painstakingly creating a counternarrative and in enacting a different vision of political life and ethics. The next section follows the notion of inheritance and its intergenerational circulation in terms of the labor of reckoning the past with the present through idioms of kinship and acts of care. I contend that all three aspects of inheritance are oriented toward emergent futures, whether the future in question relates to a movement, individual activists, or continuing legacies.

INHERITING A LEGACY, INHERITING AN ARCHIVE

Later in the summer of 2016, Gloria and I began conducting oral history interviews for the archival project, which includes a collection of curated materials: oral history interviews, pamphlets, posters, handbills, poetry, and songs to consolidate a movement's collective memory. The activists and I are annotating the materials we will collect over time and contextualizing them in activists' reflections on past events, particularly moments when these materials were produced, envisioning the archive as intentionally in process. This archive is meant to be digitized, which allows the possibility of reaching out to feminists in other parts of the world.

The digital form also offers possibilities for young people in India to engage with this archive. Older members of the movement perceive a younger generation of Dalit women, who could potentially become feminist activists in the future, as experiencing an ease with digital technology. Gloria referred to them as the "WhatsApp generation"; they may be more likely to appreciate a legacy if it is consolidated in digital form. Simultaneously, this also attends to older activists' nostalgia. Their yearning to narrativize the past can be realized in a form that is both accessible as well as amenable to revision. In this sense, the aesthetics of digital technology resonate with Dalit visions for a democratic future: knowledge in digital form can be produced and accessed by anybody, and can be reshaped in the event that alternative narratives emerge.

This section examines the intersection of archives and political legacy in terms of inheritance. My narrative begins with Gloria and my quest to find two older activists, Arputhamma and Pichamma, who "retired" from the DWM. We wanted to map their activist journeys and use this opportunity to think more about how oral histories and other materials could be brought together to animate this archive. As forerunners of Dalit women's activism in Arakkonam, Arputhamma and Pichamma's legacies preceded them. The DWM wanted these legacies in a form that could be inherited by future generations of Dalit women.

While the idiom of "inheritance" has received considerable attention in academic scholarship, I find it useful to understand Dalit inheritance of activist legacy through a careful reading of Yukiko Koga's conception of "double inheritance" (Koga 2016). Writing from the context of China's contemporary relationship with Japan and Japanese imperialism, Koga understands Chinese inheritance of a colonial legacy characterized in the present through an economy of guilt and redemption: *"Double inheritance* presents itself not as a trace of the past, such as a legacy or memory, but as a reckoning with the present that comes with compounded losses and accrued interests on debt over time" (25). Koga's conceptualization of this category calls upon two distinct but related processes: on the one hand, there is the inheritance of a legacy or memory, but on the other, there is also a regime of values that indexes the ways the past constructs the present. This "reckoning" of the past in, and with, the present requires a particular form of ongoing ethical labor that necessarily has to be performed by different generations of activists (Koga 2016, 25; also Benwell 2016). This ethical labor of laying claim to movement genealogies and consolidating fractured notions of belonging becomes integral to imagining a future with possibility. The potential future of a movement, then, depends on a value regime that indexes the movement's legacy as valuable to younger generations of activists, who will be expected to perform the ethical labor of sharing a mutually intelligible world with their forerunners (Benwell 2016).

Concerns around the future of a movement raise questions as to *who* can inherit a legacy. Older activists must perform the labor of identifying a next generation that can lay claim to this legacy, to forge a sense of belonging through a place-based ethics of care. The DWM is knit together by kinship-based claims on each other (Haraway 2016): political solidarity here is imbricated in idioms of kinship through which they allow themselves to care for each other and feel cared for. These idioms of kinship are derived from both fictive and filial forms of Tamil kinship. For example, activists within the DWM often see Beulah, the leader of the movement, as an older sister or a generous aunt who would perform the duties expected of corresponding filial kin. Saroja Amma, an activist in her seventies who has been around since the inception of the movement, said that Beulah had paid for her grandson's school fees through the 1990s. "That is *why* she is like family," said Saroja Amma. "She does not expect me to pay this back. She took care of my grandson like she would her *own* nephew." Kinship relationships are deepened through activist labor, rather than natal and filial ties as the only conduits of "relatedness" (Carsten 2000). Yet idioms of kinship signify these ties, rendering activist cohesion as contingent on *how* people understand themselves to be related to one another.

Like Saroja Amma, DWM activists also frequently refer to Beulah as an older sister or a generous aunt. Gloria has a narrative similar to Saroja Amma's. In the late 1980s, Gloria was a fieldworker for a small civil society organization that received infrastructural assistance from the Churches of South India (CSI), working on primary education issues, when Beulah spotted her speaking at a seminar in the neighboring town of Vellore. Beulah Akka approached Gloria a few weeks later. "Akka asked whether I want to be part of the movement; she said she saw a lot of *potential* in me." If Akka had not been at that meeting and had not heard her make the speech, Gloria might not have had an activist career. "Beulah Akka is like the older sister I never had," she said, somebody constantly looking out for her. The *indebtedness* that Gloria feels toward Beulah emerges from that moment of recognition—of potential—which then stretched on through assurances that Gloria is capable of more by investing in training her and sending her abroad to meet other human rights defenders. "Whatever I am today, I owe it all to Akka," Gloria said conclusively, marking Beulah's status in her life as a caring older sister. In turn Gloria allows herself to be cared for by Beulah Akka in a manner akin to an older relative in a better economic or social position. The economy of debt maps onto an economy of care: the labor of care generates an indebtedness, which points to a temporal future in which it can be repaid. As we shall see in later sections, the currency of repayment—care—is intergenerational and oriented toward a future. In providing care to older activists, younger activists perform a place-based ethic of care toward the future of the movement.

Similarly, when reminiscing about her first few years with the movement, Chandra Amma, another older activist, spoke about DWM's decision to take in young Dalit girls dealing with sexual assault whose families were unable to provide them with support. In "adopting" these girls, women in the movement had not just given them a home but provided them with resources to go to school, helped them with homework, arranged to perform the subcaste-specific rites that correlate with menarche ceremonies, and bought them new clothes for Pongal and Deepavali.[8] These acts of care inform the everyday lived experience of belonging to a movement and investing in its future.

The economy of care allows activists across generations, particularly a younger generation, to lay claim to the movement's past, marked by legacy, and the movement's future, as their inheritance. Legacy can be construed as a site where the consolidation of memory and imaginaries for the future converge, bound together through idioms of inheritance, kinship, and care. Acts of care come with expectations for the future: in repaying the debt of care, performing the ethical labor of reckoning the past with the present, and caring for each other in the present, activists invest the future with possibility. As evinced in the next section, the anxiety that activists experience has to do with the foreclosure of future possibility and the breakdown of intergenerational care networks in a rapidly changing economy where the march of neoliberal market structures can no longer be sustained by the DWM family.

THE CHALLENGES OF SUSTAINING A NETWORK OF CARE

As Gloria and I approached the first settlement where Arputhamma and Pichamma lived, we arrived at a village main square. A few middle-aged men were hanging out on the cemented area around the biggest tree, chatting. Gloria seemed anxious: she did not have a personal long-term connection with either of them, though the DWM as a collective front did. We stopped to ask for directions to Pichamma's house. Gloria was met with many questions that she had not prepared for: How do you know her? Does she know that she is going to have a visitor today? Do you know her niece who takes care of her? Gloria was especially flustered at the last question, murmuring that if there was a niece, she had never heard of her from other activists. It seemed to me that for the first time, Gloria's self-perception was being gently troubled: she seemed anxious that the intimacy she expected to have between herself and past DWM activists was absent, with nothing else to fill that void.

After a fair amount of navigation—mostly trial and error—we reached a house that happened to be the "niece's" residence. Gloria eased up a bit when we realized that the woman was not really a relative, just someone that Pichamma considers niece-like and who looks out for her, helps her buy groceries, and assists her when she needs to go to the doctor in the nearest town. She guided us to Pichamma's home, and Gloria pointedly said that she can "take it from here." We went on to have a detailed conversation with Pichamma, reminiscing and feeling nostalgic for the good old days when they all got arrested for protesting against the Indian military intervention in Sri Lanka, spending many nights in jail, teaching the female constables all about social injustice and how they were going to fight it all their lives. Toward the end of our visit, Pichamma suggested that we walk around the settlement looking for Arputhamma. It seemed curious that Arputhamma would be anywhere but her house in the middle of an afternoon in June, the summer sun beating down on the dry, barren terrain of north Tamil Nadu. Gloria must have wondered, too, as she asked why we need to go looking for her in the first place. "You will see," said Pichamma nonchalantly. "She is not okay."

A few doors from her residence, Arputhamma was lying spread-eagle and muttering incoherently to herself, half her body spread out on the outer cemented perimeter of the shack, her toes skimming the untreated drain water. The niece hurried over to help her up. Pichamma quickened her pace, balancing on her makeshift walking stick the best she could. Arputhamma continued to mutter incoherently. Pichamma was desperately trying to explain to her that people from the "big town" were visiting and had come looking for them, her tone unmistakable from a nanny trying to cheer up a cranky toddler. Amid this, Gloria was peppering Pichamma's explanations with suggestions for a long interview, saying that we were all eager to listen to her talk about the old days of protest and being arrested. At this point, Arputhamma started beating her chest and flailing, repeatedly saying, "Leave me alone, I don't know anything . . . I don't have anything to tell you." She was obviously disturbed at the sight of strangers. Gloria looked crestfallen: "But don't you remember anything at all? You remember Beulah, don't you? Beulah who set up the DWM, Beulah who was so supportive when you all wanted to set up women's support groups?" In all her flailing, Arputhamma's *sari* had come undone. The "niece" went over to cover her up, as Gloria murmured to Pichamma that maybe if we took her inside and gave her a drink of water, she might feel better and be willing to talk. Pichamma looked defeated. "I told you that she wasn't okay." Feeling discomfited, I tried to convince Gloria to let this go.

Neither of us uttered a word on the drive back to the DWM office. In the passenger seat next to me, Gloria looked despondent. A couple of times I wondered if I should say something comforting. After all, it must have come as a shock to witness women like Pichamma and Arputhamma, whose legacies preceded them, utterly helpless. A week later, I managed to catch Gloria on her own, after she returned from a fact-finding trip in another district. I wanted to talk to her about that troubling afternoon and simultaneously reassure her that we could annotate the history of the movement in a way that does not pressure older activists to talk if they did not feel up to it. Gloria's only response was this: "Most people have some 'insurance' by the time they become old. They invest in their children and grandchildren, and in turn they look after them. When they invest in this collective, it becomes *our* job to look after them . . . and we *failed*."

Evident in Gloria's lament is the fear of attenuation: of future potential, of networks of care, and the failure to do right by a legacy. As the last two sections have demonstrated, the labor of care, informed by kinship idioms, is intertwined with inheritance, the ability to lay claim and secure belonging, and, finally, with future possibilities of a movement. Later that summer, as I was talking about the logistics of the archive, I noticed that the despondent look from the drive had returned. When I asked if something was the matter, Gloria said, "This archive will tell younger women what has been sacrificed to make their lives better, what we fought for our daughters to have." In this context, to sacrifice something for another's life to flourish is an act of care. It is to ensure that another generation of women have something to inherit, call their own, and forge a sense of belonging to generations past, rooted in the place that absorbed this labor. Gloria's aspiration is for this archive to mediate this sense of belonging and to enact an ethic of care toward older and younger generations. The next section furthers this argument by engaging the shifts in sociopolitical landscape that cause spatial and temporal disarray, making activists anxious about the movement's future.

GENERATIONAL ANXIETIES

Arasi often joked that as long as there were no new recruits in the DWM who showed signs of staying on in the long term, she would always be considered a "young activist" despite rapidly approaching forty. This lament was reflected in Gloria's ponderings about the priorities of young Dalit women, their interest in working in factories, and the lack of a defined younger generation to take over the mantle of DWM. "Do young women know that the reason they were able to go to high school (and in many cases, college) is because *we* fought hard? Why do they imagine that government empowerment programs is the reason they are able to do the things they want to do?" Building on Gloria's and others' concerns, this section engages why activists turn toward performing the ethical labor of consolidating memory and legacy. In a rapidly shifting sociopolitical landscape, it becomes all the more important to perform memory-work and remember. In conducting this memory-work, activists work toward a place-based ethic of care, toward a shifting landscape in which they try to forge a sense of belonging, and toward the people who animate that landscape (Till 2012). Acts of remembering, in this context, require activists to historicize their movement with urgency, before connections to place, kin, and future aspirations start to fade. I rely on two ethnographic narratives that illuminate the sites of anxiety in greater detail: one has to do with inter-generational shifts in the form, rather than solely the content, of activism, and the other with economic restructuring that accompanies neoliberal shifts in the sociopolitical landscape of Tamil Nadu.

In summer 2016, Tamil Nadu was shaken by the murder of a young woman in Chennai. She was murdered as she waited to board the Chennai local train one morning on her way to work. Tamil media and most of Tamil society speculated that the killer was an ex-lover, or maybe a young man whose advances she had spurned. Even though the feminist activist community had no illusions about the pervasiveness of violence against women in Tamil society, it still came as a shock. Beulah uneasily reflected that not much had changed since she first started activist work in the 1970s; if anything, it felt like gendered violence was sprouting heads that feminists had to learn to tackle anew.

In Chennai and Arakkonam, there were protests—big and small—throughout the summer. Every women's rights organization had put out a statement, as had every political party in Tamil Nadu. Articles were written and circulated about an extant culture of misogyny in the state that allows for such incidents to take place. Many young women in Tamil Nadu were demanding that the state administer capital punishment to the attacker, citing the Nirbhaya rape case that occurred in Delhi in 2012. The question of capital punishment as retributive justice for rape and sexual assault occupies controversial terrain in India, and has been a site of moral and ethical dilemma. Across the country, feminists stand firm that capital punishment is a form of state violence, reflective of the state's paternalism and patriarchy, the same logics that normalize sexual violence in the first place (Baxi 2000; Dutta and Sircar 2013). While the state features substantively in debates within feminist discourses, there is unanimity that it is a cultural and political artifact, an institution that is an object of analysis. Feminist common sense also dictates that demands made on the state should be arrived at through collective discussion of moral ambivalence with a focus on how power and its various negotiations; the stand on capital punishment is a classic example.

Gloria was not sure whether women in their twenties—feminist or not—were working through political uncertainties in the same ways when conducting activism. She was unsettled by the demand for capital punishment. "What gives us the right as a democracy to ask the state to take away a citizen's life?" she opined. "This is a lack of civility [*anākarīkam*]." *Nākarīkam* implies the condition of being civilized, while *anākarīkam* implies an absence of civility. Gloria used the word *anākarīkam* in the context of a polity that refuses a moral dialogue about life and death, especially in the context of the state having power over life. Additionally, Gloria was also upset that young political women lacked a sense of regional history. As an example, she cited the way they articulated their political demands as removed from any knowledge of histories of feminist struggle in Tamil Nadu. Evident in Gloria's discontent is the fear that future generations may occupy a world that she may not have the political markers for, or that her world and the ethical labor she enacts may be incomprehensible to younger women.

This brings us to the second concern that demonstrates intergenerational anxiety. Neoliberal economic restructuring ushered in sizable foreign capital investment and precipitated a number of special economic zones (SEZ) in Tamil Nadu through the 1990s and early 2000s. Global concerns with SEZ corridors, large multinational corporations' crackdown on attempts to mobilize factory workers, and management's anxieties surrounding the possibility of political dissent have generated a wide array of scholarship (Dutta 2009; Ong 2006; Roy 2009). Arakkonam's proximity to the industrial corridor has meant that these industries look to surrounding districts, including Arakkonam, for factory labor, often young Dalit men and women. Offering seductive future possibilities for the next generation of Dalit women, these workplaces cultivate imaginaries of middle-class aspirations and offer a facade of these imaginaries materializing into reality: drawing an income, setting aside part of it for their families, owning smartphones (whom Gloria repeatedly referred to as the "WhatsApp generation"), or going to the movies. However, this also comes at a price. Collectives like the DWM and left political parties in Tamil Nadu are prevented from organizing fellow workers in these spaces.[9] Employees demonstrating any sign of radical politics or dissent are watched closely.

There is also a shift in how neoliberal workplaces restructure employees' relationships with place—of work, of home—that poses a conundrum for how sustained collective action can be enabled. This precipitates the need for younger women to discover new ethics of care for a place that is home, and its inhabitants. For previous generations, the places where they lived, performed labor, and conducted activism bled into each other, structuring care accordingly. For example, an earlier movement generation worked in agricultural land surrounding village hamlets, whereas today young women have to travel an hour each way to get to their workplaces. "Look at all these buses. They are here to pick up the girls," said Gloria one morning as we drove past the highway. Further, DWM activists who inhabit place and feel a sense of collective responsibility to reclaim spaces as Dalit women are not allowed to mobilize workers within SEZs.

A disconnect between spaces of work and home, albeit in a contested way, requires reconfiguring relationships with place and the routines that animate it. These young women's mothers, aunts, and grandmothers—who had largely performed agricultural labor on upper-caste land—had formed the village-level base for DWM's activities in the 1970s and 1980s. In each village, a group of women functioned as cohorts for which the DWM arranged training sessions on issues as wide-ranging as human rights, land acquisition, gender, and sexuality rights. They would join mass protests, form networks with other political actors such as Communist party workers, liaise with state functionaries such as the collector's office, the police, the land revenue office, and doctors and nurses at the primary health center and government hospital. Their everyday lives were punctuated by rhythms of activist labor as much as tilling land, performing domestic labor, or raising children. In sum, these social worlds mapped onto each other and were grounded in place and locality. They were perceived as belonging to a *radical* grassroots movement, which was imbued with the hope of living in a more equitable world in the future.

The possibility of a collective future prematurely foreclosed constantly shadows the anxiety regarding the legacy of a more radical past. Further, everyday ethical labor in political organizing and social reproduction of schooling another generation of activists are moored in a place-based ethics of care. For the DWM, place is collectively made and inhabited based on a set of shared social and political ethics (Till 2012, 8). According to Karen Till, these ethics denote an obligation to care for place as a means to care for each other. In a similar vein, Anna-Kaisa Kuusisto-Arponen contends that place-making is about forging collective identities and concurrent practices that reiterate identity in an intimate and embodied manner (Kuusisto-Arponen 2009). For Kuusisto-Arponen, the consolidation of "fragmented memories" in collective narration and reiteration elicits what she calls a "sense of place": the ethical labor, in her narrative, is located in the active transfer—and repetition—of affects and practices to a next generation, to create a sense of claim or ownership to an identity group and heritage, and a sense of place-based belonging (549).

For the DWM, even if a younger generation cannot inhabit place in the same way, acquainting them with the legacies that infuse the Arakkonam landscape will give them a sense of place, of a political culture that may have completely changed in a few decades. And to do that, an archive becomes important: memory-work is the enactment of a place-based ethics of care (Till 2012). The archive performs the work of witnessing and being witnessed: the act of weaving this past—one that activists feel nostalgic for—into a narrative clearly assigns roles of "narrator" and "audience," or the one being witnessed and the ones who perform the witnessing, respectively. Through this archive, nostalgia for a radical past that seems anachronistic to the present acquires narrative shape and form. Nostalgia is accorded with legitimacy, itself an act of political care.

CONCLUSION: LEGACY AND COLLECTIVE MEMORY

This chapter explores what prompts Dalit activists of the DWM to construct an archive that consolidates memory, narrates their histories, and offers a tactile and material past for future generations to inherit. I discussed this in the context of intergenerational care, idioms of inheritance that ensure permanence to activist legacy, and reconciling anxieties that have to do with intergenerational shifts in political visions and material conditions of life that enact a place-based ethics of care. Through this discussion, I have traced the shifting spatialities and temporalities of activist landscapes, grounded in enactments of labor, care, and place-making.

In *Localization of Memories*, Maurice Halbwachs (1992, 53) argues, "What makes recent memories hang together is not that they are contiguous in time: it is rather that they are part of a totality of thoughts common to a group, the group of people with whom we have a relation at this moment." Collective memory then becomes spatial, as much as temporal, as it is collectively embodied, even if Halbwachs would contend that it is *individuals* within the collective who remember and recall. This has a bearing on legacy. If we understand collective memory to be spatial, a disturbance in spatial contiguity, as Gloria posits of activism, renders "remembrance" in disarray. To remember is to perform the labor of care toward memory-work. Spatial contiguity then becomes a prerequisite for legacies to exist, or rather, to *go on*, and be inherited. It is in recognizing Arputhamma and Pichamma as legendary figures, whose legacies are repeatedly passed on to generations, that networks of care for people and place can be animated.

This calls for us to return to Koga's (2016, 25) "reckoning with the present." Gloria's yearning, where she wants the past to inform the present (and the future) *differently*, is what Svetlana Boym would characterize as "prospective nostalgia," one where "fantasies of the past, determined by the needs of the present, have a direct impact on the realities of the future" (Boym 2007, 8). A robust archive that brings together histories of how Dalit women enacted place-making ensures a material form to the past, with the hope that it informs the present and future to reenact an ethic of care. Gloria catches herself yearning for the WhatsApp generation to be aware of the legacies of women like Arputhamma and Pichamma and, in a few years, Beulah and herself as well, and think about what this all means as they perform assembly line tasks. She would like for the DWM to be not spectral to a present but actively "reckoned" with through memory-work (Till 2012). She would like for the DWM, its legacy, and the values it stands for as it lays claim on the state to take away a man's life as a sentence for rape to rethink their political legacies. Most importantly, she would like for the present to accommodate a way by which young women would care for *her*, if there ever comes a time when she stops remembering what she labored for all her life.

In reflecting on this, Gloria is clearly identifying her anxiety of a discontinued legacy as central to the economy of care. In finding Arputhamma lying abandoned that summer afternoon, Gloria is struck by her own generation's role in this project. Despite intimate kinship ties to the past and present of DWM, this infrastructure seems to have broken down, disrupting the landscape of activism. This also poses challenges for the futures that this movement can aspire to: Without another generation of young Dalit women, or another cohort of Dalit feminists, who could perform the emotional labor of care for an older generation of activists and keep DWM's legacy alive? An archive forged with intent upholds the legacy that younger generations could inherit and reenact toward building a future. In doing so, activists further the thrust of Dalit studies, and Dalit politics more broadly, by bearing witness to the past and using it to reckon with the present, orienting pasts and presents toward enacting future aspirations by forging a collective ethic.

NOTES

1. The Dalit Women's Movement is a pseudonym, as grassroots movements run by Dalit women have been threatened in India's current political climate. India's right-wing political regime punishes any citizen or group engaged in political dissent. State sanctions are harsher when dissenters belong to marginalized groups and are already politically, socially, and economically vulnerable.
2. While it literally translates to "older sister" in Tamil, *Akka* is also an honorific given to women who are older or who occupy a higher status in a social hierarchy. Despite hierarchy, Akka signifies a degree of kinlike intimacy toward the bearer of the honorific.
3. I recognize that there is a plethora of literature on feminist methods and feminist engagement with the field that productively engages Nagar's observation, including Smith (2016), from which I have learned immensely.
4. I thank Kumi Silva for raising this concern of assuming a shared feminist commitment in her talk on "Discomfort Feminisms" (keynote panel, Feminist Geography Conference 2017, Department of Geography, University of North Carolina at Chapel Hill).

5. Anti-caste mobilization predates the formation of the particular category of Dalit and associated activism (Geetha and Rajadurai 1998; O'Hanlon 2002).
6. There is an array of scholarship addressing untouchability and caste within worker's rights organizing and left party politics in India. One work that foregrounds the shift in lower-caste and Dalit women's subjectivities through their engagement with movements fighting for peasant worker's rights and land rights in Telangana, southern India, is Vasantha Kannabiran and K. Lalitha (1990), "That Magic Time: Women in the Telangana People's Struggle."
7. Maharashtra is a hub of Dalit political assertion, given that it is home to Babasaheb Ambedkar's legacy. Dr. B. R. Ambedkar is the pioneer leader of Dalit politics. To commemorate this legacy, the Women's Studies Center at the University of Pune (Maharashtra) fought to be named after Savitribai Phule, a nineteenth-century caste and gender ideologue from the region.
8. Pongal, the festival of harvest, and Deepavali, the festival of lights, are significant markers of the Tamil calendar and are celebrated all over the country.
9. Despite Gloria's skepticism of social media and digital technology, young Dalit women who worked at Microsoft's factory decided to collectivize and strike in 2013–2014. They communicated with each other using digital technology, used social media to popularize a street play on worker exploitation, and participated in creating a podcast. These organizing efforts were successful for a period, until the Microsoft factory closed down for reasons beyond the scope of this chapter. However, it is noteworthy that while workers were able to forge solidarity with younger factions of left parties, as well as middle-class activists from Chennai with a history of participating in labor struggles, solidarity was not possible with movements such as the DWM, for reasons not articulated explicitly. All organizing was done near the factory, while being careful about the jurisdiction of SEZ laws regarding political mobilization on SEZ land.

REFERENCES

Ahmed, Sara. 2004. "Affective Economies." *Social Text* 22 (2): 117–39.
Alone, Y. S. 2017. "Caste Life Narratives, Visual Representation, and Protected Ignorance." *Biography* 40 (1): 140–69.
Alvarez, Sonia E. 2009. "Beyond NGO-ization?: Reflections from Latin America." *Development* 52 (2): 175–84.
Baxi, Pratiksha. 2000. "Rape, Retribution, State: On Whose Bodies?" *Economic and Political Weekly* 35 (14): 1196–1200.
Benwell, Matthew C. 2016. "Encountering Geopolitical Pasts in the Present: Young People's Everyday Engagements with Memory in the Falkland Islands." *Transactions of the Institute of British Geographers* 41 (2): 121–33.
Boym, Svetlana. 2007. "Nostalgia and Its Discontents." *Hedgehog Review* 9 (2): 7–18.
Carsten, Janet, ed. 2000. *Cultures of Relatedness: New Approaches to the Study of Kinship.* Cambridge: Cambridge University Press.
Dutta, Debolina, and Oishik Sircar. 2013. "India's Winter of Discontent: Some Feminist Dilemmas in the Wake of a Rape." *Feminist Studies* 39 (1): 293–306.
Dutta, Madhumita. 2009. "Nokia SEZ: Public Price of Success." *Economic and Political Weekly* 44 (40): 23–25.
Geetha, V., and S. V. Rajadurai. 1998. *Towards a Non-Brahmin Millennium: From Iyothee Thass to Periyar.* Calcutta: Samya Publishers.
Guru, Gopal, ed. 2011. *Humiliation: Claims and Contexts.* New Delhi: Oxford University Press.
Halbwachs, Maurice. 1992. *On Collective Memory.* Chicago: University of Chicago Press.
Haraway, Donna J. 2016. *Staying with the Trouble: Making Kin in the Chthulucene.* Durham, NC: Duke University Press.

Jain, Kajri. 2010. "Taking and Making Offence: Husain and the Politics of Desecration." In *Barefoot across the Nation: Maqbool Fida Husain and the Idea of India*, edited by S. Ramaswamy, 198–212. New Delhi: Yoda Press.

Kannabiran, Vasantha, and K. Lalitha. 1990. "That Magic Time: Women in the Telangana People's Struggle." In *Recasting Women: Essays in Indian Colonial History*, edited by Kumkum Sangari and Sudesh Vaid, 180–203. New Brunswick, NJ: Rutgers University Press.

Koga, Yukiko. 2016. *Inheritance of Loss: China, Japan, and the Political Economy of Redemption After Empire*. Chicago: University of Chicago Press.

Kuusisto-Arponen, Anna-Kaisa. 2009. "The Mobilities of Forced Displacement: Commemorating Karelian Evacuation in Finland." *Social & Cultural Geography* 10 (5): 545–63.

Nagar, Richa. 2002. "Footloose Researchers, 'Traveling' Theories, and the Politics of Transnational Feminist Praxis." *Gender, Place & Culture* 9 (2): 179–86.

Nagar, Richa. 2014. *Muddying the Waters: Coauthoring Feminisms across Scholarship and Activism*. Champaign: University of Illinois Press.

O'Hanlon, Rosalind. 1988. "Recovering the Subject: Subaltern Studies and Histories of Resistance in Colonial South Asia." *Modern Asian Studies* 22 (1): 189–224.

Ong, Aihwa. 2006. *Neoliberalism as Exception: Mutations in Citizenship and Sovereignty*. Durham, NC: Duke University Press.

Purushottam, K., Gita Ramaswamy, and Gogu Shyamala, eds. 2016. *The Oxford India Anthology of Telugu Dalit Writing*. New Delhi: Oxford University Press.

Raiford, Leigh. 2009. "Photography and the Practices of Critical Black Memory." *History and Theory* 48 (4): 112–29.

Rao, Anupama. 2009. *The Caste Question: Dalits and the Politics of Modern India*. Berkeley: University of California Press.

Ravikumar and Azhagarasan, eds. 2012. *The Oxford India Anthology of Tamil Dalit Writing*. New Delhi: Oxford University Press.

Rawat, Ramnarayan Singh, and K. Satyanarayana. 2016. *Dalit Studies*. Durham, NC: Duke University Press.

Rege, Sharmila. 1998. "Dalit Women Talk Differently: A Critique of 'Difference' and Towards a Dalit Feminist Standpoint Position." *Economic and Political Weekly* 33 (44): WS39–WS46.

Roy, Ananya. 2009. "Why India Cannot Plan Its Cities: Informality, Insurgence and the Idiom of Urbanization." *Planning Theory* 8 (1): 76–87.

Satyanarayana, K., and Susie Tharu, eds. 2011. *No Alphabet in Sight: New Dalit Writing from South India*. Dossier 1: Tamil and Malayalam. New Delhi: Penguin Books.

Satyanarayana, K., and Susie Tharu, eds. 2013. *Steel Nibs Are Sprouting: New Dalit Writing from South India*. Dossier 2: Telugu and Kannada. New Delhi: Penguin Books.

Smith, Sara. 2016. "Intimacy and Angst in the Field." *Gender, Place & Culture* 23 (1): 134–46.

Tartakov, Gary M., ed. 2012. *Dalit Art and Visual Imagery*. New Delhi: Oxford University Press.

Till, Karen E. 2012. "Wounded Cities: Memory-Work and a Place-Based Ethics of Care." *Political Geography* 31 (1): 3–14.

Tronto, Joan C. 1993. *Moral Boundaries: A Political Argument for an Ethic of Care*. New York: Routledge.

CHAPTER 11

FROM THE WOMEN'S MOVEMENT TO THE ACADEMY: FEMINIST URBAN PLANNING, 1970-1985

Bri Gauger

The rise of feminism in the United States converged with a pivotal moment in urban planning's history. Urban space was a central component of social justice struggles in 1960s and 1970s America, as widespread unrest over race and class oppression exploded into rebellions in cities like Los Angeles and Detroit. As the civil rights, gay liberation, anti-war, and environmental movements were enacted at the community scale, urban planning, a profession responsible for shaping the built environment, was bruised and battered by the very public failures of urban renewal. Pressure from social movements afforded institutional and political opportunities to redefine urban planning as a discipline rooted in social justice, and feminist scholars, many of whom were active in the women's movement, were at the forefront of this charge. My research, based on oral interviews, feminist planners' scholarship, and institutional analysis, reveals women's roles in pushing the field to consider social aspects of planning that had been deemphasized since the birth of the profession. Feminist planners produced knowledge in creative ways to draw attention to their perspectives and to insert gender into planning discourse.

Leveraging extensive on-the-ground experience with social movements and community planning, women entering the planning academy for the first time in the 1970s employed a gendered perspective to advocate for equity and inclusion in their field. Bolstered by the women's movement and federal funding for their graduate education, this emergent group of planning scholars engaged feminist critiques about the gendered division of labor and postwar suburban life. Feminist planners pushed the field to rethink relationships between urban space and social norms. Their organizing ties and experience in neighborhood activism enabled them to connect social and human struggles to oppressive structures and systems through the physical form of the built environment and the political process of planning. As one scholar told me, "I was brought to community development because of my feminism." Shared experiences in grassroots feminist and other social movements motivated this group of women to dedicate their academic energies to change planning theory, practices, and institutions.

To trace how ideas traveled between feminism and planning, I move between personal, institutional, and intellectual perspectives gathered from interviews, archival sources, and published scholarship. In this chapter, I draw from eighteen oral history interviews I conducted with some of the first women to become planning scholars in the US and Canada. I analyzed scholarship (including monographs, edited volumes, dissertations, and journal articles) written by my interviewees and others publishing about gender in planning during this period who I did not have the opportunity to interview. While not fully inclusive of this first generation of women to enter the planning academy, the sources referenced here are reasonably comprehensive and representative. Overall, the actors under consideration in this essay earned their doctorates and obtained their first faculty jobs in the 1970s and early 1980s. Aside from two women of color, both of whom are African American, the group consists of white women from primarily middle- or upper-class backgrounds. While their disciplinary backgrounds varied, and they were not united as a formal group during this period, feminists built a coalition to make sure gender was on the map in urban planning.

Primary documents from the archives of academic planning organizations include governing board meeting minutes, committee reports, and documentation on the formation of special interest groups. I draw from internal correspondence and educational materials produced by several short-lived but influential feminist planning and design collectives. I also integrate a variety of primary sources gathered from personal collections of interviewees, including posters and proceedings from feminist planning conferences, bibliographies circulated among feminist scholars, and syllabi from planning courses on women and gender. I used interviews and archival sources to identify other individuals and institutions that shaped feminism's impact in the field through formal and informal practices of knowledge sharing. Collecting personal and intellectual narratives that speak to strings of influence, barriers, and responses provides context for the priorities early feminist scholars articulated and offers insights into tactics employed for institutional and systemic change.

Combined, these sources reveal that feminism in planning encompasses more than participating in women's movement activities or publishing scholarship on gender. Feminism appears in at least three modes in the planning academy during this period: as an activist practice, as a critical theoretical orientation, and as a set of institutional demands. These overlapping and mutually constitutive areas of action provide a framework through which to understand these women's experiences and influence in planning. In this chapter, I show how feminists intervened in this specific historical moment of the 1970s and early 1980s through their personal and activist commitments and backgrounds, theoretical interventions, and specific institutional tactics. I focus on ways that feminist activists in the academy shifted planning discourse by producing knowledge in creative and interdisciplinary ways, shaping topics in the field, and altering institutional structures. After outlining the broader social and disciplinary context for this period, I highlight how these women's personal and professional backgrounds led them to urban planning. I describe the emergence of a gender lens for planning through early feminist scholarship and then examine the tactics and venues that women used to collectively produce knowledge across disciplinary boundaries.

WOMEN ENTER THE PLANNING ACADEMY

Many of the women I interviewed agreed that a driving force behind their individual choices to pursue careers in academia was a combination of support for women in higher education and funding made available for urban research. As women began to enter planning faculty jobs and PhD programs in substantial numbers in the 1970s, the pressure that social movements brought to bear on American cities created opportunities to study urban social problems in the US. The first generation of women in the planning academy benefited from (and later fought to protect and expand) structural supports for gender equity and women's advancement in the academy, as well as grant funding for education and research on topics relevant to urban inequality.

National executive and legislative measures intending to increase the number of women in the academy and public service were implemented during this period. In 1967, President Johnson signed an executive order expanding affirmative action programs to include women (though, as with initial legislation in the 1964 Civil Rights Act, there was no mechanism for enforcement until the 1972 passage of the Equal Employment Act) (Leonard 1989). Title IX, designed to end gender discrimination in education by protecting people in education programs that receive federal financial assistance, passed in 1972.

In addition to hiring requirements that allowed women to gain a foothold in the academy, the Johnson and Carter administrations provided grants for research on community-level urban and women's issues through the Economic Opportunity Act of 1964, the National Institutes of Health, the Department of Transportation, and Health and Human Services. Several women I interviewed also took advantage of research funding from entities like the United Nations' Ryder Commission and the Women's Unit at the Department of Housing and Urban Development (HUD) during the 1970s and early 1980s.

Women I interviewed leveraged these structural supports for their careers. As one planning scholar recalled, "I went to the sociology department and I went to the planning department and I said, 'You need women, you need to fill these affirmative action slots.' . . . There was one senior woman in the entire school of architecture, and she had come in as a full professor. One. So, I went to the chairs of both departments and I said, . . . 'Each of you can give me a part-time appointment and you'll be credited for a new woman and I get a real job.' And so that was another way I created a job for myself and also that's why I've always acknowledged the importance of affirmative action. Had it not been for affirmative action there would have been no pressure at all to hire me."

Urban planning's normative and theoretical commitments were beginning to shift at the same time as education and institutional policies for women began to change. Feminists were often attracted to the field of planning in the 1970s and early 1980s because an emerging redefinition and expansion of planning goals, issues, and scales appealed to their experiences and skills. In the postwar period, planning had been characterized by grand-scale physical planning and design, technocratic expertise, and top-down decision-making. Modernist planning's desire for rationalism and efficiency left little room in the profession for attention to social issues or political processes, particularly at the neighborhood or community scale. When feminist activist scholars began entering the academy in the 1970s, however, social movement pressure and their own political organizing experience expanded the discipline beyond a singular focus on physical land use to include political activism for oppressed groups (Ritzdorf 1995; Zapata and Bates 2015).

Feminist planners, who were heavily involved in grassroots political action before and during their graduate educations, joined a disciplinary context where other professional planners were beginning to embrace the deeply political nature of their work and call for broader recognition of the power dynamics and structures that intersect in local neighborhoods. Their participation in women's movement activities like consciousness-raising and anti-domestic violence work, as well as their respective commitments to civil rights, anti-war, labor, environmental, and gay liberation organizing on campuses and in communities, gave them firsthand experience with spatialized struggles for justice. David Harvey's (1973) foundational text *Social Justice and the City* exposed how implicit planning assumptions served to perpetuate inequality, and new planning models emerged that espoused redistributive visions of planning as a way to achieve social equity (Davidoff [1965] 2012; Krumholz 1997).

Planners for Equal Opportunity (PEO), a professional interest group formed in 1964 by a group of radical social activists that included Frances Fox Piven, "wanted planners to take a stand against racist policies and acquire the skills for addressing the urban crisis" (Sutton 2017, 38). PEO distributed a newsletter and convened annual conferences between 1966 and 1972 that often explicitly agitated against the agendas set at mainstream planning conferences. In 1969, for example, PEO members staged what they called a "coup" of the American Institute of Planners (AIP) conference in New York, sitting in to draw attention to racial discrimination perpetuated by planning. Their disruptive tactics were intentional. One meeting agenda noted, "To call attention to the need for reforms and changes, our position papers and action recommendations must be a provocative and lively exposition of realities" (Planners for Equal Opportunity 1969).

PEO focused most of its energies around racial injustice but also participated in actions advocating for women as a group. The American Society of Planning Officials (ASPO) conference program had for years included a "Women's Program" advertising activities such as "tours, TV productions, museums and shopping" for wives of conference attendees. In 1970, PEO members threw their weight behind a withering press release composed at an impromptu meeting by women at the conference that year. The document "condemn[ed] the misuse of women in planning and other occupations, deplore[d] the planning that is done—by men," and "scorn[ed] this ill-conceived conference." It continued, "While the profession claims to be trying to humanize its practice, the Conference panel topics and the resource people are a denial of this claim. Discussions of the inner city, of minorities in the profession, of land use policies, and of neighborhood planning all affect women and community people intimately" ("Women and Planning: A Condemnation" 1970).

Partly due to pressure from groups like PEO, the nascent national academic planning organization, the Association of Collegiate Schools of Planning (ACSP), named an affirmative action program that targeted both women and minority groups as its first priority in 1973 (Association of Collegiate Schools of Planning 1973). Among other factors, this policy contributed to a broader sense of openness and possibility for women at a time when academic planning programs were rapidly expanding and when institutional and intellectual disciplinary commitments were malleable. Critiques of rational planning and emerging disciplinary commitments to equity signaled to feminist activists that urban planning would be a good field in which to pursue their interests in social aspects of the built environment.

The emerging social focus of planning, which these women would continue to foster throughout their careers, drew the attention of feminist activists from a wide range of specialties and disciplinary backgrounds, who told me that planning appeared more open to addressing social issues than their home disciplines. One scholar, coming from sociology, explained to me that when she was taking courses in housing, they were always geared toward policy programs instead of "about what it does to people. The people part never came with the content. . . . I wanted the stories, I wanted to see . . . what it does to people, and I think that's how I also got closer to women's stuff." Since few schools offered doctorate degrees in urban planning before the 1960s, the majority of both male and female planning faculty in the 1970s obtained their PhDs in other fields. Attracted by planning's permeable theoretical and institutional boundaries, feminists came from an array of disciplines, including architecture, environmental psychology, geography, political science, history, sociology, and English literature. Despite the lack of a common degree or shared disciplinary departments, most of my interviewees shared experiences with spatialized struggles and were committed to community-level approaches to understanding and changing the built environment.

Jacqueline Leavitt, a feminist leader in UCLA's Planning Department for many decades, chose the field of urban planning over architecture because she believed in its "ability to support social movements through both rigorous research and ethical practice" (Planners Network 2008). While pursuing her doctorate at Columbia, Leavitt had been involved with the National Congress of Neighborhood Women (NCNW), a group advocating for public housing by building "a social change movement of grassroots women living in poor and working class urban and rural communities" (National Congress of Neighborhood Women n.d.). After relocating to California, Leavitt joined a group of women that included Sheila de Bretteville and Dolores Hayden at the Women's Building Los Angeles, founded in 1973 as a feminist art and education community center from which the group also established the interdisciplinary feminist journal *Heresies* in 1977.

Unlike in traditional postwar planning positions, women were not an anomaly in grassroots and community-based organizations during the 1960s and 1970s. They occupied leadership roles and addressed precarity in housing, education, and access to resources that planning as a field was only beginning to consider. These forms of women-led community activism shaped feminist scholars' research and the ways they disseminated their points of view. They leveraged their experience working on social issues at the community scale throughout their careers in order to revitalize and redefine issue areas that had been deemphasized by postwar planning. Antiracist organizing had forced planning to contend with its social aspects and outcomes, and once their feet were in the door, feminists continued to push that project forward.

FEMINIST PLANNING SCHOLARSHIP

As the urban nature of social movements opened up planning to consider new normative goals and tasks for planners to engage with, feminist planning scholars leveraged their extensive experience with grassroots planning through community organizations to bring attention to social aspects of planning through their scholarship. They used a gender analytic to examine the relationships between planning, social structures and norms, and the built environment. Many scholars took cues from feminist thought to critique the lack of social reproduction in Marxist theory, calling for expanding the definition of "work" to include domestic and community labor, reproduction, and elder care (Fainstein 2005; Hayden 2002, [1980] 2005, [1984] 2012; Markusen 1980; Milroy 1991). Topics focused on women's household work and its connection to housing and urban forms like suburbanization, engaging in larger conversations about women entering the paid workforce and other changes to family structures. This group of primarily white women employed feminism as a critical orientation focused on questions of gendered power, structure, and agency, but during this period rarely questioned the many assumptions built into the category of "woman."

Some feminist planning historians looked at city planning history through the lens of gender and related concepts like domesticity and rationality, exposing the ideological work that planning performs to fulfill its desires for social order and professionalism (Boyer 1983; Wright 1980). The majority of historical scholarship during this period highlighted women's previously unrecognized contributions to social and community planning through housing movements from the early twentieth century through the Progressive and New Deal eras (Birch 1978, [1983] 1994; Hayden 1978, 1981). This work reveals the gendered origins of the profession of city planning, in which men delegitimized women's involvement in areas like housing advocacy while consolidating the profession around technical aspects that women had little access to. The long tradition of women's efforts to tether city planning to social issues at the neighborhood scale allowed feminists to reclaim housing advocacy and community development activities under the purview of planning in the 1970s. One interviewee reminded me that near the beginning of her career "urban history was just in its infancy, and city planning history didn't exist," so their work came at an opportune time to shape the field.

Other scholars offered a vision of feminist research that took a stand against oppression (Milroy 1991), actively critiqued planning's role in structural and symbolic disadvantage to women (Fainstein 2005), and propelled planners to engage directly in advocacy (Leavitt 1986; Sandercock and Forsyth 1992b). The promise of feminist planning lay in binding equity to the built environment at the neighborhood scale, where women historically had a higher degree of self-determination and influence. In the inaugural issue of the interdisciplinary feminist journal *Frontiers*, which she helped found during her first faculty job at the University of Colorado, Ann Markusen (1975) addressed the theme of "women and work" by directly linking to the economic demands of the women's movement and the community provision of services at the neighborhood level.

In addition to drawing attention to individual women and social aspects of planning that had been overlooked or disregarded, feminist planning scholarship focused on spatial outcomes of gendered norms. Feminist research highlighted various ways the built environment reproduces the gender imbalance in labor and economic opportunities and reifies gendered expectations about space and reproduction. These perspectives contrasted sharply with modernist planning ideals of scientific rationality that held sway through the 1950s. Feminist scholarship vehemently rejected notions of objectivity, renouncing the idea of planning as an arm's-length practice and arguing instead that planners are complicit in perpetuating inequality through the built environment (Leavitt 1986; Rosenbloom [1978] 2005; Milroy 1991; Ritzdorf 1994; Saegert 1980; Sandercock and Forsyth 1992b). Policy and regulatory frameworks and planning tools are therefore not value neutral (Forsyth 2011; Hirt 2014) and neither are the planning institutions and processes that create and enforce them (Ritzdorf 1994). Only by confronting this perceived neutrality, feminists argued, can planners illuminate the ways social and political relationships, language and discourse, and the built environment all structure (and are structured by) gendered identities, relations, and expectations.

Marsha Ritzdorf, who left a professional planning career to complete a PhD at the University of Washington in 1983, exemplified this through her work on municipal zoning, one of the primary tools that planners use to regulate land use development. Although often viewed as a technical planning mechanism, zoning is instead a system laden with values. Traditional zoning practices that regulate housing type, form, and placement contain ideological orientations about gender roles, impeding "both the creation of innovative housing and the formation of alternative families" (Ritzdorf 1985, 183). As Ritzdorf's later publications made clear, hegemonic family values and definitions are embedded in zoning ordinances that define and enforce household composition rules and place compounded barriers on female-headed and minority-headed households (Ritzdorf 1994, 1997, 2000).

Prior to the 1990s, however, this type of intersectional analysis was rarely present in feminist planning scholarship. Much of the early feminist planning literature linked gendered inequalities to the physical and symbolic separation of the public and private spheres (Leavitt 1980; Saegert 1980; Wekerle 1980, 1985) and asserted that as a result women experience urban environments and planning processes differently than men. Planners adversely affect women when they zone childcare out of suburban neighborhoods or design transportation systems around malecentric employment patterns, for example (Birch 1985; Markusen 1980; Wekerle 1980).

The prevalence of Marxist perspectives led to integrated class analysis at times and some scholars confronted race and class head-on without a simultaneous gender analysis (Fainstein and Fainstein 1974; Thomas 1985; Wolch 1980). However, in most cases scholarship focused on women neglected to note the wide range of women's experiences beyond age. While enumerating the double burden placed on women by the segregation of the city from the suburb, feminist analyses left intact many problematic assumptions embedded in the category of woman. Analysis of the economic and social shifts contributing to women's "double day" and resulting spatial outcomes assumed women to be white, middle-class, and heterosexual, for example. Scholars leveraged discourse around segregation to draw attention to women but shifted the conversation from race to gender instead of examining how those oppressions interacted with each other.

A few contrasting examples exist. A 1984 study by Leavitt and Saegert, published in the radical journal *Social Policy*, placed the experiences of poor women of color firmly at the forefront (Leavitt and Saegert 1984). Leavitt and Saegert began their research with African American women in landlord-abandoned properties in Harlem while participating in Birch's housing seminar at Hunter College, and they later cowrote a book based on the work (Leavitt and Saegert 1990). Catherine Ross, who joined Georgia Institute of Technology's planning faculty in 1976 and was one of the few African American women in the planning academy during this period, provided another notable exception in a study that analyzed both race and gender variables while studying community members' attitudes toward public transportation (Ross 1985).

Scholarship about gender from this period often did not acknowledge race at all. When it did, authors tended to mention race more as a footnote rather than as a system of oppression intertwined with gender (see Leavitt 1986; Saegert 1980; Wekerle 1980). A few publications indicate that feminists made a conscious decision to subsume race to gender in their scholarship, arguing that research was already being directed toward so-called minority groups and the poor (Birch 1985; Leavitt 2003; Markusen 1975; Wekerle 1981). The sheer lack of women in the planning profession and academy (Leavitt 1986) indicates that it made sense to women in the early years to consider themselves as a unified group (a strategy institutionalized in the planning academy during the late 1980s to mixed results; see Gauger forthcoming). Mirroring broader trends in the women's movement, feminists were attempting to bind women together through shared experiences such as the need for and access to childcare, for example.

Feminists achieved a higher profile for women's interests and needs in planning by stressing the importance of social aspects and outcomes. Despite the fact that many feminist planners were steeped in community-level engagement with diverse populations through their research and activism, their scholarship often elided discussions of race. They introduced gender as a frame of analysis for planning research and theory but often treated "woman" as a universal category, which further masked structural and experiential variations among women.

TACTICS FOR FEMINIST KNOWLEDGE PRODUCTION

Women faced tremendous challenges in the planning academy. Despite some increased institutional and federal support, women had to overcome daunting obstacles in an often dismissive or hostile academic environment. Those starting careers in the 1970s were commonly the only woman in an otherwise male department and usually several decades younger than most of their colleagues. Many of the women I interviewed were handed an outsize amount of responsibility as junior scholars, such as being asked to head up high-profile initiatives like research centers. Too often, university administrators handed them these "privileges" with few on-the-ground resources to help with the learning curve, and they often faced active resistance when leading such initiatives. As one scholar hired in 1972 reported, "I was in this horrible environment where I was young and the only woman. And as it turned out the reason I seem to have gotten hired was that a group of graduate students who were women made a lot of trouble and noise to the dean saying that this was shameful there were no women. And so, to placate them, I got hired." According to several interviews, male faculty and graduate students often took credit for their ideas, overtly stole their work, and participated in more insidious behaviors like refusing to cite publications authored by women. One female scholar told me, "Men just don't cite women," indicating that such attitudes pervade even today. Some of the women I interviewed benefited from supportive male faculty leadership who encouraged them to write about gender, but in many cases, gender was considered "anathema," as one interviewee told me.

How did feminists produce and circulate knowledge in this disciplinary climate? Women planners made space to develop, disseminate, and debate feminist ideas when the establishment did not provide room for them. The first women to become planning faculty would eventually espouse diverse perspectives on planning processes and implementation over the course of their careers, but in the 1970s and early 1980s they banded together as a marginalized group to highlight inequities and to put gender on the radar in a male-dominated discipline. The resulting visibility of feminist ideas and activism in the planning academy occurred because women employed a variety of tactics for their own survival. They formed collectives, convened conferences, created publishing opportunities, and worked to institutionalize their demands for gender equity. When faced with marginalization in the planning academy, feminist planners took matters into their own hands to ensure that their intellectual and pedagogical network grew.

Even outside of activist circles, women formed working relationships for the practical reason that there were so few of them and they found each other easily. Working across disciplines at the university level, they advocated for each other's careers to gain institutional footholds by strategically serving on tenure committees. They formed local women's writing groups and reading groups, which functioned as forums for sharing ideas and provided informal support networks.

Groups of women in environmental design fields like architecture and planning formed collectives centered around feminist principles and practices. Ranging from experimental groups to formal organizations, collectives attracted professionals and academics alike and served as research groups and platforms for advocacy. For example, the Women's School of Planning and Architecture (WSPA) was founded in 1974 as a feminist "summer school" of

environmental design that ran short-term interdisciplinary educational semi-
nars semiannually around the US (Weisman 1992). WSPA's seven founders
took an explicitly separatist approach and envisioned the group as a concrete
link between the women's movement and architecture and planning education
in the US. They focused on translating tactics from the women's movement
into pedagogical and research innovations for the design professions, such as
breaking down hierarchies through collaboration in the formation and execu-
tion of the retreats' educational programming (Cahn 2014). The group aimed
to gather participants from "the widest possible range of ages and experiences"
(Women's School of Planning and Architecture, n.d. a) and adopted affirmative
action measures to "draw more low-income and minority women into the network," including active recruitment and partial fee subsidies (Women's School
of Planning and Architecture, n.d. b).

Dolores Hayden, a prominent feminist architect and planning scholar, was
instrumental in starting Women in Architecture, Landscape Architecture,
and Planning (WALAP) in the greater Boston area while she was on faculty at
MIT. WALAP was more focused on the academy than WSPA, often directing
advocacy efforts at Harvard and MIT departments. WALAP members took a
practical approach: the group's objectives included increasing the "influence
of women felt in the design and planning professions," making the "influence
of the design and planning professions felt in the environment," and generating a "meaningful way that women can work together to further such goals"
(Women in Architecture, Landscape Architecture, and Planning, n.d.). WALAP
hosted open meetings for professional women that integrated consciousness-
raising practices and maintained a nonhierarchical model. From these meetings, they identified interest areas of the membership, such as education and
professionalism, gender discrimination in employment, and political action on
specific community issues. They accumulated a mailing list of nearly 250 names
by 1972 (Women in Environmental Planning and Design 1972a), to which they
circulated a newsletter with meeting minutes, updates on campaigns, and job
advertisements.

WALAP members also applied direct pressure to institutions in the name
of professional equity, urging the Harvard dean and the Graduate School of
Design (GSD) to fix discriminatory practices in hiring, citing the absence of
women faculty in the GSD and calling for affirmative action measures (Women
in Environmental Planning and Design 1972b; Women in Architecture,
Landscape Architecture, and Planning 1972a). They wrote letters to the Board
of Registration of Architects arguing that women were disproportionately affected by certification requirements for qualifying work hours, and collectively

published a 1972 article in *Architectural Forum* laying out a case for flexible work schedules (Women in Architecture, Landscape Architecture, and Planning 1972b). Though they took different approaches, WSPA and WALAP shared goals, such as fostering networks to expand the feminist knowledge base across disciplines and providing a platform from which to agitate against the mainstream profession and academy.

In addition to participating in collectives, many women in the 1970s and 1980s taught undergraduate and graduate courses devoted specifically to gender and urban space. With titles such as Gender and the City, Women in Planning and Design, and Planning for Spatial Justice in the City: Women and Urban Change, the courses were cross-listed to a variety of departments and were often cotaught with women's studies faculty. While a graduate student in the early 1970s, Gerda Wekerle helped to design Northwestern University's first women's studies course, and later her Women and Environments course at York University in Toronto attracted students before a women's studies department existed at that institution. Eugenie Birch, an associate professor at the time, cotaught a Women and Housing seminar with Donna Shalala and Frances Levinson at Hunter College between 1981 and 1984. The seminar was funded by the Ford Foundation, made national policy recommendations at the Democratic Platform Committee in 1984, and would lead to a 1985 edited volume, *The Unsheltered Woman: Women and Housing in the 80's* (Birch 1985).

Women used formal and informal channels to circulate syllabi as well as to compile bibliographies on gender and planning as they began to form a canon for research and teaching. At least one bibliography was distributed formally by the national professional group, the American Planning Association (APA), with support from APA's Planning and Women Division (founded in 1979 to lend legitimacy to gender issues in planning practice) and funding from HUD's Office of Policy Development and Research (Coatsworth 1981). In addition, interviewees' personal collections demonstrate the existence of alternative, more informal networks of knowledge circulation, as women mailed and faxed annotated reading lists to one another.

By organizing panels at mainstream planning conferences on topics such as Feminist Contributions to Planning and Changing Roles and Expectations of Women: Implications for Policy, feminists provided knowledge-sharing and networking opportunities that generated further collaboration. Women also organized their own interdisciplinary conferences specifically dedicated to gender and planning. Organizations like WALAP provided resources and served as platforms to publicize the events, as was the case with the 1973 Women in Housing conference organized by students at Harvard's Graduate School of

Design. Over the next several years, conferences on women in architecture and design took place around the country (Hayden and Wright 1976; Leavitt 1999). Feminist Planners and Designers (FPD) at UCLA was an influential student group that hosted yearly conferences on a gender theme for almost a decade, starting with the 1979 Planning and Designing a Non-Sexist City conference (Leavitt 1999). UCLA's Planning Department, which employed such figures as Leavitt and Hayden, was an influential site for challenging and honing feminist planning knowledge by the mid-1980s, and FPD would exert later direct influence on ACSP policy (Association of Collegiate Schools of Planning 1987).

The United Nations Human Settlements meetings were important venues for building international networks during the 1970s and '80s. After the 1976 meeting in Vancouver, for example, Gerda Wekerle reflected, "For many of us, there was a great sense of excitement and joy to discover women (and some men) from other countries who also viewed urban issues as feminist issues. We felt that we were witnessing the birth of an exciting new interdisciplinary field—one that combined an interest in the urban environment with feminist analysis and consciousness" (Wekerle, Peterson, and Morley 1980, xiii). As was the case with the collection *New Space for Women* (Wekerle, Peterson, and Morley 1980), edited volumes often served as a way to document shared ideas from a conference, particularly during this time when publicizing conference proceedings was rare. Interdisciplinary edited volumes were instrumental in helping define research, the relationship of gender roles to the built environment, and urban design (Berkeley and McQuaid 1989; Birch 1985; Keller 1981; Little, Peake, and Richardson 1988; Wekerle, Peterson, and Morley 1980). Some groups started their own publications, such as the newsletter *Women and Environments* that Wekerle cofounded, to serve a need for nonacademic publications for an audience of women's activists and NGO workers who felt left out by both feminist and planning literatures.

In addition to creating discursive spaces through conferences, feminist planners were strategic about collaborative publishing choices. As part of a concerted effort to build women's studies across disciplines, new interdisciplinary feminist journals formed in the mid-1970s, such as *Quest: A Feminist Quarterly*, *Heresies*, *Frontiers*, and *Signs: Journal of Women in Culture and Society*. Feminist planning scholars such as Ann Markusen, a regional economist and planning scholar at the University of California, Berkeley in the late 1970s, worked alongside members of women's studies programs to raise the profile of environmental design and spatial disciplines among feminists in the broader sphere. Several feminist journals featured discussions of women and space in special issues, including *Centerpoint*'s 1980 issue "Women: The Dialectic of

Public and Private Spaces" and *Heresies'* 1981 issue "Making Room: Women and Architecture."

Sometimes these opportunities arose out of local feminist activist ties, as was the case with *Heresies* and the Women's Building in Los Angeles. At other times a scholar recruited them, as when women's studies pioneer Catherine Stimpson reached out to a number of feminist planners and designers to produce a 1980 supplemental issue of *Signs* focused on the role of women in urban politics and community organizations. One of the contributors gave credit to Stimpson for what would become a well-cited piece, telling me that she "would have never written that article" if Stimpson had not contacted her "out of the blue." The issue, which was republished a year later as a book with a grant from HUD's Office of Policy Development and Research, formed a watershed moment for many feminist planners, who saw it as evidence for the mutually beneficial relationships between feminists and planners. Along with Hayden's *Grand Domestic Revolution* (1981), this *Signs* issue was named by many women I interviewed as the most formative publication for that period in their intellectual development.

Another strategy for building feminist scholarship in planning-related disciplines was producing special issues of mainstream journals devoted to women, such as the 1978 special issue of the *International Journal of Urban and Regional Research* titled "Women and the City." Ellen Perry Berkeley, one of WSPA's cofounders, leveraged her position as a senior editor at *Architectural Forum* to feature two feminist articles in a 1972 issue, including a piece advocating for flexible work schedules written by WALAP members. In the case of a 1983 special issue of the *Journal of the American Planning Association*, "Planning and the Changing Family," one of the scholars involved told me that the benign title rhetoric was a "feint." She said, "To get the editors to do it we talked about general issues, but all the articles were written by women about women!" In order to center women's perspectives, contributors strategically used language about the family (writing, for example, about changing structure, forms, and definitions of family in relation to urban planning topics). Inserting a gendered perspective required women to employ creative tactics for visibility.

CONCLUSION

While planning had previously been a top-down process enacted along rational-scientific principles, social movement pressure helped to reorient the field toward social and subjective aspects of planning at the neighborhood and community scale. Many forces contributed to these shifts, but the oral histories, archival documents, and published scholarship analyzed here reveal that feminist planners contributed significantly to the disciplinary values of engagement, participation, and advocacy that characterize the field today. Women raised the profile of feminist perspectives through educational collectives and advocacy groups and by strategically organizing conferences and publishing opportunities in planning and related fields. Though the discourse was largely limited to white middle-class women's needs and experiences, feminists were a catalytic force for social justice efforts in planning by creating spaces to introduce gendered power differentials and push back against technocratic ideals.

Feminist planners introduced a gender analytic into planning research and literature. By the mid-1980s, when Doreen Massey declared that feminism was "clearly on the agenda in geography" (Women and Geography Study Group of the IBG 1984, 11), women's and gender issues were likewise visible in planning discourses and institutions. By banding together as a marginalized group in the academy, feminists fostered spaces for knowledge sharing, made it more common to study women's experiences in planning, and achieved a basic level of topical representation in the discipline. Their backgrounds in community advocacy allowed them to insert underrepresented topics like housing and childcare into planning. In addition to influencing subject matter, feminist planners encouraged new ways of conceiving of and imagining the discipline by affirming social perspectives and expanding the role of activists and community organizers at a time when city planning departments housed much of the recognized knowledge production in the field.

The conception of gender emerging from feminist planning scholarship of the 1970s and 1980s centered social perspectives and questions of power. Just as feminist geographers argued that the social construction of space produces a gendered built environment that reifies difference (Hanson and Pratt 1995; Little, Peake, and Richardson 1988; McDowell 1999), feminist planners criticized their profession for its role in reproducing gendered inequalities. Ritzdorf (1995, 105) wrote that underlying feminist work is a recognition that "gender is a significant aspect of the cultural, social, political, and economic construction of reality." If the professional practice of planning (as well as research about planning) always contains an implicit set of values and attitudes about the role of women, as Ritzdorf argues, then questioning the assumed neutrality of planning formed a cornerstone of feminist work. Publications from the 1990s would reflect this most explicitly (see Milroy 1991; Ritzdorf 1994; Sandercock and Forsyth 1992), but by introducing gender as an analytic for examining power differentials, early feminist planners used gender to highlight inequitable practices and policies.

While this gender framework united their scholarship, the effort to put gender on the table in planning collapsed women's experiences into a falsely universal category. In highlighting the role of norms, feminists were really only focusing on one manifestation of that norm—the changing roles and expectations of middle-class white women in suburban contexts. Feminists inserted gender discourse in a way that elided connections to race and class oppression, despite often working on the ground in research and advocacy contexts where those intersections were evident in high relief.

Despite these blind spots, feminist practices of knowledge sharing in the 1970s and early 1980s opened up space for intersectional perspectives and epistemological interventions in the decades that followed. Feminist analysis evolved past its initial siloed focus on gender to encompass social equity viewed through a gendered lens. Scholars incorporated gendered power analysis into their research as a starting point to ask questions about the intersections of race and class with gender (Blumenberg 1998; Dubrow and Goodman 2003; Irazábal and Huerta 2016; Markovich and Hendler 2006; Milroy 1991; Parker 2012; Rahder and Ahtilia 2004; Ritzdorf 1994; Roberts 2018; Sandercock 1998; Sandercock and Forsyth 1992b; Spain 1990, 2016; Thomas 2018; Thomas and Ritzdorf 1997). Others foregrounded connections and contradictions with sexuality (Bauman 2002; Doan 2011, 2015; Dubrow and Sies 2002; Forsyth 1997; Frisch 2002; Quinn 2002) and interrogated the notion of the public and its multiple roles in planning (Beebeejaun 2017; Sandercock 2000). Early feminists also set the stage for planning scholarship that challenged the dominance of quantitative methods by valuing experiential knowledge and interpretive methods and seeking to break down the barrier between activism and academic careers (Markusen 2015; Parker 2016; Porter et al. 2012; Ritzdorf 1993, 1995; Sandercock 1995; Sandercock and Forsyth 1992a; Sweet and Escalante 2015, 2016), as well as transferring that practice into planning pedagogy (Forsyth 1995; Ritzdorf 1993; Thomas 1996, [2008] 2016).

While some scholars from subsequent generations would use gender to advance social equity through an intersectional lens, another focus emerged in the late 1980s that carried feminist planning further. Many women's priorities shifted to the institutionalization of gender equity within the planning community and, unlike the radical tactics employed in the 1970s and early 1980s, institutionalization efforts were often not informed by an inclusive agenda. Individualized mentoring became a top strategy to satisfy professional motivations but resulted in institutional gains that primarily benefited white women. Despite increased attention to the interconnectedness of race and class along with gender, there was very little forward movement on inclusion of people of color in the academy. Because feminist efforts in planning focused largely on career equity, much of the radical import of their initial work has been lost. While early feminist planners were not blind to structures, they had not yet developed the capacity to hold each other accountable when it came to challenging dominant structures in the planning academy. Nevertheless, by contributing to new discourses and practices fostering attention to social problems and power dynamics, feminist planning scholars helped to lay groundwork for a more inclusive and just planning practice.

REFERENCES

Association of Collegiate Schools of Planning. 1973. "Minutes of the Executive Committee Meeting." Washington, DC. US 90-6, Box 1, Folder 1.4a. Association of Collegiate Schools of Planning records, Archives and Rare Books Library, University of Cincinnati.

Association of Collegiate Schools of Planning. 1987. "Minutes of the Executive Committee Meeting." Los Angeles, CA. US 98-1, box 1, folder 27. Association of Collegiate Schools of Planning records, Archives and Rare Books Library, University of Cincinnati.

Bauman, John F. 2002. "Race, Class, Gender, and Sexuality in Planning History: A Look at Trends in the Literature." *Journal of Planning History* 1 (3): 225–29.

Beebeejaun, Yasminah. 2017. "Gender, Urban Space, and the Right to Everyday Life." *Journal of Urban Affairs* 39 (3): 323–34.

Berkeley, Ellen Perry, and Matilda McQuaid. 1989. *Architecture: A Place for Women*. Washington, DC: Smithsonian Institution Press.

Birch, Eugenie Ladner. 1978. "Woman-Made America The Case of Early Public Housing Policy." *Journal of the American Institute of Planners* 44 (2): 130–44.

Birch, Eugenie Ladner, ed. 1985. *The Unsheltered Woman: Women and Housing in the 80s*. New Brunswick, NJ: Center for Urban Policy Research, Rutgers University.

Birch, Eugenie Ladner. (1983) 1994. "From Civic Worker to City Planner: Women and Planning, 1890–1980." In *The American Planner: Biographies and Recollections*, edited by Donald A. Krueckeberg, 2nd ed., 469–506. New Brunswick, NJ: Center for Urban Policy Research.

Blumenberg, Evelyn. 1998. "Gender Equity Planning: Inserting Women into Local Economic Development." *Journal of Planning Literature* 13 (2): 131–46.

Boyer, M. Christine. 1983. *Dreaming the Rational City: The Myth of American City Planning*. Cambridge, MA: MIT Press.

Cahn, Elizabeth. 2014. "Project Space(s) in the Design Professions: An Intersectional Feminist Study of the Women's School of Planning and Architecture (1974–1981)." PhD diss., University of Massachusetts Amherst.

Coatsworth, Patricia A., ed. 1981. "Women and Urban Planning: A Bibliography." Office of Policy Development and Research, US Department of Housing and Urban Development.

Davidoff, Paul. (1965) 2012. "Advocacy and Pluralism in Planning." In *Readings in Planning Theory*, edited by Susan S. Fainstein and Scott Campbell, 3rd ed., 544–55. Malden, MA: Wiley-Blackwell.

Doan, Petra L., ed. 2011. *Queerying Planning: Challenging Heteronormative Assumptions and Reframing Planning Practice*. Farnham, Surrey; Burlington, VT: Ashgate Publishing Limited.

Doan, Petra L. 2015. *Planning and LGBTQ Communities: The Need for Inclusive Queer Spaces*. Planning and Lesbian, Gay, Bisexual, Transgendered, and Queer Communities. New York: Routledge, Taylor & Francis Group.

Dubrow, Gail Lee, and Jennifer B. Goodman, eds. 2003. *Restoring Women's History through Historic Preservation*. Baltimore: Johns Hopkins University Press.

Dubrow, Gail Lee, and Mary Corbin Sies. 2002. "Letting Our Guard Down: Race, Class, Gender, and Sexuality in Planning History." *Journal of Planning History* 1 (3): 203–14.

Fainstein, Norman, and Susan S. Fainstein. 1974. *Urban Political Movements: The Search for Power by Minority Groups in American Cities*. Englewood Cliffs, NY: Prentice Hall.

Fainstein, Susan S. 2005. "Feminism and Planning: Theoretical Issues." In *Gender and Planning: A Reader*, edited by Susan S. Fainstein and Lisa J. Servon, 120–38. New Brunswick, NJ: Rutgers University Press.

Forsyth, Ann. 1995. "Diversity Issues in a Professional Curriculum: Four Stories and Some Suggestions for Change." *Journal of Planning Education and Research* 15 (1): 58–63.

Forsyth, Ann. 1997. " 'Out' in The Valley." *International Journal of Urban and Regional Research* 21 (1): 38–62.

Forsyth, Ann. 2011. "Queerying Planning Practice: Understanding Non-Conformist Populations." In *Queerying Planning: Challenging Heteronormative Assumptions and Reframing Planning Practice*, edited by Petra L. Doan, 21–52. Farnham, Surrey; Burlington, VT: Ashgate Publishing Limited.

Frisch, Michael. 2002. "Planning as a Heterosexist Project." *Journal of Planning Education and Research* 21 (3): 254–66.

Gauger, Bri. Forthcoming. "Urban Planning and Its Feminist Histories." PhD diss., University of Michigan.

Hanson, Susan, and Geraldine Pratt. 1995. *Gender, Work, and Space*. International Studies of Women and Place. London and New York: Routledge.

Harvey, David. 1973. *Social Justice and the City*. Johns Hopkins Studies in Urban Affairs. Baltimore: Johns Hopkins University Press.

Hayden, Dolores. 1978. "Two Utopian Feminists and Their Campaigns for Kitchenless Houses." *Signs* 4 (2): 274–90.

Hayden, Dolores. 1981. *The Grand Domestic Revolution: A History of Feminist Designs for American Homes, Neighborhoods, and Cities*. Cambridge, MA: MIT Press.

Hayden, Dolores. 2002. *Redesigning the American Dream: The Future of Housing, Work, and Family Life*. New York: W. W. Norton.

Hayden, Dolores. (1981) 2005. "What Would a Nonsexist City Be Like?: Speculations on Housing, Urban Design, and Human Work." In *Gender and Planning: A Reader*, edited by Susan S. Fainstein and Lisa J. Servon, 47–64. New Brunswick, NJ: Rutgers University Press.

Hayden, Dolores. (1984) 2012. "Nurturing: Home, Mom, and Apple Pie." In *Readings in Planning Theory*, edited by Susan S. Fainstein and Scott Campbell, 3rd ed., 358–83. Chichester; New York: Wiley-Blackwell.

Hayden, Dolores, and Gwendolyn Wright. 1976. "Review Essay: Architecture and Urban Planning." *Signs: Journal of Women in Culture and Society* 1 (4): 923–33.

Hirt, Sonia A. 2014. *Zoned in the USA: The Origins and Implications of American Land-Use Regulation*. Ithaca, NY: Cornell University Press.

Irazábal, Clara, and Claudia Huerta. 2016. "Intersectionality and Planning at the Margins: LGBTQ Youth of Color in New York." *Gender, Place & Culture* 23 (5): 714–32.

Keller, Suzanne Infeld, ed. 1981. *Building for Women*. Lexington, MA: Lexington Books.

Krumholz, Norman. 1997. "Urban Planning, Equity Planning, and Racial Justice." In *Urban*

Planning and the African American Community: In the Shadows, edited by June Manning Thomas and Marsha Ritzdorf, 109–25. Thousand Oaks, CA: Sage Publications.

Leavitt, Jacqueline. 1980. "Women in Planning: There's More to Affirmative Action than Gaining Access." In *New Space for Women*, edited by Gerda R. Wekerle, Rebecca Peterson, and David Morley, 219–34. Boulder, CO: Westview Press.

Leavitt, Jacqueline. 1986. "Feminist Advocacy Planning in the 1980s." In *Strategic Perspectives on Planning Practice*, edited by Barry Checkoway, 181–94. Politics of Planning Series. Lexington, MA: Lexington Books.

Leavitt, Jacqueline. 1999. "Gendered Planning: Inside/Out?" *Critical Planning Journal* 6 (Spring): 110–13.

Leavitt, Jacqueline. 2003. "Where's the Gender in Community Development?" *Signs: Journal of Women in Culture and Society* 29 (1): 207–31.

Leavitt, Jacqueline, and Susan Saegert. 1984. "Women and Abandoned Buildings: A Feminist Approach to Housing." *Social Policy* 15 (1): 32–39.

Leavitt, Jacqueline, and Susan Saegert. 1990. *From Abandonment to Hope: Community-Households in Harlem*. Columbia History of Urban Life. New York: Columbia University Press.

Leonard, Jonathan S. 1989. "Women and Affirmative Action." *Journal of Economic Perspectives* 3 (1): 61–75.

Little, Jo, Linda Peake, and Pat Richardson, eds. 1988. *Women in Cities: Gender and the Urban Environment*. New York: New York University Press.

Markovich, Julia, and Sue Hendler. 2006. "Beyond 'Soccer Moms': Feminist and New Urbanist Critical Approaches to Suburbs." *Journal of Planning Education and Research* 25 (4): 410–27.

Markusen, Ann R. 1975. "The Economics of the Women's Movement." *Frontiers: A Journal of Women Studies* 1 (1): 42–52.

Markusen, Ann R. 1980. "City Spatial Structure, Women's Household Work, and National Urban Policy." *Signs* 5 (3): 23–44.

Markusen, Ann R. 2015. "How Real-World Work, Advocacy, and Political Economy Strengthen Planning Research and Practice." *Journal of the American Planning Association* 81 (2): 143–52.

McDowell, Linda. 1999. *Gender, Identity and Place: Understanding Feminist Geographies*. Cambridge, UK: Polity Press.

Milroy, Beth Moore. 1991. "Taking Stock of Planning, Space, and Gender." *Journal of Planning Literature* 6 (1): 3–15.

National Congress of Neighborhood Women. n.d. Home page. Accessed October 5, 2017. http://neighborhoodwomen.org/.

Parker, Brenda. 2012. "Gender, Cities, and Planning: Looking Back and Looking Forward." In *The Oxford Handbook of Urban Planning*, edited by Randall Crane and Rachel Weber, 609–33. Oxford: Oxford University Press.

Parker, Brenda. 2016. "Feminist Forays in the City: Imbalance and Intervention in Urban Research Methods." *Antipode* 48 (5): 1337–58.

Planners for Equal Opportunity. 1969. "PEO Annual Meeting Conference Drafting Workshops." Box 1, Folder 6. Planners for Equal Opportunity records, Division of Rare and Manuscript Collections, Cornell University Library.

Planners Network. 2008. "Progressive Planning Profile: Jacqueline Leavitt." January 3, 2008. http://www.plannersnetwork.org/2008/01/progressive-planning-profile-jacqueline-leavitt/.

Porter, Libby, Leonie Sandercock, Karen Umemoto, Lisa K. Bates, Marisa A. Zapata, Michelle C. Kondo, Andrew Zitcer, et al. 2012. "What's Love Got to Do with It? Illuminations on Loving Attachment in Planning." *Planning Theory & Practice* 13 (4): 593–627.

Quinn, Kelly. 2002. "Planning History/Planning Race, Gender, Class, and Sexuality." *Journal of Planning History* 1 (3): 240–44.

Rahder, Barbara, and Carol Ahtilia. 2004. "Where Is Feminism Going in Planning? Transformation or Appropriation?" *Planning Theory* 3 (2): 107–16.

Ritzdorf, Marsha. 1985. "Zoning Barriers to Housing Innovation." *Journal of Planning Education and Research* 4 (3): 177–84.

Ritzdorf, Marsha. 1993. "The Fairy's Tale: Teaching Planning and Public Policy in a Different Voice." *Journal of Planning Education and Research* 12 (2): 99–106.

Ritzdorf, Marsha. 1994. "A Feminist Analysis of Gender and Residential Zoning in the United States." In *Women and the Environment*, edited by Irwin Altman and Arza Churchman, 255–79. Human Behavior and Environment 13. New York: Springer US.

Ritzdorf, Marsha. 1995. "Feminist Contributions to Ethics and Planning Theory." In *Planning Ethics: A Reader in Planning Theory, Practices, and Education*, edited by Sue Hendler, 104–19. New Brunswick, NJ: Center for Urban Policy Research.

Ritzdorf, Marsha. 1997. "Family Values, Municipal Zoning, and African American Family Life." In *Urban Planning and the African American Community: In the Shadows*, edited by June Manning Thomas and Marsha Ritzdorf, 75–89. Thousand Oaks, CA: Sage Publications.

Ritzdorf, Marsha. 2000. "Sex, Lies, and Urban Life: How Municipal Planning Marginalizes African American Women and Their Families." In *Gendering the City: Women, Boundaries, and Visions of Urban Life*, edited by Kristine B. Miranne and Alma H. Young, 169–82. Lanham, MD: Rowman & Littlefield.

Roberts, Andrea R. 2018. "Interpretations & Imaginaries: Toward an Instrumental Black Planning History." *Planning Theory & Practice* 19 (2): 283.

Rosenbloom, Sandra. (1978) 2005. "Women's Travel Issues: The Research and Policy Environment." In *Gender and Planning: A Reader*, edited by Susan S. Fainstein and Lisa J. Servon, 235–55. New Brunswick, NJ: Rutgers University Press.

Ross, Catherine. 1985. "The Influence of Race and Gender on Perceptions of Community Impact." *Environmental Impact Assessment Review* 5 (2): 169–79.

Saegert, Susan. 1980. "Masculine Cities and Feminine Suburbs: Polarized Ideas, Contradictory Realities." *Signs: Journal of Women in Culture and Society* 5 (s3): S96.

Sandercock, Leonie. 1995. "Voices from the Borderlands: A Meditation on a Metaphor." *Journal of Planning Education and Research* 14 (2): 77–88.

Sandercock, Leonie. 1998. *Making the Invisible Visible: A Multicultural Planning History*. California Studies in Critical Human Geography. Berkeley: University of California Press.

Sandercock, Leonie. 2000. "When Strangers Become Neighbours: Managing Cities of Difference." *Planning Theory & Practice* 1 (1): 13–30.

Sandercock, Leonie, and Ann Forsyth. 1992a. "Feminist Theory and Planning Theory: The Epistemological Linkages." *Planning Theory* 7/8: 45–49.

Sandercock, Leonie, and Ann Forsyth. 1992b. "A Gender Agenda: New Directions for Planning Theory." *Journal of the American Planning Association* 58 (1): 49–59.

Spain, Daphne. 1990. "The Effect of Residential Mobility and Household Composition on Housing Quality." *Urban Affairs Review* 25 (4): 659–83.

Spain, Daphne. 2016. *Constructive Feminism: Women's Spaces and Women's Rights in the American City*. Ithaca, NY: Cornell University Press.

Sutton, Sharon E. 2017. *When Ivory Towers Were Black: A Story about Race in America's Cities and Universities*. New York: Fordham University Press.

Sweet, Elizabeth L., and Sara Ortiz Escalante. 2015. "Bringing Bodies into Planning: Visceral Methods, Fear and Gender Violence." *Urban Studies* 52 (10): 1826–45.

Sweet, Elizabeth L., and Sara Ortiz Escalante. 2016. "Engaging Territorio Cuerpo-Tierra through Body and Community Mapping: A Methodology for Making Communities Safer." *Gender, Place & Culture* 24 (4): 594–606.

Thomas, June Manning. 1985. "Neighborhood Response to Redevelopment in Detroit." *Community Development Journal* 20 (2): 89–98.

Thomas, June Manning. 1996. "Educating Planners: Unified Diversity for Social Action." *Journal of Planning Education and Research* 15 (3): 171–82.

Thomas, June Manning. (2008) 2016. "The Minority-Race Planner in the Quest for a Just City." In *Reading in Planning Theory*, edited by Susan S. Fainstein and James DeFillippis, 4th ed., 443–63. Malden, MA: Wiley-Blackwell.

Thomas, June Manning. 2018. "Josephine Gomon Plans for Detroit's Rehabilitation." *Journal of Planning History* 17 (2): 97–117.

Thomas, June Manning, and Marsha Ritzdorf, eds. 1997. *Urban Planning and the African American Community: In the Shadows*. Thousand Oaks, CA: Sage Publications.

Weisman, Leslie. 1992. *Discrimination by Design: A Feminist Critique of the Man-Made Environment*. Urbana: University of Illinois Press.

Wekerle, Gerda R. 1980. "Women in the Urban Environment." *Signs: Journal of Women in Culture and Society* 5 (3): 188–214.

Wekerle, Gerda R. 1981. "Women House Themselves." *Heresies: A Feminist Publication on Art and Politics* 3 (3): 14–17.

Wekerle, Gerda R. 1985. "From Refuge to Service Center: Neighborhoods That Support Women." *Sociological Focus* 18 (2): 79–95.

Wekerle, Gerda R., Rebecca Peterson, and David Morley, eds. 1980. *New Space for Women*. Westview Special Studies on Women in Contemporary Society. Boulder, CO: Westview Press.

Wolch, Jennifer R. 1980. "Residential Location of the Service-Dependent Poor." *Annals of the Association of American Geographers* 70 (3): 330–41.

Women and Geography Study Group of the IBG. 1984. *Geography and Gender: An Introduction to Feminist Geography*. London; Dover, NH: Hutchinson in association with Explorations in Feminism Collective.

"Women and Planning: A Condemnation." 1970. Press release. Box 3, Folder 50. Planners for Equal Opportunity records, Division of Rare and Manuscript Collections, Cornell University Library.

Women in Architecture, Landscape Architecture and Planning. 1972a. "An Open Letter to Members of the Harvard Graduate School of Design Association." June 15, 1972. Ellen Perry Berkeley personal papers.

Women in Architecture, Landscape Architecture, and Planning. 1972b. "The Case for Flexible Work Schedules." *Architectural Forum* 137 (2): 53–66.

Women in Architecture, Landscape Architecture, and Planning. n.d. "By-Laws." Ellen Perry Berkeley personal papers.

Women in Environmental Planning and Design. 1972a. "Women in Architecture, Landscape Architecture, and City Planning in the Boston-Cambridge or Suburban Area." Ellen Perry Berkeley personal papers.

Women in Environmental Planning and Design. 1972b. "Letter to Dean Kilbridge, Graduate School of Design, Harvard University." February 4, 1972. Ellen Perry Berkeley personal papers.

Women's School of Planning and Architecture. n.d. a. "Informational Flyer." Box 1, Folder 11. Women's School of Planning and Architecture Records, Sophia Smith Collection of Women's History, Smith College.

Women's School of Planning and Architecture. n.d. b. "Draft Statement of WSPA Goals and Policies." Box 1, Folder 14. Women's School of Planning and Architecture Records, Sophia Smith Collection of Women's History, Smith College.

Wright, Gwendolyn. 1980. *Moralism and the Model Home: Domestic Architecture and Cultural Conflict in Chicago, 1873–1913*. Chicago: University of Chicago Press.

Zapata, Marisa A., and Lisa K. Bates. 2015. "Equity Planning Revisited." *Journal of Planning Education and Research* 35 (3): 245–48.

CHAPTER 12

CHALLENGING ANGLOCENTRIC FEMINIST GEOGRAPHY FROM LATIN AMERICAN FEMINIST DEBATES ON TERRITORIALITY

Sofia Zaragocin

Challenging the epistemic dominance of Anglocentric feminist geography is not a linear process of knowledges from "below" disrupting knowledges from "above." The flow of place-based knowledges is multidimensional and lived through subject positions that are often transcultural. This chapter addresses how we can discuss feminist geography in places where intellectual traditions do not converge on the same questions or share the same trajectory. Specifically, this chapter makes the case for a decolonized translocation (Alvarez 2014) of feminist geography to question the field's epistemic privilege while allowing for nuanced conceptualizations of what constitutes feminist geography. This insight stems from being a decolonial feminist geographer in Ecuador, a country that has had limited engagement with critical geography debates—even those currently unfolding in Latin America. As a child immigrant to the United States, then an adult migrant from the United States back to Ecuador, I embody an uncomfortable set of relations, positioned amid uneven postcolonial flows of knowledge. Moving back and forth between different localities, I have witnessed how epistemes are profoundly place-based. Through border crossings and transcultural personal experiences, I found a conceptual home in the tradition of feminist geography because it emphasized place and space as determinant factors in gender relations. Nevertheless, returning to Ecuador, a country with a distinct intellectual tradition, required confronting a new set of questions regarding the flow of knowledge between unequal planes of knowledge production. The persistent absence of a transnational feminist dialogue with geographic peripheral feminisms (from places like Ecuador) and these locales' respective conceptions of time-space, body-territory, and land-based epistemologies is a matter of concern. Meanwhile, place-based critiques of feminist geography as prioritizing Western ontological perspectives and as written primarily in English offer their own claims to ways of knowing.

However, lines of knowledge production in feminist geography do not travel and follow a neatly divided north-south binary. Feminist geography in the global South is not inherently decolonial, and not all Anglophone feminist geography is Anglocentric (a term I describe below). For example, I have spoken of a *decolonized* feminist geography in Ecuadorian academic circles, where there seems to be an acceptance of feminist geography but a rejection of the decolonial. Specifically, I have been questioned in different academic panels and informal conversations in Ecuador for bringing topics like settler colonialism, Indigenous feminist theories from the US and Canada, and Sara Ahmed's citation policies concerning the institution of white men in the academy, as these theories have been interpreted as "muy gringo" (too American). It is from this ironic and paradoxical place that I have inhabited epistemic discomfort. This chapter is my attempt to productively work through this problem space. Ultimately, as a means to counter the Anglocentricity of feminist geography, I propose translocation to achieve decolonial processes of knowledge construction but emphasize that in my experience on panels and in the classroom this approach does not always lead to the acceptance of decolonial theory as a preferred approach to knowledge production in Ecuador. However, in this context decolonization in geographical knowledge construction cannot wait for all to be on board or to be convinced of its urgency and, in turn, new theories to emerge. The process of working toward decolonization is just as relevant as the resulting theories.

Theory not only moves and is encountered through written texts, but it is also shaped by embodied experiences. A feminist politics of translation draws on the travels of the heterogeneity of Latinx peoples or Latinidades in the United States, Latin America, and Caribbean (Alvarez 2014). This framework of translating theory speaks to what happens when one or more place-based systems of thought encounter one another, affecting not only theoretical frameworks but also those involved in creating these dialogues. Through the figure of a transloca—a role I myself embody—I explore how understanding processes of transporting and translating a discipline to another part of the world can be framed as part of a reflexive decolonial translocal feminist politics (Alvarez et al. 2014). Transloca as praxis is suggested as a means of grappling with the colonial implications of translation and the epistemological mobility of feminist geographical theory. Given the continued Anglocentricity of feminist geography, those engaged in transforming it must partake in a decolonized methodological praxis influenced by translocation. For the particular case of Ecuadorian academic and activist-research communities, this must be taken up in dialogue with the existing Latin American feminist debates on territory in ways that I will show below. Translocation is required for furthering the conceptual overlap between Anglocentric feminist geography and Latin American feminist debates on territory. This implores a particular decolonial politics of translation that is embodied between a wide range of subject-agents at multiple scales and spaces (Laos Montes and Buggs 2014, 397). Translation in this context is not just linguistic but implies taking responsibility for the process of making conceptual work available to other audiences. Translocation embraces multidirectional crossings and movements of feminist ideas, practices, and embodiments through multiscalar analysis of power across all of the Latin/a Americas (Alvarez et al. 2014; Lao-Montes and Buggs 2014). Moreover, the embodiment of translocation is possible through the figure of translocas, a metaphor for the epistemological mobility that links the physical displacement of women through place and a resulting conceptual madness stemming from constant movement that acknowledges the intimate linkages between place, body, and knowledge construction (Alvarez 2014). Translocas disrupt linear understandings of place-based knowledge construction through an embodiment of being constantly "out of place" (Alvarez 2014). Drawing from my experience as a transloca, I argue that the process of transforming Anglocentric versions of feminist geography through Latin American feminist debates on territoriality lies somewhere between translocation and decolonization.

In the case at hand, a feminist politics of translation in the Latin/a Americas involves creating a conversation between feminist geography as it is understood in its Anglocentric formations and an emerging feminist geography in Latin America centered on the question of *territorio* (territory) and *territorialidad* (territoriality). Territory and its derivations have been the preferred form of spatial practices and dimensions of social movements as well as interventions of place-based development in Latin America (Lopez, Robertsdotter, and Paredes 2017). As will be discussed in this chapter, Latin American feminist debates on territory have focused on (a) dialogue between decolonial and feminist communitarian frameworks, (b) the gendered effects of extractivism on territory and territorialized gender-based violence concepts, and (c) social cartography and thematic maps on gender-based violence. Meanwhile, Anglocentric feminist geography is understood as geographical knowledge that prioritizes literature produced in the English language and from Western ontological viewpoints, even from intellectual traditions outside the global North. I am making a specific distinction with existing literature on the dominance of Anglophone feminist geography, which has been criticized for its reproduction of Anglo-American hegemony in the field (García Ramon, Simonsen, and Vaiou 2006), in order to emphasize decolonizing knowledge production critiques outside the North-South binary. Feminist geography literature travels through messy epistemic geographies, further complicated when taking into account current decolonization debates. There are different strands of Anglophone geography, including those that engage with decolonial geographical literature in great length, so it is not solely an issue of language or place of publication. Feminist geography literature written in other languages, such as Spanish and Portuguese, has reproduced Anglocentric feminist geography in ignoring theoretical production in places that speak these languages outside of Western Europe. The question of where and how feminist geographies travel is key to decolonizing processes for the field. This gap is further widened when we take into account the theoretical production that does not consider itself feminist geography but shares similar conceptual inquiries, prompting questions about what is considered as feminist geography and who decides this. Decolonization of geographical knowledge implies that we not take for granted a preconceived definition of decolonization *and* feminist geography. While feminist geography is still published mainly in English and taught primarily in the global North, this critique is relevant in an emerging Latin American feminist geography alongside Latin American feminist debates on territory.

Despite feminist scholars across the Americas having approached trans-locality and decoloniality as complementary processes that are profoundly place-based (Alvarez 2014; Laos Montes and Buggs 2014), in geography this discussion has yet to materialize. I suggest that amid efforts to decolonize geographical knowledges in human geography (Naylor et al. 2018; Radcliffe 2017), the concept of translocation (Alvarez 2014), derived from feminist politics of translation in Latin America or the "Latin/a Americas" is necessary for the field. Decolonization and translocation are complementary processes through which theory is embodied, and it is from this experience that I will speak. The emphasis found in feminists' politics of translation in the Latin/a Americas on decolonization adds to the discussion in human geography, and it is in this translation zone (Apter 2006) that Latin American feminist debates on territoriality can come into productive dialogue with Anglocentric and Latin American notions of feminist geography. Pluralizing place-based systems of knowledge production and decolonizing feminist geography implies intellectual alliance building (Zaragocin 2018). This, in many ways, has been addressed by the theoretical proposition of translocation, as I will address below.

TRANSLATION, TRANSLOCALITY, AND THE *TRANSLOCAS* OF FEMINIST GEOGRAPHY IN LATIN AMERICA

In my identity as a transloca, my feminist geographical inquiries occur within two spaces in Ecuador: both as a member of the Critical Geography Collective of Ecuador and an academic affiliated with gender departments at two national universities at different moments of my career (University of Cuenca and the Latin American Faculty of Social Sciences, known as FLACSO-Ecuador). These two forms of intervention draw attention to the emerging landscape of knowledge production in Ecuador on feminist geography. The Critical Geography Collective of Ecuador is a collective of geographers (both human and physical) and nongeographers who engage in research-activism, create counter-maps, analyze social issues related to natural resource extraction, and, more recently, investigate gender-based violence. A joint mission to utilize critical geography methods for radical social change is what brings us together. It is about *doing* critical geography alongside existing feminist and ecological social movements. Our work stemming from gender-based violence is positioned as engaging feminist geography, and along with input from other feminist collectives we have produced thematic maps on femicide and the criminalization of abortion in Ecuador. Civil society organizations currently use the collective's thematic maps as tools to mitigate gender-based violence in the country. Moreover, the collective has also carried out political advocacy measures such as developing a political manifesto on femicide that was delivered to the national congress as countrywide debates on the new gender-based violence law unfold (Zaragocin, Silveira, and Arazola 2018). Feminist geography interpreted by the Critical Geography Collective of Ecuador and partner feminist collectives reclaims counter-mapping as a feminist geographic tool for confronting gender-based violence. The result has been a counter-practice of translation and translocation, through which counter-hegemonic narratives about gender and feminisms can evolve (Costa 2014).

Meanwhile, in Ecuadorian academia, geography has primarily been taught from a positivist and utilitarian perspective (Zaragocin, Moreano, and Alvarez 2018). A sustained tradition in human geography is lacking, making the work of the Critical Geography Collective of Ecuador central in propelling national interest on social cartography, feminist geography, and socioterritorial disputes concerning extractive industries. An ever-growing interest in feminist geography is opening up the field of human geography in Ecuadorian universities. In this scenario, universities have approached the collective for advice in the development of curricula for future undergraduate and graduate degrees in critical geography, as well as for the participation of its members in academic panels and conferences. In February 2018, I taught the first feminist geography course at FLACSO-Ecuador, a leading social science postgraduate university in the country. The course gathered sixteen students from existing master programs as well as from other universities in the country. Aside from teaching, research between activists and academics on feminist geography has also emerged. For example, the map on the criminalization of abortion was a result of a joint research project coordinated by FLACSO-Ecuador, along with the Critical Geography Collective of Ecuador and Surkuna, a feminist human rights organization that has long fought for the depenalization of abortion. Alongside this project, the collective has promoted various academic panels on feminist geography in Ecuadorian universities, including one sponsored by the journal *Gender, Place & Culture* on a recently published manual on feminist geography methodologies.

Given the predominance of Anglocentric feminist geography, developing feminist geography from a translocal perspective and from collective and academic spaces in Ecuador necessarily implies that it be done from a decolonizing perspective. Not doing so would reinforce unequal planes of knowledge construction and epistemic privilege. However, if feminist geography in collective, activist, and academic spaces in Ecuador has often been receptively received and engaged, decolonial perspectives have not. Activist and academic spaces currently engaging with feminist geography methods and concepts do not necessarily reject the decolonial, but they are explicitly hesitant to engage the decolonial as it is perceived as originating externally. Broadly, there remains a lack of engagement with decolonization in critical geographical knowledge production. In instances where I have spoken of a *decolonized* feminist geography in Ecuadorian academic circles, there is a simultaneous rejection of the decolonial and acceptance of feminist geography. The feminist geography aspect of a decolonized feminist geography has been applauded for its innovative concepts and ways of presenting long-existing gender-based violence data in a way that has captivated the attention of sectors of society historically apathetic to critical engagement. The decolonial part of a decolonized feminist geography, however, has provoked a much different reaction, reflecting long-standing ambivalence to existing decolonial approaches in the region. The more critical geographical scholarship that has emerged has been largely limited to a focus on Marxist geography, which reflects prevailing intellectual traditions in Ecuadorian social sciences more generally. In this way, the decolonial brings up existing tensions and resistance to the type of decolonization known and adopted regionally such as that originated in the modernity-coloniality-decoloniality school (Lander 2002; Mignolo 2000; Quijano 2000). For many geographers, literature on decoloniality is deemed as something from the global North and hence not relevant for the Ecuadorian context. Therefore, what becomes difficult and uncomfortable in geography circles is promoting not a feminist geography but a *decolonial* feminist geography. This is precisely where translocation, as understood by Latin/a American feminist politics of translations, is needed regarding Anglocentric feminist geography in contexts outside the global North. Specific attention is needed to ensure that in the translocation process, a decolonial process be implemented as it draws productively on both critical Anglocentric feminism and decoloniality. If a decolonial perspective is not brought into the process of translocation, then white Anglocentric feminist geography can be reproduced outside of places where this particular type of knowledge production resides.

AN EMERGING ANGLOCENTRIC FEMINIST GEOGRAPHY IN LATIN AMERICA AND LATIN AMERICAN FEMINIST DEBATES ON TERRITORY

Challenging the Anglocentricity of feminist geography is invariably a decolonizing project. However, in the "translation zone" (Apter 2006) described above in collective and academic spaces, it has also become apparent that few Latin American territorial feminist debates explicitly identify as decolonial. This prompts the question: Is it possible to decolonize geographical knowledge construction without using decolonized concepts? At this moment and based on my experience in different settings in Ecuador, I suggest that not only is this possible, but it should be encouraged when decolonization is understood as a process of converging and translating embodied theory. The disruptions provoked in considering Ecuador as a settler state, for example, productively bring up topics concerning race, ethnicity, and *mestizaje* that are severely sidelined in the Ecuadorian academy.

However, introducing concepts like settler colonialism and decoloniality into these Ecuadorian spaces makes legible the very real and personal geographies of knowledge production. As a transloca, being tainted as "too American" is also extremely painful, for my lived experience transporting theory from one place to another did not start in the academy but rather in early childhood. As many scholars have noted, decoding cultural and language barriers for migrant parents is part of everyday life that we later come to understand as translocation (Espinal 2014). Similarly, questions arise as to why I bring another entry point on decolonization pertaining to other regions, when what was expected of my interventions as a feminist geographer in these academic spaces were contributions solely on feminist geography. Being simultaneously in the collective and academic spaces is part of the transloca embodiment that I hold. For I am a transloca in both the collective and the academy, and my dual role is both heightened and a result of the multiple places I have lived and, now, create knowledge from.

The disassociation from Western universal ontologies and epistemologies currently promoted in geographical knowledge production is resisted by the majority of Ecuadorian academia as well as by the transloca project. This is due in part to the importance and conceptual dependence on Western universalizing mega-narratives that have dominated leftist-oriented Ecuadorian social sciences. Marxist geography through the work of David Harvey has been taken up by various universities in the country, giving him an honorary teaching post at the Central University of Ecuador and a short-lived summer school and research program at the Ecuadorian Institute of Higher Education. In this scenario, bringing up feminist geography has been challenging, and a decolonial feminist geography even more so. What makes systems of thought prominent in part is the refusal to let others into the conceptual discussion, a dynamic that has been discussed in terms of postcolonial geographies (Sharp 2009) that manifests in Ecuadorian academic circles. Translocation, then, is full of contradictions, since the flow of knowledge creation is literally *all over the place*. In these scenarios, would translocas such as myself be at fault for not making it explicit that the concepts used for decolonization of geographical knowledge are not in fact decolonized to begin with? This question arises in situations as those mentioned here, where my positionality as a transloca does not coincide with the conceptual priorities of the context, and to which I hold ambivalent sentiments of belonging. This furthers the idea that the process of decolonization serves as a legitimate starting point for geographical knowledge production. Critical geography, more than any other discipline, has questioned the containment of space, and so it is important that as a field we not equate the geographies of the global South with the production of theory that is inherently decolonial. Decolonial inquiry helps to address the Anglocentricity of feminist geography, but there are other elements alongside decolonization, such as translocality, that are part of the conceptual toolkit available for challenging dominant systems of thought. In particular, translocality looks to insert feminist notions of territory originating from Latin America into these decolonial and Anglocentric feminist conversations.

In places where total dissociation from Anglophone feminist geography is not an option, such as the scenario presented above, the feminist radical politics of decolonization already part of the translocation proposal presented here must be emphasized. In this case, feminist geography in either its Anglocentric formations or its emerging Latin American traditions requires a radical feminist politics of decolonization that "seeks to challenge the 'hierarchies of rule' and the colonial legacies of race, gender, class, sexuality and nation that constitute modern/colonial constellations of power" (Lao-Montes and Buggs 2014, 382). Moreover, translocal feminist discourses and imaginaries—including ideas, projects, and movements across borders, nations, and identities— promote "the notion of translocality [that] combines multiple mediations of self, power, and culture that link local, regional, national, and global scenarios, configuring a more complex concept of location and perspective that we conceptualize as a decolonial politics of translocation" (Lao-Montes and Buggs 2014, 382). A decolonial politics of translocation is mainly concerned with combating intersecting spheres of injustice as it practices a politics opposed to racism, imperialism, capitalism, patriarchy, and heteronormativity (Lao-Montes and Buggs 2014).

There are at least three conceptual lines that analyze feminist spatialities and debates on territory in Latin America (Zaragocin, Moreano, and Alvarez 2018). The first is the academic production of feminist and gender geography within the intellectual traditions of critical geography in Brazil and Argentina (Lan 2016; Veleda da Silva 2016; Veleda da Silva and Lan 2007), with an incipient tradition in Mexico (Ibarra Garcia and Escamilla-Herrera 2016). Feminist geography approaches in Latin America have engaged with Anglocentric feminist geography primarily with the work of Linda McDowell and Doreen Massey, largely due to the fact that these are the texts available in Spanish and open-sourced. Feminist geography texts produced in Spain and Portugal are also heavily cited in these emerging feminist geography traditions (Nelson 2016). A recent Ibero-Latin American edited collection brought together Spanish and Portuguese feminist geographic traditions with those already established in Latin America (Silva, Orna, and Chimin 2017). That is, what makes up Anglocentric feminist geography is not only Anglophone feminist geography but also literature produced in other languages and geographies outside of the US and UK. Emerging feminist geography traditions in the region are also tied to processes of institutionalized critical geography and political ecology perspectives. Brazil, Argentina, and Mexico have long-standing critical geography intellectual traditions, with academic departments that can sustain feminist geography discussions, something that is not possible in the rest of the region. Feminist geography, then, is produced in parts of Latin America where critical geography traditions already exist, and in dialogue with dominant places of knowledge production (Anglophone and otherwise). Meanwhile, in the rest of Latin American countries, the emerging Latin American feminist and gender geographies have had limited conceptual dialogue with longstanding Latin American debates on territory.[1] The moving of ideas and texts take place through specific material forms making them translocal and present a particular scenario for scholars and activists who self-identify as translocas. The implications of a limited conceptual dialogue across geographically diffuse conceptual lines of analysis truncates cross-cultural knowledge production and the sharing of concepts for those different intellectual traditions involved.

The second conceptual line of analysis concerning feminist spatialities in Latin America consists of feminist debates on territory, addressed in Bolivia, Colombia, Ecuador, Guatemala, Mexico, and Uruguay.[2] Latin American feminist debates on territory can be summarized in the following three ways: dialogue between decolonial and feminist communitarian frameworks; the gendered effects of extractivism on territory and territorialized gender-based violence concepts; and social cartography and thematic maps on gender-based violence. In all three discussions, territory and the body are the preferred analytical scales, with varying degrees of interconnectedness and overlap. Communitarian feminism (Cabnal 2010; Paredes 2010), an Indigenous feminist framework that displaces the individual and replaces it with a communal subject agency, has a specific approach to territory referred to as *cuerpo-territorio* or body-territory. Body-territory is fast becoming a central tenet of contemporary Latin American feminist theory and politics based on Indigenous ontologies of space and decolonial understandings of the gendered body, promoting a decolonized embodied ontology (Zaragocin 2018). *Cuerpo-territorio* places the community and territory as a single subject of political agency that resists and identifies violations against Indigenous women's bodies and territories as part of the same process (Cabnal 2010; Miradas Críticas del territorio desde el Feminismo 2014, 2017). This merging of body and space from a decolonial feminist furthers the discussion on the possibility of a decolonial turn in political geography (Zaragocin 2018).[3] Meanwhile, decolonial feminisms (see Paredes 2008) have promoted the concept of Abya Yala as an alternative Indigenous name for what is today known as Latin America, framing a geopolitics and a place for an emerging feminist decolonial epistemology (Espinosa Miñosa, Gómez, and Ochoa 2014; Zaragocin 2017). Alongside these emerging Latin American feminist frameworks, parallel debates on territory exist concerning extractivism, gender-based violence, and the creation of masculinist spaces. A recurring debate on extractivism's reconfiguration of gender and economic relations of populations in the region has yielded two positions. Feminist collective spaces point to the body as the first territory, as well as the (re)patriarchalization of territory based on the masculinization of territory due to the preponderance of extractivist industries that produce a particular gender-based violence affecting primarily women's bodies and their spaces (Miradas Críticas del territorio desde el Feminismo 2017). Others have questioned the linear assumptions between gender-based violence and extractivism, and the essentialisms associated with a gendered territory (Jenkins 2015; Ruales and Zaragocin forthcoming; Ulloa 2016). The latter has made room for nuanced tales of encounters between women's territorial movements and extractive industry, as well as the government and industry's strategic use of essentialized ideals of gendered places. Latin American feminist debates on territory are being applied to aquatic space through *agua-territorio* (water-territory) that relates territory to water not as equivalents but as part of an indivisible formation (Panez Pinto 2018) and in relation to feminist geography perspectives (Colectivo de Geografía Crítica del Ecuador 2018).

The third conceptual line of analysis on feminist territorialities in Latin America is the link between territory and gender-based violence, suggesting different narratives on territorialized violence. Latin America is home to some of the world's most violent spaces, including the highest homicide rates and the most dangerous cities in the world (Segato 2014). In this scenario, decolonial feminist scholar Rita Segato contends that the colonial relationship between bodies and territories persists, however, with contemporary forms of corporeal destruction producing *femi(geno)cidio* or femicide-genocide (Segato 2011, 2014). Also, following a colonial analysis of territory, Julieta Paredes (2008) equates sexual violence on the body of Indigenous women with the colonization of ancestral lands through the concept of *colonial penetration*. Territorialized gender-based violence is also depicted through a resurgence of social cartography and thematic mapping to denounce systemic gender-based violence, provoking new theorizations of geographies of gender-based violence, such as those concerning femicide and the criminalization of abortion (Zaragocin, Silveira, and Arazola 2018). Various feminist collectives in the region use thematic maps on gender-based violence to further their political and theoretical objective of drawing attention to the continuum of gender-based violence.

While feminist geography as a discipline is not (yet) institutionalized in Ecuadorian universities, feminist debates on territory have long existed in social activism and the peripheral spaces of Latin American academia. The three conceptual lines I mentioned concerning feminist spatialities in the region coexist but are just starting a dialogue that will hopefully be sustained into the future. What happens when feminist territorial debates in Latin America meet Anglocentric feminist geography traditions and emerging feminist geographies in the rest of Latin America? Who gets to be part of this conversation, and what are the implications of translating and placing these different intellectual traditions in dialogue? These questions add to the discomfort mentioned previously concerning the decolonization of feminist geography in the global South. Pursing feminist geography thinking and praxis in Ecuador has meant entering into dialogue with existing feminist debates on territory among activists and members of civil society and academics, across borders and disciplines. It has necessarily meant seeking out common praxis and dialogue.

In the winter of 2018, the syllabus for my course on feminist geography brought together the three strands of conceptual analysis. I could have produced a syllabus and taught solely from Anglophone literature, and therefore partaken in the production of Anglocentric knowledge construction of feminist geography. However, from a decolonial imperative to knowledge construction, I taught feminist geography from these three strands separately with methodological exercises meant to provoke conceptual linkages. During one particular class on social cartography of the body, I asked students to develop bodymaps that could depict both oppression and resistance from a transloca epistemology.

Four very different bodymaps were produced from distinct ontological notions of the body as territory, resulting from varying degrees of interconnectedness of the concepts covered in the course. The students and I marveled at seeing the four bodymaps produced reflecting distinct feminist geography perspectives and notions of Latin American territorial feminist debates. The first body map was considered by all to be reflective of a Western urban feminist geography and the last representative of *cuerpo-territorio*, where the lines blurred between space and corporeal experience based on the theoretical proposal of communitarian feminism (Cabnal 2010). The other two maps incorporated different elements of Anglocentric and Latin America feminist geography, as well as Latin American feminist debates on territory. Once the bodymaps were assembled and presented in class, we were able to dissect the different intellectual traditions embedded in them. My students and I considered the methodology decolonial; however, not all the maps were conceived with decoloniality in mind. These reflections were possible from the implementation of a transloca epistemology, suggestive of an important conceptual link between decoloniality and translocality that I further explore below.

DECOLONIALITY OR TRANSLOCALITY FOR FEMINIST GEOGRAPHY IN LATIN AMERICA?

Decolonizing geographical knowledges represents a problem space for geography (Jazeel 2017; Radcliffe 2017). As Tariq Jazeel (2017) has stated, decolonizing geographical knowledge is now every geographer's problem and no longer solely an issue belonging to postcolonial geography. Different accounts of accountability in geographical knowledge construction are at the heart of this discussion, which demands that all geographers acknowledge how their place of enunciation matters for the decolonization of the settler colonial project (Daigle 2018). The decolonial conversation that I am specifically proposing is not only with Anglocentric feminist geography in the global North, but it is also targeted to all those directly or indirectly involved in this theoretical discussion. Decolonizing geographical knowledge production means that we must be aware of the plurality of conversations occurring, even from spaces that do not consider themselves decolonial or part of the critical geography tradition. What I am suggesting is contrary to what several scholars have now shown to be a key feature of decolonization for geography, namely the recent emphasis on delinking the field from particular epistemological fronts, particularly Western, universalizing, and masculinist ontologies (Jazeel 2017; Noxolo 2017; Sundberg 2003). The Ecuadorian case characterized by openness to Anglocentric feminist geography and resistance toward *decolonial* feminist geography, amid rich feminist territorial debates in the region, suggests that new strategies and concepts should be deployed. This can happen without compromising the *decolonial process* of translocation, considering the course of action just as important as the theorized results out of these uncomfortable intimacies. As in the example above of four different body-maps resulting from a transloca epistemology, the methodology implemented was considered decolonial because it resulted from dialogue among different ontological perceptions of space, territory, and corporeal experiences. Only one body map was identified as decolonial, but all bodymaps resulted from a decolonized methodology invoked by a transloca epistemology. The students did not identify the three other bodymaps as decolonial, reflecting a process of geographical knowledge in which decolonial practices (not theory) are strongly tied to self-determination and intellectual sovereignty. In this way, translocation does not propose a total delinking from, but rather provokes articulations between, diverse place-based epistemologies, "linking geographies of power at various scales (local, national, regional, global) with subject positions (gender/sexual, ethno/racial, class, etc.) that constitute the self" (Lao-Montes and Bugg 2014). Therefore, the implementation of a transloca epistemology, which asked the students to position themselves as translocas in the construction of the bodymaps, resulted in decolonized methodologies. I suggest, then, that challenging Anglocentric feminist geography's dominant status lies somewhere between the delinking proposed in decolonizing geographical knowledge production and a counter-practice of translation found in translocation.

To challenge feminist geography's Anglocentricity does not imply solely disconnecting from dominant Western ontologies and creating knowledge *from* Indigenous, black, subaltern populations but also, through translocation, pluralizing the traffic between different place-based systems of thought. And while I applaud recent decolonization efforts in global centers of academic power, I urge geographers located primarily in these places to not assume that knowledge produced in the South is always decolonial. For example, despite the MCD's (Modernity, Coloniality, and Decoloniality group) intricate relationship to Latin America (Asher 2013), in some Latin American countries, these conceptual lines are sidelined. The decolonial turn in human geography and political ecology is severely limited in Latin America, as noted by several geographers in the region (Betancourt 2017). In this scenario, with different degrees and levels of decolonization in countries like Ecuador, where critical geography has not yet been institutionalized, a feminist geography canon needs to emerge through both translocation and decolonization processes, as has been proposed in terms of a Latin American politics of translation across the Americas (Alvarez 2014). Doing so resolves some of the risks involved in converging two or more systems of knowledge production. For starters, it obstructs the domestication of decolonial theory in Western academic spaces. A constant flow of transloca ideas, activities, and questions decenters epistemic trends and privileges within contained spaces. Allowing for a praxis in decolonial knowledge also places attention on decolonial place-based alternatives that are already occurring (Zaragocin 2018). The rich feminist debates on territory already under way in the region and briefly mentioned here need to represent a primary point of entry for the conversation between Anglocentric and Latin American feminist geographies. Intensified dialogue and theorizing *from* territorial feminist debates

in Latin America means bringing together floating commonalities and differences among feminist geographies in Latin America and beyond.

CONCLUSIONS

Anglocentric feminist geography's lack of engagement with non-Western notions of spatial identities and subaltern feminist politics is not new. The three
conceptual lines of feminist spatialities mentioned—Latin American feminist debates regarding territoriality, Anglocentric feminist geography, and an
emerging feminist geography in the region—confront both unequal and postcolonial flows of geographic knowledge production, as well as resistance to decolonial theory in many academic spaces outside of the global North. It is far
less complicated to transport an Anglocentric feminist geography to a country
like Ecuador, where the intellectual tradition has not existed. However, translocation of the field amid recent decolonization inquiries and existing decolonial feminist paradigms, such as those mentioned in this article, requires
an emphasis on the *decolonial process* of knowledge production. Translocation
allows for this. I have drawn on the use of a transloca epistemology, and my
own embodiment of the term, to show how scholars and activists can use
translocation to provoke decolonization in knowledge construction. It is in
generating disruptions of our place-based systems of knowledge, in that in-
determinacy of where we think and do feminist geography, that decolonization methods are most vital. This implies that we must also be open to the
possibility that decolonization be present in knowledge construction but not
in resulting theory.

In response to some of the questions posed in this chapter, I contend that
it is possible to decolonize Anglocentric feminist geography without decolonial
concepts, placing equal emphasis on the *process* as we often do on theoretical products. This also implies that, as geographers, we can embrace dynamics with the hope and end goal of decolonization of geographical knowledge
production, even under uncertain and uncomfortable theoretical encounters.
The epistemic privilege of certain feminist spatialities over others is, as Jazeel
(2017) mentions in relation to human geography and decoloniality, everyone's
problem space. The dialogue that is commencing among these feminist spatialities needs to ensure a decolonial process whereby the reproduction of theories
does not recreate colonial blind spots and inequalities in knowledge production. I have proposed one way of doing this through the delinking proposed
in decolonizing geographical knowledge production and a counter-practice of
translation.

NOTES

1.   Notable exceptions include Astrid Ulloa's work on territorial feminisms (2015, 2016). Ulloa groups some of the approaches mentioned above as territorial feminisms, defining them as "the territorial-environmental struggles that are led by indigenous, afro-descendant and peasant women, and that focus on the defense of the care of the territory, the body and nature, and in the criticism of development processes and extractivism . . . based on a vision of the continuity of life articulated in their territories" (Ulloa 2016). For Ulloa, extractivisms relate to the bodies-territories of women as processes of appropriation and dispossession.
2.   There is limited overlap in some places on feminist geography and feminist debates on territory. For example, Sara Smith's (2012) intimate geopolitics was recently highlighted in a manual on body-territory methodology produced by the Miradas Feministas sobre el Territorio Collective in Ecuador (2017).
3.   It is important to note that not all communitarian feminisms consider themselves decolonial. In a recent feminist studies conference in Ecuador, Lorena Cabnal narrated her experience prior to considering herself a feminist, and stated that she is going through a similar process with decoloniality.

REFERENCES

Ahmed, Sara. 2017. *Living a Feminist Life*. Durham, NC: Duke University Press.

Alvarez, Sonia. 2014. "Introduction to the Project and the Volume/Enacting a Translocal Feminist Politics of Translation." In *Translocalities/Translocalidades. Feminist Politics of Translation in the Latin/a Américas*, edited by Sonia Alvarez, Claudia de Lima Costa, Verónica Feliu, Rebecca Hester, Norma Klahn and Milie Thayer, 1–18. Durham, NC: Duke University Press.

Alvarez, Sonia, Claudia de Lima Costa, Verónica Feliu, Rebecca Hester, Norma Klahn, and Milie Thayer. 2014. *Translocalities/Translocalidades: Feminist Politics of Translation in the Latin/a Américas*. Durham, NC: Duke University Press.

Apter, Emily. 2007. *The Translation Zone: A New Comparative Literature*. Princeton, NJ: Princeton University Press.

Asher, Kiran. 2013. "Latin American Decolonial Thought, or Making the Subaltern Speak." *Geography Compass* 7: 832–42.

Betancourt Santiago, Milson. 2017. "Colonialidad territorial y conflictividad en Abya Yala/América Latina." In *Ecología Política Latinoamericana. Pensamiento crítico, diferencia latinoamericana y rearticulación epistémica,* edited by Héctor Alimonda, Catalina Toro Pérez, and Facundo Martín, 303–352. Ciudad Autónoma de Buenos Aires: CLACSO; México: Universidad Autónoma Metropolitana; Ciudad Autónoma de Buenos Aires: Ciccus.

Cabnal, Lorena. 2010. *Feminismos diversos: el feminismo comunitario*. Madrid: ACSUR-Las Segovias.

Colectivo de Geografía Crítica del Ecuador. 2018. *Geografiando por la Resistencia Feminista como práctica espacial*. Quito.

Costa, Claudia. 2004. "Feminismo, Traducao, Transnacionalismo." In *Poéticas e Políticas Feministas*, edited by Claudia de Lima Costa and Simone Pereira Schmidt, 187–96. Florianópolis: Mulheres.

Daigle, Michelle. 2018. "Embodying Relations of Accountability in Settler Colonial Contexts." In Lindsay Naylor, Michelle Daigle, Sofia Zaragocin, Margaret Marietta Ramirez, and Mary Gilmartin, "Interventions: Bringing the Decolonial to Political Geography." *Political Geography* 66: 199–209.

Espinal, Isabel. 2014. "El Incansable Juego/The Untiring Game: Dominican Women Writing and Translating Ourselves." In *Translocalities/Translocalidades: Feminist Politics of Translation in the Latin/a América*, edited by Sonia Alvarez, Claudia de Lima Costa, Verónica Feliu, Rebecca Hester, Norma Klahn, and Millie Thayer, 95–106. Durham, NC: Duke University Press.

Espinosa Miñoso, Yuderkys, Diana Gómez Correal, and Karina Ochoa Muñoz, eds. 2014. *Tejiendo de otro modo: Feminismo, epistemología y apuestas descoloniales en Abya-Yala*. Popayan: Universidad del Cauca.

Ibarra García, María Verónica, and Irma Escamilla-Herrera, eds. 2016. *Geografías feministas de diversas latitudes: Orígenes, desarrollo y temáticas contemporáneas*. México: Universidad Nacional Autónoma de México.

Jazeel, Tariq. 2017."Mainstreaming Geography's Decolonial Imperative." *Transactions of the Institute of British Geographers* 42: 334–37.

Jenkins, Kathy. 2015. "Unearthing Women's Anti-Mining Activism in the Andes: Pachamama and the Mad Old Women." *Antipode* 47 (2): 442–60.

Lan, Diana. 2016. "Los estudios de género en la geografía argentina." In *Geografías feminista de diversas latitudes: Orígenes, desarrollo y temáticas contemporáneas*, edited by María Verónica Ibarra García and Irma Escamilla Herrera, 55–71. México: Universidad Nacional Autónoma de México.

Lander, Eduardo. 2000. *La colonialidad del saber: Eurocentrismo y ciencias sociales*. Buenos Aires: CLACSO.

Lao-Montes, Agustin, and Mirangela Buggs. 2014. "Translocal Space of Afro-Latinidad: Critical Feminist Visions for Diasporic Bridge-Building." In *Translocalities/Translocalidades: Feminist Politics of Translation in the Latin/a Américas*, edited by Sonia Alvarez, Claudia de Lima Costa, Verónica Feliu, Rebecca Hester, Norma Klahn, and Milie Thayer, 381–400. Durham, NC: Duke University Press.

Lopez, Maria Fernanda, Andrea Robertsdotter, and Miriam Paredes. 2017. "Space, Power, and Locality: The Contemporary Use of Territorio." *Journal of Latin American Geography* 16 (1): 43–67.

Mignolo, Walter. 2000. *Local Histories/Global Designs*. Princeton, NJ: Princeton University Press.

Miradas Críticas del territorio desde el Feminismo. 2014. *La vida en el centro y el crudo bajo tierra. El Yasuní en clave feminista*. Quito, Ecuador.

Miradas Críticas del territorio desde el Feminismo. 2017. *Mapeando el Cuerpo-Territorio. Guía Metodológica para Mujeres Que Defienden Sus Territorios*. Quito: Abya-Yala.

Naylor, Lindsey, Michelle Daigle, Zaragocin Sofia, Margaret Marietta Ramirez, and Mary Gilmartin. 2018. "Interventions: Bringing the Decolonial to Political Geography." *Political Geography* 66: 199–209.

Nelson, Lise. 2016. "Geografía feminista anglosajona: Reflexiones hacia una geografía global." In *Geografías feministas de diversas latitudes: Orígenes, desarrollo y temáticas contemporáneas*, edited by María Verónica Ibarra García and Irma Escamilla Herrera, 21–54. México: Universidad Nacional Autónoma de México.

Noxolo, Patricia. 2017. "Decolonial Theory in a Time of the Recolonisation of UK Research." *Transactions of the Institute of British Geographers* 42: 342–44.

Panez Pinto, Alexander. 2018. "Agua-Territorio en América Latina: Contribuciones a partir del análisis de estudios sobre conflictos hídricos en Chile." *Rev. Rupturas* 8 (1): 201–24.

Paredes, Julieta. 2010. *Hilando Fino: desde el feminismo comunitario*. La Paz: Mujeres Creando Comunidad.

Quijano, Anibal. 2000. "Coloniality of Power, Ethnocentrism, and Latin America." *Neplanta* 1 (3): 533–80.

Radcliffe, Sarah. 2017. "Decolonising Geographical Knowledges." *Transactions of the Institute of British Geographers* 42: 329–33.

Ruales, Gabriela, and Sofia Zaragocin. Forthcoming. "De-géneros y territorio, ¿Tiene género el territorio?" In *Cuerpos, Territorios y Feminismos*, edited by Tania Cruz and Manuel Bayón. Quito: Abya-Yala e Instituto de Estudios Ecologistas del Tercer Mundo.

Silva, Maria Joseli, Marcio Jose Ornat, and Aldies Baptista Chimin Jr., eds. 2017. *Diálogos Ibero-LatinoAmericanos sobre geografías feministas e das sexualidades*. Uvaranas, Ponta Grossa: Todapalavra Editora.

Segato, Rita. 2011. "Femi-geno-cidio como crimen en el fuero internacional de los Derechos Humanos: el derecho a nombrar el sufrimiento en el derecho." In *Feminicidio en América Latina*, edited by Rosa Linda Fregoso and Cynthia Bejarano. México, DF: UNAM-CIIECH/Red de Investigadoras por la Vida y la Libertad de las Mujeres.

Segato, Rita. 2014. "Las nuevas formas de la guerra y el cuerpo de las mujeres." *Sociedad e Estado* 29 (2): 341–71.

Sharp, Joanne. 2009. *Geographies of Postcolonialism*. Los Angeles: Sage.

Smith, Sara. 2012. "Intimate Geopolitics: Religion, Marriage, and Reproductive Bodies in Leh, Ladakh." *Annals of the Association of American Geographers* 102 (6): 1511–28.

Sundberg, Juanita. 2003. "Masculinist Epistemologies and the Politics of Fieldwork in Latin Americanist Geography." *The Professional Geographer* 55 (2): 180–90.

Ulloa, Astrid. 2015. "La resistencia territorial en América Latina." *Perspectivas Latinoamericanas* 1: 39–42.

Ulloa, Astrid. 2016. "Feminismos territoriales en América Latina: Defensas de la vida frente a los extractivismos." *Nomadas* 45: 123–39.

Veleda da Silva, Susana, and Diana Lan. 2007. "Estudios de geografía del género en América Latina: un estado de la cuestión a partir de los casos de Brasil y Argentina." *Documents d'Analisi Geogràfica* 49: 99–119.

Veleda da Silva, Susana. 2016. "Geografías feministas brasileñas un punto de vista." In *Geografías feministas de diversas latitudes: Orígenes, desarrollo y temáticas contemporáneas*, edited by María Verónica Ibarra García and Irma Escamilla Herrera, 71–94. México: Universidad Nacional Autónoma de México.

Zaragocin, Sofia. 2017. "Feminismo decolonial y Buen Vivir." In *Feminismos y Buen Vivir: Utopias Descoloniales*. Cuenca: Universidad de Cuenca.

Zaragocin, Sofia. 2018. "Decolonized Feminist Geopolitics: Coloniality of Gender and Sexuality at the Centre of Critical Geopolitics." In Lindsay Naylor, Michelle Daigle, Sofia Zaragocin, Margaret Marietta Ramirez, and Mary Gilmartin, "Interventions: Bringing the Decolonial to Political Geography." *Political Geography* 66: 199–209.

Zaragocin, Sofia, Melissa Moreano, and Soledad Alvarez. 2018. "Presentación del dossier. Hacia una reapropiación de la geografía crítica en América Latina." *Iconos. Revista de Ciencias Sociales* 61: 11–32. http://dx.doi.org/10.17141/iconos.61.2018.3020.

Zaragocin, Sofia, Manuela Silveira, and Iñigo Arazola. 2018. "Hacia una Geografía del Femicidio en Ecuador." In *Appropiaciones de la ciudad: Género y Producción Urbana la reivindicación del derecho a la ciudad como práctica espacial*, edited by Maria Gabriela Navas Perrone and Muna Makhlouf de la Garza. Barcelona: Editorial Pollen.

CHAPTER 13

INTERVIEW WITH LATOYA EAVES, NOVEMBER 2018

Editors: In your remarks at the 2017 Feminist Geography Conference, you spoke of discomfort in two ways: as helpful for pushing us into new ways of thinking, and as how we come to understand that our bodies are not always welcome in certain spaces. Could you elaborate on these different ideas of discomfort? Do you see them as related? What is the role of discomfort in your own work? How do you work with discomfort when you actively work to create and hold space for others?

Eaves: Fundamentally, feminist inquiry draws attention to uncomfortable spaces. Having conversations about domination through exclusion and pushing for legibility in feminist and gendered spatial relations are central to redefining or providing relief to spatial discomforts. When I teach, I often draw attention to the everyday ways that people and structures resist yielding power. In other words, I teach how to analyze and deconstruct comfort.

Comfort is a primary factor in the maintenance of power, hierarchies, and structures of domination. Therefore, the origins of my thinking around the two areas of discomfort that you posed in the question, which are complementary, lie in interrogating the spaces of comfort. I find discomfort to be necessary to thinking and doing differently. At the most basic level, though, drawing attention to the spaces of discomfort is an insufficient mode of operation. Rather, the interrogation of comfort yields more revolutionary opportunities for feminist inquiry. Analyzing comfort shows where the boundaries of spaces are located, which yield the barriers to access or lack of welcome for our bodies in certain spaces. It also reveals complicity in hegemonic forms and the maintenance of political power.

In my own work, discomfort allows for renovating ideas about Black space and agency. Comfort is undergirded by dominant spatial practices, so to make

Black space legible—particularly queer Black space—transforms the hegemony of comfort. A dominant faculty of comfort is the use of separation and deterministic characteristics. I use discomfort to resist that enactment. I demand consideration of the roles and contributions of queer Black women in spatial production. I have found this is an uncomfortable analytical frame in geography, including among some supporters of my work and activism. This reality creates more urgency for analyzing bodies and spaces that are generally rendered ungeographic. I religiously adhere to the proverb "none of us are free until all of us are free." As such, it is imperative to hold space in the spaces of discomfort and build coalitions, which both troubles comfort and continuously draws attention to the revolutionary praxis of alliances.

Editors: Your scholarship engages and contributes to what often seem to be three subfields: queer geographies, Black geographies, and feminist geographies. Does it feel like there are distinct conversations in each of these subfields? What are the intersections, tensions, and divergences between them? How do you navigate the relations between these subfields, and how does this navigation shape your work?

Eaves: I think that is a fair assessment of where my engagements and contributions largely center. Yes, I do find there are some distinctions, which can give some difficulty when pursuing intellectual projects. The primary issue that I encounter surrounds the assumed limitations that tend to be imposed from one subfield to another. However, I argue that they have much to contribute in conversation with each other. Black, queer, and feminist disciplinary approaches provide critical inquiry of sociospatial interactions and allow for an interrogation of axes of power and structures, as they coincide and interrelate. Additionally, they contribute to a deeper and more nuanced knowledge of the local, which enhances an understanding of the intricacies of space and place. Further, I would argue that a discourse on space and place is incomplete if the variance of human attributes and their attendant nodes of spatial production are not fully considered. With only one facet of an individual space or place considered, the notion of knowledge is only a partial, deterministic one. To reiterate, the relationships between feminist, queer, and Black geographies are necessary and productive for their individual disciplinary philosophies on social life and human interactions in space and place. That might be the most exciting aspect of navigating all three discourses—by wrestling with the opportunities that they yield for intellectual and theoretical endeavors. The epistemologies of feminist geographies, Black geographies, and queer geographies have material implications. As such, I find that any prescription to these ideologies must be undertaken very carefully. And the union of these disciplinary frameworks in my empirical practice is important. They collectively formulate approaches that fundamentally resist space and place in hegemonic constructions. They disturb the structures that produce normative, essentialist notions of space and place and partial histories.

Editors: We have been very excited to see the development of the Black Geographies Specialty Group of the American Association of Geographers (AAG). Your work has been crucial to its emergence. How do you think the formation of this specialty group and its growing institutional strength will impact Black Geographies and a new generation of scholars? What key questions are driving scholars in the group now, and what do you hope for the future?

Eaves: I appreciate the excitement! The past couple of years have been both affirming and surreal. The surrealism comes from how quickly everything developed. I submitted the petition to the AAG for the Black Geographies Specialty Group (BGSG) in fall 2016, which was after spending a couple of years organizing sessions and conversations that developed during my doctoral program as well as creating the Black geographies reading list. At the time of the Feminist Geographies conference in May 2017, we had just held our first business meeting at the AAG meeting in Boston. A few months later, I was told that Black geographies would be a featured theme at the AAG 2018 meeting in New Orleans and was asked to select a cochair and committee. Needless to say, the past few years have been a whirlwind and the response has been overwhelming—in the most positive way.

The development of the BGSG has been very impactful for the discipline and for the new generation of scholars, which feels really odd to say given that I identify strongly with that category. Like I mentioned, Black geographies was one of three featured themes at the AAG 2018 annual meeting in New Orleans. Beyond that, a Black geographies symposium was held in October 2017. The Anti-Blackness in the American Metropolis symposium was held in November 2018. The special issue of *Southeastern Geographer* (Bledsoe et al. 2017) on Black geographies has been frequently cited in scholarly work and assigned in course syllabi. Lately, there have been postdoctoral and tenure-track positions specifically calling for Black geographies scholars. To reiterate, the past couple of years have escalated Black geographies into a formidable movement. I should note that I was also honored to work with a wonderful group of people in their formation of the Latinx Geographies Specialty Group. The BGSG and LGSG have become a support system and collaborators for each other, and I am excited about the future of Latinx geographies.

This movement has also made clear that scholars, both new and established, have been hungry for the type of spaces that Black (and Latinx) geographies create(s). I am consistently astounded by the volume of emails I receive from undergraduate students across the nation who are interested in shifting the perspective from "geographies of race" to Black geographies. There *is* a difference, which brings me to looking at the future and the key questions component. If you read the opening chapter to *Black Geographies and the Politics of Place*, you will find how Blackness has been positioned within the discipline—in broad, essentialist terms that are mapped onto reductionary spaces (McKittrick and Woods 2007). Black geographies resist the categorical mapping of difference and curate theoretical and empirical approaches to the production of space. These serve to renovate global worldviews and offer alternative geopolitical concerns. The future and the next generation will solidify the epistemological foundation of Black geographic thought and resist the definitive demarcations brought by "geographies of race."

Editors: At the conference you ended your panel remarks with a set of questions to yourself: "LaToya, have you set aside your methods and let the people's methods become the driving force of your work? Who have you talked to today, and did they have anything to do with academia? Have you made your work public? Where is your area of discomfort today, recognizing that you are working in a world that was never meant to accommodate you? Is this about you, or is this about everyone else?" We were deeply taken with these questions, and wanted to know how you arrived at them. Do you still ask yourself these questions today, or have they changed? How do they reflect your perspective that research is also part of your activism and your everyday life?

Eaves: Quite frankly, my questions arise out of observing and reflecting on my everyday life. I resist the idea that research is objective and disengaged. I argue instead that we are all complicit in the systems that dominate our lives, in some form or another. I say that because I often tell people that I exist in a liminal arena, constantly crossing back and forth between borders, networks, and communities. Gloria Anzaldúa's "ni de aquí, ni de allá" (neither from here nor from there) resonates strongly for me here. I live in a suburban neighborhood outside of Nashville. I work for a predominantly white, large public university in the United States Southeast. On our campus, Black faculty and faculty of color comprise less than 10 percent of who a student sees when they enter a classroom or walk into a department. The primary textbooks of the discipline are Eurocentric and colonial. I am active in the AAG, which is not dissimilar from working on my campus.

Then I go home to the community where I grew up and to my family members. There is a stark contrast between home and work for me, which is the first signal of my personal politics and motivations. I grew up in a predominantly Black neighborhood down the street from an old textile mill. The indigenous knowledges of the people in my small-town neighborhood—the ways they navigated, shifted, and produced space, institutions, and networks—represent an enduring set of lessons that are beautifully captured by Clyde Woods's blues epistemology (Woods 1998).

Of course, I am not alone in this experience. There are many Black and Brown folks who express similar experiences. I simply want to provide this context so that you can see where my work and that set of questions has its origins. They represent the ways I am grappling with how to settle my own sense of place and how I might enact them more broadly. This is my area of discomfort—being "ni de aquí, ni de allá." Because of my discomfort, I am more quickly drawn to how the world might be reshaped in order to expand into the liminality.

I try to spend time in the community as often as possible, whether it is attending church on Sunday mornings, eating at the Black-owned Jeff's Family Restaurant in my town, or by attending an event organized by the Nashville Feminist Collective. I have also intentionally shaped a regular social circle that does not include academics. These spaces become important for me because they help me survive the institution of higher education and geography while also pushing my research into a public collaborative liberation project.

Editors: As you mentioned in your remarks, intersectionality has become a buzzword of late, and even more so in the year since you spoke. How can we pursue intersectionality (drawing on Vivian May's work) that is reflective of lived experience, speaks to the effects of structures in our lives, and goes beyond the simple citational politics of *saying* intersectionality so you don't have to *do* intersectionality (to paraphrase from Ahmed's work on diversity)? In your presentation you said, "My research never stopped because it's my lived experience." How do you do intersectionality, and what does it look like?

Eaves: What I think Vivian May's *Pursuing Intersectionality, Unsettling Dominant Imaginaries* (2015) asks us to do is to avoid dilution and a misunderstanding of intersectionality. It seems to me that intersectionality has been far more utilized as a way to talk about a reductive category of gender, race, class, or sexuality. Meaning, it often seems the configurations of intersectionality seem to be less concerned with historical, institutionalized oppressions and their effects on one's identity mediations in society and more about an additive multiculturalism-style framework that operates to explain differences. But intersectionality is much more revolutionary, which my friend Caryl Nuñez and I took up in an unpublished paper responding to the question, What is intersectional about intersectionality now? When Crenshaw coined the concept (as it is often phrased), she was building on decades of Black women's organizing and critique. Interestingly, the concept itself mirrors what the Combahee River Collective called "identity politics." Keeanga-Yamahtta Taylor draws attention to the Combahee River Collective's "A Black Feminist Statement" and its impact by using identity politics:

> The CRC made two key observations in their use of "identity politics." The first was that oppression on the basis of identity—whether it was racial, gender, class, or sexual orientation identity—was a source of political radicalization. Black women were not radicalizing over abstract issues of doctrine; they were radicalizing because of the ways that their multiple identities opened them up to overlapping oppression and exploitation. Black women's social positions made them disproportionately susceptible to the ravages of capitalism, including poverty, illness, violence, sexual assault, and inadequate healthcare and housing, to name only the most obvious. These vulnerabilities also made Black women more skeptical of the political status quo and, in many cases, of capitalism itself. In other words, Black women's oppression made them more open to the possibilities of radical politics and activism. (Taylor 2017, 8)

My thinking aligns with what Taylor describes here in that, for me, intersectionality requires an interrogation of the "unmarked," which May discusses in her text. So rather than merely drawing attention to the nondominant identity markers, I insist on using it to dismantle the systems of oppression that mark nondominant conditions. In my view, intersectionality is supposed to cause discomfort. It draws attention to the ways we operate in domination, displacement, and oppression, which fundamentally shape how we produce space and enact agency. So in my everyday life, I am not just reminded of the systems of oppression at play in my lived experiences, but I also insist on ways to resist them and move toward the necessary dismantling of those systems.

REFERENCES

Bledsoe, Adam, LaToya Eaves, and Brian Williams. 2017. "Introduction: Black Geographies in and of the United States South." *Southeastern Geographer* 57 (1): 6–11.

May, Vivian M. 2015. *Pursuing Intersectionality, Unsettling Dominant Imaginaries*. New York: Routledge.

McKittrick, Katherine, and Clyde Woods, eds. 2007. *Black Geographies and the Politics of Place*. Toronto and Cambridge: South End Press.

Taylor, Keeanga-Yamahtta. 2017. *How We Get Free: Black Feminism and the Combahee River Collective*. Chicago: Haymarket Books.

Woods, Clyde Adrian. 1998. *Development Arrested: The Blues and Plantation Power in the Mississippi Delta*. London and New York: Verso.

CHAPTER 14

CALLING ALL COLLECTIVES: INTERVIEWS WITH FEMINIST GEOGRAPHY COLLECTIVES

The Feminist Coven at University of Kentucky; Great Lakes Feminist Geography Collective; Annie Elledge, Caroline Faria, Dominica Whitesell (the Feminist Geography Collective at University of Texas at Austin); Danya Al-Saleh and Elsa Noterman (Women in Geography University of Wisconsin–Madison); FLOCK University of North Carolina at Chapel Hill

At the 2017 Feminist Geography Conference held at the University of North Carolina at Chapel Hill, the Feminist Geography Collective at the University of Texas at Austin (UT Austin) proposed a session titled Calling All Collectives. Their call for papers invited potential participants to reflect on their experiences in forming feminist collectives within and across universities. These UT Austin geographers asked how feminist collectives can be maintained in geography departments as they also encouraged participants to reflect on the barriers that limit such organizing in university spaces. Building off this Feminist Geography Conference session, we invited four feminist geography collectives to complete open-ended interviews. Two of these collectives—the UT Austin Feminist Geography Collective and the Great Lakes Feminist Geography Collective—participated in the 2017 conference panel session. Members from the University of Kentucky's feminist coven and the Women in Geography (WIG) group at the University of Wisconsin–Madison who were also at the conference also contributed to this set of interviews.

In writing the questions for these interviews, we recalled our own experiences in FLOCK, a collective of graduate students and faculty members in

Geography at UNC Chapel Hill (of which all four of this book's editors are founding members). We hope each collective's careful reflections on their histories, motivations for organizing, and interventions aimed at both departments and universities can serve as a helpful guide for those considering organizing or joining a feminist geography collective, as well as for those already in such collectives. Responses attest to the difficulties of organizing and sustaining a space of cooperation within universities where established department routines often foreclose such forms of interaction. The collectives interviewed here publish together, edit one another's work, and organize workshops and colloquia hoping to foster more hospitable work places. They hold forums and conduct surveys within their departments to disclose those senses of discomfort, uneven divisions of labor, forms of harassment, and microaggressions that persist across and in geography departments. Such interventions aim to center the exclusionary legacies and barriers to success haunting academia and intentionally seek to counter the demobilizing refrain that "things [in the department] have gotten better." Other groups center ephemeral ethics of care and support and have no interest in formal institutionalization or recognition. Instead, they view their shared relations as capable of making demands that can challenge established norms and push the boundaries of our imagination beyond familiar solutions. These interviews reflect varied responses and maneuvers deployed in the face of difficult—and often hostile—institutions. All of these collectives levy explicit demands at their departments, universities, or the discipline of geography and aim to prefigure more caring, just, and attentive spaces through collaboration.

We start this section with interviews from the four collectives. We conclude with a reflective piece about our own experiences as members of the FLOCK collective at UNC Chapel Hill. In our own section, we recount the history of a zine created by FLOCK that traced histories of organizing for racial justice at UNC Chapel Hill. We use the zine project as a way to consider our own successes in collectively organizing but also to acknowledge the difficulties of maintaining collective cohesion and momentum as a group after we released the zine. The interviews reproduced here and FLOCK's story productively explore questions of accountability and intervention. As a cohesive section, we hope the interviews and FLOCK's story encourage geographers to consider the transformative potential, and limitations, of feminist cooperation within and beyond departments and universities.

THE FEMINIST COVEN AT UNIVERSITY OF KENTUCKY
Jess Linz and Araby Smyth

FLOCK: Can you provide us with some basic background on the feminist coven and its history? What were your initial intentions or aspirations for coming together?

Feminist Coven: The feminist coven is both a theoretical orientation and real relationships between graduate students. Practically speaking, it is an informal network of friends at the University of Kentucky and other campuses, and it is also the notion that as graduate students together we can alchemize our power in ways that resist our maligning in the patriarchal environment of the academy.

The feminist coven was not planned. We started referring to it in spring 2017. It has origins in previous experiments with autonomous feminist spaces both inside and outside the university. One of them, a group called Speeding Vaginas,* gathered woman-identified students across disciplines at the University of Kentucky for monthly parties. The coven is a zeitgeist that has been passed down through the spunky generations of feminists at the University of Kentucky. Feminist graduate students that came before us never shrank themselves. They are people who say what they think, take leadership roles, and mentor. They set precedent for the unruliness of the feminist coven.

The feminist coven is not a formal group that has regular meetings. It is not an institutionalized entity with a bank account or a student group number. It is amorphous and emergent, appearing when necessary. In an article we wrote, we describe it as "a pack, a band, a swarm: something admittedly imperfect itself, which carves spaces out of larger structures for alternative conventions to incubate" (Smyth, Linz, and Hudson 2020, 855). As such, we are not interested in individualized lean-in solutions, practical advice for making it, or the comforts of professionalization. Rather, the feminist coven is a call to our colleagues to ditch the individualized norms of the neoliberal university. These

---

* Woman-identified collective at University of Kentucky that was birthed out of reading *A Thousand Plateaus* and finding inspiration in the critique of lack in the following lines: "Physicists say that holes are not the absence of particles but particles traveling faster than the speed of light. Flying anuses, speeding vaginas, there is no castration" (Deleuze and Guattari, 1987, 32).

norms are rooted in the history of the university as a violent site of imperialism, racism, and patriarchy. Each day we hear about the gender and racial wage gap, depression among graduate students and recent grads, the precarity of students and contingent labor of adjuncts, and the scourge of sexual harassment in the academy. We see the potential for radical change in the networks of rebels that spring from different campuses. Rebels who speak out, demand alternative futures, act in creative new ways, and passionately defend each other. Our aspiration is to turn academia upside down. We envision and build a radically different future that ensures the mutual flourishing of our fellow friends and colleagues.

We call ourselves a coven because we are conjuring both the caring and threatening energy of witches. During the feudal era before capitalism, witches were key people who held knowledge about women's reproductive health. Their spells were a form of extralegal power when marginalized people lacked the right to adjudication. Witches were perceived as a threat to the emergence of capitalism and patriarchy. Therefore, the witch hunts punished witches, disciplined women's bodies, and ultimately were a part of the move to capitalism that confined women to reproductive work (Federici 2004). We call ourselves a coven because we fiercely care for our fellow graduate students who subvert the university with their bold actions, and in doing so we pose a threat to the neoliberal university.

FLOCK: How have conversations or interventions changed over time? At what level or site have your conversations or interventions been directed (your home department, the university more broadly, the publishing industry)? Can you reflect on the successes and limitations of those organizing efforts, conversations or interventions?

Feminist Coven: Our interventions are directed at people in the university. We seek conversations with students across departments and between students and faculty, staff, and the administration. For example, we encourage each other to speak out in seminar, mentor younger students, scheme new formats for social events. We nominate each other for awards, hold our ground on demanding that known sexual harassers be removed from syllabi, bring up #MeToo in department meetings and with guest speakers, push within the department and the college for more trans- and child-friendly environments, wage campaigns to decolonize the canon, fight for increased graduate student wages across departments, and call out whiteness in higher education.

Being bold in this way takes a great deal of courage and a bit of audacity, so we recognize that to cultivate those feelings in an austere and competitive environment, we need one another. We cultivate the strength and gumption to do all of this by affirming each other, sending each other goofy GIFs and memes in digital communication, throwing dance parties with bonfires, driving out to the countryside to watch the full moon rise, and orchestrating primal screams in each other's backyards and on campus when we just want to explode. The interstitial and collective spaces of these practices conjure the glue that holds us together to be powerful and confident when we make uncomfortable assertions to our superiors and colleagues. The care we practice on each other emanates through the difficult things we say. Our bite is infused with our love for each other and our hope that academia can be otherwise. Through these practices, our orientations to one another cut through the invasive fear and scarcity that plague us, and we envision this also changing the structures that enclose us.

FLOCK: What are some of the challenges to forming and sustaining a collective space in the university? How do you maintain this space and ensure continuity?

Feminist Coven: The work of the feminist coven is challenging, imperfect, and situated in this time and space, for competition is seductive and no collective space is ever completely inclusive. Resisting the disciplining forces of professionalization requires nimble creativity and an ever-changing configuration of autonomous space making. Therefore, despite everything we are building, we are not trying to establish an institutional version of the feminist coven. We want to be a force that can warp the institution, not impose permanent structures. We do not anticipate that the feminist coven will even necessarily still exist when this book is published, but we do expect that it will have left its traces on the University of Kentucky and beyond, and made new openings for some other formation to emerge in its stead. The coven is an opening that's been made by different people at different times. It has had various manifestations through its genealogy, and while it may feel right for the current moment, we don't anticipate that groups of students that follow will have the same needs. With the change in contexts, the pressure to create permanent structures (even if they are radical) is unhealthy for the vitality of the community bearing those burdens. Therefore, we resist the temptation to aim at permanence. There is beauty and power in ephemerality, and we will not fight for the continuity of the feminist coven in this particular configuration—for becoming part of the university, becoming watered down, means death.

FLOCK: Have there been particular texts that you all have read together?

Feminist Coven: The short answer to this question is no, and the exception is that we held one formal reading group in 2017 of Sara Ahmed's *Living a Feminist Life*. However, there are other readings that circulate among us, which people have read or have a working knowledge of, due to the way that they appear in conversations among us. A considerable number of us read articles in *LIES: A Journal of Materialist Feminism* last year, and other common texts include *The Managed Heart, Caliban and the Witch, Joyful Militancy,* and *This Bridge Called My Back.* The Speeding Vaginas came directly out of a line from Deleuze and Guattari's (1987) *A Thousand Plateaus,* and this book certainly inflects many of our members' politics. One text that comes from our immediate context and which shaped the emergence of this coven is "Not Everyone has (the) Balls" by Carrie Mott and Sue Roberts (2014). That text cast a spell over the University of Kentucky, giving us the clearance to be a bit unacceptable and witchy.

FLOCK: Can you offer additional advice to existing feminist geography collectives or those looking to form them in the future?

Feminist Coven: We are charged by the idea that the time for benevolence is over: "The goddess is not doing it anymore. The trial is coming to an end. The grace period is slowly drawing to a close. The queen is about to move on the chess board" (Teish 1981, 255).

Our first piece of advice is to throw out the rule book. Abandon the definition of appropriate behavior in the university. Be loud and disruptive when your voice is not heard. The time for patience and practicality has passed; it is time to be hideous, to make impractical demands, to shift the expectations and shift the whole structure. "We must be loud enough to expose the secrets of our departments and institutions, and strong enough to protect the speakers" (Smyth, Linz, and Hudson 2020, 874).

Our second piece of advice is to reimagine and prioritize care, friendship, and solidarity. It is so easy to be fractured. Especially in disciplines that practice fieldwork, graduate school builds and breaks relationships, and loneliness and depression thrive. To this we say: do everything you can to be connected. Conjure trust where you only seem to find suspicion. Listen to one of our contributors, who suggests falling in love with your best friends and then figuring out what an unconventional relationship like that looks like. Be stubborn and banish isolation and loneliness with collectivity. Back each other up and hex naysayers: gatekeeping against illegible care and labor fractures trust.

And while you're at it, have a fucking blast! As our rebellious acts subvert the university, find strength in the solidarity of new forms of friendship. Make spaces to feel, to step out of the race, to relax. Lean into the awkwardness of being around other people until it breaks through. Laugh at each other's jokes. #actlikeyouknow until you know. "Stop comparing yourself to other people" (personal communication with Roberts, 2019). Ask what new ways of being can emerge from the in-between spaces of our everyday actions right now. If you wait too long 'til after the work is done or the position secured, it will have come and gone so take a breath. Grab your friend. Blur your eyes until you see it!

Suggested Readings

Ahmed, Sara. 2017. *Living a Feminist Life*. Durham: Duke University Press Books.

Bergman, Carla, Nick Montgomery, and Hari Alluri. 2017. *Joyful Militancy: Building Thriving Resistance in Toxic Times*. Chico: AK Press.

Deleuze, Gilles, and Felix Guattari. 1987. *A Thousand Plateaus: Capitalism and Schizophrenia*. Minneapolis: University of Minnesota Press.

Federici, Silvia. 2004. *Caliban and the Witch: Women, the Body and Primitive Accumulation*. Brooklyn: Autonomedia.

Hochschild, Arlie Russell. 2012. *The Managed Heart: Commercialization of Human Feeling*. Berkeley: University of California Press.

LIES: A Journal on Materialist Feminism. https://www.liesjournal.net/.

Moraga, Cherrie, and Gloria Anzaldúa, eds. 1981. *This Bridge Called My Back: Writings by Radical Women of Color*. Berkeley: Third Woman Press.

Mott, Carrie, and Susan M. Roberts. 2014. "Not Everyone Has (the) Balls: Urban Exploration and the Persistence of Masculinist Geography." *Antipode* 46 (1): 229–45. https://doi.org/10.1111/anti.12033.

Smyth, Araby, Jess Linz, and Lauren Hudson. 2020. "A Feminist Coven in the University." *Gender, Place & Culture* 27 (6): 854–80. https://doi.org/10.1080/0966369X.2019.1681367.

Teish, Luisa. 1981. "O.K. Momma, Who the Hell Am I? An Interview with Luisah Teish." In *This Bridge Called My Back: Writings by Radical Women of Color*, edited by Cherrie Moraga and Gloria Anzaldúa, 247–59. Berkeley: Third Woman Press.

GREAT LAKES FEMINIST GEOGRAPHY COLLECTIVE

Emily Billo, Winifred Curran, Roberta Hawkins, Beverley Mullings, Alison Mountz, Kate Parizeau, Margaret Walton-Roberts, and Risa Whitson

FLOCK: Can you provide us with some basic background on the Great Lakes Feminist Geography Collective and its history? What were your initial intentions or aspirations for coming together?

Great Lakes Collective: The Great Lakes Feminist Geography Collective emerged from an *Antipode*-sponsored regional workshop organized by Alice Hovorka, Alison Mountz, and Roberta Hawkins. The workshop, which hosted approximately twenty-five people, was designed to bring feminist geographers from both sides of the Canada–US border in the Great Lakes region together to meet for two days in Guelph, Ontario, in May 2013. Participants included tenured and tenure-track faculty, postdoctoral fellows, and faculty on limited-term contracts. The organizers hoped that the workshop would facilitate a cross-border network of scholars designed to foster support and collaboration. The initial idea for this gathering and the network was to counter the isolation that critical feminist scholars and marginalized people often experience in their own departments and universities.

During the workshop, the group decided to form the Great Lakes Feminist Geography Collective and move forward with various projects. One of the reasons that we think the workshop culminated in the forming of a collective was due to its structure. It was very loosely structured, modeled on the "unconference" that organizers had read about online. No one presented their research or anything formal. Instead, participants agreed on discussion topics of importance over email in the weeks before the workshop. Topics included teaching, work/life balance, mental health in the academy, and research challenges. People were then assigned topics to talk about for a few minutes each. Participants were also asked to take turns chairing sessions. Organizers also scheduled generous amounts of informal time for meals, snacks, and networking/socializing so that people reported feeling rejuvenated instead of exhausted at the end of the two days.

The last part of the workshop involved brainstorming future projects in small groups. Before leaving, people signed up to the projects they were interested in working on. These could be papers, conference presentations/panels, or activist interventions, etc. From there, we moved to an email list where group members could coordinate different projects. Some tangible things came out of this, like the paper on slow scholarship (Mountz et al. 2015); several international conference sessions and a special issue on mental health in the academy organized by collective members (Mullings, Peake, and Parizeau 2016; Parizeau et al. 2016), as well as the formation of the American Association of Geographers (AAG) Task Force on Mental Health; activist postcards handed out at the 2014 AAG; and a paper on feminist mentoring currently being written by yet another collective-within-the-collective. The collective remains loosely structured. Members use the listserv to propose projects or interventions, and different members choose to participate as they are able and interested.

FLOCK: How have conversations or interventions changed over time? At what level or site have your conversations or interventions been directed (your home department, the university more broadly, the publishing industry)? Can you reflect on the successes and limitations of those organizing efforts, conversations, or interventions?

Great Lakes Collective: Recently, several of us met at the 2017 AAG annual meeting, with another small group meeting at the 2017 annual meeting of the Canadian Association of Geographers. Upon reflection, we agreed that it seems the collective has continued on with a focus on three main issues: mental health and well-being, feminist critical questioning of labor processes, and witnessing and calling out around issues of underrepresentation, silence, and absence (i.e., who is not here—a conversation that opened the workshop and continues as we write). This does not mean that interests are limited to these areas, but that—organically, in the spirit of the collective's initial formation—these have remained a focus of ongoing collaborative work.

We have tried interventions at a variety of scales, in various iterations, and with various members of the collective, from distributing postcards listing statistics about the gender breakdown of geography at the AAG, to the collectively written articles on slow scholarship in ACME (Mountz et al. 2015) and the "Breaking the Silence" special issue in the *Canadian Geographer* (Parizeau et al. 2016) that reflected many of the issues that arose in our original workshop. The process of writing that article forced many of us to interrogate the ways in which we don't always follow our own advice when it comes to responding to the accelerating pace of academic work. This, in turn, led us to look at the ways we could bring slow scholarship to our departments and students, as well as our own practices. For those of us in positions with some degree of power, such as department chairs or graduate directors, we feel a deep responsibility to try to bring slow scholarship into being in a substantive way.

We feel that our interventions have been successful in raising awareness of critical issues currently facing the discipline and the academy. The sessions and writing on mental health have resulted in increased awareness in the discipline around this issue, and its institutionalization through the development of a listserv to discuss mental health in academia (MHGEOG-L@lists.queensu.ca), the AAG Task Force on Mental Health in Geography, and its recent proposal to establish a standing Committee on the Status of Mental Health in Geography. Authors of articles in "Breaking the Silence" learned recently that several of their papers on wellness, well-being, and mental health counted among the top twenty downloads from the journal in recent years. Similarly, the paper on slow scholarship has had enormous readership in geography and outside of the discipline, which, according to both our experience and the communications that we have received, has prompted conversations, workshops, and colloquia both within and beyond the universities and countries where we are based. Another outcome of the collective is that it has allowed many of our members to expand the focus of their published work, creating space for those who identify personally as feminist geographers, but whose job description and previous research did not necessarily reflect this, and encouraging them to more explicitly engage in what is feminist about their research. So while our whole collective has not yet been able to reconvene in person, it has continued to work in different formats and at different scales.

One thing we did strategically was to write about our collective. We wrote a report for *Antipode* and a report for the Geographic Perspectives on Women and Canadian Women and Geography specialty group meetings and newsletters. We also funneled some of our funding to the first Feminist Geography conference, which was held in Nebraska in 2014, and held a workshop on strategies of resistance based on the slow scholarship paper. This event was very well received by attendees, who were energized by the opportunity to share their experiences and collectively develop strategies of resistance to the neoliberal and corporatist practices emerging at their institutions. Reaching out and (where possible) supporting other groups/institutions and getting our name out there is one way that we were able to gain some sort of legitimacy—for example, to link our work on tenure and promotion applications to newsletter pieces. This is one way to make this feminist organizing work visible beyond the publications that emerged from our collective.

FLOCK: What are some of the challenges to forming and sustaining a collective space in or across universities? How do you maintain this space and ensure continuity?

Great Lakes Collective: There are some opportunities built into our loose structure; not everyone is committed to participation, and clusters can form loosely around specific issues of interest. But this structure also poses a number of challenges.

Leadership is a critical challenge in a context in which there is no formal organizational structure. Some initiatives have been proposed (monthly writing support group, and writing for more popular audiences, for example) that have not been followed up on because while people have expressed interest, no one has been able to take the lead in organizing. This was not the case with the projects that came directly out of the workshop (where leaders did emerge), but seems to be more of an issue with ongoing or new initiatives.

Another main challenge from an organizing perspective is how to grow the network. Because the collective was formed from a face-to-face meeting, a lot of rapport was built. A specific challenge related to growing the network involved the establishment, maintenance, and membership of a listserv. For some time, we did not add anyone to our listserv who had not been at the workshop, even if they lived in the region, because they did not know the group and the group did not know them. We had established rapport and trust that enabled political projects and discussions to unfold across a closed list. This was of course exclusionary. We decided to try to address this problem by asking any feminist geography faculty in the region interested in joining the listserv to just introduce themselves. However, there continue to be questions around the size of the collective and its makeup. Right now, it is narrowly comprised of people in faculty positions (not all permanent), but no students. We have had discussions over the years about how to involve students and enlarge the network. This has happened informally at conference meetings at the AAG and CAG, but we have collectively resisted a desire to formalize any kind of belonging to the network. Yet at the same time, the loose nature of the collective has been an advantage, in that it has been able to work openly and morph in some ways into new forms/groups as needed to address issues raised in the original workshop (mentioned above).

A third challenge is how to meet again. The workshop happened five years ago now, and a face-to-face, dedicated meeting (not one happening in the cracks and crevices of the AAG or CAG) would be ideal and exciting to revisit conversations five years on. Many of us have not been able to see each other face-to-face in some time. Resources in the form of time and money are the key challenge here. Without regular meetings or contact, it takes one or more people to initiate projects or ideas and others to join. Sometimes it is hard to keep that momentum going without face-to-face interaction.

One of the strategies that the mental health group has employed to maintain momentum and to ensure continuity is to schedule meetings and conference sessions at events that we tend to attend anyway, such as the AAG and CAG annual meetings or at feminist geography conferences. These sessions are often loosely structured and informal, allowing us to block off time in our event calendars to dedicate to this topic, but also to show up and be together without too many expectations of preparatory work.

FLOCK: Have there been particular texts that you all have read together?

Great Lakes Collective: While we have not organized formal reading groups, those of us who have written together have sometimes suggested texts for the collaborative to read in order to inform our collective writing. Among the works that have gotten us thinking and writing collectively are Harriet Hawkins's reflections on mentoring and self-care (2018), the series on women and power in the academy in the *Chronicle of Higher Education*, and just about anything by Sara Ahmed.

FLOCK: Can you offer additional advice to existing feminist geography collectives or those looking to form them in the future?

Great Lakes Collective: Do it. The very fact of the collective has proven meaningful and sustaining to us, even if the goals and outcomes have not always been set in advance. There will invariably be some bumps and tensions along the way, but we have so much to learn from each other, and, for many of us, the ability to draw upon the expertise and empathy of other like-minded academics has been one of the best experiences in our professional lives. It helps to combat the isolation that is too often a feature of academic work, and is particularly useful for understanding our own struggles within a larger context. Similarly, for those of us who work in departments that do not explicitly recognize a feminist approach or for those of us who were not hired to teach feminist geography classes, the collective offers an important network and informal space to exchange ideas and remain committed to the goals of advocacy and action through a collaborative approach.

For those of us who were in the early stages of our career, the collective was a particularly important space, as it enabled us to listen to and learn with more senior colleagues. For this reason, we would advocate for collectives that span student, faculty, and research positions and that continue to call attention to processes of marginalization in the academy. While not all of us continue to hold current faculty positions within the region, we continue to draw on connections with the collective as a foundation for professional support.

For those of us considered "midcareer," the two-day event also provided the opportunity to reflect and engage in important, needed conversations about the work that we do. This was both rejuvenating and inspiring, realizing what a collective can accomplish in two days, and what seeds might be planted for unknown outcomes and collectives that emerged in the months and years to come.

Suggested Readings

Chronicle of Higher Education. n.d. "The Awakening: Women and Power in Academia."
    Accessed August 2, 2018. https://www.chronicle.com/interactives/the-awakening.
Hawkins, Harriet. 2018. "On Mentoring: Reflections on Academic Caring as Feminist
    Practice. Gender and Feminist Geographies Research Group." Accessed August 2, 2018.
    http://www.gfgrg.org/on-mentoring-reflections-on-academic-caring-as-a-feminist
    -practice-by-harriet-hawkins/
Mountz, Alison, Anne Bonds, Becky Mansfield, Jenna Loyd, Jennifer Hyndman, Margaret
    Walton-Roberts, Ranu Basu, Risa Whitson, Roberta Hawkins, Trina Hamilton, and
    Winifred Curran. 2015. "For Slow Scholarship: A Feminist Politics of Resistance through
    Collective Action in the Neoliberal University." *ACME, International E-Journal for Critical
    Geographies* 14 (4): 1235–59.
Mullings, Beverly, Linda Peake, and Kate Parizeau. 2016. "Cultivating an Ethic of Wellness in
    Geography." *The Canadian Geographer/Le Géographe canadien* 60 (2): 161–67.
Parizeau, Kate, Laura Shillington, Roberta Hawkins, Farhana Sultana, Alison Mountz,
    Beverly Mullings, and Linda Peake. 2016. "Breaking the Silence: A Feminist Call to
    Action." *The Canadian Geographer/Le Géographe Canadien* 60 (2): 192–204.

FEMINIST GEOGRAPHY COLLECTIVE AT UT AUSTIN

Annie Elledge, Caroline Faria, and Dominica Whitesell

FLOCK: Can you provide us with some basic background on the Feminist Geography Collective at UT Austin and its history?

Feminist Geography Collective at UT Austin: Our collective brings together faculty, graduate, and undergraduate students from within and beyond the discipline of geography. We strive to foster healthy and vibrant academic spaces for women, and particularly women of color, to engage in feminist geographic research. We are not the most radical a feminist collective can be. We have found ourselves working within the neoliberal constraints of the discipline as a strategy to survive, thrive, and support one another. However, we do have a broader vision of a more just discipline. For us, the journey there centers a feminist practice where mentorship and research are inseparable, and where students are sheltered from, can thrive within, and are supported to challenge the racisms, sexisms, and other structural violences of the discipline.

Dominica: In terms of how we work, we have always viewed research and mentoring as inseparable. Peer mentoring operates across career stages and is based on our different skills and experience. Caroline took the lead at first in guiding us on grant writing, fieldwork, and publishing. I mentored Annie on writing her first literature review, presenting at conferences, and now applying to grad school. As we grew, she started to mentor new undergrads in writing AAG abstracts, developing projects, making posters, and conducting more basic research work. Stuff I had taught her, and Caroline had taught me. Now as new members join, and as we each learn new skills, we all start to mentor more junior members down the line.

Annie: But while we do tend to mentor "down" in this way, we want to also stress the multilateral flows of knowledge. More junior members have brought skills in web design, popular writing, archive development, and critical cartography, and they have taken the lead in teaching us. Those contributions have extended the scope of our work dramatically and in exciting ways. We try to each value our own unique and diverse skill sets, areas of expertise, and embodied experiences, using them to strengthen the group as a whole. We feel this is essential both to the success of the collective and to the depth and rigor of the work. We always stress the collaborative nature of our work, and we make sure to credit our members and the wider group. We celebrate each other's successes as our own.

FLOCK: What were your initial intentions or aspirations for coming together?

Dominica: For me they feel very basic: we loved our work and we wanted, *needed*, to build a feminist community. Folks in UT geography are doing important work with social justice implications, but we were reaching out to faculty in women's and gender studies, sociology, English, and elsewhere to have explicitly feminist conversations. We wanted to make a home for ourselves in our department and to build a community of feminist geographers at the undergraduate, graduate, and faculty levels. Caroline had tried recruiting new feminist graduate students and faculty, but it was challenging. Feminist work is still too often met with suspicion, misunderstood, seen as too "political" or not rigorous enough. We learned that there are so many structural challenges around faculty and graduate recruitment. After a few years trying, we needed another strategy. We knew there were fantastic undergraduates at UT and that many women (in particular) longed for feminist spaces. So we decided to start there, to build from within.

Caroline: Before we formed the collective, I had no experience with research "labs" as such. I did most of my research alone up to that point or co-wrote with close colleagues and friends. And while I had always taken a very hands-on role in mentoring students, this was usually done on a one-on-one basis. It was rewarding, and remains central to my work, but as we know it is emotional labor and incredibly time-consuming. It is also largely unrecognized and devalued labor (in terms of metrics for tenure and promotion) that women and minority faculty spend many more hours on. Like many similar institutions, UT is affected by the same neoliberal shifts many of us are experiencing, and the promotional pressures to publish are intense. While my research and mentoring work has always been intertwined, in the past my mentoring-based relationships rarely led to publications or other "outputs." And that was fine. But in 2015 I started to realize the tenure requirements were going to be more demanding. And I also had my son. Juggling publishing, my commitment to mentoring and quality teaching, and being part of his life was hard. Of course, this is a familiar story for anyone caring for family or friends, and again this is work disproportionately done by women. It is a work model that is unsustainable and unhealthy, as feminist geographers and others have been telling us for a while now (Berg, Huijbens, and Larsen 2016; Caretta et al. 2018; Hawthorne and Meché 2016; Mountz et al. 2015; Peake and Mullings 2016). The tenure and promotion statistics for women, and particularly women of color, are bleak—at UT and across geography as a discipline (Kobayashi 2006, 2007; Kobayashi, Lawson, and Sanders. 2014; Sanders 2006). I knew I needed a healthier way to work. To share the mentoring labor out, and also to create a supportive feminist space for research.

Dominica and Annie: Definitely one of the unexpected insights of the collective is that we have developed empathy for how power works and disciplines us differently across the life course. As students, we now see that, as you move along in your career, things actually get busier, the pressures get more intense, the responsibilities for others and the juggling get crazier. And for Caroline, I think she is more aware of the intense pressures students today are under. It might seem naive, but that was not something we really understood before. That empathy brings a sense of responsibility to care for one another, including for Caroline. We understood that in being there for one another as students, we were easing the burden on her. In doing that caring work, we created this space of encouragement and affirmation that had been so difficult to find on such a large university campus. We made a space where we, as women, could get hands-on research experience, share our ideas, and connect with others excited by feminist approaches. The opportunity to be mentored and to mentor others provided us with the confidence and support necessary to thrive within the discipline and outside of it.

Caroline: Reading our words, of course it is clear that despite the different career and life stages we are at, our experiences all speak to the structural violences that remain so prevalent in academic and wider life: the devaluation of care work, the uneven work of mentoring, the neoliberal metrics of success that widen racial, class, and gender divides, and the trivialization of feminist work, and of women's ideas, that can lead us to work harder and think less of ourselves. The collective was a space for us to do the work that we found nourishing, exciting, and fun, that shielded us from, to paraphrase Minelle Mahtani (2014), the "toxicities" of academia.

FLOCK: How have conversations or interventions changed over time?

Caroline: Most notably, our collective has adjusted to build an explicitly antiracist feminist space. Our projects and our praxis demand that racial power is unveiled and confronted. However, during our first year we struggled with racial justice, both in small, everyday discussions about the racial makeup of our peers and departments, and in broader conversations around systemic inequality. While passionate about feminist ethics of care and mentorship, we weren't attentive enough to the ways we ourselves perpetuated systems of racial violence. One way we saw that was in our recruitment. Our first round of recruiting was informal and primarily focused on geography and international relations/government students that Dominica and Annie knew. We had fantastic new recruits, and they all identified as white. Even though we thought of ourselves as *critical* scholars, our lack of explicit attention to race and power during the recruitment reproduced the overwhelming whiteness of our respective disciplines (Berg 2012; Faria, Henderson, and Torres 2018; Kobayashi 2006).

Annie: We met to reflect and collected some useful resources on building diversity in academia. We decided to respond through our messaging on the website and in our next recruitment drive. Extending our reach beyond geography, we strategically reached out to and recruited from more diverse departments and programs such as the Center for Women's and Gender Studies, the African and African diaspora department, the Teresa Lozano Long Institute of Latin American Studies, and the Middle Eastern studies department. We created a more formal application "advert" that specifically encouraged scholars of color to apply and asked applicants to talk about their commitments to antiracist and feminist work. We also sought to make our collective more inclusive (and antiracist) by ensuring that members either receive academic credit and/or financial compensation for their work. We try to work with various work schedules and provide compensation for, say, our end-of-semester dinners and research trips to ensure that students are not inhibited by funds, which is often (though not always, of course) a concern for minority students. As a direct result of these efforts, our collective is now actually majority minority at each career stage. And we are now more deliberate about creating a space that is not dominated by white bodies and norms of whiteness (not always but often the same). This is an important step to ensuring that the future of geography is inclusive, innovative, and better reflective of our world.

Dominica: This shift in our membership and our more deliberately intersectional approach has dramatically shaped our discussions, the work we do, and the questions we ask more broadly. It forces us to constantly reflect on and be attentive to intersectional systems of power. In the process, we have become better equipped to *recruit, support, and retain* scholars of color. In our most recent end-of-semester reflection, our newer members each remarked on how the collective transformed their perception of geography as they gradually felt more space and support. Our collective is in a constant process of learning and unlearning, and while we have much work still to do to make our collective racially and socially just, we are excited and proud of the progress we have made.

FLOCK: At what level or site have your conversations or interventions been directed (your home department, the university more broadly, the publishing industry)? Can you reflect on the successes and limitations of those organizing efforts, conversations or interventions?

Dominica: We strive for visibility as a way to build communities within and outside of our university. Though it sometimes felt like we were talking to ourselves (not at all a bad thing), we were also in conversation with our department, college, university, and wider discipline. Ranging from publicly announcing our successes on departmental blogs to presenting our work in various college-wide research competitions and publishing in geography journals, we strategically engaged on multiple scales to survive and thrive within the context of hostilities, fear, suspicion, and/or misunderstandings around feminist work.

Annie: Caroline has pushed us to be proud of and vocal about our work and success. So often women are told to keep quiet in the name of modesty. Forget that. We wanted to see and be seen at UT and in the discipline as geographers.

We deliberately meet in a glass-walled room in the middle of the department. We make visible the awards, honors, and grants we earn. We encourage each collective member to present a poster of their original research at AAG. We put our posters up in the walls of our department and in the corridors that lead to it. We post news items about our achievements to our departmental website, include reference to the collective in any public-speaking opportunities, give conference talks about our work, and have started to write articles and give other kinds of public interviews about our work. In addition to showcasing what feminist research can look like, we have adopted this hypervisible model in order to affirm and make overt our place within geography.

Caroline: We are starting to sound a bit colonial! But there is another motivation too. We hope that this visibility will further encourage people who might not have been attracted to the discipline (and particularly women of color) to consider classes, doctoral tracks, and careers in the field. The visibility makes it possible for the discipline to be remade for and invigorated by women and women of color. It challenges the whiteness of the discipline in healthy and disruptive ways. But it has to be meaningful, and I think it is. Several of our new members have already said they learned about and began to consider the university and department because they came across our website. We certainly recognize that not all collectives want to be visible, invisibility can be protective. But for us, advertising the collective and our success has allowed us to gain recognition for our work, to carve out some space for ourselves. And it has encouraged students to *see themselves* in the discipline and to join us. We feel it is vital to re-present and reimagine geography to the world and to one another.

FLOCK: Have there been particular texts that you all have read together?

Caroline: Finding common intellectual ground at the start is so important, but it has been hard. Most students are not coming in as geographers and if they are they have very little, if any, feminist foundations. At the start we had students reading sections of my NSF proposal alongside Dominica's undergraduate thesis. We paired this with Gillian Rose's *Visual Methodologies* (2016) and Mountz and Hyndman's "Feminist Approaches to the Global Intimate" (2006) so that students could learn more about the foundations and methodologies of our approach. These did give a crash course in the basic theory and methods we were working with, and the empirical details of the field site, but it was a very narrow introduction of what feminist geography is/can be. It was also a lot of reading and maybe a bit advanced for the students. We've re-thought that a lot. Now we introduce the projects to members ourselves and, maybe twice a semester, integrate in a reading or lecture to discuss together.

Dominica: As the political scope of the collective became clearer—challenging academia's racist and sexist violences—we have started to more deliberately share, reference, and watch antiracist feminist work. As such, our new reading list includes the former pieces and expands upon them by incorporating more work that specifically speaks to racial power and is written by women of color. This list includes formative pieces such as Kobayashi's "Anti-Racist Feminism in Geography: An Agenda for Social Action" (2007), Mohammad's " 'Insiders' and/or 'Outsiders': Positionality, Theory and Praxis" (2001), Mahtani's "Challenging the Ivory Tower: Proposing Anti-Racist Geographies within the Academy" (2006), and Mollett's "Anti-Racist Geography" (2017). We know that the reading list is political, and we've been inspired by Christen Smith's #CiteBlackWomen project. We want the readings to reflect our commitment to support women of color by making sure we are engaging with and recognizing the influence of their work.

Annie: Something I have really enjoyed is that we now incorporate lectures and videos into meetings, in addition to or instead of academic readings. We livestreamed Minelle Mahtani's talk on toxic geographies at last year's Critical Geography conference, and went to lectures by Pavithra Vasudevan and Martina Caretta when they were on campus. Looking beyond geography, we've also attended several talks by feminist and critical race scholars across campus. Further, we've begun cosponsoring visits, like Katherine McKittrick's last spring, and have invited graduate and postgraduate speakers from Switzerland and Germany. We hope in the future to expand by adding other creative feminist expressions such as performance art and activist events.

Caroline: We want to use the collective to showcase the varieties and possibilities of feminist work. These alternatives are also useful because they help balance the increasing demands on already-tired students. There's a lot of important and exciting work out there, but this isn't a feminist geography class. We did create a curriculum of sorts, but we're rethinking that and instead building a set of references, videos, and podcasts our students can engage with. One goal is to extend the website to include these resources and to link to established lists like the black geographies and feminist geography collections. That's a project for the fall!

FLOCK: Can you offer additional advice to existing feminist geography collectives or those looking to form them in the future?

UT Austin: As feminist faculty you are probably already doing so much of what forms the foundation of a collective like ours: caring labor, connecting people, building mentoring resources, listening and sharing ideas, worrying about and striving for different geographic futures. Maybe you are already in a sort of collective if you are part of wider feminist geography communities. For us, it was about stopping the struggle to model ourselves on what we were told/felt was valued, and start with what we loved, what was important to us.

As we have noted, our collective has grown and changed significantly in the mere two years since we formalized. And we are still learning. But we are not starting out of nowhere, nor are we alone. We owe much to other feminist geography collectives such as those found at the University of Georgia, the University of North Carolina at Chapel Hill, and the regional Great Lakes Collective. We have looked to and connected with these groups who have longer histories and who have inspired us greatly. Though our collectives all may look different, we share a common goal: a desire to build supportive, antiracist, and feminist spaces. There are many ways to effect change. Find what works for your group and go forward.

And here we recognize that in many ways we *are* still working within a neoliberal, patriarchal system. Our focus on helping members succeed in terms of professional metrics (grants, awards, papers, etc.) also works to reinforce that system. We also know that in many ways we have adopted a "lab model," but one with critical foundations. We sometimes even use that name, calling ourselves the UT Feminist Geography "lab" when we know "collective" will not register or will be received with suspicion. By co-opting the term, we also feel that we are challenging the basic assumptions of what a lab is and reclaiming its feminist potential. Maybe this is a bit optimistic. But we read Katz's work on minor theory (1996) (perhaps too generously, but hopefully she won't mind) as a sort of permission to disrupt the major with these modest, quiet but powerful moves.

We can already see small ripples of change within our department and college, and in ourselves. While geography (including the subfields of critical and feminist geography) remains very white, we have built a majority-minority space, and we're doing the work we love in a way that feels restorative and energizing. We are being recognized as innovative scholars (in 2017 Annie won the social science thesis award for the College of Liberal Arts, and Dominica was awarded an NSF Graduate Research Fellowship). But more importantly, we see and feel that our ideas are important. *Who* is making knowledge matters, and we feel we have a space where we can ask different questions and build new geographic futures.

Suggested Readings

Berg, Lawrence D. 2012. "Geographies of Identity I: Geography—(Neo) Liberalism—White Supremacy." *Progress in Human Geography* 36 (4): 508–17.

Berg, Lawrence D., Edward H. Huijbens, and Henrik Gutson Larsen. 2016. "Producing Anxiety in the Neoliberal University." *The Canadian Geographer* 60 (2): 168–80.

Caretta, Martina Angela, Danielle Drozdzweski, Johanna Carolina Jokinen, and Emily Falconer. 2018. " 'Who Can Play This Game?' The Lived Experiences of Doctoral Candidates and Early Career Women in the Neoliberal University." *Journal of Geography in Higher Education* 42 (2): 261–75.

Faria, Caroline, Bisoal Falola, Jane Henderson, and Rebecca Torres. 2018. "A Long Way to Go: Collective Paths to Racial Justice in Geography." *The Professional Geographer* 71 (2): 364–76.

Hawthorne, Camilla, and Brittany Meché. 2016. "Making Room for Black Feminist Praxis in Geography." *Society and Space*. September 30, 2016. http://societyandspace.org/2016 /09/30/making-room-for-black-feminist-praxis-in-geography/.

Katz, Cindi. 1996. "Towards Minor Theory." *Environment and Planning D: Society and Space* 14 (4): 487–99.

Kobayashi Audrey. 2006. "Why Women of Colour in Geography?" *Gender, Place & Culture* 13 (1): 33–38.

Kobayashi, Audrey. 2007. "Anti-Racist Feminism in Geography: An Agenda for Social Action." In *A Companion to Feminist Geography*, edited by Lisa Nelson and Joni Seager, 32–40. Oxford: Blackwell Publishing.

Kobayashi Audrey, Victoria Lawson, and Rickie Sanders. 2014. "A Commentary on the Whitening of the Public University: The Context for Diversifying Geography." *The Professional Geographer* 66 (2): 230–35.

Mahtani, Minelle. 2006. "Challenging the Ivory Tower: Proposing Anti-Racist Geographies within the Academy." *Gender, Place & Culture* 13 (1): 21–25.

Mahtani, Minelle. 2014. "Toxic Geographies: Absences in Critical Race Thought and Practice in Social and Cultural Geography." *Social & Cultural Geography* 15 (4): 359–67.

Mohammad, Robina. 2001. " 'Insiders' and/or 'Outsiders': Positionality, Theory and Praxis." In *Qualitative Methodologies for Geographers: Issues and Debates*, edited by Melanie Limb and Claire Dwyer, 101–17. London: Routledge.

Mollett, Sharlene. 2017. "Anti-Racist Geography." In *International Encyclopedia of Geography: People, the Earth, Environment and Technology*, edited by Douglas Richardson, Noel Castree, Michael F. Goodchild, Audrey Kobayashi, Weidong Liu. and Richard A. Marston, 182–85. Washington, DC: Wiley-Blackwell and the Association of American Geographers. https://doi.org/10.1002/9781118786352.wbieg1083.

Mountz, Alison, and Jennifer Hyndman. 2006. "Feminist Approaches to the Global Intimate." *Women's Studies Quarterly* 34 (1/2): 446–63.

Mountz, Alison, Anne Bonds, Becky Mansfield, Jenna Loyd, Jennifer Hyndman, Margaret Walton-Roberts, Ranu Basu, Risa Whitson, Roberta Hawkins, Trina Hamilton, and Winifred Curran. 2015. "For Slow Scholarship: A Feminist Politics of Resistance through Collective Action in the Neoliberal University." *ACME: An International Journal for Critical Geographies* 14 (4): 1235–59.

Peake, Linda, and Beverly Mullings. 2016. "Critical Reflections on Mental and Emotional Distress in the Academy." *ACME: An International Journal for Critical Geographies* 15 (2): 253–84.

Rose, Gillian. 2016. *Visual Methodologies: An Introduction to Researching with Visual Materials.* London: SAGE Publications.

Sanders, Rickie. 2006. "Social Justice and Women of Color in Geography: Philosophical Musings, Trying Again." *Gender, Place & Culture* 13 (1): 49–55.

WOMEN IN GEOGRAPHY (WIG), UNIVERSITY OF WISCONSIN-MADISON

Danya Al-Saleh and Elsa Noterman

FLOCK: Can you provide us with some basic background on WIG at UW-Madison and its history? What were the original members' initial intentions or aspirations for coming together?

WIG: Women in Geography, more often called WIG, is a long-standing organization that supports and unites female-identified graduate students, faculty, and staff affiliated with University of Wisconsin–Madison's geography department. There is no official agreement over when the collective was founded, although most of WIG's early members agree it happened during the mid-1980s. WIG was established to serve as an informal space to support "women in geography" at UW-Madison. While not initially labeled as an explicitly feminist collective, WIG emerged in a departmental and broader disciplinary context that was notoriously sexist and anti-feminist. Meetings often took place off campus, and were focused on building a supportive space for women in an otherwise hostile environment (Rosenfeld 2017).

It has been difficult for us to get a sense of the original WIG members' intentions and the ways in which WIG organizing efforts have changed over time since the 1980s. Both of us joined the department within a context of departmental change in leadership and more explicit attempts to acknowledge the legacies of sexism in the department. Currently, the history of the collective is mostly referenced through side comments about "the bad old days." In this narrative, WIG emerged as a survivalist safe space in an inhospitable climate. For this reason, the mantra in WIG has been that, with the retirement of certain tenured faculty (the "old guard"), conditions have improved, particularly for (primarily white cisgender heterosexual) women.

WIG is actually a unique formation within geography departments, particularly in the US. While resembling the more prevalent Supporting Women in Geography (SWIG) groups, WIG has continued to maintain the collective as a separate space for female-identified people in the department, although recently it has become explicitly inclusive of genderqueer as well as cis and trans women. As WIG became an established departmental institution, it has been and continues to be organized via an annual rotation of graduate student coordinators, which, along with the regular shuffling of academic schedules, has created challenges for continuity year to year as well as the maintenance of historical memory.

FLOCK: How have conversations or interventions changed over time? At what level or site have your conversations or interventions been directed (your home department, the university more broadly, the publishing industry)? Can you reflect on the successes and limitations of those organizing efforts, conversations, or interventions?

WIG: WIG's organizing has historically been and continues to be mostly directed toward making change at the departmental level. As co-coordinators and members of WIG, one of our main obstacles to organizing in the department was the repeated, and often demobilizing, refrain that "things have gotten better." While it is important to recognize the work of those who came before us, we found that this statement functioned to obscure ongoing departmental and disciplinary marginalization that WIG members were regularly sharing among the collective. Additionally, a consistent challenge of WIG organizing involves how to bring the issues raised in WIG discussions into the broader department. We found that it was important to do so not only to build strategic visibility, but also because other geography graduate students, including international students, LGBTQ+ students, and students of color, share differentially in the exclusionary experiences discussed by members of WIG.

One recent means by which WIG members sought to involve the wider community in discussions and to cultivate solidarities was through the creation of a "climate" survey. A growing interest of many WIG members in moving from sharing individualized experiences of exclusions, anxieties, and harassment toward collective change called for a broader discussion of the department's climate. We were concerned, however, with how to build on experiential knowledge to improve the department without placing a burden on individuals to do so publicly. In order to elicit recommendations for improvement in the geography department based on experiential knowledge, some members of WIG put together an anonymized climate survey for geography graduate students during spring 2017.

While not assuming that complex experiences could be fully captured quantitatively, WIG's survey was created in order to push the wider department to discuss sexism, homophobia, and racism as systemic issues rather than individual, isolated cases. The survey addressed issues that had emerged in the WIG collective, including how respected and included graduate students feel in the department, uneven divisions of labor, the existence of harassment and microaggressions, where and who graduate students go to for support and resources, and obstacles to graduate student success (broadly defined). After compiling and internally discussing the survey results, WIG organized a department-wide forum to discuss the results of the survey and the issues it raised (and missed), and to collectively generate an action plan for the community.

The survey not only started important conversations about ongoing exclusions and marginalization in the department but also led to specific changes in policy and practices, including the formation of a permanent climate committee in the department. However, it also underlined that while things have improved for some people in the department, there are serious ongoing challenges that not only require attention at the departmental level but also extend beyond to the campus and academic communities at large. These challenges demand sustained organizing and the building of solidarity with other departments and campuses. The experience has also affirmed the importance of organizing on the departmental level, a tactic that was suggested in the early formations of radical geography.

FLOCK: What are some of the challenges to forming and sustaining a collective space in the university? How do you maintain this space and ensure continuity?

WIG: One of the challenges of WIG organizing as a collective is the nebulous category of "professional development." The precarity surrounding the academic job market—as well as the resulting anxieties—has been accompanied by a demand for professional development opportunities. With the increasing entrepreneurial orientation of the university, students and faculty are encouraged to take individual responsibility for their future success (Slaughter and Rhoades 2009).

Following this phenomenon, a recurrent theme in WIG over the years that we have participated is a demand for professional development among graduate students. At times, WIG members' interest in professional development activities has been focused on specific topics, such as CV writing assistance and job talks. Most often, however, professional development is used as a catchall category to signify a hand-wringing desire to "be prepared" in the face of an increasingly uncertain future in academia. The irony is that professionalization activities, which focus on strategies for "succeeding," frequently elide the structural causes of uncertainty. Instead, these activities place responsibility for narrowly defined success in the lap of anxious, alienated individuals. Strategies for organizing an alternative—one that rejects the metrics for success meted out by an institution that cannot escape its colonial, racist, transphobic, sexist, homophobic, and ableist legacies—are not captured in normative professional development frameworks.

For these reasons, one of our goals in WIG was to organize professional development events that supported attendees and acknowledged their needs while simultaneously highlighting structural inequities and ways to strategically organize our departments. For example, during 2016–2017, WIG hosted a series of professional development events. These events were coordinated with a speaker series (organized by Dr. Erika Marin-Spiotta and the Earth Science Women's Network), which brought three prominent women of color earth scientists to share their work at UW-Madison. WIG coordinated a number of concurrent events with these visiting speakers, including career-trajectory workshops that were open to the general campus community.

The workshops tackled a number of topics related to each speaker's experiences, including navigating the academic and nonacademic job markets and mentoring students from traditionally underrepresented communities. Many of the issues discussed were individual focused, such as how to successfully complete large writing projects. However, the workshops also addressed the ways academic work is still tied to exclusionary legacies in academia. Along these lines, speakers shared their personal struggles with lack of diversity in their departments and universities, alternative academic careers, intersectional strategies for organizing at the departmental and disciplinary levels, and mentoring.

While these workshops did not entirely escape the paradigms of professional development pervasive in WIG and universities more generally, they did provide a glimmer of the possibility for feminist alternatives. Instead of privileging discussions of how individuals can survive in academia by becoming "professionalized," these workshops emphasized broader systemic issues, such as racism and sexism, that erect barriers within academia—and the ways these can be resisted in everyday settings. Moving forward as participants in WIG, we are concerned with the ways professional development paradigms promoted by neoliberalizing universities consume the organizing potential of collectives like WIG. While we personally reject professionalization for erasing the ways in which racism, sexism, ableism, homophobia, and transphobia erect barriers in academia, we found it important to acknowledge the ways the recurring calls for professional development from WIG members signal a need for intersectional feminist organizing in departmental spaces. We are interested in exploring how we might sustain feminist modes of organizing that provide the support that students seek out in the form of professional development without collapsing the potential of collective resistance and cultivation of alternative modes of being in academia.

FLOCK: Have there been particular texts that you all have read together?

WIG: Since the graduate students coordinating the group shift on a yearly basis, the group does not consistently spend time collectively reading texts. The collective's focus and organizing has shifted with the interests of those participating and coordinating WIG. Most often, members of the collective will share relevant articles and texts, based around recent group discussions, on WIG's listserv.

However, during the time we co-coordinated WIG, we were able to read and discuss sections of Sara Ahmed's *Living a Feminist Life* (2017). This reading has been useful for us in relation to the collective's recent organizing in the department, specifically to identify and work against the ways in which institutional memory make it difficult to change the department. Ahmed (2012, 2017), in her work on universities and diversity work, has expressed the regeneration of institutional memory through the metaphor of brick walls. Institutions are hard—they regenerate walls that operate as structured barriers: "a system is working when an attempt to transform that system is blocked" (Ahmed 2017, 97). Even minor or counter institutions, such as WIG, build and regenerate brick walls. For WIG, this operated through the absence of collective memory that enabled the continuous circulation of the depoliticizing statement that "things have improved." We found that the lack of collective memory has both paralyzed WIG's organizing potential and erased the collective's historic role in improving departmental life.

Inspired by the reading, we designed and wore WIG T-shirts that attempted to recognize an alternative history of WIG as "feminist killjoy," rather than a space for survival. Sara Ahmed defines the killjoy as the feminist figure who is always perceived to be causing problems: "however she speaks, the one who speaks as a feminist is usually heard as causing the argument. Another dinner ruined. Institutions also have tables around which bodies gather. Some more than others are at home in these gatherings" (Ahmed 2017, 99). Proclaiming WIG as a killjoy in a public manner was an important strategy in shifting WIG members' (including ourselves) understanding of the collective's role in the department. The T-shirts had an unexpected and powerful effect on WIG and its departmental presence. Not only was this a mode of building strategic visibility by cultivating an outspoken killjoy position, but it also was a way for other students, faculty, and staff (who wore WIG T-shirts as well) to express solidarity with the collective's organizing.

FLOCK: Can you offer additional advice to existing feminist geography collectives or those looking to form them in the future?

WIG: Begin where you are. So often when identifying structural and historical challenges of the academy or even the discipline, it is easy to become overwhelmed and not know where to start. Organizing on a departmental level allows for a grounded means of both understanding how we are all enrolled and complicit in the continuation of injustices and inequities in academia and identifying spaces for wrenches to be thrown in the gears of our workplaces in order to instigate change.

With that said, it is possible to identify already-existing institutional spaces to organize for change in your department. If you are part of an existing group, be open to challenging your institutionalized history. A group that did one thing in the past can be reoriented to do completely different things in the future. This can get complicated, especially when these spaces have established institutionalized histories and roles. Once something like WIG gets institutionalized, it becomes more difficult to mobilize the space as a collective to make change. For instance, WIG has historically supported "women in geography" (largely white, female-identified people), and has not been used for intersectional, antiracist organizing in the department. However, because WIG had an established and well-known institutional presence, it is arguably a powerful site from which to develop a more intersectional feminist geography collective.

Whether you plan to form a new feminist geography collective or build on an existing collective, do an inquiry into historical and contemporary organizing in your department and campus and keep a record of your organizing efforts. This will help build historical memory and critical solidarities that can inform and sustain your efforts going forward. The absence of historical memory of organizing in the department, while in some ways freeing for WIG, also placed a burden on the collective to regularly reinvent the wheel.

Be open to different strategies and tactics for organizing and community building. Seemingly simple activities, like creating T-shirts, hosting potlucks, or replacing photos of department "founding fathers" with current community members, can be surprisingly powerful mobilizing tools with unexpected effects. Projects that are seemingly amicable to departmental life and draw on normative discourses, such as department climate surveys and professional development programming, can also be enrolled to do more radical work by redefining their terms and outcomes.

Suggested Readings

Ahmed, Sara. 2012. *On Being Included: Racism and Diversity in Institutional Life.* Durham, NC: Duke University Press.

Ahmed, Sara. 2017. *Living a Feminist Life.* Durham, NC: Duke University Press.

Rosenfeld, Heather. 2017. "Beyond the Old Boys Club? Gender Relations at UW-Madison Geography from the 1970s to the Present." In *Surviving Sexism in Academia: Strategies for Feminist Leadership*, edited by Kristi Cole and Holly Hassel, 106–26. New York: Routledge.

Slaughter, Sheila, and Gary Rhoades. 2009. *Academic Capitalism and the New Economy: Markets, State, and Higher Education.* Baltimore: Johns Hopkins University Press.

FLOCK COLLECTIVE AT UNC CHAPEL HILL

In April 2017 about forty people gathered in a campus meeting room for an event titled "Struggles for Racial Justice at UNC: A Lunch and Roundtable Conversation." Organized by a group of graduate students and faculty members in the geography department known as the FLOCK Collective, we sought to foster discussion about student activism for racial justice on campus. In the months leading up to the event, FLOCK created a zine that explored and contextualized histories of racial activism at UNC CH and highlighted ongoing student-led struggles. In this moment student activists were demanding the removal of a confederate statue located on our campus's main quad. Just two years earlier a group of primarily undergraduate students—The Real Silent Sam Coalition—campaigned for the removal of William Saunders's name from the campus building housing the geography department. Saunders had been a university trustee and a member of the Ku Klux Klan in the late 1800s. For decades, students had engaged in a number of creative protests and awareness raising campaigns about Saunders's connection to the KKK. The 2014 movement proposed renaming the building to Hurston Hall to honor Zora Neale Hurston. In 2015, university administrators voted to change the name of the building but tepidly chose the neutral, whitewashing moniker Carolina Hall over the more creative one offered by Carolina students.

Thus, it was from within a time of both triumph and defeat for campus activists, and of knowing that change is almost always limited by institutional responses, that FLOCK conceptualized our zine project. We did not intentionally come together to create this zine, but instead were inspired to challenge norms and institutional practices at our university as we collectively shared a skepticism toward depoliticized university-sponsored campaigns for diversity. After a few months of semi-regular meetings, we applied for a grant offering funding to campus projects that used art to explore local activism. We organized brainstorming meetings that brought together students, staff, and faculty across the campus. Wrestling with a number of different ideas and interventions, we ultimately decided to create a zine that centered the historic and contemporary campaigns of student activists. We imagined this zine as a way to move beyond anemic and apolitical institutional approaches to diversity that centered whiteness as the norm and fetishized the diverse campus as a metric or checkbox. Through the zine we highlighted how student activists insistently discover histories in campus archives that are either denied, dismissed, or conveniently forgotten by UNC CH administrators. We aimed to celebrate the works of generations of student visionaries who suffused the landscape of our Southern institution with historical and political meaning, rupturing the narratives that denied or failed to acknowledge the active role monuments and buildings such as Silent Sam and Saunders Hall played in continuing racial injustice and violence.

We launched the zine during the April 2017 racial justice roundtable. We envisioned this event and the zine release as a way to foster conversation between campus activists across generations. We invited a handful of former students whose names had emerged during our archival work on racial justice campaigns during the 1960s, 1970s, 1990s, and early 2000s. We also invited more recent activists and representatives from key student organizations. At the event, students from across these generations shared their experiences and reflected on the successes and failures of their movements and campaigns. Among the most generative moments occurred when older former student activists spoke directly to younger generations to offer encouragement, advice, and strategies. Inspired by these stories of organizing across generations, we were also dismayed by the historic continuity with which campus administrators evaded student demands and deflected responsibility for addressing injustices on campus. Across these historical moments continuities emerged: repeated stories of broken promises from administrators, the dismissal of student activists as naive young people unaware of how universities actually functioned, and the neutralizing of radical and progressive student demands into largely meaningless gestures toward diversity.

The yearlong zine project and this event represent FLOCK's most productive period. In the years since, FLOCK has continued to meet sporadically. We have made some attempts to revive a reading group, participated in AAG meeting sessions as a collective, and participated together on a panel at the 2017 Feminist Geography conference. Disrupted by the rhythms of academic life—summers away, losing founding members to graduation, dissertation fieldwork, faculty leave, pressures to write other proposals, books, and seminar papers—we often wonder whether our collective needs to have a project to provide it coherence and a purpose. We have collectively asked what it means to prioritize other academic work, often framed through expressions of guilt in abandoning FLOCK. Campus activism has continued with renewed vigor. In August 2018, direct action toppled the confederate statue. While individual members have broadened relationships and networks with other campus organizations and campus activists, as a collective FLOCK has not participated in organizing on campus since the April 2017 event.

We hope that the zine, as a material object, lives on to inspire future students. We have taken steps to reprint hundreds of copies, have distributed them in our classes, deposited them in campus archives, circulated them at the AAG, given them to prospective graduate students, and brought them on trips to other conferences and universities. At the beginning of the 2017 school year, undergraduate students passed out zines at a campus event welcoming incoming first years. As a traveling pedagogical object, the zine has the capacity to live beyond our feminist collective and foster conversations about campus activism as it attests to students' potential to transform the university. Similarly, the process, collaboration, organization, and research that produced the zine deepened our relationships with one another and introduced frameworks and concrete histories that continue to shape our thinking on racial justice in our classes, department, and the university as a whole. But FLOCK continues to struggle with questions of continuity and incorporation as new cohorts of students and faculty join the department. It remains an ongoing project for FLOCK to preserve accumulated institutional knowledge and trust established over shared time while welcoming new members and being flexible and open to new iterations of the collective to take the work in new directions.

AFTERWORD

Lorraine Dowler

Feminist Geography Unbound not only examines how spaces and places are gendered and racialized but shines a new and honest light on the fractures within feminist geography. This book's importance cannot be overstated, as the editors and authors advance a reflective path forward for feminist geographers that demands we engage with discomfort and vulnerable bodies within our feminist praxis. To this end, the book challenges us to strive for a praxis that avoids "flattening or erasing" the struggles of some bodies over others (Gökarıksel et al., introduction). Discomfort can provoke anxiety and embarrassment, which is often accompanied by fear and anger for the source of these emotions. However, there is a difference between affective discomfort and our emotive response to it. To secure an unbounded feminist geography, we must recognize the consequences of nullifying discomfort and instead validate how comfort normalizes our relationships with control, power, and even the status quo. The authors point to a future feminist geography that dislocates the discomfort/comfort binary in order to "undermine dominant power structures" and "contribute to a re-presentation of geography" (Gökarıksel et al., introduction). Therefore, if we as feminist geographers want to reorder societies rightly, and liberate bodies and create more just futures, we then must welcome a discomfort feminism that does more than pay lip service to theories of intersectionality.

To subvert the uneven "distribution of discomfort," this book interrogates racialized and gendered framings, to destabilize social norms that "are structured to make those in power feel comfortable and the marginalized uncomfortable" (Gökarıksel et al., introduction). The collection highlights different bodily experiences while also being mindful of a shared vulnerability that stems not only from institutional policies and politics but also from the unspoken vulnerabilities inherent within feminist geography. This is a vital curation for the field because as LaToya Eaves guides us, "Comfort is a primary factor in the maintenance of power, hierarchies, and structures of domination . . . I find discomfort to be necessary to thinking and doing differently" (ch. 13). Instead of advocating for comfortable forms of feminist solidarity, in chapter 5, Valdivia et al. point to more differentiated systems of understanding in the configuration of a *social skin*. For the authors, this way of envisioning a collective is an inclusive process to incorporate non-Waorani collaborators into their search for humanity. The authors recognize that no language can capture the "politics and poetics" of the encounters across different bodies. They suggest this social skin allows for intimate embodied ways of knowing that centers Waorani ways of being in discussions of justice and humanity rather than eclipsing their lives with neoliberal sound bites of inclusion and diversity. The authors welcome the discomfort of an uneven social skin that bunches up and gathers when trying to realize the vulnerabilities inherent to other worlds.

Significant ways of encountering discomfort require that all collaborators be radically vulnerable. In chapter 2, Carrie Chennault demonstrates that alliances, especially when conducting field research, must embrace vulnerability evenly across all communities. This form of vulnerability requires feminist scholars to openly acknowledge the discomfort of privilege, complicity, silence, and injury to our collaborators to envision nonhierarchical solidarities. This praxis is echoed in the interviews with feminist collectives who advocate for horizontal relationships such as evenly valuing the crucial institutional memory of senior members alongside the skills of more junior members (see the interview with Elledge et al., this volume).

Welcoming discomfort is potentially a shameful and uneasy undertaking. Sofia Zaragocin (chapter 12) reminds us that feminist geography must acknowledge its place within the North-South binary, and its predisposition to thinking that feminist scholarship in the global South is inherently decolonial. Similar to a "social skin" that appreciates how gendered and racialized bodies remain rooted to a genealogy of injury, Zaragocin examines how the translocation of harms among diverse place-based peoples can speak to the geographies of justice in meaningful ways. A "decolonized translocation" of feminist geography has the potential to destabilize the artificial binary between the global North and South as it recounts with place-based specificity a commonality of gendered and racialized damages.

As a strategic act of resistance, feminist geographers have historically made visible the violence often eclipsed in the private sphere with framings of whose voices can be mapped onto public space. However, as Cofield and Doan make evident in chapter 3, common public areas such as bathrooms reaffirm the contemporary buoyancy of the gendering of binaries such as of male/female. This, in turn, weakens access to fundamental human rights for those individuals who do not fit neatly into these categories. Therefore, banal acts such as entering a public bathroom dehumanize transgender and gender-nonconforming individuals. Paradoxically, the adherence to binary systems by social activists can destroy the gendered social justice that they seek. Feminist organizations can exacerbate the vulnerability of individuals who are excluded by bifurcated gendered thought. As Abigail Barefoot asserts in chapter 8, when so-called radical feminist organizations adhere to male/female binaries of inclusion, they actively exclude trans women from membership. In this way, radical feminists create discomfort for trans women who are left even more vulnerable by having to claim their inclusion into women-only spaces. Petra Doan (chapter 9) affirms that revisiting one of the tenets of a feminist praxis, feminist standpoint theory, makes visible the specificity of the discomfort of the worlds we are experiencing.

Black feminist scholars draw attention to representational choices as sources of discomfort/comfort. Understanding how power shapes knowledge production is critical to feminist perceptions of space, and yet as Pavithra Vasudevan suggests in chapter 1, it is often reduced to a speculative exercise or sadly a confessional of one's bodily privilege. This becomes intensified when non-Black scholars speak to issues of social justice in ways that obsessively link the binaries of white/Black to power/powerless. Non-Black scholars must recognize their comfort with white institutional and stereotypical norms of victimhood and suffering that furthers Black victimhood.

Antiracist and decolonial understandings of reflexivity are inherent to Tia-Simone Gardner's understanding of *human workability* (chapter 6). When examining how living small on the landscape can be linked to a history of spatial justice strategies, Gardner's tiny house project embodies a lineage of Black feminist intention. In the form of spatial reflexivity, Gardner acknowledges alternative spatial lineages and charges non-Black feminist scholars to become collaborators rather than rivals for academic authority. Gardner urges antiracist and decolonial researchers to respond to past collective injuries when proposing future paths. Similarly, Anusha Hariharan (chapter 10) explores ways to bind activist communities together. This type of cooperative building is critically important when questioning who is included in institutional knowledge in a public archive, and whose experiences have been erased. Most importantly, Hariharan asks how these experiences can be reclaimed and reimagined by way of a feminist praxis.

Similarly, Bri Gauger argues in chapter 11 that revisiting strategies for collective resistance, especially reflexive strategies that subvert the public/private binary, can provide powerful mappings for future institutional change. However, as Melanie Yazzie and Andrew Curley remind us in chapter 7, gender binaries were and remain a strategy to employ other forms of hegemonic institutional schemes, such as capitalism, that in turn facilitate the larger project of settler colonialism and US nationalism. Yazzie and Curley indict feminist scholarship for its comfortable mapping of white gender roles onto Native American communities to promote capitalist forms of social reproduction. For this reason, the destabilization of heteronormative patriarchy cannot be abolished in Native American communities without abolishing capitalism.

The feminist geography exacted in this book indicts the racialized and gendered nature of places. As Kumi Silva makes transparent, "Racially othered bodies are essentialized through originary geographies that we are never able to leave behind" (ch. 4). By demonstrating the inextricable relationality of vulnerability, comfort, and discomfort, this important book advances an alternate future for feminist geography, one that rightly embodies intersectional justice, bodily autonomy, and nondominant solidarity.

CONTRIBUTORS

Dayuma Albán is a PhD candidate in cultural anthropology at the University of North Carolina at Chapel Hill. She has worked in the Ecuadorian Amazon for eighteen years, supporting projects of health and interculturality, gender, and environment and researching oil extraction and gender dynamics. Her dissertation examines Waorani women's political organization in response to territorial and social changes caused by oil extraction in their territory in the Ecuadorian Amazon.

Danya Al-Saleh is a PhD candidate in the department of geography at the University of Wisconsin–Madison. Her research combines insights from feminist economic geography, critical university studies, and political ecology to examine the relationship between US higher education and the oil and gas industry in Qatar. Her work has been supported by the National Science Foundation; the Center for Culture, History and Environment; the Foreign Language and Area Studies Fellowship; and UW-Madison's Holtz Center for Science and Technology Studies.

Kati Álvarez is an ethnohistorian and sociologist based in Ecuador. She received her MA in sociology and PhD in history of the Andes from FLACSO Ecuador. She has worked on issues of land and resource use, territory, local economies, and oil in the Ecuadorian Amazon since 2001. She teaches at the Centro Panamericano de Estudios e Investigaciones Geográficas (CEPEIGE) and in the jurisprudence department at the Universidad Central of Ecuador.

Abigail Barefoot is a doctoral candidate in women, gender, and sexuality studies at the University of Kansas. Her research interests include gender-based violence within activist groups and the role of restorative/transformative justice frameworks in community building. As both a cisgender scholar and an activist, Abigail works on trans* inclusion within the field of women's studies and beyond through developing trans* inclusive pedagogy strategies and as a founding member of the Trans* Studies Reading Group at the University of Kansas. Her chapter in this volume connects her research on building community and her desire to help end transphobia in feminist spaces.

Alicia Weya Cawiya is a Waorani from Ecuador. She is a former leader of the Waorani Nationality of Ecuador (NAWE) organization and of the Association of Waorani Women of Ecuador (AMWAE). She has led several fights for the defense of Waorani territory, of Waorani women's rights, of peoples in voluntary isolation, and of the environment.

Carrie Chennault is a postdoctoral fellow and School of Global Environmental Sustainability leadership fellow at Colorado State University. Her interdisciplinary research draws on feminist geography and critical food studies to examine the political ecologies of US agrifood practices and food justice activism. Past and current projects have focused on alternative food systems, prison agriculture, emergency food networks, grassroots movements, and the changing roles of US land-grant universities and Cooperative Extension. Engaging feminist geographies, Carrie's research critiques uneven power relations while looking to radical vulnerability, emotion/affect, the body, and daily relational life in constituting coexperimental modes of social transformation.

Rachael Cofield is a queer geographer currently working on her PhD at Florida State University. Born and raised in Georgia, she hopes to integrate study of the US South with queer geography. She's interested in how Southern identity and queer identity intermingle and present new opportunities for a queer Southern future. Her work envisions the South as a region plagued by a problematic past but also as an open playing field for change, wherein intersectionality, difference, and queer futurism play an important role in building a different South. Her dissertation project centers on place-making and daily life of LGBTQ-identifying community members in Atlanta, Georgia, and seeks to explore the ways intersectional identities operate to create urban queer and Southern place as a response to gentrification of queer neighborhoods.

Andrew Curley (Diné) is an assistant professor in the school of geography and development at the University of Arizona. He studies natural resources, energy, colonial infrastructures, and water rights for Indigenous nations. His previous publications were on the moral economy of Navajo coal workers, western water law as colonial enclosure, and green development as hybrid neoliberalism. Andrew is writing a book on resource sovereignty and the legacy of coal for the Navajo Nation.

Petra Doan is professor of urban and regional planning at Florida State University. She conducts research on transgender experiences of the city and explores the relationship between urban planning and the wider LGBTQ community. Most notably, she has edited two books: *Queerying Planning: Challenging Heteronormative Assumptions and Reframing Planning Practice* (Ashgate, 2011) and *Planning and LGBTQ Communities: The Need for Inclusive Queer Space* (Routledge, 2015). She also has published a number of related articles in *Gender, Place & Culture, Women's Studies Quarterly, Environment and Planning A*, the *Journal of Planning Education and Research, Progressive Planning*, and *International Review of Urban and Regional Research*.

Lorraine Dowler is professor of geography and women, gender, and sexuality studies at Penn State University. Her research examines everyday violent processes that are at the heart of the life of any nation. She aims to explore the role of hypermasculine state practices in everyday life, private spaces, and the lives of women and other nonprivileged individuals. For this reason, her research focuses on how individual vulnerabilities to violence are rendered invisible through spatial processes such as border making, cultural privilege, militarization, and nationalism. She is the author of several publications focusing on gender and war in Northern Ireland. Her current research project is a feminist examination of the critical geopolitics of the Cold War, the War on Terror, and the New Military. As part of this analysis, she has conducted extensive interviews with women who trained to be astronauts during the NASA Mercury program, contemporary women firefighters, and female soldiers returning from Iraq and Afghanistan.

LaToya Eaves is a native of Shelby, North Carolina. She earned her PhD in the department of global and sociocultural studies at Florida International University in Miami. Her small-town, Southern upbringing informs her research, which centralizes Black geographies and women of color feminisms in order to engage ideologies of race, place-based politics, and the discursive formation of the US South and the Atlantic world. She is specifically interested in the interplay of these three ideas from the positionality, knowledges, and place-making of queer Black women. LaToya is an assistant professor in the department of geography at the University of Tennessee, Knoxville. She is founder and past chair of the Black Geographies Specialty Group with the American Association of Geographers (AAG). She has been active in both the AAG and the National Women's Studies Association for a number of years, having served in leadership positions in both organizations.

Annie Elledge received her BA in international relations and global studies and government from the University of Texas at Austin. In fall 2020 she joined the doctoral program in the department of geography at UNC Chapel Hill. Her research examines the intersectional geographies of beauty and tourism-based development. She has begun publishing this work, with her first article in *Environment and Planning D: Society and Space*. She is cofounder of the University of Texas at Austin Feminist Geography Collective.

Caroline Faria is a feminist geographer in the department of geography and the environment at the University of Texas at Austin. Her research engages postcolonial and intersectional feminist approaches to understand nationalism and neoliberal globalization, with a focus on the Gulf–East African region. She is cofounder of the University of Texas at Austin Feminist Geography Collective.

Feminists Liberating Our Collective Knowledge (FLOCK) was formed in 2016 by a group of geographers at UNC Chapel Hill as an effort to sustain the momentum built by decades of student visionaries in the movement for racial justice on campus and the movement for renaming the geography building Hurston Hall.

Tia-Simone Gardner is an artist, educator, and Black feminist scholar. Her creative and scholarly practice are interdisciplinary strategies and engage ideas of ritual, iconoclasm, and geography. Gardner grew up in Birmingham, Alabama, and received her BA in art and art history from the University of Alabama at Birmingham and an MFA in interdisciplinary practices and time-based media from the University of Pennsylvania. She recently received her PhD in feminist studies from the department of gender, women, and sexuality studies at the University of Minnesota. She is currently working on a project on Blackness and the Mississippi River, as well as expanding her dissertation, "Sensing Place: House-Scale, Black Geographies, and a Humanly Workable City," into an artist book and a series of site-specific installations. Gardner lives in Minneapolis, Minnesota, where she is an assistant professor in the department of media and cultural studies at Macalester College.

Bri Gauger is a postdoctoral researcher in gender and the built environment at Chalmers University of Technology. She completed a master's degree in planning at the University of Southern California and a PhD in urban and regional planning with a graduate certificate in women's studies at the University of Michigan. Bri's research examines the ways planning interacts with social norms at the intersections of gender, race, and class. Her dissertation, "Urban Planning and Its Feminist Histories," traces the history of feminist thought and women's activism in urban planning by examining how insurgent and institutional practices have shaped the various meanings of feminism in the discipline. Drawing on original oral history interviews, archival research, and published scholarship, the project explores how ideas and strategies have traveled between feminism and planning and examines the legacy of feminism in planning's political and intellectual history.

The Great Lakes Feminist Geography Collective is a cross-border, regional network of geographers that originated with the 2013 Great Lakes Feminist Geography Workshop in Guelph, Ontario. The collective includes approximately twenty-five faculty who collaborate around issues of mental health and well-being, feminist critiques of labor processes, and issues of representation within geography. Members of the collective have been active in organizing and publishing around themes of slow scholarship, mental health, and mentoring.

Banu Gökarıksel is professor of geography and global studies and the Caroline H. and Thomas S. Royster Distinguished Professor at the Graduate School of the University of North Carolina at Chapel Hill. She has an adjunct appointment with Duke University's gender, sexuality, and feminist studies department. She served as coeditor of the *Journal of Middle East Women's Studies* (2014–2018) and codirector of the Duke Middle East in Europe summer program in Berlin (2018). She is the recipient of the 2018 American Association of Geographers Enhancing Diversity Award and the 2017 University of North Carolina at Chapel Hill Chapman Family Teaching Award. Her research analyzes the politics of everyday life and questions of religion, secularism, and gender with a focus on bodies and urban space. Her current projects include the current political dynamics of encounter and difference in Turkey (funded by the National Science Foundation), the gender politics of right-wing nationalism and feminist interventions (in the US and Turkey), and the refugee and migrant spaces of difference and belonging. She is a member of the FLOCK Feminist Geography Collective.

Anusha Hariharan is a PhD candidate in anthropology at the University of North Carolina at Chapel Hill. She has engaged with queer and feminist movements in India since 2007. Her dissertation work examines friendship, care, and ethics of solidarity-building among feminist activists and Christianity's role in enabling social justice activism in southern India.

Michael Hawkins is a PhD candidate in the department of geography at the University of North Carolina at Chapel Hill. He received his MA from the same department in 2017 for a project exploring the gendered legacies of US militarism in Subic Bay, Philippines. His dissertation research explores historic and contemporary contestations over the production of space and the time of labor at the Port of Manila. He is a member of the FLOCK Feminist Geography Collective at UNC.

Jess Linz is a PhD candidate in the department of geography at the University of Kentucky. Her dissertation research is on the affective dimension of gentrification and residential displacement in Mexico City, supported by a Fulbright-García Robles fellowship. She has published on gentrification, affect theory, feminist politics of resistance in the academy, and the affective politics of internet memes in *Geoforum*, *Environment and Planning D: Society and Space*, *Gender, Place & Culture*, and *GeoHumanities*.

Flora Lu is the Pepper-Giberson Endowed Chair and Professor of Environmental Studies at the University of California, Santa Cruz and provost of Colleges Nine and Ten. Flora began conducting research in the Amazon as an undergraduate in 1992. As an ecological anthropologist, she is interested in human/environment dynamics in tropical rainforests, the political economy of oil extraction, resource governance, and household economics. Her longitudinal fieldwork among Indigenous communities in northeastern Ecuador has been featured in two programs on the National Geographic Channel, funded by $2.5 million in external grants, and published in four books and three dozen articles and chapters.

Christopher Neubert is a PhD candidate in the department of geography at the University of North Carolina at Chapel Hill and a National Science Foundation graduate research fellow. His current research examines how masculinity and whiteness have shaped everyday political life in agricultural communities in the US Midwest. He is a member of the FLOCK Feminist Geography Collective.

Elsa Noterman is a junior research fellow at Queens' College in the University of Cambridge. As a critical geographer, Elsa examines collective struggles over precarious spaces of social reproduction—particularly those related to "vacant" property and housing commons, as well as to forms of critical study and pedagogy on the edge of academia. Her research has been supported by the National Science Foundation and the American Council of Learned Societies.

Manuela Omari Ima Omene was born in the Intangible Zone of the Ecuadorian Amazon and grew up in Teweno. From a young age she has been involved in Waorani organizational work. She directed tourism and organization, and served as president of the Association of Waorani Women of Ecuador (AMWAE) and later as its coordinator. These experiences shaped her commitment to the defense of women's and territorial rights and the lives of the Tagaeri-Taromenane. Manuela believes that a sustainable economy cannot be achieved through petroleum but only through local initiatives led by Waorani women. She will always resist the advance of the oil frontier because it contaminates the forest and usurps Waorani territory and ancestral lifeways.

Kumarini Silva is associate professor of communication at the University of North Carolina at Chapel Hill. She is the author of *Brown Threat: Identification in the Security State* (University of Minnesota Press, 2016) and coeditor of *Feminist Erasures: Challenging Backlash Culture* (Palgrave UK, 2015) and *Migration, Identity, and Belonging: Defining Borders and Boundaries of the Homeland* (Routledge, 2020). Her current research extends the exploration of racialized identification in *Brown Threat* to unpack how affective relationships, especially calls to and of love, animate regulatory practices that are deeply cruel and alienating.

Sara Smith is associate professor of geography at the University of North Carolina at Chapel Hill. She is a feminist political geographer interested in the relationship between territory, bodies, and the everyday. Her research seeks to understand how politics and geopolitics are constituted through intimate acts of love, friendship, and birth. She has researched these questions in the Ladakh region of India's Jammu and Kashmir State in relation to marriage and family planning, and is now engaged in a project on marginalized Himalayan youth. She also pursues this agenda in the national (US) and global context through futurity and difference. She is a member of the FLOCK Feminist Geography Collective. She has authored two books, *Intimate Geopolitics: Love, Territory, and the Future on India's Northern Threshold* and *Political Geography: A Critical Introduction.*

Araby Smyth is a PhD candidate and instructor in the department of geography at the University of Kentucky. Her research interests are in feminist economic and political geography. Her doctoral dissertation is about migration, remittances, and gendered communal participation in an Indigenous town in Mexico, and it is supported by the National Science Foundation, Society of Woman Geographers, and a PEO Scholar Award. She has published in *Gender, Place & Culture* and *Geoforum.*

Gabriela Valdivia is professor of geography at the University of North Carolina at Chapel Hill. Her work focuses on how states, firms, and civil society appropriate and transform resources to meet their interests, and how capturing and putting resources to work transforms communities in Latin America. Her project *Crude Entanglements* draws on feminist political ecology to examine the affective dimensions of oil production. She is coauthor of the book *Oil, Revolution, and Indigenous Citizenship in Ecuadorian Amazonia,* which examines the political ecology of the Ecuadorian petro-state since the turn of the century.

Pavithra Vasudevan is an assistant professor of African and African diaspora studies and women's and gender studies at the University of Texas at Austin. Pavithra's research addresses toxicity as a manifestation of racial violence, capitalist entanglements with state and science, and the abolitional possibilities of collective struggle. As a critical performance ethnographer, Pavithra develops arts-based collaborations with affected communities and is interested in collective knowledge production bridging political thought and grassroots organizing. She is a founding member of the FLOCK Feminist Geography Collective and the Hurston Collective for Critical Performance Ethnography at the University of North Carolina at Chapel Hill. At UT Austin, she is a core faculty member of the Feminist Geography Research Collective and advises the emergent Environmental Justice Collective.

Dominica Whitesell is a doctoral student in the department of geography and the environment at the University of Texas at Austin. Her research, funded through the NSF Graduate Research Fellowship, examines the economic and political geographies of clothing and fashion in Uganda. Drawing from intersectional theory and global intimate approaches, she employs creative cartography and other feminist geovisualization methods. She has published on this work in *Environment and Planning C: Politics and Space*. She is cofounder and current member of the UT Austin Feminist Geography Collective.

Melanie K. Yazzie (Diné) is assistant professor of Native American studies and American studies at the University of New Mexico. She does historical research at the intersections of feminist studies, queer studies, Native American studies, Diné studies, and environmental studies.

Sofia Zaragocin is an assistant professor in the international relations department of Universidad San Francisco de Quito, with research interests on decolonial feminist geography and processes of racialization of space. She has written on geographies of settler colonialism along Latin American borderlands, feminist geography, and mapping gender-based violence in Ecuador. She is currently working on a hemispheric study on the hydrosocial cycle, women, and mining along the Americas. She is also part of the Critical Geography Collective of Ecuador, an autonomous interdisciplinary group that seeks territorial resistance through a wide range of sociospatial geographical methodologies.

INDEX

ableism, 118, 134, 285
abortion, 176, 239, 240, 245
Abya Yala, 244
academia
   diversity/representation in, 269, 276,
     285, 289
   the division of labor/labor practices in,
     262, 269, 284
   exclusion and marginalization in, 262,
     268, 272, 283, 284, 285, 286
   hostility toward feminism in, 276, 277,
     282
   mental health in (depression, isolation),
     264, 266, 268, 269, 271, 272
   mentoring in, 229, 268, 272, 273,
     274–76, 280, 285
   and minority faculty/scholars of color,
     256–57, 275, 277, 278
   and professional development, 284–85
   and professional metrics, 275, 280, 285
   sexual harassment in, 7, 168–69, 262,
     264, 283, 284
   See also feminist collectives; precarity,
     economic: in academia; tenure
adjuncts. *See* precarity, economic: in
   academia
affirmative action, 135n3, 215–16, 217, 224
African Americans
   in academia, 254–57
   housing of, and racial justice, 117–21,
     124, 125–26, 130–32
   scholars who center, 16
   and solidarity with Asians, 35
   in the South, interpreting subjectivities
     of, 41–42
   See also anti-Black violence; Black
     feminism; Black Power movements;
     Black studies; Black suffering; Black
     vernacular architecture; Black
     women
Afrofuturism, 14
aging, 14–15, 133
   elder care, 219
agriculture, US
   and racialized inequities, 8–9, 49–54
agua-territorio, 245

Ahmed, Sara, 266, 272
   on academia as an embodied terrain of
     struggle, 18
   and affective economies, 194
   on antiracism, 51, 58, 62, 257
   on the cultural politics of emotion, 9, 70,
     77, 82, 182
   on the feminist killjoy, 58, 88
   on happiness in a neoliberal, patriarchal
     world, 1, 14
   on how orientations matter, 30, 34
   and identity as a "construction-in-prog-
     ress," 29
   on institutional memory and barriers,
     286
   on racialized violence, 36
Albán, Dayuma, 10, 11, 16, 18, 30, 95–115,
   292
Alcoa plant (Badin, NC), 27, 28, 31–32, 38–42,
   43
Al-Saleh, Danya, 282–88
Álvarez, Kati, 10, 11, 16, 18, 30, 95–115, 292
Amazon, Ecuadorian, 95–115
Ambedkar, Bhimrao R., 191, 193, 194, 211n7
American Association of Geographers (AAG),
   255–56, 257, 268, 269, 271
American Institute of Planners (AIP), 217
American Planning Association (APA), 225
American Society of Planning Officials
   (ASPO), 217
AMWAE, 102, 104, 105–6
angling (as a practice), 51, 55, 56
Anglocentrism/Eurocentrism, 6, 10, 235–50,
   257
Anglophone feminist geography, 236, 238,
   243–44
Anglophone literature, 246
Anti-Blackness in the American Metropolis
   symposium, 255
anti-Black violence
   Asian Americans as complicit in, 30
   implications of studying, as a Brown
     scholar, 8, 16, 27–44
   and migration, 131
   See also antiracism; Black suffering
anti-Muslim racism and violence, 4–5, 44n1

www.ingramcontent.com/pod-product-compliance
Lightning Source LLC
Chambersburg PA
CBHW050335270326
41926CB00016B/3460